STRANGERS IN OUR MID
SEXUAL DEVIANCY IN POSTWAR ONTARIO

Contemporary efforts to treat sex offenders are rooted in the post–Second World War era, in which an unshakable faith in science convinced many Canadian parents that pedophilia could be cured. *Strangers in Our Midst* explores the popularization of the notion of sexual deviancy as a way of understanding sexual behaviour, the emergence in Canada of legislation directed at sex offenders, and the evolution of treatment programs in Ontario.

Popular discourses regarding sexual deviancy, legislative action against sex criminals, and the implementation of treatment programs for sex offenders have been widely attributed to a reactionary, conservative moral panic over changing sex and gender roles after the Second World War. Elise Chenier challenges this assumption, arguing that, in Canada, advocates of sex-offender treatment were actually liberal progressives. Drawing on previously unexamined sources, including medical reports, government commissions, prison files, and interviews with key figures, *Strangers in Our Midst* offers an original critical analysis of the rise of sexological thinking in Canada, and shows how what was conceived as a humane alternative to traditional punishment could be put into practice in inhumane ways.

(Studies in Gender and History)

ELISE CHENIER is an assistant professor in the Department of History at Simon Fraser University.

STUDIES IN GENDER AND HISTORY

General editors: Franca Iacovetta and Karen Dubinsky

STRANGERS IN OUR MIDST

Sexual Deviancy in Postwar Ontario

Elise Chenier

UNIVERSITY OF TORONTO PRESS
Toronto Buffalo London

© University of Toronto Press Incorporated 2008
Toronto Buffalo London
www.utppublishing.com
Printed in Canada

ISBN 978-0-8020-9226-7 (cloth)
ISBN 978-0-8020-9453-7 (paper)

Library and Archives Canada Cataloguing in Publication

Chenier, Elise Rose, 1967–
    Strangers in our midst : sexual deviancy in postwar Ontario / Elise
Chenier.

    (Studies in gender and history)
    Includes bibliographical references and index.
    ISBN 978-0-8020-9226-7 (bound)   ISBN 978-0-8020-9453-7 (pbk.)

    1. Paraphilias – Ontario – History – 20th century.   2. Sex
offenders – Ontario – History – 20th century.   3. Paraphilias – Treatments –
Ontario – History – 20th century.   I. Title.   II. Series.

    HV6593.C3C44 2008   364.15′30971309045   C2008-901781-1

University of Toronto Press acknowledges the financial assistance to its
publishing program of the Canada Council for the Arts and the Ontario
Arts Council.

This book has been published with the help of a grant from the Canadian
Federation for the Humanities and Social Sciences, through the Aid to
Scholarly Publications Programme, using funds provided by the Social
Sciences and Humanities Research Council of Canada.

University of Toronto Press acknowledges the financial support for its
publishing activities of the Government of Canada through the Book
Publishing Industry Development Program (BPIDP).

To my mother, Marie

Contents

Acknowledgments

This book was a long time in the making, but it would have taken even longer, and have been much less rewarding, were it not for the support of family, friends, and colleagues. From the very moment I decided to explore the history of sexuality, I enjoyed the intellectual support and encouragement of an remarkable group of scholars and activists. First among them are Kathryn McPherson and Craig Heron, who together convinced me that history is where I belong. Maureen Fitzgerald, Amy Gottlieb, Steven Maynard, and Gary Kinsman have been constant companions, and continue to be sources of intellectual and political inspiration. In the process, they have also become very dear friends. Becki Ross, Canada's poster girl for queer studies, cheered my earliest efforts in the field. Karen Dubinsky, my supervisor at Queen's University in Kingston, championed this project from the beginning and pushed me to finish. She also helped me become a better writer and thinker. I am grateful for her careful supervision of the thesis, and for her support in seeing the manuscript through the publication process. Ian McKay and Constance Backhouse provided insightful commentary on the manuscript at critical stages; their contributions helped me to clarify and sharpen significant aspects of my argument. Marc Stein, who served as the external examiner of the thesis, has stayed with me, and with this manuscript, to the very end. His generosity as both a friend and a scholar is limitless, and my debt of gratitude is a pleasant burden to bear.

Some of the people about whom I write were exceptionally generous with their time. Many granted me in-person interviews, shared copies of obscure and unpublished books and articles, and pointed me toward material I might not otherwise have discovered. Bertha Shvemar generously shared her memories and her personal files on the Parents Action League. Dr Edward Turner and Hans Mohr of the Toronto Psychiatric Hospital's Outpatient Forensic Clinic were particularly forthcoming about their experiences working in the field of forensic sexology in the late 1950s and 1960s. William Marshall of Queen's University, Harold Barbaree of the Clarke Institute, and Karl Hanson also provided me with useful information about the field of sex offender treatment and research. So too did Richard Steffy, who ran the Mimico Pedophile Treatment Program. Steffy surprised me with a wonderfully rich but unpublished book-length study of the program, and he gave thoughtful answers to all of my questions about his controversial treatment program.

For more than two decades a dedicated group of volunteers, and donors, have kept the Canadian Lesbian and Gay Archives alive. This institution is one of the most important resources available to young and established scholars, and I have benefited tremendously from their expertise and from the intellectual community they provide. I am especially appreciative to have the friendship of Harold Averill, Ed Jackson, and Don McLeod, all of whom have welcomed me into the archives community, and who play a crucial behind-the-scenes role that fosters queer historical scholarship in English Canada. Staff and volunteers at the Queen Street Mental Health Archives are a vital resource to anyone working in the field of the history of psychiatry in English Canada, and I benefited from their knowledge and expertise. Their annual Research-in-Progress seminars as well as the Madness Film Festival bring together and foster new scholars and interesting scholarship. I am fortunate to have enjoyed a brief but intellectually stimulating relationship with the late Cyril Greenland who spent many years pondering the role of sex in our society.

I am tremendously grateful for the assistance provided me by the dedicated staff at the Archives of Ontario. Stormie Stewart, Leon Rabinowitz, Dan Bryant, and the support staff made my research experience as smooth as possible, and socially pleasurable. It was during my time there that my ordinary friendship with historian Mary MacDonald became extraordinary. Her research on Grandview School for Girls served as a source of inspiration. Equally important was her wicked sense of humour, which saved me from becoming utterly overwhelmed by the feelings of despair one necessarily battles when trawling though prison and sex offender treatment records. Mary and I were half of the mostly monthly 'Diss'n'Dine' group. I grew, and this project benefited immeasurably, as a result of the trenchant criticism and intellectual scrutiny that Mary, Sheila McManus, and Amanda Glasbeek brought to some of these chapters. Each of these women proved to be masters of the art of offering critical advice with affection and enthusiasm.

One of the most tremendous opportunities to come my way during the course of researching this project was made possible by a Canada–U.S. Fulbright Scholarship. The scholarship allowed me to spend nine months in the archives of the Kinsey Institute for Research in Sex, Gender and Reproduction. Archivist Jennifer Corbin and the indispensable Ruth Beasley worked hard to provide me with difficult-to-access material. Paul Gebhard offered interesting details about some of the work undertaken by Kinsey Institute staff in the 1960s, and Director John Bancroft and Jennie Hamburger made sure my visit was comfortable and productive.

This project also benefited from funding provided by the Social Sciences and Humanities Research Council, the Hannah Institute for the History of Medicine, the Canadian Federation of University Women, Queen's University, the Visiting Scholar program of the McGill Centre for the Research and Teaching on Women, Simon Fraser University's Publications Fund and the Canadian Federation for the Humanities and Social Sciences Aid to Scholarly Publishing Program.

In the fall of 2001 I took up a postdoctoral fellowship at McGill University in Montreal. Members of the Montreal History Group invited me to present some of the material in this book, and I am thankful for their warm response and thoughtful comments. My host, Susanne Morton, and Brian Young, Jarrett Rudy, Andrée Lévesque, Magda Fahrni, Tamara Myers, and Denyse Baillargeon became good friends and were marvellous colleagues. The community they have created is a model of how richly rewarding an academic life can be. Perhaps the best feature of that life is the generosity we can show to each other. Others who were similarly generous with their time and work were Simon Cole and Stephen Robertson, two historians whom I have never met, but who did not hesitate to share with me their own research. Thanks also to Lara Harvester, Rachel Torrie, and Jonathan Bujeau for undertaking important research for this project. While I am entirely responsible for what has happened to that research, there are some people who make it look so much better than it might have otherwise. I am deeply indebted to Jennifer Coffey whose love of the English language, and whose passion for good writing, contributed greatly to the clarity of my prose. I am also thankful for the hard work put in by the staff at the University of Toronto Press, including most especially my editor Jill McConkey and the remarkably skilled Andy Carroll, who also copy-edited this manuscript.

Historical scholarship has its own particular rhythm which can, at times, seem painfully slow. Our friends and colleagues are what make the challenging moments in our writing and research bearable. Some of the people who have made a foxtrot feel like flamenco are Helen Harrison, Scott Rayter, Patrizia Gentile, Franca Iacovetta, Carolyn Strange, Cy-Thea Sand, Paige Raibmon, Alexander Dawson, Mark Leier, and Roxanne Panchasi. Some read and commented on chapters of this book, and some were just there to hang out and not work at all. Lynn Farrell was closest to me and to this project for much of the time it took to complete it. A constant source of support, Lynn regularly helped me reconnect to my original purpose by reminding me why this project mattered. Thank you.

The decision to pursue an academic career was made possible only because of the love and support of my family. Words cannot express how grateful I am to my mother, Marie Chenier, to my sisters Laura Tilley and Yvette Moriarity, my brother-in-law Keith Tilley, my niece Nicole and nephews Sheldon Rye and Derek, and, most especially, my daughter Natasha. Indeed, of all the people in my life, Natasha has made the greatest sacrifices, but I like to think that she also has the most to gain in return. Her daily queries about my progress, and her regular inducements to 'keep going' have kept me buoyant in the roughest waters. We are made better people by each other.

We can do something about . . .

SEX CRIMES

By Ken Johnstone
Standard Staff Writer

SCIENCE

Preventive education and science can combine to combat sex offences.

WHAT are we doing about sex crime?

Canada, along with the United States, is faced today with a steadily mounting wave of sex offences that range from the relatively trivial but significant act of "indecent exposure" to rape and murder. There is scarcely a city of any size in the Dominion that hasn't suffered in the last few months from at least one shocking instance of our complete inability to protect our young and cure our sick. For sex crimes, in the last analysis, consist of just those two failures. Yet, protection can be given children, and sex offenders can be cured.

The latest recorded Dominion Government figures reveal that in one year there were 428 convictions for indecent exposure, 279 convictions for indecent assault, 83 for carnal knowledge, 46 for incest, 23 for rape and attempted rape, 189 for sodomy. Yet this is the barest fraction of actual cases that occurred and went either unpunished or even unreported.

The writer recently interviewed the director of an establishment which employs a large number of drivers. One of them was accused of having assaulted a four-year old child. When faced with the accusation, he admitted the fact, went on to state that it was his custom to commit such an act each month. The parents of the child, fearing that the affair would create an indelible impression in the child's mind if pursued into the courts, refused to prosecute. Without the parents' support, the police could make no case. The driver was discharged, found employment elsewhere. And perhaps the most unhappy footnote to the whole story was that the driver in question was a married man, a war veteran with a child of his own. There is no existing machinery, medical or legal, to handle such cases.

Another instance was given me by a prominent juvenile court judge. He was faced with a case of a little girl, 11 years of age, who had been assaulted, impregnated and given a venereal disease. The man who committed the act had been caught on the spot. But the child's parents refused to prosecute because of the unhappy publicity that would attend the case. So the man was convicted of — indecent exposure.

The same judge said flatly to me: 'What is the use of sending these men to jail? They are mentally sick and no jail sentence, no lashes will cure them. On the contrary, jail only too frequently provides a breeding place for perverted sexual practices.'

So, on the one hand a fog of reticence covers many of the sex crimes which occur daily, and on the other hand our method of dealing with convicted sex criminals does nothing to remedy the situation. One judge went so far as to blame the fear of apprehension as a cause of sex murders. He said: "The sex pervert cannot help committing the act, no amount of fear for the consequences will stop him. But he will murder the child to prevent his own discovery at the time of the act. That is the horrible tragedy of our present law."

The records show, too, that there is an inevitable progression of minor sex offences in the history of most sex criminals. Bussey, the Owen Sound murderer, had five previous convictions on minor sex offences leading up to his final act of murder. John Staley, executed recently at Lethbridge for a sex murder, had a half-dozen previous convictions for sex offences.

I have before me the record of one inmate of Burwash Industrial Farm. His career began in 1926, with a two-year sentence. In the last 21 years he has been sentenced a total of 17½ years for five separate sex offences, and when his latest 18 months term is up, who knows whether he will stop short of murder to commit the inevitable offence that deranged sexual impulses drive him to? Only one thing is certain; he will be back unless in the meantime we find some way of curing people like him.

IS THERE a solution? Recently the Arlene Anderson case, the mutilation and murder of a helpless crippled child, shocked Toronto into action. The Board of Police Commissioners called together a committee to study the problem of sex offenders. Probably the most important discovery of that committee was that it had already been anticipated a month previously by another committee formed on the initiative of the Canadian Penal Association's dynamic president, J. Alex Edmison, KC. An expert body, this group is making an exhaustive study of the problem from every aspect. Its preliminary report will be public property within weeks. Some idea of the scope of the inquiry and the many sides to the problem of sex crime can be gained from a consideration of the committee and its program, which is financed by the Kiwanis Club of Toronto.

Chaired by Alex Edminson and with secretary R. H. Carpenter provided by the Canadian Penal Association, the committee includes Dr. Kenneth Rodgers for the Canadian Welfare Council, Dr. L. P. Gendreau for the Department of Justice, Chief Constable John Chisholm

Continued on Page Sixteen

Most English Canadians learned about sexual deviancy and its treatment from journalistic news coverage. This illustration, which accompanied a 1948 *Montreal Standard* story on just that issue, successfully captured the key elements in the construction of the sexual deviancy problem in a single, striking image. Courtesy *Montreal Standard*, 10 January 1948, 4.

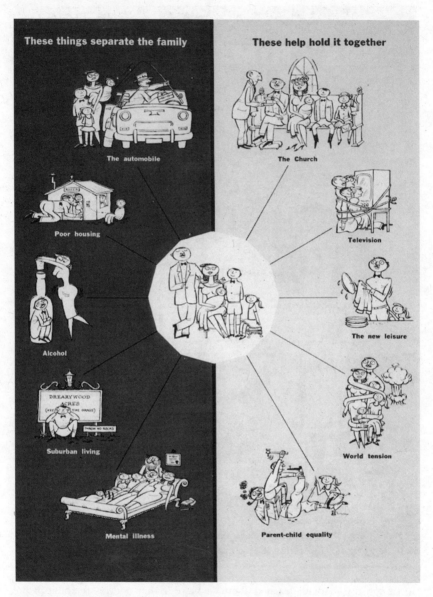

As this illustration shows, the threat of nuclear war was good for family life. Fear of planetary destruction underpinned the movement for progressive reform, and many postwar parents believed that mental health was the ultimate weapon against war, instability, and social distress. Courtesy *Maclean's*.

Angered by sex crimes

against children,

four housewives — guided by some

of the nation's best medical

and legal brains — have set

a ball rolling that promises

to knock a hole in official apathy

and give Canada a fresh start

in tackling this nationwide problem

BY JUNE CALLWOOD

The Parents' Action League (Toronto) in session. From left: Mrs. Ethel Dorfman, Mrs. Bertha Shvemar, Mrs. Isobel Mills and Mrs. Ethel Hahn.

THE PARENTS

LAST FEBRUARY in Toronto an eight-year-old child, Judy Carter, disappeared while walking home from school. For forty-three days police and civilian volunteers dragged ice-choked rivers, tramped through frozen ravines, searched tawdry boarding-houses and peered under debris in vacant lots. In the long weeks before her body was found, strangled by a still unknown killer, it was assumed that the little girl had been the victim of what society used to call a sex maniac, later termed a sex pervert and currently calls a sex deviate or sex offender.

The apparent nature of the crime touched off a wave of revulsion across the country—as sex crimes always do—and brought out demands, freshened by anger and fear but as ancient as the Book of Genesis, that the law, police or doctors do something to remove the menace of the sex criminal. Usually such outbursts of public feeling soon die out, having accomplished absolutely nothing. This one resulted in something almost unprecedented—the formation of a militantly hopeful organization called the Parents' Action League with a businesslike plan for protecting Canada's children against sex criminals and, where possible, for protecting the criminals against themselves.

No crime stirs public opinion so quickly and uneasily

Author Callwood (second row, far left) attends PAL meeting in suburban school hall when aims were first presented to general public last May.

STRIKE BACK

Still fresh in parents' minds was the tragedy of Judy Carter whose body was found after a long search on the bank of a river near Markham, Ont.

AGAINST SEX CRIMINALS

The horrible possibility that one's own child might become a victim sold newspapers and magazines, and roused the public to take action. The Parents Action League represented the ideals of postwar citizenship, and it easily attracted media attention. Courtesy *Maclean's*.

The
Strange One

A report from the Parents' Action League of Ontario.

The Parents Action League advocated a rational, informed approach to the problem of sex crime, but as the cover of their widely distributed information pamphlet shows, they were not above fear mongering to get their point across. (Pamphlet in author's collection.)

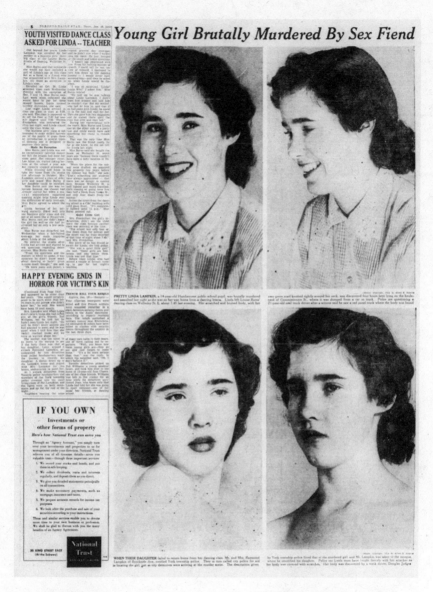

These portraits of fourteen year old murder victim Linda Lampkin contributed to the *Toronto Daily Star*'s characterization of her as a sexually precocious teenager. Readers rejected the implication that she was anything less than an innocent victim. 19 January 1956. Courtesy *Toronto Star*.

STRANGERS IN OUR MIDST:
SEXUAL DEVIANCY IN POSTWAR ONTARIO

Introduction

As society's most vulnerable members, children rely on adults for protection, and when we fail, we feel it keenly. When this happens, we are also more likely to feel obligated to swiftly take actions we think will provide children with greater protection. In this sense, the current popularity of sexual predator laws in the United States and the implementation of a national sex offender registry in Canada appear to reflect a basic human impulse to protect the weak and punish the wicked, an impulse that seems to stand outside of history. No matter in what historical period they occur, sexual offences against children lead us to ask what it is that would cause people to commit such horrible crimes. Concepts of innocence and evil and ideas about human nature are susceptible to historical change, however, and answers to these questions are always shaped by the political and cultural climate in which they are asked. That context ultimately determines the solutions we devise. In the post–Second World War era, men who committed sex crimes against children were popularly referred to as 'strangers in our midst.' The phrase evokes Canadian Methodist J.S. Woodsworth's well-known 1909 anti-immigration book, *Strangers within Our Gates, or Coming Canadians.* Concerned that eastern European and other non-Anglo immigrants threatened to erode Canada's British character and undermine social stability, he argued that the future of the nation depended on the assimilation of Canada's foreign population.[1] Woodsworth renounced his position soon after, but the image of the 'stranger in our midst' endured. The phrase is a Christian trope typically used to urge congregants to reach out to and embrace members of an isolated and perhaps misunderstood community, most often immigrants, and it is still used in this manner today. For a brief period of time, however, the stranger in our midst referred to sex deviants.[2] In the 1950s and

60s in Canada and the United States, a surge in public concern over sexual assaults against children led everyday citizens to demand new, innovative methods for dealing with the problem. By the mid-1950s, popular consensus held that sex criminals suffered from a mental disorder, not a criminal indifference to humanity. They needed help, not punishment.

Strangers in Our Midst tracks the historical roots of contemporary sex offender treatment programs and examines the historical construction of the male sex offender. Prevailing criminal sexual stereotypes, particularly that of the pedophile as being unable and unwilling to exercise control over his sexual impulses, are a product of a specific set of social concerns, conditions, and values articulated by Canada's English-speaking parents of the baby boom generation. This book is not a history of sex offenders, nor is it a history of victims of sexual assault, though both of these historical subjects haunt these pages. It tells the history of sexual deviation, one of the most important modern concepts that continues to shape how we think about sexuality to the present day.

Forensic sexology has its roots in the nineteenth century, but sex remained a relatively marginal field of study until the post–Second World War era, when changing sexual mores, popular and state support for the mental health movement, and the demographic spike in the number of parents raising young children converged to lend widespread support for criminal sexual psychopath legislation.[3] Adopted only in Canada and in twenty-nine American states, sexual psychopath laws signalled an important shift in the way the criminal justice system dealt with sex offences. No longer were perpetrators of sex crimes regarded only as criminals deserving punishment. Those who committed crimes of a sexual nature were viewed as pathological victims of a mental aberration for which traditional forms of punishment were neither a cure nor a deterrent. Men determined by the courts to be 'sexual psychopaths' were subject to indeterminate criminal sentences to be served in prison (in Canada and some American states), or to civil commitment to a hospital or mental health institution (in most American states) so that psychiatric and other forms of reformative and rehabilitative 'treatment' could be provided until the inmate was deemed 'cured' or at the very least unlikely to repeat his offence.

Sex psychopath laws seemed a perfect solution to the newly discovered problem of recidivism among sex offenders who victimized children, but the law displeased many of the experts who were responsible for its administration.[4] Psychiatrists complained that sexual psychopathy was a meaningless legal construct that had no basis in medical science; that there was no logic in singling out sex criminals for treatment; and, most concerning, that there were no known methods for treating sexual deviation. Legal experts argued that passing out indefinite sentences based on psychiatric testimony violated the offender's civil rights. Proponents insisted that if an opportunity for providing treatment was created and treatment methods were explored, there was hope that a cure could be found. In Canada and in more than half of the American states, the optimists carried the day.

Sexual psychopath laws no longer exist in their original forms, due in part to persistent campaigning for their repeal.[5] However, the change is largely in name alone. In Canada, for example, the 1948 criminal sexual psychopath law became the 1961 dangerous sex offender law, which became the dangerous offender law in 1977. 'Sex' may have been dropped from the name, but since 1977 the majority of offenders in Canada designated as 'dangerous offenders' committed a sex crime against non-family members. Criminal sexual psychopath legislation is still with us, only in different forms.

The history of sexual deviation and sex offender treatment has tremendous contemporary relevance, yet it has attracted only limited attention from historians.[6] This is partly because in North America the history of sexuality in the twentieth century has been largely concerned – and for good reason – with the devastating legacy of the medicalization of sexuality for gays, lesbians, and, more recently, transgendered people.[7] As historian Philip Jenkins noted, the mid-century sex crime panic had 'bleak implications' for homosexuals.[8] Even for those who were not subjected to medical and psychotherapeutic treatment, self-defined homosexuals, as well as other sexual 'outsiders' such as transvestites, transsexuals, and bisexuals were medically and culturally defined as mentally ill, and were widely perceived to be a serious threat to the safety of others, including children. The consequences could be devastating, such as the loss of employment, family, and friends. In order to survive, some passed as heterosexual; others escaped by suicide.[9]

While there is good reason to focus on lesbian and gay experience, by extricating homosexuality from the broader category of sexual deviancy we limit our ability to fashion effective tools for responding to contemporary issues around human sexuality, the law, and the regulation of sex offenders.[10] Sexual psychopath laws and the promotion of sexual deviation treatment had much further-reaching effects. For example, it was heterosexual sex offences against women and children that propelled the public to demand sexual psychopath laws, but assumptions about the anti-homosexual, socially conservative roots of sexual psychopath laws have meant that the history of activism around sexual assault in the 1950s has been virtually ignored. Moreover, Canadian historians have ignored the significant differences between the sexual politics in Canada and those in McCarthy-era United States, where in some places the sex crime problem focussed equally, if not primarily, on male homosexuality, as was the case in Boise, Idaho.[11] In Canada, however, the public and media focus was much more squarely on sex offenders whose victims were children. Indeed, only two sexual psychopath and dangerous sexual offender cases are known to have involved offenders for whom the substantive charge resulted from consensual sex with another adult male.

One of them was George Everett Klippert, a gay man whose admission, during an arson investigation, of having had sex with other men resulted in his being convicted of gross indecency. He was subsequently found to be a dangerous sexual offender.[12] Sociologist Gary Kinsman argues that Klippert's case helped to speed up the process of legal reform regarding the decriminalization of homosexual acts.[13] The Supreme Court of Canada's 3–2 ruling against Klippert's appeal of the dangerous sex offender legislation became headline news and galvanized emerging gay rights activists. Even the Court's written decision hinted that it was time for Parliament to consider following England's 1967 Sex Offenders Act, which decriminalized homosexual acts between consenting adults. Klippert lost his appeal, but his case was a turning point in the public debate about homosexuality. It was a decisive step forward in the fight for equality for gays and lesbians.

The early vision of sexual liberationists, however, was about much more than achieving equality. Gay and lesbian-feminist liberationists aimed to destabilize the homosexual/heterosexual dichotomy. They envisioned a future where such distinctions would disappear altogether. More than that, all types of the liberationist critique of the pathologization of sexuality included sex deviants, not just lesbians and gay men. For example, more than five years after the decriminalization of homosexual acts, Gays Ottawa and the National Gay Rights Coalition wrote to the federal government and denounced the treatment of sex offenders as 'barbaric and inhumane,' and demanded that dangerous sex offender legislation be repealed.[14]

This book returns us to that early vision by reinserting the medical construction of homosexuality within the broader context of the history of sex deviation. Instead of extricating homosexuality from the grip of forensic sexology, this project casts a critical gaze on the entire system of sexual classification. This may appear to be a step backward in the evolution of the history of sexuality, a field that began as part of a broader political project aimed at countering and correcting the myths and misconceptions medical science created by lumping homosexuals with pedophiles and other criminal sex offenders; liberating homosexuality from myth, superstition, and censure to take its rightful place in life's rich pageant is a central goal of this historical field. But rather than reprove the incisive criticisms of its predecessors, this book documents how the conflation of homosexuality with other sexual deviations occurred in the first place, and in so doing reveals how early medical studies of homosexuals continue to underpin modern understandings of criminal sexual behaviour, particularly pedophilic behaviour.

Despite my determination to avoid paying a disproportionate degree of attention to homosexuality while researching and writing this book, I found it at almost every turn. Medical doctors, psychiatrists, psychologists, lawyers, judges, the police, prison administrators, and even inmates kept leading me back to it for two key reasons. First, homosexuality was what medical scientists knew the most about, or so they thought. And second, in prison, discipline took precedence over psychotherapy, and homosexuality was considered a much more pressing problem than pedophilia or other deviations. But it is important to resist the persistent pull toward a homosexual centre when looking at sexual deviation. A broader lens that takes in the whole of the 'sex deviant' population will deepen our historical understanding of the popularization and impact of the medicalization of sexuality. For example, while it is certainly true that gay men were unfairly targeted by the postwar sex crime panic over assaults against children, this was never the intended effect of either the judiciary, medical experts, or the thousands of parents who demanded that Canada adopt a sexual psychopath law.[15] Similarly, in the annals of homosexual history, the successful campaign to have the American Psychiatric Association remove homosexual sex from the *Diagnostic and Statistical Manual of Mental Disorders* is considered a victory of homosexual rights organizations, but this victory needs also to be understood within the wider context of the antipsychiatry movement, and the forgotten role played by the failure of sex offender treatment in this process.[16] It was not just that homosexuality was 'liberated.' Psychiatry's grip on sexuality was loosened, even if only slightly.

Strangers in Our Midst is a study of the growth and expansion of forensic sexology during a period of unprecedented public and state support. It examines the theories and ideas sexologists produced, and documents how they were applied in clinical and carceral settings. The spectre of treatment for sexual deviants continues to haunt the cultural imagination, but precisely what treatments were used, why medical practitioners employed them, and in what contexts, have yet to be systematically documented or fully explained. Some of the more sensational methods, such as electroconvulsive therapy and lobotomy, have become emblematic of the injustices endured by marginalized and medicalized sexual 'outsiders.' Yet, at one time, these treatments were seen as promising tools that would bring an end to social unhappiness and to unnecessary pain and suffering endured by victims of sexually deviated desires. My primary aim is to show the range of social and political processes through which psychiatric treatment came to be seen as the best way to address the problem of sex crimes, and to examine how mental health experts attempted to meet the demand for treatments, while at the same time to attend to the ways these programs became mechanisms of control and regulation.

The history of the criminal sexual psychopath in Canada formally begins in 1947 when the British Columbia Provincial Organization of Parent-Teacher Associations (BCPTA) determined that the most modern and effective response to a man who had sexually assaulted a Vancouver child was not imprisonment, but medical treatment.[17] Inspired by American sex psychopath laws, the BCPTA won over H.C. Green, the Vancouver South member of Parliament, who first brought their demands to the attention of the House of Commons in April of that year. Just one year later, a Canadian version of criminal sexual psychopath legislation was unanimously passed through Parliament and into law. The law was based on the assumption that sex perverts could be cured by psychiatric or medical treatment. And despite the minister of justice's concern that the law was impractical (since there was no known cure for sexual perversion), public and political pressure led even him to support its passage.

In a high-profile campaign opposing the execution of convicted U.S. murderer Caryl Chessman, one protestor succinctly captured the tenor of the times with a placard that read 'Love not Hate, Justice not Revenge, Psychotherapy not Cyanide.'[18] It is a reminder that the psychotherapeutic solution extended beyond the sex crime problem and influenced a wide range of postwar prison and justice reform movements. Throughout the 1950s and 1960s in English-speaking Canada and in parts of the United States, public support for mental health treatment was at its peak. As Canadian forensic sexologist Hans Mohr saw it, the Second World War had made it difficult to continue to see madness as individual pathology. The mass middle class embraced the age of the expert and proved receptive to mental health experts who extended a message of optimism and hope.[19] Providing therapy rather than administering punishment appealed to members of English-Canada's middle class, who were also, of course, busy reading the latest child-rearing manuals, which advocated precisely the same approach to parenting.[20]

The heady optimism that characterized the postwar enthusiasm for a mental health approach to solving social problems came to an end with the rise of the antipsychiatry movement of the late 1960s and 70s. The assault on psychiatry came from a number of corners including gay rights organizations, women's liberation groups, ex-psychiatric patients, and even members of the profession itself.[21] Critics denounced treatment programs as an extension of the prison's culture of repression. High-profile media exposés and books like Nicholas Kittrie's 1971 *The Right to Be Different* revealed that, behind the walls of some of the largest U.S. prisons, the helping professions were conducting atrocious experiments on the most disenfranchised and powerless people in the nation.[22] Singled out for special attention were electroconvulsive and aversion therapies, both of which were employed in the treatment of sex deviation. Immortalized by Stanley Kubrick's 1971 film adaptation of Anthony Burgess's 1962 novel *A Clockwork Orange*, in which a violent sex offender volunteers for treatment in exchange for early release, aversion therapy fell into disrepute.[23] These revelations had their intended effect on both sides of the Canada–U.S. border. Support for treatment dwindled, funding for such programs dried up, and a law and order approach filled the breach. Century-old images of the psychiatrist as an evil, self-serving asylum keeper were revived, invasive treatments were denounced as mind control, and the profession was scandalized. Prisoner's rights advocates denounced the treatments as a sham and, even worse, as an extension of the state's oppressive regime. Support for therapeutic confinement rapidly declined. Treatment teams continue to work with certain groups of inmates, including sex offenders, but the idea that prisons will one day be abolished and replaced by hospitals is met with ridicule today. In the 1950s, however, it was greeted with enthusiastic support by everyday citizens who shared a profound faith in the ability of modern medicine to solve complex social problems.[24]

This book is divided into two parts. Part 1 explores the contentious history of criminal sexual psychopathy as a medico-legal concept, and part 2 examines the history of treating for sexual deviation in postwar Ontario.

The first chapter tracks the progress of the concept of the sexual psychopath from its origins in late nineteenth- and early twentieth-century psychiatric thought up to its enshrinement in the Criminal Code of Canada in 1948. Historians have attributed the emergence of the sexual psychopath and sexual psychopath laws to the disruption of family life during the Depression, to postwar anxiety about masculinity and the demobilized soldier, and to a resurgence of social conservatism in response to changing sexual and gender mores brought about by the Second World War. Tracing sex psychopath laws through the long history of legal and criminological reform, however, tells a different story about the postwar era. In Canada, the campaign for psychiatric treatment for sexual deviation had more in common with late nineteenth- and early twentieth-century liberal progressive reform movements than it did with cold war conservatism.

Chapter 2 shows how the popularization of psychiatric ideas about sex offenders was driven by a public willingness to see sex deviation as the result of bad parenting, and to regard sex criminals as emotionally deviated and in need of treatment, not punishment. Compassionate understanding was the order of the day, at least for everyday citizens who demanded a re-examination of the way crimes were handled by the state. The parent activism that fuelled this campaign is further evidence that the retrenchment thesis and the myth of domestic quiescence, both of which have come under increasing scrutiny, misrepresent the complex social politics of the postwar era.[25] While not explicitly feminist in their analysis of the problem, women put sexual violence back on the public agenda and into popular discourse. In so doing, they challenged the discourse of sexual shame that kept families from pursuing criminal charges against perpetrators of child sexual assault. As contemporary readers well know, contesting fundamental beliefs about the meaning and experience of sexual assault is not without its complications. Historians have shown how, for example, the collapsing of pedophilia and homosexuality was one of the major features of the social and political movement that supported criminal sexual psychopath legislation. This chapter reveals how the supposedly generalized hysteria about homosexuality that marked this period can be more clearly delineated by closely examining the very particular way that local police forces responded to anxiety about repeat sex offenders whose victims were children, and how the ambiguity of the new and poorly understood terms 'sex deviate' and 'sexual deviation' contributed to the collapsing of sexual difference and sexual danger.

Four years after the 1948 passage of criminal sexual psychopath legislation, critics noted that the law was little used. A sustained public pressure campaign demanding that the federal government investigate why convicted sex offenders were not being sentenced under the law resulted in the 1954 creation of the Royal Commission on the Criminal Law Relating to Criminal Sexual Psychopaths. Chapter 3 examines the range of testimony offered to the commission by medical and legal experts, social service workers, and 'concerned citizens,' most of whom were members of women's councils and parent-teacher associations, from across the county. The transcripts offer a glimpse of how the problem of sex crime was constructed and contested by citizens and experts alike, and allows us to gain a much clearer picture of where Canadian psychiatrists sat regarding sexual matters. Significantly, most psychiatrists opposed the legislation on the grounds that it lacked medical legitimacy. Expert and lay testimony combined with the commission's final report allow us to reconstruct the intellectual and ideological foundations of the sex offender treatment programs that the state would later introduce.

The 1950s was a period of tremendous growth for forensic sexology, but not because there was an explosion of medical interest in sexuality or because of advances in psychiatry, psychology, or any other field of medical science or mental health. Indeed, treatment staff had the impossible task of treating a population so recently identified that almost nothing was known about them. Moreover, treating 'the mad and the bad' – people whose crimes were attributed to mental instability, aberration, or illness – was one of the least appealing fields of psychiatric work, and sex deviants were the least palatable among them.[26] Those who worked in this field were forced to be creative, and many became champions of a permissive approach to understanding human sexuality.

The permissive approach popular among many postwar forensic sexologists made a positive contribution to homophile and later gay liberation movement politics. Experts like R.E. Turner, who headed Canada's first and, in the 1950s and 60s, its only clinic for the treatment of sexual deviation, argued that homosexuality should not be subject to criminal prosecution. Homophile activists regarded Turner and others like him as an ally, not an enemy. Only by widening our lens to include an analysis of forensic sexologists' responses to heterosexual offences, however, can we begin to see the negative consequences of the permissive approach. The chapters in part 2 of this book reveal how the model of human sexuality that accepted homosexuality as a harmless deviation from a social norm also normalized forms of heterosexual violence. Both parts must be understood to grasp the whole. Bringing the insights of both the history of sexuality and feminist histories of sexual violence to bear on the period allows us to better appreciate the full impact of postwar forensic sexology.

These issues are the focus of chapter 4, which examines the work undertaken at the Toronto Psychiatric Hospital's Outpatient Forensic Clinic, an internationally respected sex deviation treatment clinic whose staff pioneered new treatment approaches and research methods and contributed to the development of new ways of thinking about human sexuality. Like other progressive sexologists of the time, Forensic Clinic staff popularized an approach to understanding sexual deviation that combined the theories and concepts of Sigmund Freud and Alfred Kinsey. This will come as a surprise to those who are familiar with the work of these two key twentieth-century thinkers. Kinsey repudiated Freud's theories. Kinsey's system of measuring and charting sexual behaviour attempted to undermine the moralism that underpinned modern sexological thought. As we shall see, an unlikely hybrid approach that drew on both Freudian psychoanalysis and Kinsey's quantitative methodologies and critique of sex norms became one of the most popular ways of understanding sex crime in the decades after the Second World War.

The history of sex deviation treatment in Ontario was overdetermined by the different institutional cultures and fiscal policies of the provincial governmental departments in which they were housed. The Ontario Department of Reform Institutions was the first in Canada to create a sex offender treatment program. Indeed, Canada's federal government, which was responsible for criminal sexual psychopaths and dangerous sex offenders, created its first sex offender program in 1973, almost twenty years after Ontario created its first provincial prison and civilian hospital treatment programs, and more than thirty years after criminal sexual psychopath legislation was added to the Criminal Code of Canada. The fate of this provincial program, from its beginnings in 1954 to the end of the last remaining program in 1973, is the subject of chapter 5. In contrast to the public's enthusiastic support of mental health experts, most prison administrators were adamantly opposed to softening the traditional military-style approach to running prisons and managing prisoners. I argue that the implementation of any program of reform, including sex deviation treatment programs, was fatally undermined by the conflict between those who managed the reformatory system and those who attempted to provide psychological treatment for inmates. By the end of the 1950s, Ontario's prison-based therapeutic programs were used for punitive, not reformative, purposes. The story this chapter tells is yet another reminder of how well-intentioned reform programs can have stunningly repressive effects.

Once inside the prison, treatment experts hired to provide therapeutic services for sex offenders discovered an elaborate sexual culture in male prisons that challenged their modern theories about human sexual behaviour. Prison sex culture was organized according to a pre–Second World War model that regarded effeminate men as homosexual and the masculine men who have sex with them as heterosexual. Early sexologists adopted this model as their own, but after the Second World War, 'gender inversion' was largely abandoned and 'sexual deviancy' was adopted in its stead. According to this new model, all same-sex sexual activity was homosexual. Prisoners did not see it this way, however. These different systems of organization are discussed in chapter 6. I argue that experts' response to prison sex culture reveals modern sexology's inability to grasp the intimate relationship between sex, gender, and power. It also shows how the 'diddler,' prison slang for a person who had sexually assaulted a child, emerged as a specific social type as a result of changes in the way gender, sexuality, and identity were understood.

In pre–Second World War Canada, psychologists were experts in administering and devising psychometric tests and were not deemed qualified to provide counselling or other services. After the war, psychologists saw their role in the provision of mental health services expand considerably, and by the end of the decade they were providing counselling, publishing studies, and offering expert advice to the media, parents, and anyone else interested in what they had to say. Psychiatry also underwent considerable changes in this era. Before the Second World War, Canadian psychiatry was still a very small field, and in English Canada was dominated by men like C.K. Clarke, who not only abjured Sigmund Freud and psychoanalysis in general, but who also exerted tremendous control over university curricula. The 1950s was also a time when the discipline of psychiatry became more formally regulated: in mid-decade, medical doctors wanting to specialize in psychiatry were required to fulfil certain training and testing requirements; previously one had only to do post-graduate training in a mental hospital to be considered a psychiatrist. Psychologists and psychiatrists were drawn more closely together as they became mutually interested in psychoanalysis. Moreover, as we shall see in the case of psychiatrists, many combined older biological ideas about criminal and sex aetiology with more modern Freudian ideas. Thus, for our purposes at least, the distinctions between psychiatrists and psychologists are less meaningful by profession and more meaningful by the ideas they professed. Throughout this study, I use the term 'mental health expert' to refer to all of those who possessed a graduate degree in medicine, psychology, or social work, and an interest in the subject. At the time, this was all that was required to be an 'expert' on sex deviation.

As the public became more familiar with the language of mental health expertise, so too did public discourse evolve. In the 1950s, the 'sex pervert' became the 'sex deviate,' and then the 'sex deviant,' and only became the 'sex offender' in the 1970s. I use 'deviate,' 'deviant,' and 'sex offender' as they appeared in the records under study. To reduce visual noise I have generally avoided using quotes around these terms, but as this book argues, part of the problem with the term 'sexual deviation' was its ambiguity. Therefore, I have attempted to provide clarification as much as possible, and where possible, throughout the text.

PART ONE

Theories

chapter one

Criminal Sexual Psychopathy: The Birth of a Legal Concept

In the spring of 1947, Mrs Geraldine M. had had enough. During a Saturday shopping excursion in downtown Toronto, a man had exposed himself just as she and her daughter boarded the bus home. Two days later, her daughter came home in 'a hysterical condition. One of those indecently exposed male creatures had approached her.' Mrs M. related these events in a letter to Russell Kelly, Ontario's minister of health. She wrote the minister not only to express anger and fear, but to share some very specific ideas about what the Ontario government should do with sex perverts.[1] 'We have raised our children with a chaste and modest upbringing in a Christian home,' she argued, 'and we feel that this class of men's childhood may have been sadly neglected, thus causing them to be what they are ... Any right thinking person,' she continued, 'is forced to believe there must be ... some brain disease to cause them to act in such a manner.' For this reason, 'such men needed treatment [because] jail meant nothing to this type.' She was not alone in her thinking. As Canada set out to rebuild itself after the exhaustive effort to win the Second World War, sex crimes against children emerged as one of the most urgent social problems of the day, and the sexual psychopath, a pathological character popularized in the United States in the interwar years, appeared as the new sexual villain.

Like most sex crime panics, the post–Second World War frenzy was fuelled by sensational media coverage of sexual assaults and, in rare instances, the disappearance and murder of a child. In Canada, the first widely reported attack was the murder of seven-year-old Roddy Moore in Vancouver, and was soon followed by the murder of two small boys in Winnipeg. But, perhaps because the victim was a girl, or was disabled, or was from Ontario where the national media and federal government were more likely to take notice, it was the 1947 murder of Toronto's Arlene Anderson that pushed the level of media coverage and public outrage over the top.[2] Perceiving a dangerous threat out of control, Canadians looked to the government for a quick and meaningful response. While the call for action was predictable, what was unique to this era was the construction of the problem. Curiously, Mrs M. did not, as one might have expected, send her letter to the Department of Justice. Instead, she directed her comments to the minister of health. That she did so places her at the forefront of an epistemological shift in the way Canadians were to think about sexual danger. In the years following the Second World War, sex offenders were regarded as more mentally disturbed than criminally culpable, and the sex crime was regarded as a major mental health problem waiting to be solved.

All across Canada, citizens embraced criminal sexual psychopath legislation as the solution. First introduced in the state of Michigan in 1937, criminal sexual psychopath laws were premised on the notion that repeat sex offenders were neither deterred nor reformed by incarceration because their actions were driven by an uncontrollable impulse to commit their horrible crimes. Those who accepted this interpretation of sex crimes, and sexually deviant behaviour in general, believed that the answer was to eliminate the impulse, or, in popular lay terms, cure the disease. Thus, sexual psychopath laws married psychiatric expertise in the area of mental illness with the court's ability to confine, resulting in the incarceration of certain sex offenders until they were deemed cured by a psychiatrist. Although sexual psychopath laws were adopted in the late 1930s by only a handful of states in the American northeast, public support for these laws resumed with fervour at the end of the Second World War. In 1948 members of Parliament unanimously passed criminal sexual psychopath legislation into the Criminal Code of Canada, and by the end of the 1950s, twenty-nine American states had adopted some version of the law.

This chapter tracks the genealogy of criminal sexual psychopath legislation within the context of the evolving relationship between the law, psychiatry, and the increasing popularity of mental health as a palliative to a wide range of post–Second World War political and social problems. I begin with a brief overview of the conjoining of psychiatry and the law in Britain, Canada, and the United States, covering the period from the medicalization of insanity to the introduction of psychopathy and 'therapeutic confinement.' Next, I examine how Canadian and American social reformers pushed for changes to the administration of justice by advocating for the adoption of positivist criminological concepts, including the idea that criminal behaviour was the product of a mental disturbance or disorder. Acceptance of this notion was dependant on psychiatry's perceived ability to treat or cure these disorders. As this chapter shows, psychiatrists were reluctant to claim curative abilities, but they nonetheless remained committed to the medical and mental health model of sexual deviation. The consequences would prove to be far-reaching, extending well beyond the control of the very same professionals who helped set, and keep, the wheels in motion for the better part of the twentieth century.

The legal concept of psychopathy was a long time in the making, its roots stretching back into the mid-nineteenth century. Up to that time, insanity functioned as an exculpatory legal defence, offering absolution to adjudged lunatics for their illegal acts, and relieving them of criminal responsibility. A wide range of people were considered by the court qualified to testify as to the sanity of the accused, including friends, family, community members, and even the jailer who held the prisoner for trial.[3] That changed after 1843, when a British jury acquitted Daniel M'Naghten for the murder of Sir Robert Peel's private secretary. Public and political outrage at the decision resulted in a demand for the clarification of the insanity defence, and the law lords were asked to draw up new guidelines. By this time, psychiatrists had elaborated considerably on the subject of lunacy; years of observing and studying both asylum inmates and incarcerated criminals had provided the opportunity to catalogue and quantify a wide range of manifestations of madness.

Partial insanity was one of the conceptual inventions that psychiatrists, including those who advised the law lords, thought worthy of the court's consideration. Partial insanity posited that one could comprehend both good and bad, but also suffer a disorder of emotion and volition, or an 'irresistible impulse.' This finding was backed by ongoing observations of both asylum inmates and criminal populations that demonstrated that punishment alone did not always act as a deterrent. If the purpose of incarceration was to effect reformation, it was unconscionable to send to prison someone for whom it would have absolutely no useful effect. Indeed, through the eyes of a medical practitioner, if the convicted criminal's actions were driven by an impulse stronger than his (or her) own free will, a sentence of confinement was scientifically unsound and inhumane.

The M'Naghten rules, as they came to be known, enhanced the status of psychiatrists as scientific and medical experts on human behaviour, and the courts became an important source of new patient referrals.[4] But England's law lords rejected the concept of partial insanity as a legal defence on the grounds that it undermined *mens rea*, the foundation upon which the law rested.[5] The M'Naghten rules determined that unless it could be proved that one was unable to discern right from wrong, accused criminals would be held legally, if not medically, responsible for their actions. Canada immediately adopted the M'Naghten rules, as did the majority of the United States.[6] However, the District of Columbia and seventeen states accepted partial insanity, or 'irresistible impulse,' as a legitimate legal defence, thus leaving the door open for the creation of new ways of dealing with persistent offenders.

The primary concern of the courts is to determine whether the accused committed the crime. It remained up to psychiatrists to try to understand why the crime was committed, and they were not alone in their quest. As the nineteenth century drew to an end, social and moral reform movements in Canada and the United States gained popular and political momentum. Though most concerned themselves with problems associated with urban neighbourhoods, some looked further down the line along which many of their charity recipients travelled. The few that dared investigate were all horrified by what they discovered. Prisons and asylums shared many of the same devastating qualities: men, women, and often children were housed together in buildings that were invariably run down, unsanitary, cold, damp, overcrowded, and dangerous. For even the least-attentive observer, it was immediately clear that no one could possibly leave such a place improved.

If the social reform movement was about anything, it was about improvement, and its advocates rejected the tenets of classical criminology that held that criminals deserved punishment. Instead, social progressives and moral reformers championed the ideas of theorists like Enrico Ferri, a vigorous advocate for the application of anthropology and criminal sociology in the justice system. Positivist criminologists saw the 'dangerous classes' not as a single homogenous mass but as a heterogeneous collection of a wide variety of criminal types. For Ferri and others, progress in criminal justice depended on the proper classification of prisoners. By sorting the young from the old, the experienced from the inexperienced, the violent from the non-violent, the less hardened could be saved from further corruption, and appropriate programs of reform could be tailored to the needs of different groups of offenders. Ferri argued that delinquents should be regarded in the same manner as hospital patients and the insane, and that prisoners should be held only as long as it took to effect a cure.[7] Tailoring programs for reform demanded a more flexible approach to sentencing, allowing inmates early release or a prolonged period of confinement, depending on their progress. Thus, positivist penologists introduced what was to become the cornerstone of therapeutic confinement: the indeterminate sentence.[8]

Social progressives and moral reformers in Canada, the United States, and Britain embraced positive penology. Of particular concern was the class of criminal who, by a persistent refusal to conform to the bounds of society, regularly and repeatedly found himself or herself in jails, prisons, and reformatories. Improved record-keeping methods and the popularization of social scientific research revealed that for some prisoners, law-breaking activities were habit forming. For reform-minded citizens, widespread recidivism provided incontrovertible evidence that prison did not always have the desired deterrent effect. If cities were to be saved from their downward spiral into degeneracy, new approaches to crime and delinquency were required. Women, the young, and, to a lesser extent, alcoholics were most likely to be sympathetically perceived as victims of the pleasures and dangers of the city, as suffering from a 'disease of the will,' or as succumbing to a combination of both.[9] It was for their benefit that Canada's moral reformers and America's social progressives called for a more compassionate and less punitive stance.

In response to the problem of recidivism, habitual-criminal legislation was introduced into British law in 1908. However, it was based on the premise that it was the criminal that failed to reform in prison rather than the prison that failed to reform the criminal. Indeterminate sentences were imposed not to allow for flexible sentencing deemed necessary to implement a program of rehabilitative reform and reclamation, but simply to allow the state to hold a criminal beyond the expiration of the original sentence as a preventative measure.

In contrast, many northern and western American states showed a greater willingness to experiment with positivist criminology. In 1909 psychologist William Healy founded the Chicago Juvenile Psychopathic Institute, which provided therapy for children and adolescents and gave advice to the city's new juvenile court. The Chicago clinic became the prototype for similar legal tribunals. In 1911 the Massachusetts legislature passed the Briggs Act, enshrining the 'defective delinquent,' a medicalized version of the habitual criminal, into law. This first generation of psychopathic legislation did not distinguish between types of criminal offences; virtually anyone deemed likely to reoffend could be included. To earn such a dubious distinction, the concurring testimony of two psychiatrists was required, despite the fact that the law was aimed at those who could not be diagnosed as mentally deficient. Defective delinquent laws were quickly adopted by other states. By the early 1930s, all but two American states had their own version of the Chicago clinic.[10]

Well attuned to developments in the United States, English Canadian social reformers monitored the progress of criminological innovations like Chicago's Juvenile Psychopathic Institute with great interest, and in 1920 Toronto set up a similar court clinic to service the Juvenile Court established only eight years earlier.[11] It was an experiment that combined the insights of psychiatry, psychology, and social work with the regulatory methods of the justice system. Juvenile delinquents were sent for psychometric testing by a psychologist, a family background check was conducted by a social worker, and a psychiatric interview completed the subject's file. This team of experts would then prepare a report with a sentencing recommendation for the court.

Although the defective delinquent was a novel legal invention, it drew on an established medical concept. Mid-nineteenth-century psychiatrists developed nuanced understandings of the form and content of insanity, dividing it into five main types. Moral insanity referred to those who were intellectually unimpaired but who were 'incapable of conducting themselves with decency and propriety in the business of life.'[12] When eugenics came into vogue in the latter half of the century, moral insanity was recast as 'constitutional psychopathic inferiority,' indicating that an inability to comply with the demands and expectations of the prevailing social order was, to use modern terminology, genetically encoded. Most psychiatric assessments tended to attribute criminality to low mental scores on the battery of tests administered during the assessment and classification phases in the processing of delinquents, and the psychopathic personality was most commonly applied to those who did not fall into that category. Consequently, one of the more unsettling features of psychopathy was a propensity toward criminal acts accompanied by an above-average intellect. The ability to appear normal to the untrained eye made the psychopath an even more threatening character. Of course, all of this served to make psychiatrists that much more essential to the criminal justice system. Without them, psychopaths were free to roam the streets and commit their heinous crimes undetected.

Because psychiatric and social work services were first integrated into the criminal justice system at the family and juvenile court level, defective delinquency and psychopathy were medico-legal labels applied to youthful offenders. In the early twentieth century, psychopathy was also applied to adult women, most of whose 'problem' behaviours were non-violent violations of sex and gender norms. In fact, when sexuality and psychopathy were first explicitly linked in American criminal law in 1920, it was to address the problem of female sexual immorality.[13] The integration of psychopathy with the criminal law depended on the willingness of the courts to regard some offenders as incapable of exercising control over their actions. Characterizing the commission of certain crimes as the lack of self-control was most likely to win the sympathy of judges when the perpetrator was either female or a minor, and especially if one could argue that she or he lacked the kind of character-building education and moral upbringing necessary for resisting evil temptations. With the help of social progressives and moral reformers whose protective concerns focused on those they deemed most endangered by industrialization and urbanization, women and children were more likely to be cast as victims of circumstance, and consequently to be in need of help rather than punishment.

The experience of the Great Depression proved just how elastic the concept of psychopathy was. As historian Estelle Freedman has argued, economic and social stresses on traditional family arrangements triggered concerns about masculinity. Large groups of unemployed men riding the rails and women left alone to provide for their children aroused public anxiety about the dangers of 'men adrift' from the taming rewards of breadwinner masculinity and the feminizing influence of the family.[14] In urban centres like New York City, however, homosexuals were singled out as both sign and symbol of the dangerous excesses of the 1920s. Conservative forces successfully argued that a return to order and stability required the elimination of all forms of corrupt behaviour, including that which had been allowed to flourish in small pockets of many metropolitan cities, but especially in New York where a vibrant drag entertainment scene attracted thousands of onlookers.[15] Mayor Fiorello LaGuardia rode this platform to power in 1933. His campaign to rid the city of its 'unsavoury' elements explicitly targeted homosexual cruising spots and drag queen culture.[16]

As the prostitute gave way to the sex criminal as the emblem of social disorder, experts and politicians recast the problem of uncontrollable impulses to reflect male, not female or juvenile, behaviour. In the 1930s, male homosexuality was characterized as a pernicious social evil. Though not limited to New York City, New York did play a central role in linking

homosexuality, particularly as it manifested itself in nonconforming gender behaviour, with violent and dangerous sexual acts. Beginning with
the founding of the Bureau for Social Hygiene in 1911, New York was the
North Americana hub for new social scientific research on sexual behaviour. Supported with funding from John D. Rockefeller, the bureau
undertook a program of 'study, prevention and amelioration of those
social conditions, crimes, and diseases which, adversely, affect the well-
being of society.'[17] Until LaGuardia's electoral victory, its staff focused on
providing sex education, preventing venereal disease, and stemming
prostitution, then the emblematic social evil caused by urbanization,
industrialization, and commercialized leisure. According to Jennifer
Terry, in the 1910s and 20s homosexuality was marginal to the research
interests of bureau staff. Where it emerged, she argues, re-searchers
tended to interpret it less as pathological and more as a sign of the problems of heterosexuality.

In 1935, however, the research agenda took a significant turn. Both
Rockefeller and the bureau threw their support behind the creation of a
committee whose sole focus was the study of homosexuality. Also based
in New York City, the Committee for the Study of Sex Variants at-tracted
a sizable number of high-profile specialists based in universities, hospitals, and clinics throughout the American northeast and in California.
Committee members viewed homosexuality as both a medical disorder
and a social problem, and their research ultimately strengthened the
bridge between formal systems of regulation and medical science.

In 1937 the New York State legislature and LaGuardia called on forensic psychiatrists to help create assessment and treatment facilities whose
purpose was to cure psychopathic sex criminals. The criminal sexual psychopath – the offspring of a perceived threat to national morality and
sexual safety, and the medical construction of the (homo)sexually deviated offender – shared all of the features of its predecessor, the defective
delinquent: able to distinguish right from wrong but persistently socially
non-compliant due to an 'irresistible impulse'; of normal or even above-
average intelligence; unable to profit from experience, and a recidivist.
What made him different was that he was always male and 'appeared to
be a sex pervert or degenerate or to suffer from a mental disorder with
marked sex deviation and tendencies dangerous to the public safety.'[18]
Though sexual psychopath laws varied from state to state, and Canada
ultimately made its own revisions to suit the particular needs of its criminal code, all such laws defined their subjects as needing treatment, and,

once deemed a sexual psychopath, a convicted sex criminal was incarcerated in a prison, a psychiatric hospital, or both, until he was assessed as no longer a threat to the community. Because of the way sexual psychopath legislation drew a link between sexual acts, uncontrolled behaviour, dangerousness, and recidivism, sex offenders came to be viewed as a much greater threat than other types of criminals.[19]

Members of the Committee for the Study of Sex Variants, and other sexologists who followed, articulated a new scientific discourse about sex that would underwrite the sex crime panic of the mid-twentieth century.[20] When J. Edgar Hoover, the director of the Federal Bureau of Investigations, declared a 'War on Sex Crime,' the American media increased its focus on stories of sex-related social and moral conflicts and turned to medical and psychiatric experts for explanations for local crimes.[21] But sexual deviancy was still a marginal (and stigmatized) area of medical expertise. Concerns over morality in the modern world may have paved the way for the expansion of psychiatric inquiry into the realm of everyday life, but New York's bureau and committee aside, the bulk of North America's psychiatric patients continued to either reside in dreary asylums or to face criminal charges, and very few experts were committed to studying 'sex problems.'

In Canada, for example, the opening of the Toronto Psychiatric Hospital (TPH) in 1925 represented a victory for doctors eager to apply their expertise in the mainstream hospital system, but men and women facing criminal charges continued to make up a large portion of the patient body. Of 3,622 patients admitted to the TPH between 1929 and 1933, almost half were court referrals.[22] Of those, 150 were charged with sex offences. In 1933 Senior Assistant Physician A.J. Kilgour undertook a study of this particular group and published his findings in the same year. Sexual delinquency, Kilgour claimed, was a much greater problem than most people recognized. The 150 people referred to the clinic were but a fraction of the 1,100 sex-related charges laid in Toronto during the same period. The good news, however, was that the courts were showing a greater recognition of the psychological aspects of sex offending; the number of court referrals to the TPH clinic was on the rise.

Kilgour was not the first Canadian psychiatrist to weigh in on matters concerning sex, but he was the most modern. Ontario psychiatrist Joseph Workman, his successor Daniel Clarke, and later C.K. Clarke and Richard Maurice Bucke were all instrumental in fuelling the masturbation insanity scare in Canada.[23] The masturbation scare reflected national anxieties about declining birth rates among the Anglo-Celtic majority and, in the United States and Canada, the concomitant increase in immigration from non-British 'races.' But a much more comprehensive intervention into the realm of sexuality was under way in Europe, and it built on psychiatrists' now established role in the criminal courts. The first encyclopaedic text on sexology was Richard von Krafft-Ebing's 1886 *Psychopathia-Sexualis: A Medico-Forensic Study*.[24] Written as a courtroom guide, *Psychopathia-Sexualis* was the foundation upon which future sex researchers would sort, quantify, and organize a wide spectrum of sexual behaviours into types. For criminologists, the text was a tremendous advance toward the modernization of crime and punishment. Sex laws were artefacts of an earlier age, rooted in medieval ecclesiastical law that made no distinction between different types of moral offences that sexologists regarded as categorically exclusive. In Canada, for example, buggery between two male adults and fornication between a human and an animal were the same crime. Similarly, the Criminal Code drew clear distinctions between heterosexual intercourse with a female under fourteen, with a female between fourteen and sixteen, and with a female over sixteen, but homosexual sex between two consenting adult males was punishable under the same sections as were same-sex sexual assaults on a child or young adult.[25]

Inconsistencies such as these drove many early sexologists to become law-reform advocates, Krafft-Ebing included.[26] Some simply sought a clarification of existing laws, but others struggled to have certain laws repealed, particularly those relating to consensual homosexual acts. Most raised questions about the state's role in regulating morality. A.J. Kilgour's 1933 study took up the mantle in Canada, but while his publication stands alone in the Canadian literature, he joined the growing chorus of medical experts who were inspired by new research into the sexual habits and behaviour of everyday people. This new generation of specialists took a decidedly modern stance in their approach to sexuality. As historian Elizabeth Lunbeck cogently argues, early twentieth-century psychiatrists fashioned themselves as harbingers of a value-free scientific future. Casting off the false modesties and repressive tendencies of the Victorian era, the science of sex would liberate the masses from undue shame and stood to increase human happiness by releasing men and women from the restraints of myth and misconception propagated by religious dictum and social convention. Apprehending sex as a straightforward fact was a defiant strategy meant to align the profession with science and medicine and to 'signal psychiatrists' and social workers' unflinching modernity.'[27]

Kilgour's contribution to the growing body of international literature on sexuality was both defiant and self-avowedly modern. He challenged some of the most deeply held beliefs about sexual morality, and also refuted eugenics, a system of scientific thought supported not only by the country's medical elite, but by some of the most prominent social reformers of the day – a decidedly pro-psychiatry constituency.[28] Many are given to believe, Kilgour argued, that 'there is but one pattern of normal sex life and any straying from that path was abnormal.' New research, however, showed that 'there are as many [paths] as there are individuals.' Rather than use this as evidence of the erosion of morality, Kilgour drew on history to show that sexual and moral norms were constantly changing. Using homosexuality as an example, he made the increasingly commonplace observation that earlier civilizations accepted and even celebrated sex between men. Embracing sexual diversity, to use a modern term, was necessary 'not only [as] a matter of justice to those who may vary from the conventional form in sex conduct, but also because it increases the stability of the whole moral system.'[29] Kilgour's proposition was radical in its time, especially given the lack of an intellectual or political community that might stand in support of his conclusions.

Although the medical pathologization of sexuality is by now a well-documented twentieth-century phenomenon, the centrality of homosexuality to Kilgour's argument bears consideration. The medical and psychiatric study of sex was built not on violent sex crimes but on sexual acts that merely deviated from accepted norms. In fact, much of the expert theorizing about human sexuality and the subsequent designation of sex 'norms' sprung from medical studies of men who engaged in sex with other men.[30] The focus on male homosexuality was driven by the growing acceptance of a pathological view of male same-sex practices. Apart from cases of insanity, criminal court judges and justices of the peace were increasingly willing to entertain psychiatric assessments and sentences to treatment over more traditional punishments such as whipping and imprisonment. Starting in the early twentieth century, men who were charged with gross indecency and buggery also began to hire medical experts to testify in their defence.[31] In contrast, criminal charges against women for sexual acts with other women were extremely rare. Lesbians constituted only a small portion of subjects examined by sexologists, and appear not to have figured at all in Kilgour's study. That sex knowledge was to a large extent built up around male homosexuality had a great deal to do with the court's acceptance of psychiatric assessments of men who had sex with men.

Anticipating his critics, Kilgour scrutinized his subjects for physical and other social defects, considering even nationality, place of birth, religion, and ancestry. According to him, no single feature emerged to explain any of the sexual deviations. He reported no signs of physical degeneration; on the contrary, many of his subjects were 'athletic' and 'robust.' The sample showed only that sex offenders represented a typical cross section of society. Most of his subjects first engaged in sexual misconduct by introduction, not inclination, and, for at least half of them, Kilgour attributed the crime to an unsatisfactory sex life caused by '(1) exaggerated sexual desire; (2) diminished sexual ability; (3) interference with normal sexual activity because of moral, medical, and social restraint or marital dysharmony.'[32] Kilgour maintained that sexual behaviour was learned, not congenital. Although many likely rejected his conclusions, his assessment would prevail in the second half of the twentieth century and would later inform therapeutic programs intended to re-educate and normalize sex offenders.

If the problem was not sexual practices but society's narrow definition of normalcy, Kilgour asked his readers to consider the extent to which the law should intervene in matters of sexual misbehaviour. As we shall see, after the Second World War Canadians showed that they were more willing than ever to rely on Parliament to keep the country safe from the threat of sexual danger.

On 3 July 1947, Vancouver South Member of Parliament Howard C. Green stood in the House of Commons waving a copy of a recent resolution passed by British Columbia's organization of Parent-Teacher Associations (BCPTA). Like so many other Canadian women's organizations, the BCPTA was concerned about the perceived rise in attacks on children and called for the creation of a separate institution for the detention and treatment of 'psychopathic' sex criminals. Bringing the petition to the attention of the House, Green demanded to know when the government intended to take action against the 'alarming increase in Canada in moral offences against children.'[33]

Federal government officials had, in fact, already begun to look into treatment programs currently under way in the United States. Earlier that spring, psychiatrist Charles 'Chick' George Stogdill, the director of the Department of Health's Mental Health Division, and Major General Ralph B. Gibson, the commissioner of penitentiaries, embarked on a study of sex crime and the sexual psychopath statutes south of the Canadian border. Shortly thereafter, the Penitentiaries Branch of the Federal Department of Justice appointed psychiatrist Dr L.P. Gendreau as deputy commissioner, signifying the department's long-awaited move toward applying the principles of reformation through therapeutic intervention. Together Gendreau and Stogdill toured the few northeastern U.S. facilities created to diagnose and treat sexual psychopathy, but discovered that most treatment experts were wholly pessimistic about their ability to cure sexual deviation. At the treatment facility in Springfield, Missouri, the superintendent told Gendreau he was ready to give up. 'They are hard bricks,' he explained, 'and most of them do not want the treatment to begin with.'[34] Indeed, in 1947 there was absolutely no evidence to suggest that any treatment methods currently in use could be, or should be, applied to treat sexually deviated offenders.[35]

Armed with research conducted by Gendreau, Stogdill that produced by and his own legal advisors, Minister of Justice Ilsley rejected Green's demand for U.S.-style sex laws and treatment programs. Citing a 1946 article from the British *Journal of Nervous and Mental Diseases*, Ilsley argued that psychiatrists themselves were highly sceptical of their ability to effect cures for sex deviants.[36] However sound his arguments, he stood alone against the tide of pro-mental-health forces vigorously supported by the newly formed Mental Health Division of the Department of Health. At the war's end, the federal government had made mental health a cornerstone of its reconstruction program.[37] In both the United States and Canada, psychiatrists and psychologists exerted considerably more influence in the state organization of both the war effort and reconstruction than at any time in the past. The Mental Health Division assured psychiatric experts like Ewen Cameron that they would have a prominent place at the funding table. Over the next ten years, millions of dollars were allocated to support the development and maintenance of mental health research and programs across the country. Annual funding for research alone rose from $25,000 in 1947–48 to $175,000 in 1949–50.[38] By 1954 the federal and provincial governments combined spent more than $30 million on mental health.[39]

Established by the Department of Health in May 1945, the purpose of the Mental Health Division of the federal Department of Health and Welfare was to disseminate information and coordinate mental health efforts throughout Canada. Although health is a field of provincial jurisdiction under the British North America Act, it was hoped that coordination at a national level would greatly enhance service provisions as well as facilitate the sharing of ideas and research.[40] Largely a promotional office, the division's task was to collaborate with the Canadian Broadcasting Company (CBC) and the National Film Board (NFB) to educate the public, to create and distribute literature, to give public addresses to 'stimulate interest,' to furnish advice to the provinces, and to provide professional advice to other federal government services, including the Department of Justice, Immigration Medical Services, Civil Service Health, and so on.

Obstacles to building a top-notch mental health program in Canada were identified during the very first Federal-Provincial Conference of Mental Health Directors in 1946. First, there was a serious shortage of trained personnel. Only McGill University, the University of Western Ontario, and the University of Toronto offered diploma courses in psychiatry, and many graduates continued to seek post-graduate training in Britain and the United States. Because of the dearth of research opportunities and the low income potential for psychiatrists in Canada, some never returned. Mental health advocates pressed the federal government to pass something along the lines of the U.S. National Neuropsychiatric Act, which provided funds for students and grants to the hospitals and clinics that trained them. A national program would eliminate the uneven distribution of training facilities across the country and help 'keep good men in Canada.'[41] Because the provinces maintained control of health care, the federal government was unable to directly fund mental health training or programs. It could, however, provide grants to the provinces who were free to administer them as they saw fit. The federal government responded by establishing a grant system to be funded federally and administered by each province.[42]

For leading Canadian psychiatrist D. Ewen Cameron, the grant scheme was not nearly enough to build a robust national mental health program. Cameron dreamed of a national research centre where a steady funding base would provide secure jobs, promote research, and enhance the prestige of the profession, and he proposed his own Allan Memorial Institute for the honour.[43] In his submission to the Department of Health and Welfare, Cameron reminded his readers that mental health is recognized as a major national problem because of 'the extraordinary cost to the individual and to the public of caring for the hospitalized psychiatric patient'; because of the decrease in labour power; and because of its impact on 'civilian morale; marriage; delinquency; absenteeism; human motivation; [and] geriatrics.' The centralization of a national research program was sensible, efficient, and cost-effective, standing a good chance of saving the nation from its worst social problems. The proposal received serious consideration, but was never acted upon. Ten years after the establishment of the Mental Health Division, the livelihood of many research personnel remained temporary and insecure.[44]

The federal government might have washed its hands of the issue once the provincial research grant cheques were in the mail, but one thing it had a very firm hold on was the promotion of mental health issues to the general public. Advocates were keenly aware of the need to 'sell' mental health.[45] Not only did they have to convince the public that the problem of mental health was of concern to everyone, but they also had to destigmatize the notion of seeking help for personal problems, as well as change the image of psychiatry (a field that at least one news editor complained was loaded with 'too many quacks').[46] One of the ways advocates set out to do this was to solicit help from the media. They requested that the CBC and other news services fashion reports on 'the mentally ill, mentally defective, epileptic and alcoholic persons so that the reader or listener will not feel that there is any stigma attached to such illness,' and asked that they avoid using the word 'insane' and stop referring to hospital patients as 'lunatics, looneys, inmates, [or] ... "crazy."'[47] This was not an attempt to interfere with journalists' ability to remain objective, they insisted, but rather to simply 'create a desirable attitude' towards mental health and psychiatry, to 'remove the shroud of mystery, the aura of despair.'[48]

The campaign had some effect: in 1946 the Manitoba Film Censor Board banned the new thriller *Shocked*, starring Vincent Price as a killer psychiatrist, on the grounds that it 'prostituted the role of psychiatrists and psychiatry in general.'[49] By the mid-1950s, CBC radio and television, as well as the NFB, featured mental health issues in their programming. The NFB produced educational and professional training films on a variety of psychiatric and psychological issues, including child rearing, group dynamics, and treatment programs for prisoners; the CBC ran regular features and weekly programs covering a spectrum of mental health issues affecting Canadians, especially topics relating to child development. The message was getting out. A 1949 report on public education in mental health revealed that one member of a community health committee complained, 'If I hear any more about "mental health" I'll scream.'[50]

But what exactly was the message? Psychiatrists had spent more than a hundred years quantifying and qualifying lunacy in its myriad manifestations, but they were no closer to a cure. The increasingly complex systems of classification and diagnosis were followed by efforts to standardize psychiatric nomenclature into a general nosology, the *Diagnostic Statistical Manual*, which helped to ensure that psychiatrists across Canada and the United States were speaking generally the same language. Psychiatrists, however, did not enjoy any of the late nineteenth-century successes general medical practitioners savoured. New discoveries in bacteriology and germ theory had dramatically advanced medicine's ability to heal the sick and injured, but apart from advances in the identification of general paresis, psychiatry enjoyed no comparable breakthroughs. Experiments with insulin and electric-shock therapies proved that they had limited effect, and lobotomy had a too high mortality rate to be used extensively. Psychiatry, in other words, knew quite a lot about all sorts of disorders of the mind and body, but knew not how to cure or even, in most cases, ameliorate the conditions so many patients suffered from.

The Advisory Committee to the federal Mental Health Division of the Department of Health and Welfare took a cautious position from the outset. Composed of at least one representative from each of the nine provincial governments, and seven psychiatrists from university departments, including D. Ewen Cameron, director of the Allan Memorial Institute at McGill University, and A.B. Stokes, chairman of the Department of Psychiatry at the University of Toronto, committee members made their professional deficiencies a matter of record. Commenting on everything from treatment methods to a basic understanding of the nature of some mental conditions, they stated in their committee resolution, 'there are extensive basic defects in present psychiatric knowledge ... If all persons suffering from the various forms of mental ill-health were fully treated by all available methods at the present time we would still be left with a large number of ill patients.'[51] Why then was the federal government willing to adopt criminal sexual psychopath legislation, which was premised on the ability of psychiatrists to cure sexual deviation, when no such cures existed?

Given the lack of concrete solutions that mental health and medical experts offered, Justice Minister Ilsley's reservations about adopting criminal sexual psychopath legislation appear well-founded, especially considering that sexuality was one of the most underdeveloped areas of research. Interwar efforts toward research and treatment were made in the United States and Europe, but studies such as A.J. Kilgour's were almost unheard of in Canada. This was largely a result of the influence of C.K. Clarke, Canada's pre-eminent psychiatrist during the first quarter of the twentieth century, who dismissed Freud precisely because of his unorthodox views about the nature of human sexual development.[52] Even in some university classrooms, talking about sex could have severe consequences. Norman Jellinger Symons, chairman of the Department of Psychology at Dalhousie University, taught a course in dynamic psychology. As part of the course, Symons solicited dreams from his students and would 'provide them with full-blown Freudian interpretations.' Horrified, the university administration demanded his resignation.[53] By the late 1950s, discussions about sex remained somewhat controversial. In 1959 a prospective PhD student from Queen's University in Kingston was reassured by a faculty member: 'Young man, you may *describe* sex, you must never *advocate* it.'[54]

Keeping sex respectable might have been good for the national soul, but it left no intellectual foundation upon which to build a treatment program for sex offenders. When in 1947 a series of murders and sex assaults against children became national news headlines, the Canadian Penal Association decided to do for the federal government what ten American state legislatures had done for themselves: organize a committee to undertake a comprehensive study of the problem. Using funds provided by the Kiwanis Club of Toronto, the association brought together a cross section of Canadian experts in medicine, law, and education to form the Committee on the Sex Offender. Representing governmental, academic, and professional volunteer organizations were Dr L.P. Gendreau, the newly appointed deputy commissioner of penitentiaries in the Department of Justice; Dr J.D.M. Griffin, medical director of the National Committee for Mental Hygiene (soon to become the Canadian Mental Health Association), and J. Alex Edmison, King's Counsel and president of the Canadian Penal Association. Joining this esteemed panel were a handful of Toronto-based experts, including members of the University of Toronto's Medicine and Social Work faculties; Chief Constable of Police John Chisholm; Dr Kenneth Rogers, executive secretary of the Big Brother movement, and local magistrates Robert Bigelow and Kenneth F. Mackenzie.

Three months after the committee was struck, the Committee on the Sex Offender released its *Interim Report* at a luncheon held at the prestigious King Edward Hotel in Toronto. Research about sex offenders, the chairman remarked, is 'involved and complicated,' especially, he added, because it had not been previously attempted in Canada, nor, he claimed, adequately elsewhere.[55] Hopeful that the work of the committee should prove useful to professionals in the field, members decided that the issue was best approached from three different angles: medical, legal, and educational. While the end result makes it clear that the three subreports were written entirely from the standpoint of the individual authors, what is remarkable, and most revealing, is its ultimate cohesion. Each report addressed the sexual psychopath construct and described how it should be treated (medical), determined if it could be contained (legal), and suggested how it might be prevented (educational). Though the report did not provide a single solution or approach to the sex offender problem, it defined the parameters of the debate.

Gendreau and Griffin provided independent analyses of sex crime and its perpetrators. A study in contrasts, the two subreports illustrate psychiatry's intellectual transition at mid-century from a eugenic-based biological model to an anthropological and Freudian-based behavioural model. First, Gendreau presented a single case study, one of the oldest and most common tools of his trade, to illuminate his subject. Of the many cases he could have presented, he chose to examine a man who had been in the media spotlight as the perpetrator of a sexual assault. Like most psychiatrists, Gendreau subscribed to no single theory of causality; his assessment combined eugenic and degenerative theories as well as more modern environmental and behavioural theories, the latter of which gave considerable weight to parenting as a causal factor. He described his subject's parents as 'sexually delinquent and not likely to raise their children with moral standards above their own.' They were 'of low grade stock mentally and morally.' The father created a poisonous environment, was 'morally deficient,' and had carried on an incestuous relationship with his twelve-year-old stepdaughter. The mother exacerbated the problem by being 'overindulgent and overprotective,' a post–Second World War descriptor that would increasingly come to be associated with developmental abnormalities, particularly male homosexuality.[56] In the interwar years, mothers of delinquent and especially sexually 'perverted' boys were more likely to be described in opposite terms: as uninvolved, as negligent, and perhaps even as a 'New Woman.' In the postwar period, however, the failing mother was more likely to be 'emotionally unstable.' In this particular case study, for example, the mother reportedly kept her children home from school 'for no valid reason,' which not only prevented them from receiving a proper education, but also kept them from the positive influence the school presumably offered. For Gendreau, it was clear that 'due to her own emotional deficiencies,' the mother was unwilling to allow her children to be 'normal.'

Bad parenting would become one of the most ubiquitous and enduring explanations for delinquency in the postwar era, but Gendreau's assessment reminds us how paradigm shifts are never sudden or complete, that old and new ideas, even when they are seemingly incongruent, often overlap. Gendreau conjoined a germ disease model with newer developmental models of sexuality to explain his subject's deviant behaviour. His subject was 'initiated in early life, in sexual activities along homosexual lines,' and had been in trouble with the law as a result. The original contamination, left untreated, led him to 'become a confirmed sexual invert. This is confirmed by his inability to make heterosexual adjustment.'[57] Unable to arrive at the heterosexual endpoint, the victim remained in a perpetual state of immaturity, his development into full manhood with all its attendant rights, privileges, and responsibilities thwarted.[58]

In his final assessment, Gendreau concluded that socio-economic factors unique to his subject's family led to the 'development of such an individual emotionally conditioned to such behaviour.' Unless the subject receives treatment in prison, Gendreau argued, he will most assuredly return to his practices and 'be a menace, perhaps, to a greater extent than before and commit crimes of greater magnitude.'[59] It was precisely these assumptions – that prison was not reformative, that sex offenders would reoffend and commit increasingly serious crimes, and that psychiatric treatment was the only possible method to rehabilitate (or perhaps more precisely re-habituate) the deviated offender to the norms of society – upon which the criminal sexual psychopath as a medico-legal construct rested.

But what if treatment didn't work? A well-accepted truism among therapeutic experts suggested that the better educated and more intelligent the individual, the more amenable to treatment they would be. Anticipating that his subject was not a good prospect for this reason, Gendreau argued that he should be incarcerated 'for years to come.' Thus, the preventative sentence, premised on the need to make the criminal justice system more pliable so that treatment programs would not be interrupted by the expiration of a prison sentence, was simultaneously conceived of as a means to ensure the long-term protection of society from a criminal deemed incurable. In this way, sexual psychopath legislation appealed to those who regarded the sex offender as more mentally disturbed than criminally minded, and provided for psychotherapy and other forms of psychological and medical treatment that, when contrasted with the bleak monotony of prison life and medieval methods of punishment, appear both humane and progressive. At the same time, however, sexual psychopath legislation also appeased those who wanted sex offenders incarcerated for life, and guaranteed as much by ensuring that no one deemed a sexual psychopath would be released from custody until cured, or, as some American state laws held, until judged by a psychiatrist as no longer a threat to society.

While Gendreau reinforced the image of the sex fiend as the poor, unintelligent offspring of low-grade stock, Griffin joined a growing group of scholars who challenged the most basic premise of sex research. Influenced by anthropologists like Ruth Benedict and Margaret Mead, a new generation of North American sex researchers set out to exorcise the moral assumptions embedded in popular ideas about sexuality. Critical of biological determinist theories, which were popular in many fields of medicine, including sexology, anthropologists of the Culture and Personality school sought to document cultural variation in sexual expression and practice. Most regarded personality formation as the sum total of socialization processes that varied according to the cultural norms in a given society. Gaining strength in the 1930s, this emergent body of literature was quickly adopted by sex experts in other disciplines, including psychiatry.[60]

Griffin's arguments exemplify anthropology's influence on forensic sexology. 'Ignorance, superstition, rigid taboos and violent prejudice' complicate our understanding of sexual disorders, he complained. 'So powerful have been the emotional and social repression concerning sex in our culture, that even scientific enquiry as to the actual facts has been hampered.'[61] Griffin and other experts argued that sexual practices that our culture viewed with hostility and contempt might be highly valued in other cultures. Moreover, sexual behaviour varied tremendously even in our own culture. Echoing A.J. Kilgour, Griffin argued that we could no longer sustain the illusion that 'normal' sex was static, stable, and definable. Any further advances in sex research required that we remove our sexual blinders and encourage more frank, open, and honest discussions about sex.

Griffin's subreport also diverges from Gendreau in method. By 1948 psychiatrists no longer relied on a handful of individual case studies to extrapolate some sort of understanding of sex crime and sexual deviancy. The interwar decades spawned a number of large-scale studies of the sexual habits and attitudes of Americans, including Katharine Bement Davis's 1929 study of the sexual attitudes of 2200 women and George Henry's New York sex variant study. Griffin drew on the findings of LaGuardia's New York report on sex-crime charges laid in that city.

Based on an examination of over 3000 convicted criminals, the report provided the kind of raw numbers that individual case studies, no matter how colourful, could not. As a result of these recent mass surveys, including the just-released Alfred Kinsey report on male sexual behaviour, Griffin argued that sexual activities widely considered perverted and esoteric 'are now known to occur with surprising frequency.'[62] With data collected from a cross section of middle America, scientists had the raw material they needed to strip sex of its moral embellishments and to analyze it with a science based not on social norms and values, but on the innovative systems of measurement Kinsey created. Categories like 'total sexual outlet,' a measurement of how often one engaged in any kind of sexual activity, along with Kinsey's scale that measured degrees of heterosexual and homosexual behaviour in a single individual, were two important tools that liberalized the way people thought about sex.

Kilgour, Kinsey, and Griffin agreed that there were no common features that defined the sex deviate. 'Sex offenders have no particular or easily recognizable features or stigmata to distinguish them from anyone else,' Griffin argued. 'They may be of any age, race, colour or creed. They may come from good homes or bad. They may live in wealthy or residential areas or in the slums. Their families may be criminals or respected pillars of the church.'[63] Indeed, he continued, the sexual psychopath scare was based on misinformation. According to the latest research findings, the vast majority of sex offenders were not mentally ill, and the mentally ill were not more likely to commit sex crimes. Neither were sex offenders more likely to be recidivists. An analysis of 5821 New York cases spanning nine years showed the general recidivism rate at 39 per cent, with only 9 per cent having a previous sexual offence conviction, an almost insignificant number in comparison with other crimes.[64] The sexual psychopath was a figment of the imagination of a zealous public built on sketchy psychiatric profiles similar to that offered up by Gendreau. Still, Griffin did not reject the sexual psychopath concept completely. Instead, he argued that, though they were rare, society needed protection against those who committed 'compulsive and repetitive' acts of sexual violence.[65]

Psychiatrists could not agree whether there was such a thing as a sexual psychopath, and there was little clarity about what a sexual psychopath was among those who accepted the concept. On one point, however, most everyone concurred: more sex knowledge was needed. The education subreport authored by Canadian Welfare Council member Kenneth Rogers elaborated on the growing popularity of the socialization and behaviourism schools of thought, and showed that many leading experts agreed that the sex instinct needed to be properly guided lest a young child be misled by a corrupt friend or a perverted stranger.[66] Unfortunately, frank talk about sex was as controversial in the late 1940s and 50s as it was in Jellinger's Dalhousie University psychology class of 1929, making Rogers's task a delicate one. Already Alfred Kinsey's path-breaking surveys of the sex habits of Americans were inciting censorious responses in both Canada and the United States, but among specialists and the 'intelligent public,' *Sexual Behavior in the Human Male* was enthusiastically embraced as an important breakthrough in the modernization of sex knowledge.[67] Whatever public opposition there may have been to such frank talk about sex, it was not enough to keep Canadian experts from incorporating Kinsey's findings into their own research efforts.

Though many of Kinsey's supporters fashioned themselves as modern progressives dedicated to liberating sex from the shackles of the Victorian past, some of the study's supporters found that the report confirmed what they already suspected: sexual morality needed to be policed now more than ever. Contrary to Kilgour, Kinsey, Griffin, and others who argued that what social and moral convention deemed to be normal sexual practice did not reflect the wide range of sexual activity taking place, Rogers's education subreport argued that the Kinsey data was proof positive of the urgent need for 'greater moral restraints in family, community and national life.'[68] If the basis of sexual perversion was psychogenic and not congenital, then better sex education was the key to a future free from sexual abnormality:

> By our ignorant, short-sighted and blundering treatment of the very natural
> subject of human reproduction and its relationship to the business of nor-
> mal heterosexual relationships and social living, we manufacture perverts.
> We seek to protect ourselves from sex and by so doing we have developed a
> sex-centred and sex-ridden society ... We must stop being prudes ... Sound
> sex information is the greatest single measure available for the protection
> and guidance of young people toward successful social living.[69]

For Rogers, the next and most important step in the battle against sex crime was to offer 'mass education for parenthood.' This, he argued, will give a solid foundation for proper sex education in the home.[70] The federal government agreed. In a 1950 radio report on child training, the

Honourable Minister of Health Paul Martin implored parents to take greater responsibility for training their children to live emotionally healthy lives. The home, Martin argued, 'should not only develop healthy bodies but should foster sound and stable, well-balanced personalities.' In the 1950s, promoting a healthy attitude toward sex would become a central component of parenting.

Was criminal sexual psychopath legislation the answer? According to legal expert Kenneth Mackenzie, perhaps not. In reviewing the existing American statutes, Mackenzie drew readers' attention to a number of troubling features of the legislation, including how in some states a person deemed a sexual psychopath could not be tried or sentenced for the original offence, but must be treated as insane. Regarding those states that acted otherwise, Mackenzie argued that the inconsistency – treating a person as irresponsible while at the same time providing for his punishment – was at the core unjust.[71] In Canada, the British North America Act further complicated matters. Federal-provincial responsibility for prisoners was divided: the former was obliged to care for those sentenced to two years or more, and the latter was liable for those sentenced to anything less. Dangerous and repetitive sex offenders, the object of public concern and the intended target of sexual psychopath legislation, would likely be sentenced to lengthy prison terms, and thus would be required to serve time in a federal institution. Provincial governments were responsible for matters of health, however, including mental health. Criminal sexual psychopath legislation, Mackenzie rightly pointed out, would first require that the Penitentiary Act be amended to permit those convicted to be confined in a hospital for more than two years. Provincial governments would then need to be persuaded to provide the necessary facilities, staff, and treatment programs.

The Committee on the Sex Offender never had the opportunity to propose solutions to any of the problems its report raised. By 1950 all activity on the project was suspended due to a lack of funds, the committee was never revived, and no final report was ever published.[72] It must have been a tremendous disappointment to Stuart Jaffary and the other participants who hoped to generate usable research in Canada, but for the Kiwanis, the committee had done its job. The goal of the Kiwanis was to increase public pressure on Minister of Justice Ilsley to pass some type of sexual psychopath law.[73] Shortly after the *Interim Report* was publicly released at a press conference, Ilsley introduced a slightly modified version of the Massachusetts 1947 statute.[74] On 14 June 1948, Canada's members of Parliament unanimously approved the passage of Section 1054A of the Criminal Code.

The popularity of criminal sexual psychopath legislation and of treatment as a solution to the sex crime problem grew in the post–Second World War era because of a specific set of historical conditions. As the following chapters will detail, the baby boom, the rise of mental health expertise, anxiety concerning masculinity in an era of demobilization, and the rethinking of social and sexual mores that accompanied reconstruction each contributed to public interest in the problem of sex crimes against children. It is also, however, useful to see criminal sexual psychopath legislation as one point on a century-long trajectory of psycho-medical thinking about criminality, sexuality, and legal responsibility, and as part of a long tradition of social reform that took a dim view of punishment and repression. In other words, criminal sexual psychopathy was one expression of an ongoing evolution of philosophical, legal, and medical ideas about assessing moral responsibility and regulating sexual behaviour. Sexual psychopath laws were not only the offspring of a marriage between the justice system and medicine, they were also the product of an almost century-long effort to implement the principles of positivist criminology, a project that in some quarters continues to this day.

Widespread Canadian support for what began as an American legal construct also reveals something about Canada's changing position in the post–Second World War political and cultural landscape. Though the Canadian legal system followed Britain's lead and rejected the concept of partial insanity at the end of the nineteenth century, Canadian psychiatrists kept well abreast of the evolving relationship between psychiatrists, psychologists, social workers, and the courts and prisons in the United States, and they advocated for similar advances here. For Canadian psychiatrists, the border hardly existed. A movement to create their own national professional organization did not get under way until the early 1950s, and even then Canadian psychiatrists maintained memberships in the American Psychiatric Association, attended their conferences, published in their journal, and served on their executive board. The postwar boom in university education further opened the doors of Canadian psychiatry, loosening the grip of the few dominant personalities that characterized the pre–Second World War period and allowing greater circulation of the different schools of psychiatric thought. Given this environment, Canadian psychiatrists were as involved in the creation of the sexual psychopath as were their American colleagues.

Politically and culturally, the war and the international reorganization of power that followed brought Canada under the sphere of American influence.[75] In the annals of legal history, the introduction of criminal sexual psychopath legislation stands as a material demonstration of the waning influence of the British Empire. After the Second World War, England, Scotland, Australia, and New Zealand each undertook criminal law revisions, paying particular attention to sex offences, but only Canada adopted criminal sexual psychopath legislation. Though postwar reconstruction themes were the same, geography had an effect. Psychiatrists might be going to England for graduate training, but the new young parents who demanded criminal sexual psychopath legislation were more likely reading American, not British, news. Hoover's 'War on Sex Crime,' the reintegration of demobilized soldiers, the disappearance of women from the paid labour market, the rapid development of the suburbs, and the concomitant baby boom all contributed to the erosion of the border as a meaningful cultural divide. Cold war concerns for the preservation and protection of the family were no less poignant and pressing in Canada, and the penetration of the mainstream U.S. media helped shape popular opinion in Canada as effectively as it did in the twenty-nine states that also passed some form of criminal sexual psychopath legislation. Canada's early participation in the wave of criminal sexual psychopath laws that swept through America was not a portent of the rising dominance of the United States. In this instance, it is an example of how the Canadian body politic draws many of its nutrients from the same cultural soil as the northeastern United States. In other words, Canadians did not merely follow the lead of their southern neighbours; they were equal participants in the shaping of postwar sexual politics.

Criminal sexual psychopath legislation represents a fundamental shift in the way Canadians and Americans thought about sex. It was a final and decisive victory for forensic sexologists who, since the late 1800s, struggled to take sex out of the courthouse and the church and bring it into the light of the modern scientific gaze. However, this stance should not be mistaken as a liberation ideology. As Mrs. Geraldine M. demonstrated, most Canadians who supported sexual psychopath legislation merely hoped to improve the way the justice and penal systems handled sex crimes. Though some might have individually supported the liberalization of sex in areas such as public education, sexual liberation was not what drove women like Mrs M. to pen a letter to the minister of health. However, it would be equally erroneous to imply that such individuals were interested in greater sexual repression or regulation. What people like Mrs M. wanted was for the state to recognize that sex crimes should not be treated like other crimes. She, like many others, was convinced that sexual deviants needed help, not punishment. This epistemological shift was facilitated not only by the sexual anxieties that characterized the period, but by the overall triumph of everyday psychiatry. In Canada and the United States after the Second World War, psychiatrists not only belonged in the bedroom, but also in the living room, the office, the factory floor, the courtroom, and even in the legislature.

With criminal sexual psychopath legislation in place, Canadians felt reassured that the sex crime problem was well on its way to being solved. Unfortunately, the feeling did not last long. Those who remained involved with the criminal justice system were soon complaining that the law was rarely applied, and when it was, few Canadian judges were willing to convict sex offenders to an indefinite sentence as criminal sexual psychopaths. Furthermore, in 1952 the Canadian Welfare Council formally protested the government's failure to make provisions for treating offenders, and demanded that the government establish a committee to 'study the whole matter of the sex offender.'[76] As chapter three shows, the Royal Commission on the Criminal Law Relating to Criminal Sexual Psychopaths inspired a national conversation about sex. Psychiatrists across the country endeavoured to answer the questions asked by Toronto Psychiatric Hospital's A.J. Kilgour in 1933: To what extent should the courts regulate sexual behaviour? And how do we define normal? The director of the Mental Health Division of the Department of Health and Welfare struggled with the same questions, asking, 'What's "abnormal"? What's a sex act?'[77] Once again, it was to psychiatrists and other medical experts that the state would turn. In the next chapter, we examine the critical role played by parents, particularly women, in giving shape and direction to this national dialogue.

chapter two

Social Citizenship and Sexual Danger

On 25 February 1955, eight-year-old Judy Carter didn't make it home from school. Somewhere along the short four blocks between her friend's house, where she stopped to read comics, and her parents' basement apartment in Cabbagetown, then one of Toronto's rougher working-class neighbourhoods, she disappeared. The press, the public, and even the victim's mother immediately speculated that Judy was the victim of a 'sex fiend.'[1] Hundreds of volunteers, including firemen, boy scouts, and the local Rotary Club, joined the 'Search for Judy' campaign. Tragically, six weeks later her body was discovered along a riverbank in Markham Township, well outside the city limits. An autopsy revealed that Judy was strangled with her own scarf, but she had not been sexually assaulted; her attacker was not a 'sex psychopath.'[2]

In the immediate aftermath of Judy's disappearance, two women concerned about sex attacks against children formed what became one of the most successful citizen's action groups in postwar English Canada. From their first meeting that spring until they disbanded six years later, the Parents' Action League (PAL) cited the death of Judy Carter as the single event that propelled them to launch a high-profile campaign to end sex crimes against children. Over the course of the summer of 1955, PAL became a beacon for sex crime fighters across Canada, and even parts of the United States, and in little more than a year achieved what a decade of lobbying by Canadian mental health experts could not: the creation of a research and treatment clinic for sexual deviation. The Toronto Psychiatric Hospital's Outpatient Forensic Clinic opened in May 1956, and put Canada on the sex-research map. It was a major victory for PAL, one in which its members took tremendous pride. Women had once again proved that bulldog tenacity was justice's best friend.

It was a dramatic start to what turned out to be a disturbingly formulaic story. The post–Second World War preoccupation with sexual deviancy and assaults against children bears all the markings of a classic moral panic.[3] First formulated by British sociologist Stanley Cohen, moral panics are moments when certain groups are identified as a threat to societal values and interests. According to Cohen, the threat is 'presented in a stylized and stereotyped fashion by the mass media; the moral barricades are manned by editors, bishops, and politicians and other right-thinking people; socially accredited experts pronounce their diagnoses and solutions; ways of coping are evolved, or (more often) resorted to; the condition then disappears, submerges or deteriorates.'[4] British sociologist Jeffrey Weeks popularized Cohen's model among historians of sexuality. It seemed to fit well with the history of homosexuality, prostitution, and other socially marginalized and stigmatized sexual practices, practitioners of which were made 'folk devils' during times of economic, social, and political distress. Both Canadian and American historians have interpreted the popularization of criminal sexual psychopath laws and the concomitant sex crime panics that emerged in Canadian and American cities during the late 1940s and 50s as examples of moral panics at work.[5]

But postwar culture was much more complex than the moral panic model allows, a fact that has been overlooked by historians because of their reliance on two important theories: the domestic containment thesis, which holds that family life in the postwar era was fundamentally conservative; and the moral panic model itself, which characterizes popular responses to certain social problems as 'disproportionate' to the actual problem, 'irrational,' and in some accounts, 'hysterical.' These two analytical approaches seamlessly converged, leading historians to reaffirm the prevailing perception of the 1950s as a period of stifling conformity and sexual anxiety that resulted in repressive juridical measures aimed at sex deviants, most notably male homosexuals.[6] It is revealing that, while virtually every study of the postwar sex crime panic in Canada and the United States credits citizen action groups with playing a key role in engendering social anxiety about sexual deviancy and for the subsequent passage of sexual psychopath laws, none of the studies undertake a serious examination of those groups. Perhaps this is because some of the most vocal proponents of sex law reform were members of Home and School and Parent-Teacher Associations, organizations whose activism evolved from their interest in children, family, and community life. Historians have wrongly assumed PTAs to be conservative in outlook. Failing to examine these groups in their own right has left unchallenged the moral panic model's claim that community responses to sex crimes were disproportionate to the actual problem at hand, and has assigned too much credit to the media's role in giving meaning and shape to the issue. By taking their concerns about sexual violence seriously and by re-examining these events as part of the history of activism around sexual violence, a very different picture emerges. English Canadian parent-citizens were active agents in setting the postwar sexual agenda, and they proposed progressive, not conservative, solutions to dealing with sex crime.

Post–Second World War women's and parent groups were inundated with child-rearing and family-living advice from mental health experts, most of whom were male.[7] But women were not just passive subjects of expert pronouncements; they actively championed mental health expertise, thus promoting and entrenching their cultural authority. Indeed, the influence mental health experts enjoyed in the 1950s was at the pleasure of parent groups who were instrumental in pushing local school boards and Canada's provincial and federal governments to integrate mental health expertise into government-funded services.[8] In other words, the production of mental health knowledge, particularly where it concerned child development, was a symbiotic process shared between child experts like Ontario's William Blatz and Saskatchewan's Samuel Laycock and the thousands of parents who welcomed them into their homes, their schools, and their community centres. Middle-class Canadian parents gave shape, direction, and strength to the mental health movement by identifying the type of information they wanted, by demanding that the federal government fund its production and dissemination, and, perhaps most important, by advocating new standards of appropriate behaviour in the nation through schools, child guidance clinics, family courts, children's aid societies, and other state-run agencies.[9] Because child development experts held parents, and especially mothers, responsible for their children's failure to conform to middle-class standards of proper conduct, critics have cast women as the mental health movement's victims, not as its architects. But thousands of middle-class Canadian women enthusiastically championed this reputedly misogynist field of scientific expertise, and they used it to make a variety of demands in the political sphere, including that the sexual safety of children be included in the expanding welfare state.

Like some of their maternal feminist predecessors, groups such as the Parents' Action League did not challenge traditional family arrangements. Moreover, in public presentations, newspaper and magazine interviews, and their own pamphlet, 'The Strange One,' PAL reinforced the perception that sexual danger came from outside, not inside, the family circle. They spoke about sexual assault against boys, but they did not include incest as an area of concern. In other words, they both challenged and reinforced some of the most entrenched ideas about sexual assault in public discourse. Like the feminists that came before and after them, however, they put sexual danger on the political agenda by making sexual safety a matter of public policy and community responsibility. Specifically, when postwar psychologists put emotional health on par with physical well-being, parent activists were able to recast the sexual victimization of children (and to a lesser extent, women) as a threat to social well-being. In so doing, parent activists made talking about sex not only respectable, but a civic duty, thus bridging the gap between the public and the private.

In Canada, parent activism around sex crime was an exercise in social citizenship, not a disproportionate or hysterical response to a media-produced phenomenon. Social citizenship has served as an important tool for feminist analyses of women's participation in the evolution of the welfare state, and it is usefully applied here. As many historians have shown, throughout the twentieth century women have played a key role in demanding social rights, such as state sponsorship of forms of care and protection for consumers, and women's postwar efforts to include sexual safety as a state priority is an extension of this type of political work.[10] From PAL's perspective, the state could further guarantee a healthy, happy, well-functioning citizenry by eliminating the threat of sexual danger.

The Parents' Action League embodied and promoted modern citizenship ideals of universalism and inclusiveness in their membership composition and political goals. For example, they frequently emphasized that league leaders were women of Jewish, Catholic, and Protestant faiths, as a way of reinforcing their insistence that the issue cut across traditional categories of difference and concerned virtually every Canadian citizen. Equally significant was that they chose the name Parents' Action League, not Mothers' Action League. PAL rejected the particularism of motherhood as a political identity, preferring instead to embrace the ideal 1950s domestic arrangement: mothers and fathers would take an active interest in family life. For this reason, while the term 'mother-citizens' might more properly reflect the composition of PAL and similar activist groups, I have chosen to use the term 'parent-citizens' because it better captures both the ideal and intent, if not the material reality, of the organization's ethos.

The politics of inclusion and its corollary, the well-functioning society, were most vividly expressed in the solutions that parent groups pursued. If sexual safety was cast as a social right, the way to achieve it was to eliminate the threat. In the 1950s, parent groups focused on the offender, but not in ways we might expect. PAL and others rejected punishment as the only response to sex crimes, and argued that convicted offenders should receive medical treatment, either on its own or in conjunction with a prison sentence. Convinced that prison only exacerbated antisocial behaviour, a view that reflected postwar anti-authoritarian and anti-disciplinarian values, PAL argued that psychiatric and psychological counselling were more humane, and more effective, in preventing recidivism than imprisonment alone.

Drawing on a combination of child development theory and new ways of thinking about the challenge of bridging cultural differences posed by the influx of 'new Canadians,' parent activists characterized perpetrators of sex crimes as 'strangers in our midst.' Like the 'strangers at our gates' that Methodist minister J.S. Woodsworth wrote about in the 1910s, men who engaged in deviant sexual acts were 'strange' to normal society. But while Woodsworth concluded that social stability depended on the exclusion of certain groups, the postwar view held that 'strangers in our midst' needed compassion and understanding, with the ultimate goal of assimilating them into normative heterosexual culture.[11]

PAL and other parent groups insisted that it was a duty of citizenship to learn more about 'the causes and treatment of sexual deviation,' that governments were obligated to establish and fund treatment services, and that it was the responsibility of parents to prevent their own children from becoming deviants by providing their children with a proper sex education. It was a plan of action that evolved out of ongoing consultations with medical and legal experts , and it was marked by a tremendous faith in those experts' abilities to develop effective treatment programs. Careful study, regular consultations, and constant political lobbying, not fear and insecurity, fuelled their efforts.

Of course, none of this meant that the mental health construction of and approach to sex deviation was unproblematic. But if we are to understand how it was that a marginal field of study gained such tremendous cultural currency, we need to look carefully at who supported it and why. In so doing, we find a resurgence in women's activism, not a retreat into the domestic sphere. Moreover, in many instances parent activists themselves gave the media the stories to cover, not the other way around. Indeed, as we shall see, readers challenged journalists' narrative strategies and contested the meanings both journalists and the experts gave to sex crime. Conditions and events in postwar English Canada prove the domestic retrenchment thesis and the moral panic model to be more of a hindrance than a help. When viewed as a moment in the history of women's political activism around sexual assault, the story that emerges challenges many of our assumptions about postwar Canada.

This chapter explores the history of the Parents' Action League and the extensive media coverage of the sex crime issue. PAL was not the only citizen-based group to actively participate in public discussions around sex crime, but others did so as part of a broader agenda within a larger organization. PAL's positions were no different than other parent groups, but they stood apart because they were exclusively concerned with sex crime, and for a short time became a media phenomenon in their own right. They played a key role in generating public and political support for mental health treatment for sexual deviation. The second part of this chapter examines the conditions for PAL's success, but I begin by locating the moment when the notion of sexual deviation entered popular discourse in Ontario. To do this, we must start with the murder of Maria Lypoweckyj and Olga Zacharko.

In the fall of 1954, two Eastern European refugee women were brutally murdered very near their own homes in the city's west-end 'foreign section.' According to police reports, neither victim was raped, but the first was stripped naked by her attacker. Semen stains were found on the clothes of the second. Both murders were described as the work of a 'sex fiend.' Local journalists scrambled to find an explanation: first, the murders were viewed through an ethnocentric and cold war lens that looked to the women's status as refugees, and to their potential political alliances, to explain the murderer's motives. For example, reporters from the *Toronto Telegram* immediately speculated that the brutal killings were ethno-political in origin. They suggested that the murder of Maria Lypoweckyj, the first victim, was a reprisal for her husband's anticommunist activities. A member of the Ukrainian government-in-exile, the National Republicans, he regularly contributed to their newspaper. A few days later, police revealed that Lypoweckyj's purse contained a photo of a Nazi soldier and intimate letters he wrote to her during the war. Journalists wondered if perhaps her spurned lover had slipped into the country to exact revenge. Details of the life of Olga Zacharko did not lend themselves to political intrigue quite as well, and frustrated reporters turned to the local community for answers. New Canadians were blunt in their criticism of attempts to sensationalize the events in their neighbourhood. The suspect is a man known the world over, said one. He is the man that preys on innocent and unsuspecting women.[12]

Non-immigrant women weren't buying journalists' theories either. Women's letters to the city's editors expressed fear about walking the streets at night, and criticized the police for suggesting that they should remain indoors after dark. One pointed out that the second victim was attacked during the supper hour, not under the cloak of darkness. Another argued that fewer women would be made victims of male attackers if all citizens, men and women alike, put up an 'organized front.' A heightened awareness of women's vulnerability combined with public outrage had at least one immediate result: the number of women reporting sexual assaults sharply rose.

Journalists abandoned the cold war angle and turned to one of the oldest stock characters in the modern English-language newspaper business: Jack the Ripper. Though the 1888 slayings of five women in Whitechapel bore little resemblance to events in Toronto, there seemed enough similarities to revive the image of a single crazed maniac on the loose. For example, both women were killed by strangulation, thus suggesting a single attacker, and the papers dubbed him 'The Strangler.' When the police suggested that it would have taken two men to carry Maria's body through to the narrow walkway where it was discovered, journalists characterized the attacker as having super-human strength. As in the Ripper case, local residents denied hearing anything out of the ordinary, even though the victims' bodies were found on private residential property in their own neighbourhood, and the material evidence suggested that they had struggled with their attacker. Journalists concluded that he must have muffled their screams with one hand, meaning that he must have strangled them with the other. They described him as having 'hands of steel.' Also echoing the Ripper case, Lypoweckyj's husband claimed to have received a letter from the murderer.

The Strangler narrative did not go over well either. First, the spike in reports of sexual violence suggested that the problem was endemic, not isolated. This was inadvertently confirmed by the local police who tried to quell the rising tide of anxiety by announcing that they were rounding up hundreds of sex deviates for questioning. (The 'deviates' they targeted were male homosexuals who congregated in certain city bars, restaurants, and parks, though this was never made explicit in Canadian news media.) Their strategy backfired. Residents immediately demanded to know why so many sex perverts were out on the streets in the first place.

Mental health experts had an explanation, and it was to them that reporters finally turned. Psychiatrists confirmed that while Jack the Ripper characters do exist, they are rare, and that as the police sweeps suggested, sex crime is much more widespread than was generally believed. As the experts saw it, sex crime was only a symptom of a much deeper social disease: sexual deviation. Journalists quickly learned, and disseminated, new ways of thinking and talking about sexual conflict. They stopped using the phrases 'sex fiend' and 'sex pervert' and began describing perpetrators as 'sex deviates.' When eight-year-old Judy Carter disappeared four months later, mental health expertise would be called upon once again, and would provide the interpretive lens in news reporting in Ontario and elsewhere for the rest of the decade.

Like many of her neighbours, Bertha Shvemar closely followed the Strangler stories, but it was not until the death of Judy Carter that she undertook to mobilize the province's vast network of women's and other volunteer groups into action. Because Shvemar was a mother herself, Carter's death no doubt struck closer to home than did the tragic murder of the two adult women. But children also carried a particular social and symbolic value after the Second World War. Not only were there so many of them, but for the first time they were seen as bearers of human rights, and the Canadian state bore a special obligation to provide the necessary conditions for their growth and development. Canada's reconstruction policies were designed to regenerate family life, but, as historian Dominique Marshall argues, the federal government focused on children, not on their parents. The implementation of the Family Allowance is the most obvious material manifestation of how Canada's human rights policy strove to guarantee minimum standards of life for its youngest citizens. For the first time, children were regarded as autonomous and sovereign beings.[13] As Marshall points out, these policies allowed for greater scrutiny of individual families to ensure they were meeting their children's needs. They also allowed middle-class parents to construct a special relationship with the state based on their role as parents.

Seeing children as rights-bearing citizens in need of protection opened the door to changing the way Canadians responded to sexual assaults against minors. The construction of the sex crime problem and the proposed solutions were based on a very specific conception of exactly what it was children needed protection from. As I have argued, the sex crime problem was widely conceived as a mental health problem. When the local Toronto press looked for answers to the disappearance of Judy Carter, mental health experts provided those answers for them. When Torontonians asked what kind of person would commit such a crime, it was psychologists and other behavioural experts who stood at the ready with explanations.

The postwar emphasis on psychological well-being and personality development meant that the impact of sexual assault was measured less by physical damage and more by the potential for psychic trauma, with the result that everything from encountering a neighbourhood flasher to rape could cause serious emotional problems for young victims. The same logic applied to offenders. While few people would have argued that peeping toms, men who enticed children to fondle their genitals in exchange for candy, and those who vaginally penetrated five-year-olds had committed crimes of equal degree, all were nevertheless seen to be suffering from a deviation of the normal sexual instinct, and each required the same response: psychological treatment to help cure them of their disease.

It is little surprise, then, that when Shvemar recruited her best friend Effie Hahn to form an action group, the first person they contacted was Dr Kenneth Gray, a University of Toronto forensic psychiatrist who specialized in medical jurisprudence. He immediately agreed to come on board as a member of the league's Scientific Advisory Committee (SAC).[14] In fact, PAL had little difficulty piquing the interest of leading experts and lay people alike. By the time they held their first annual general meeting, just four months after the group formed, PAL's dossier bulged with endorsements from almost a hundred different groups, organizations, and individuals, including local associations of the Liberal and the Conservative parties, myriad social service and volunteer organizations, and hundreds of Ontario parent-teacher, church, and community groups as well as individuals.[15] The SAC quickly evolved into a Who's Who of Ontario politics, academe, and the mental health profession, and included such luminaries as William Blatz and Dr Reva Gerstein of the Institute of Child Study, J.D. Griffin, the founding member of the Canadian Mental Health Association, and J.A. Edmison, Queen's Counsel, former president of the Canadian Penal Association, and assistant to the principal of Queen's University. Four members of the provincial Parliament (MPPs) – two Conservatives, a Liberal, and a member of the Canadian Co-operative Federation – sat on the board of directors, though not all at the same time. They were joined by two representatives of the Toronto branch of the Kiwanis Club, a community service organization whose interest in the sex crime issue began as early as 1947 when they provided lump sum funding to a team of psychiatrists and criminologists for a study into the extent and nature of the problem.[16] The Kiwanis men aimed to make the league a national organization.[17] Their ambitions were only partly realized: the board of directors assigned a provincial organizer, and at least three independent branches formed in London, Hamilton, and Windsor.[18] In 1956 Shvemar and co-board member Bert Rickman were invited to meet with a group of high-profile community leaders in Detroit, Michigan.[19] By February 1956, PAL had grown from a team of two into a transnationally known lobby group that successfully pressured the provincial Conservative government to open the first and only clinic in Canada for the treatment of sex deviation. As we shall see, it was a feat that some of the most senior public servants were unable to accomplish despite years of internal lobbying.

Much like the expansive network of traditional women's groups founded in the late nineteenth century, PAL was a largely female-driven and volunteer-run organization. Planning was plotted over the telephone and drawn up on the backs of envelopes, and meetings depended on members' willingness to open their homes and whip up a coffee cake. Only on rare occasions did they seek to raise money, and even these efforts were small scale, providing more publicity than cash. Everything, Shvemar explains, was donated.[20] One of the group's major donors was Conservative Party supporter John Bassett, owner of the right-leaning news daily, the *Toronto Telegram*. A quick phone call to Bassett's office resulted in front section coverage of the league's birth. Bassett also assigned his science and medicine reporter to act as PAL's official media advisor. Shvemar's familial connection to the Ontario Conservative Party through her uncle, Ontario MPP Allan Grossman, certainly helped open doors, but in the 1950s media coverage was relatively easy for local action groups to organize.[21]

Guided by the advice of their SAC, PAL's first (and until they met with success, its only) objective was to convince the Ontario government to open a sexual deviation treatment clinic. On 22 September 1955, just seven months after they formed, the league secured a meeting with the Liberal premier of Ontario, Leslie Frost, and formally presented their demands. They asked for what Ontario psychiatrists and a hundred other groups and organizations had requested since at least 1947: a clinic separate from any other institution where persons charged with sexual offences would be examined by psychologists and psychiatrists. Experts could make sentencing recommendations to the courts and provide treatment for convicted offenders. The proposed clinic would also undertake research into the causes, treatment, and prevention of sexual deviation, and act as a training facility for graduate students and medical interns.[22] Though there were no known effective treatments for sexual deviancy, the proposal was built on the firm belief that given the opportunity, resources, and staff, it was only a matter of time before properly trained researchers would find a cure.

None of PAL's demands came as a surprise to the premier. Ontario's Attorney General Dana Porter attended the league's first annual general meeting in June 1955. The event, staged at the prestigious King Edward Hotel, was given full coverage in the *Toronto Telegram*. Media interest remained high over the slow summer months: in July, well-known journalist June Callwood wrote a feature article on the group for *Maclean's*, and the August edition of the *Canadian Home Journal* ran a lead story focused on the national sex crime problem in which the league's agenda for action received significant coverage.[23] Premier Frost could not possibly have been more prepared.

PAL's appeal for a research and treatment facility was not out of line with the overall agenda in the provincial Department of Reform Institutions (DRI) in this period. Ontario showed a remarkable willingness to explore and implement new and innovative services in the province's reformatories. In 1951 they opened the Alex G. Brown Memorial Clinic for the treatment of incarcerated alcoholics, and in 1954 the program was expanded to include treatment for drug addiction. Considered experimental and leading edge for its time, both programs attracted attention and visitors from across Canada and around the world. More ribbons were cut in the fall of 1955 when the DRI opened a new, twenty-five bed Neuro-Psychiatric Clinic at the Guelph Reformatory, where inmates from institutions all over the province could receive prolonged courses of psychological and psychiatric treatment on an in-patient basis. Ontario was growing accustomed to receiving international accolades for its innovations in prisoner programming, all of which were premised on the belief that rehabilitation depended on carefully planned strategies of reform that encompassed institutional placement, work assignment, and in some cases, individual or group therapy.

By the time PAL arrived on Frost's doorstep, the DRI was well into the planning stages for the creation of a new, maximum-security unit to be built in the small town of Millbrook, northwest of Toronto. Responding to internal concerns about increased violence in provincial prisons and, in particular, to a costly riot that had erupted in the Guelph Reformatory in July of 1952, the department devised a plan to house all violent offenders separately until they, through good behaviour, earned their way back into the regular prison system.[24] After a provincially appointed Select Committee on Prison Reform tabled its report in 1954, the government decided to add a sex offender program in the new prison, thus fulfilling at least one of the committee's recommendations. Millbrook, however, was not yet built, and to date none of the prisons offered anything approaching adequate psychiatric and psychological services.

Outside the premier's office, the PAL delegation was met by a small group of press photographers and journalists who predicted the appointment would last less than half an hour. When they entered the premier's office, they were joined by the DRI's head psychiatrist Frank van Nostrand, Minister of Health Mackenzie Phillips, the Toronto Psychiatric Hospital's Dr Kenneth Gray, and two MPPs, Bill Stewart and Shvemar's uncle, Allan Grossman. All but van Nostrand were avid supporters of the group, but much to the delegation's dismay, they took up a position behind Frost and remained silent throughout the meeting. After a failed attempt to flatter his female guests into submission, Frost flatly told them that the clinic they were asking for was far beyond the provincial government's means. With seven months of intense activity behind them, including political lobbying, scientific research, board meetings, media interviews, public speaking, and petition writing, PAL refused to concede defeat. According to Shvemar, she and her co-leaguers spent three hours rebutting arguments from Frost and van Nostrand (who favoured such a clinic but resented PAL's intrusion on medical and government territory). Finally the premier fell silent. His guests sat and waited. 'It looked as though we were going to lose,' Shvemar wrote in her journal. She was wrong. The meeting ended with Frost's congratulations that they had 'got everything they wanted.' This, Shvemar triumphantly declared, was 'democracy in action.'[25]

The victory was short-lived. In a predictable display of political inertia, the government of Ontario sat on its hands in the months following the September meeting, making no effort to establish the promised clinic. Shvemar grew increasingly pessimistic. 'Some of them are the worse bunch of *liars*. They only do what they are pushed to do and otherwise they spend more time blocking progress.'[26] Three days later she wrote in her journal, 'More dilly-dallying! I think they want to put us off with one excuse after the other ... [We] need something they do not expect, but what?'[27] Unfortunately, the unexpected came on 7 January 1956 when the body of five-year-old Susan Cadieux was found frozen in the snow in London, Ontario. Although the police initially admitted the possibility that she had simply wandered away from her friends and succumbed to the cold, an autopsy confirmed that she was the victim of a sexual assault.[28]

Their faith in the democratic process somewhat bruised, PAL turned to their best ally, the media, to shame the government into living up to its promise. In a *Toronto Telegram* report covering a special emergency meeting of the league, Shvemar resorted to hyperbole: 'Do we have to have a killing in every city to make the government wheels start turning?' The group's provincial organizer claimed that they represented seventy organizations whose combined memberships accounted for close to three million Ontarians. 'We want action and we want it now,' said Director Margaret Scrivener. 'Governments have made reports, established special committees and are even holding a Royal Commission. But until legislation is introduced and passed, women and children are not safe.' PAL directors 'regard[ed] the present emergency at London as being a direct result of an inadequate government policy on sexual perversion,' and demanded a meeting with the premier.[29] Two days later, PAL was back at Queen's Park, this time as members of a newly formed provincial committee composed of the attorney general, the minister of reform institutions, and the minister of health.[30] After the meeting, plans were undertaken to create an Outpatient Forensic Clinic at the Toronto Psychiatric Hospital where sex deviants could be assessed for the courts, and treated by medical, psychological, and social work staff. It would also serve as a hub for new research on the treatment of sexual deviation. The clinic opened 1 May 1956, and in its first year staff examined almost three thousand people.[31] Set up initially as a pilot project, the clinic quickly became a permanent arm of the Toronto Psychiatric Hospital.[32]

On 8 February 1956, the Frost government granted PAL a charter in a public ceremony honouring their contribution to helping solve 'the difficult problem' of sex deviation, but PAL's work was not yet done. When the clinic opened three months later, the league maintained close ties with staff at the Outpatient Forensic Clinic. Its first and second directors, Dr P.J. Thomson and Dr R.E. Turner, sat on PAL's Scientific Advisory Committee, and PAL members served as a control group for the clinic's psychologist Daniel Paitich, whose thesis was a comparative study of attitudes toward parents among normal and sexually deviated persons.[33] By this time, PAL's board of directors were beginning to think that mental health treatment was only one part of the solution to the sex crime problem, especially where it concerned child victims. Though they never wavered from their belief that sexual deviancy was a treatable condition, the group set new goals to secure better sex education for parents, and to end the way child victims of sexual assault were treated during cross-examination in courtroom trials.

Mirroring the prescription of most postwar psychologists, PAL believed that children's normal sexual development depended on parents' ability to maintain an honest and open dialogue free of the embarrassment and shame that was too often attached to discussions about sex. The argument in favour of a more open and honest approach to dealing with sexual matters was well received after the Second World War, but the question of who should do the talking was still controversial. As Mary Louise Adams found, Ontario parents were not yet ready to hand over a job they felt still belonged to the family and the church.[34] Though PAL never took a public position on the debate, SAC member and child expert Dr Blatz was publicly opposed to sex education in schools and likely encouraged the group to focus on educating parents instead.

PAL lobbied the Mental Health Division of the national Department of Health to commission a film strip on sex crimes and sex knowledge aimed at a pre-adult audience. Although the National Film Board produced a surfeit of parent education films in this period, PAL's request was declined, perhaps because the U.S. film *Dangerous Stranger* was already in circulation.[35] PAL shifted its energy to opening an education centre where parents could learn about child sexual development and gain confidence and direction in how to talk with their children about sex-related matters. The league teamed up with the Parent Education Associates (PEA), a Toronto-based organization dedicated to providing parental 'guidance, assistance, encouragement and reassurance ... within the range of normal family living.'[36] Unfortunately, after months of intense fundraising for the centre, a PEA member absconded with the money. Preferring not to cause a scandal, PEA closed ranks and quietly abandoned its efforts to develop a sex education program. League members felt defeated and never pursued the matter again.[37]

The second major initiative undertaken by PAL was to change the way child victims were treated within the judicial system.[38] Though prepubescent female victims of sexual assault were typically portrayed as innocent victims in the media, PAL members were horrified to discover that the opposite was true in the courtroom. The structure of the criminal justice system left the victims of sexual assault at a distinct disadvantage: if the accused were considered by the courts innocent until proven guilty, then it followed that victims were considered guilty of either complicity or deception until proven innocent. As a result, children who claimed to have been sexually assaulted were subjected to aggressive questioning by defence lawyers whose singular goal was to undermine their credibility.

PAL established a legal committee to observe and report on the proceedings of sexual assault trials. Members were deeply disturbed by the cross-examination techniques used by defence lawyers. Young children were forced to recount their experiences in a room full of adults, including the perpetrator. To PAL members fully conversant in studies of child psychology, it was clear that the courtroom experience added another layer of trauma to the lives of victims. The solution was to abolish, or, at the very least, place meaningful restrictions on the cross-examination of child witnesses in sexual assault trials. Their research showed that the new state of Israel provided the remedy they sought: children gave their testimony out of court where it was recorded on tape and later played at the trial.[39]

PAL's legal advisors were not nearly as enthusiastic as were the women who had witnessed child sexual assault trials for probably the first time in their lives. SAC members like lawyer and University of Toronto professor Edson Haines were reticent to accept any proposal that would deny the defence the opportunity to cross-examine witnesses, including child victims of assault. Not only were the rights of the accused compromised in such a scenario, in the 1950s it was not unusual for accusations of sexual impropriety toward children to be dismissed as the fanciful imaginings of the complainant, especially if the charge was incest. Even medical experts were disinclined to support the prosecution of incestuous parents. Dr John Rich of the Thistletown Children's Hospital and lead researcher for an unpublished Brantford study of sexual assaults against children, and Montreal's Bruno Cormier, the director of the prestigious McGill Forensic Clinic, both maintained that parent–child incest involved complicity on the part of parent *and* victim, and should not be regulated by law.[40]

As far as PAL's law experts were concerned, cross-examination was the only way to determine the veracity of a child's claim. Eventually Haines set aside his reservations, however, and agreed to chair the controversial committee under the condition that no one speak to the media about the group's activities before they were able to present a clear plan of direction.[41] The committee members agreed, and proceeded with the court-watch and research programs. According to Shvemar, an inexperienced board member revealed details of the legal committee's activities to a news reporter, and the story appeared in the paper the following day. Furious, Haines immediately resigned, and the committee did not survive the upset.[42] Exactly when PAL's board of directors ceased meeting is uncertain, but no further actions were taken after these two projects met with failure.

In late 1956 Bertha Shvemar was diagnosed with encephalitis and stepped down from her position as league president. The remaining founding members were feeling the effects of the hard work and long hours PAL demanded, and they also scaled back their commitment. Even the SAC shrank from twelve to four members after Shvemar's departure. PAL carried on under a new president, but the new board was never able to repeat the organizational successes of the first year of PAL's existence.

Without a doubt, PAL's 'militantly hopeful' spirit, combined with the board's 'bulldog tenacity' had a great deal to do with the group's success at the provincial legislature, but there are other facets of the organization and of 1950s culture generally that contributed to the league's achievements.[43] Contrary to the well-worn stereotype, the postwar decades witnessed a resurgence of women's activism. In pre–Second World War English Canada, women's councils, the Women's Christian Temperance Union, the Imperial Order Daughters of the Empire, the Young Women's Christian Association, and similar organizations were instrumental in promoting women's interests in local and national politics. After the Second World War, however, membership declined dramatically, but not because women retreated into their suburban homes. From the mid-1940s on, women joined Parent-Teacher and Home and School Associations in record numbers. In 1946 the Canadian Home and School Federation claimed a membership of just over 77,000; by 1953 that number had more than doubled to a total of 173,000.[44] Home and School and Parent-Teacher Associations offered their largely female membership opportunities similar to those found in pre–Second World War women's organizations. Participants attended lectures, formed study groups, and lobbied for institutional change. Those who began with a focus on the classroom often turned their attention to school boards and municipal, provincial, and federal governments.

Though women's councils could still catch the attention of provincial politicians at the end of the 1950s, their effectiveness as political lobby groups was slowly eroding.[45] In their stead, the Canadian Federation of Home and School and Parent-Teacher Associations (CFHSPTA) became the unofficial political lobby group for middle-class family interests, or at least that was the position of the president who confidently proclaimed that the federation was 'destined to become one of the most powerful forces in the Dominion.'[46] Although high enrolments in PTAs demonstrated that Canadian women did not abandon their social-activist past, the Home and School movement did have important consequences for how, and by whom, that activism was directed. For obvious reasons, PTAs only attracted women with school-age children. Single women, married women without children, and older women were all excluded, with the exception of those who occupied administrative or advisory positions. The Home and School movement also had a comparatively narrower mandate: the national office promoted a social and political vision that regarded home, community, church, and school as equal partners in shaping the next generation. The CFHSPTA advocated 'good citizenship' programs that included teaching immigrants their rights as Canadian citizens as well as providing outreach to isolated families, including aboriginal peoples. The CFHSPTA's vision of Canada was inclusive rather than exclusive, and they tended to be politically neutral and ideologically liberal in outlook, concerned primarily with the trials of growing up, the challenges of parenting, and child safety issues.

A defining feature of the Home and School movement in Canada was how readily it embraced child psychology. According to Kari Delhi, understanding and improving the mother-child relationship became the central focus of Ontario's PTAs as early as 1926, a focus substantially assisted by the work of Dr William Blatz and his colleagues at the University of Toronto's Institute of Child Study. The membership of the Home and School and Parent-Teacher Associations often overlapped with that of local women's councils, creating a cross-pollination of ideas and strategies, and the two types of groups often worked together on projects of mutual interest.[47] Thus, Home and School support for the mental health movement was already in place at war's end, and many baby boom parents relied on their local association and their child development advisors for help.

Though the family had an important role to play in society, it could not go it alone, insisted the CFHSPTA's president. It was not just the good family that makes the good society, but the good society must also take care of its families, many of whom are vulnerable to corrosive external and internal forces. '*We need to reaffirm our belief in the family as an institution,*' she argued, but 'parents, too, need to feel their sense of worth. We cannot say that is the responsibility of parents and pass by on the other side. The ... family does not live in a vacuum. It needs help to solve its difficult situations.'[48] 'Help' was expected to flow from volunteer organizations as well as the federal government, in part through governmental support for mental health and child development programs.

The CFHSPTA's mandate was to teach parents the skills they needed for raising well-adjusted children who, once grown, would bear responsibility for the safekeeping of the planet in the new, atomic age.[49] Reconstruction propaganda proclaimed that fathers were going to have to play a larger role in domestic life, including child rearing, and this expectation was reflected in the association's literature. Most members, however, were women. For the young and middle-aged mother at home, the PTA provided an important social outlet, but it was also a way for women to play an active role in public life. As Nancy Christie and Michael Gauvreau describe it, English Canada's postwar culture of citizenship was grounded in a 'sense of a world of unlimited possibilities, a belief in participatory democracy, a commitment to expert knowledge, the expansion of social security, a vision of active citizenship anchored in quality of life in the private sphere, and extolling the virtue of the inner-directed personality.'[50] Cultures of citizenship were more ambiguous than conformist, and allowed for a fairly broad range of social and political identities and practices, for women as well as for men.

For child-rearing women, attending lectures and reading parenting magazines and books, all of which were chock-full of mental health information, were ways they could expand their social, political, and intellectual horizons without being criticized for neglecting home life. For women who lived in rural areas, or who were unable to afford university and college courses, the Home and School movement provided immediate access to a wide range of resources on parenting techniques, and suggestions for community improvement and other popular activities. Given Canada's vast geography and the growing rural-urban divide, the CFHSPTA brought the nation's parents together in a way few volunteer associations could. Of course, not every local group lived up to the ideals trumpeted by head office. Some earned a reputation for antagonizing teachers or for functioning as little more than a coffee klatch. Regardless, the goal of the Home and School movement was to enable parents to raise compassionate, intelligent, and aware children who could live up to the ideals of the new internationalism. On a practical level, this meant making the same educational materials available from one end of the country to the other. Consequently, Home and School and Parent-Teacher Associations encouraged homogeneity.[51]

As parent-citizens, Canadian mothers mobilized to work individually and locally for a better future for their children, and collectively and nationally to pressure their provincial, state, and national governments to supply them with the resources they felt they needed to meet their goals. For its part, PAL epitomized the best qualities that modern motherhood had to offer. Self-sacrificing, committed, hard working, and dedicated to community service, its members embodied the values and concerns of the middle-class family.

The everyday woman's role in securing a safe and peaceful future was reinforced by groups like PAL who emphasized mothers' special interests as homemakers and parents. By recycling the 'we can do it' rhetoric employed a decade earlier by wartime government recruitment agencies, PAL played up the founders' status as 'just housewives.' In their own account of the league's genesis, they wrote: 'Neither of we four Toronto wives who initiated the Parents Action League are what you might call unusual. We're each about 30 years old. We're happily married to husbands – a pharmacist, a furrier, an accountant, an insurance broker – who hate undue publicity. We all have young children.'[52] Though these hardly sound like a list of credentials, in the 1950s it was an unbeatable résumé. Women who put family interests first were the ideological heroes of the day.[53]

In a 1955 *Maclean's* feature article, the sex crime issue became a mere backdrop to a story that cast PAL members as exemplars of women's ability to get things done. Feminist journalist June Callwood's profile of the league emphasized the founders' domestic roles, and drew attention to the combination of maternal values and community involvement as part of the iconography of responsible female citizenship. She coined the term 'the PAL lunch,' referring to quickly prepared midday meals that demanded little effort so that busy mothers might get on to equally important civic duties. Rather than signalling neglect, relying on new convenience foods was a trope for the small sacrifices women and their children were learning to make in order that they might serve greater ends. In other words, shortcuts like canned and convenience foods were quite all right when your time was committed to socially redeeming tasks.[54] PAL members were not unique in their efforts to improve community and family life; they were just a particularly good example of how women could watch over the children, drop off the dry cleaning, pick up the groceries, balance the household budget, and change the world. As Callwood put it, 'take a woman and a telephone and stir.'[55]

While the availability of effective psychiatric treatment for sex offenders was a first and important step in the fight against sex crime, PAL argued that the job begins in the home. In *Liberty*, a Canadian magazine for young families, PAL exhorted, 'elimination of the sex "deviate" is up to you; not by waging a war against him, but by fighting his sickness, bred in the home and nurtured by the turned back of society. Participating in this campaign is your duty to your children. It's your insurance that your child may play freely without fear; that he or she will not be named victim in tomorrow's headlines.'[56] By mid-century, the notion that mothers had a social duty to protect and promote their children's physical health from gestation to adulthood was an entrenched North American ideal. In the early part of the twentieth century, sickness and death among children were more likely to be attributed to a mother's maternal failures than to external forces such as poverty, overcrowded living conditions, or the lack of decent medical care.[57] In the 1950s, mothers' duties expanded to include emotional safekeeping as well. As far as the urban middle classes were concerned, postwar prosperity backed up by a monthly family allowance cheque meant that food, clothing, and shelter were a given. The new 'good' mother tended to children's changing psychological needs at every age and stage.[58]

That PAL chose a gender-neutral moniker over 'Mother's Crusade' – Shvemar's first suggestion – reflects the wider North American trend away from maternalism, and toward the postwar expectation that fathers would play a much more active role in domestic life generally, and child-rearing specifically.[59] Though the 1950s are often idealized as a period of traditional family living, the marital ideal was decidedly modern.[60] Once the seat of male authority, marriage was recast as a union of equals, and motherhood as the most important career a woman could hope to have. National rhetoric claimed that women's best contribution to Canada's democratic future was raising educated and responsible citizens, a view perpetuated in a variety of mass media, including *Canadian Home and School*, the official organ of the CFHSPTA; the National Film Board of Canada; and *Chatelaine*, Canada's national women's magazine. Whether or not women left the home for paid labour, Canadian mothers were repeatedly reminded that their 'ultimate responsibility' was to their husbands and children.[61] As Annalee Golz points out, familialism was a concept that served to validate women's domestic role by casting her household and child-rearing responsibilities as '"on par with any other occupation" and equal in value to paid labour,' but the effect was to submerge women's interests within the interests of family.[62] Most fathers, it appears, did not take the active parenting role that postwar planners had anticipated.[63]

As easily as women were praised for their role as social stabilizers, they were also blamed for society's ills. Accusations that mothers were corrupting or interfering with their children's emotional progress were made as early as 1942 in American author Philip Wylie's bestseller, *Generation of Vipers*.[64] Calling the phenomenon 'momism,' Wylie argued that with husbands away overseas, the American mother was suffering from an excess of emotional feeling that was thwarting the psychological development of the nation's children. Postwar suburbs were described as incubators for momism: women were home all day, stranded in the suburbs with nothing more to do than direct all their energy toward their children. The suburban father's long commute meant longer absences from the home, further compounding children's psychological torment in the hands of smothering mothers.

Too much mothering and not enough fathering explained a wide range of social problems, but none so much as sexual deviancy. In an interview with the *Toronto Daily Star*, Dr Manfred S. Guttmacher, a Maryland-based criminal court judge and leading North American expert on sex criminals, asserted that most sex crimes are 'basically the fault of parents ... His home life, the amount of affection he received and the attitude of his parents towards sex – each of these factors can bring him one day to the disaster of committing a serious sex offence.'[65] Canadian experts were of the same opinion. In the first of a four-part 'Health Week' series on sexual deviancy, Dr John Rich claimed that behind almost every sex deviant is 'a mother whose own problems about sex have driven her to destroy in her son all self-respect and self-confidence. So who is the deviate – the man or his mother? She may be a devout woman who has never committed a crime in her life. It is evident that when we talk of deviation we should include far more people than the criminals.'[66] The idea that mothers interfered with their children's 'natural' development was a staple of the expert advice industry in Canada and the U.S. alike.[67]

As the 1950s wore on, however, some experts began paying more attention to the impact fathers had on childhood sexual development.[68] Suburban life was singled out as cause for particular concern. Dr Alistair MacLeod of the Mental Hygiene Institute of Montreal worried that the absence of men 'disrupts family life by blurring the roles of the sexes' and leaving children 'bewildered.'[69] The first director of Toronto's Outpatient Forensic Clinic, Dr P.J. Thomson, suggested that one of the causes of homosexuality was the decline of the status of the father, whose commute from the suburbs meant that children were left to be raised by the 'educated and emancipated modern American female.'[70] Daniel

Paitich, a senior psychologist at the Forensic Clinic and a specialist on the causal role of parents in giving rise to male homosexuality, argued that 'if it is possible to make one large generalization about [sex deviates] ... it's this: their relations with their fathers determine *whether* they will be deviates; the relations with their mothers determine what *sort* they'll be.'[71] Four years later, Paitich placed even more emphasis on the paternal influence. 'Momism is not so important a factor in maladjustment as it was once thought to be,' he told a *Toronto Star* journalist, 'the father plays a crucial role as "rescuer" no matter how bad the child's relationship with the mother. "I'd predict there'd be no sexual problem if a boy saw his father as an admirable, competent figure," says Paitich. "If the father is negative, cold and detached, the boy is more likely to become sexually maladjusted later in life."'[72]

Whichever parent was to blame, the quality of parents' relationships with each other and with their children, and the ease with which they filled their roles as mother, father, wife, and husband were directly reflected in their children's mental, emotional, and sexual development. The behaviour of North American parents was thrust under the psychological microscope, and articles in popular women's and parenting magazines repeatedly instructed their readers that a modern attitude toward sex included achieving a happy and 'sexually healthy' marriage, and was an essential ingredient in the normal development of a child.[73] However, even those qualities that defined a happy and sexually healthy marriage were narrowly proscribed according to psychoanalytic paradigms that encouraged married women to enjoy sex and blamed them if they did not.[74] Whatever tricks she might learn for the bedroom, when wives were mothers, a 'wholesome attitude toward sex' was required. The development of children into stable and mature adults depended on parents' ability to talk about sex frankly, plainly, and easily, with an emphasis on its biological, not erotic, components.[75]

The doctrine of 'modern sex' had its roots in the turn of the century, but in the 1950s it gained a foothold in popular culture and became widely accepted as a topic for public discussion. 'Puritans' who harboured outdated Victorian attitudes were blamed for causing sex problems in the first place.[76] In 1947, for example, a newspaper editorial described the recent Toronto showing of a 'hygienic' film titled *Mom and Dad*, 'which portrayed scenes of illegitimate birth [by Caesarean section!], social diseases, and the results of immoral conduct,' as an indication that 'we have come a long way since Victorian days.' The editor admonished adults who 'by their shame-faced conduct imply that sex should be a smirking, secret thing scrawled on walls and taught in the back seat of automobiles ... The modern trend,' he declared, 'is towards airing of the subject in an intelligent fashion.'[77] Ironically, *Mom and Dad* was one of the earliest 'sexploitation' films to use the health education genre as a means to legitimize salacious material. So long as it was couched in the discourse of modern sex, however, films like *Mom and Dad* were practically guaranteed a public screening.

Doctors who ten years earlier would have led the campaign to shut such films down were now warning that sexual silences endangered children. Writing for *Maclean's,* psychologist J.D. Ketchum warned, 'Prude is Father to the Pervert.'[78] Parents who failed to have open and honest discussions about sex with their children condemned them to a life of ignorance and unhappiness. What they don't learn at home, they will pick up on the streets and in the schoolyard where false information is rampant, he warned. It was a hard message to sell to an older generation who remained firm in their belief that *any* talk about sexual matters was immoral. New parents, however, appear to have had little difficulty accepting the doctrine of modern sex, which is not to say that they were either successful or even at ease when talking to their children about 'the birds and the bees,' but only that they knew they should. According to mainstream expert opinion, parents who shielded their children from the plain facts about sex were 'prudes' at best, and at worst were responsible for creating the socio-sexual problems that would inevitably result from the shroud of secrecy and silence. As historian Elaine Tyler May has argued, in the years after the Second World War, sex was widely regarded as a force to be contained, not repressed.[79]

PAL achieved widespread support precisely because it embraced sexual modernism. However, it soon found itself trapped by the language of scientific expertise. While those who opposed frank talk about sex were dismissed as holdovers from an earlier age, by the mid-1950s those who articulated their fears and concerns about sexual danger in more personal, experiential terms were frequently characterized as hysterical. With mental health and medical experts in firm control of what defined 'intelligent discussion about sex,' those whose sex knowledge grew from their own experiences were pushed to the margins of the public conversation. Women were not the only ones excluded. During the hearings of the Royal Commission on the Criminal Law Relating to Criminal Sexual Psychopaths, male witnesses whose opinions and recommendations drew from first-hand experience working with victims of sexual violence were ignored. In this way, the modern mental health approach, based on 'rational' and 'intelligent' thinking, was gendered male. Those whose experience and expertise were gleaned from providing services for victims of interfamilial violence were gendered female.

For those who would organize politically around sexual matters, the assumption that women tended towards hysteria was a major obstacle. PAL's success lay partly in its ability to submerge members' femininity behind the masculine authority of the Scientific Advisory Committee. Speaking at PAL's second annual meeting in 1956, SAC member and head psychiatrist of Toronto's Juvenile Court Clinic, J.D. Atcheson, applauded the group for realizing that 'action based on fear alone is not in and of itself a sufficient answer to the problem ... Although the fear is still present in all of us as parents, it has now been complemented by sound, scientific, enquiry' conducted in an 'objective' and 'detached scientific manner.'[80] Yet for all its attempts to appear modern, PAL was forced to distinguish itself from early twentieth-century empire-building moral reformers. Much to the amusement of her audience, in her presidential address at the second annual general meeting Shvemar recounted having been called 'The Do Gooders,' the 'Ladies Against Sex,' and 'The Ladies of the Purity League.' 'One gentleman playfull[y] envisioned our expansion to darkest Africa,' she continued. 'He said he sees the directors of the League along the Congo riding elephants with native pygmies marching along – carrying banners – "Join our League of Purity."'[81] Shvemar took it in stride, telling the crowd that 'we learned to laugh at ourselves with our teasers.' Indeed Shvemar often attempted to disarm PAL's critics with a combination of grace, humour, and sarcasm.[82] One unlucky psychiatrist glibly asked Shvemar, 'Are you for sex or against it?' to which she replied, 'I'll call an executive meeting and get back to you.'[83] PAL refused to be characterized as anything less than an organization of intelligent, thinking parents informed by 'objective' and 'detached' scientific enquiry.[84]

The remarkable confidence in psychiatry's ability to cure sexual deviancy was a reflection of the heady optimism of many postwar North Americans who shared a 're-awakened faith not only in the value of science ... but also in the dignity of the partnership between the scientist and the layman, the citizen.'[85] In his official report on the Fifth International Congress on Mental Health, University of Toronto professor William Line observed that 'there appears to have been demonstrated the reality of a common cause – man himself and his destiny; not merely his "welfare" in the protective sense, but man as he can and needs to become.'[86] This optimistic view defined PAL's 'where there is a will, there is a way' approach to overcoming the problem of sex crime and deviation. Major Canadian health organizations like the Canadian Cancer Society and the Canadian Mental Health Association used war-like rally cries in their speeches, press releases, and promotional literature, and PAL too deployed these familiar metaphors in its first and only publication:

> We believe that when a sufficient segment of mankind decides to do something it usually gets it done. An atom bomb was built and the Salk vaccine produced because, in the one case, large numbers of people decided they were going to win a war, and they provided the money that enabled a government to build an A-bomb; in the latter case, thousands of selfless volunteers collected assistance from millions of volunteer givers in the March of Dimes campaign. Mankind has made up its mind to beat polio. And it did ... If similar determination could be aroused to conquer the problem of the sex criminal, there is very little doubt that progress would be made in that field too.[87]

Faith in humankind's ability to conquer massive social problems was inspired by the ideals of responsible, democratic citizenship. According to PAL's Scientific Advisory Committee, science was at the ready, restrained only by the lack of political will, something Shvemar and her colleagues were determined to inspire. Fortunately, the media was ready to help them spread their message.

In his original formulation, Stanley Cohen placed considerable emphasis on the role of the news media in creating moral panics, but others have since disagreed, arguing that 'the media does not produce so much as "reproduce and sustain" the dominant interpretations of the news.'[88] Clearly the news media did not construct the criminal sexual psychopath. In the 1950s, journalists simply turned to psychiatrists as well as to police investigators when distilling meaning from violent crime.[89] Psychiatrists claimed that rather than there being a single, crazed killer on the loose, there were virtually hundreds of sexual deviants living in every city. Police responses to local sex crimes reinforced this perception of a widespread menace. As we have seen, after a reported murder or assault, local forces explained to journalists that they were rounding up all known sex deviants for questioning. Placed together, reports from the police and psychiatrists converged to create the illusion of a widespread menace.

Canadian historians of gender and sexuality in the post–Second World War era have assigned significant influence to American political and cultural life in shaping the Canadian milieu. Certainly in the 1950s, American influence grew by leaps and bounds, especially with the introduction of television. While it is often difficult to say with any certainty exactly how Canadians felt the impact of these changes, there is clear evidence that media reports originating in the United States lit fires north of the border. American historians have traced the origins of the sexual psychopath scare to the director of the U.S. Federal Bureau of Investigations, J. Edgar Hoover. Facing stiff competition from the Federal Bureau of Narcotics in the 1930s for federal dollars, Hoover was anxious to redirect public and political support to his own office. Shortly before Americans cast their attention to the war overseas, he published an article titled 'How Safe Is Your Daughter?' He claimed that sexual assaults on young girls were reaching epidemic proportions, and advocated for new and stronger laws to address the problem. Only three states passed criminal sexual psychopath laws before the United States entered the war. After the war was over, Hoover recycled the same article with a slightly different title, 'How Safe Is Your Youngster?'[90] He advised parents to organize pressure groups to urge their state legislatures to pass sexual psychopath legislation. In Quebec, McGill University's dean of law, W.C.J. Meredith, credited Hoover for 'sounding the alarm' on a problem that plagued Canada and Britain as well. 'One has only to read the newspapers,' he argued, 'to realize that sex criminals constitute a serious menace to society.'[91] Indeed, it was the republication of Hoover's article that inspired PAL president Bertha Shvemar to take action after the death of Judy Carter.[92]

But Canadian journalists had been serving their readers a steady diet of information about sexual deviation since at least 1947.[93] Two leading national magazines covered the topic in its earliest days with the publication of 'The Truth about Sex Criminals' in *Maclean's* and 'We the People vs. Sex Criminals' in *Chatelaine.*[94] Canadian experts implored the press to 'render the highest public service by maintaining a steady and even pressure of public interest in this and other mental and human problems.'[95] They complied, and the issue received regular coverage until 1957, after which time the public appetite appears to have declined. Until then, the media functioned as one of the main conduits through which sex information passed. Even Ontario's Department of Reform Institutions distributed a *Saturday Night* magazine article on sexual deviation to institutional staff as an educational tool.[96]

The educative function of the press aside, the corporate bottom line, combined with the proven aphorism that sex sells, was instrumental in PAL's success. As attractive, middle-class housewives fighting a noble battle against a serious social threat, they embodied the postwar feminine ideals of familialism and volunteerism. They put a pleasing face on stories about sexual deviancy and crimes of sexual violence, thus bridging the gap between salaciousness and responsible journalism. Only months after the murder of Judy Carter, for example, the National Council of Women criticized newspapers for 'the unwholesome exploitation of sex through detailed reports of murders, suicide and other horrors,' and passed a resolution urging the Canadian Daily Newspaper Publishers Association to 'curb sensationalism.'[97] By framing sex crime stories with the activities of a citizen's action group, the *Telegram* absolved itself of such unsavoury charges, enabling the paper 'to publish without criticism endless stories about sex crimes.'[98] As a result of the publicity, members were regularly invited to speak to a wide range of community groups, and PAL became a household name almost overnight. Ron Kenyon, the *Telegram* medical reporter assigned to cover PAL, was 'as well known in Toronto as Walter Cronkite ... Everyone was reading those stories,' he claims.

Everyone except readers of the *Toronto Daily Star*, that is. That PAL was a media product is glaringly apparent from the very marginal coverage the league received in the *Telegram*'s main competitor. The *Star*, the more middle brow of the two dailies, participated in the debates and dialogue about the sex crime panic, playing the role of responsible corporate citizen by organizing a Citizen's Forum on Sex Offenders in January 1956, right after the Cadieux murder. The *Star*'s editors invited experts to speak, government officials to attend, and its readers to mail in questions they wanted answered by the panel. In the week leading up to the forum, the paper ran a series of articles exploring the subject of sex deviation, research, and treatment options locally and around the world. Remarkably, over two thousand people made the trip to downtown Toronto's Massey Hall to hear two Canadian and two American psychiatrists answer questions about human sexual variation. The event confirmed the views of both Ron Kenyon and PAL: people were reading the stories and were highly receptive to psychiatric ideas about human sexuality.

Most historical treatments of the postwar sex crime panic focus on the conflation of homosexuality and violent sexual acts. It is true that despite experts' insistence that harmful sex offences should be treated separately from 'nuisance-type' crimes, like exhibitionism, or from sex acts that were an offence against morals, like homosexuality, 1950s main-stream journalistic discussions about sex deviation and violent sex crime went hand in hand. A typical example is Callwood's 1955 article in which she asks, 'What causes a sex deviate?' The question, 'What goes wrong in a male to cause him to choose his own sex?' was buried in a paragraph of questions about why some men rape, why some men molest 'moppets of five and six,' and why some fathers 'desire their own daughters.'[99] The conflation of homosexuality with violent sex crime is a key feature of postwar discourses about sexuality, but historians' interest in homosexuality and heteronormativity have steered them away from examining other important changes that occurred in how people thought about sexual offences against children.

Mental health treatment as an alternative or supplement to traditional penal remedies was clearly popular, but most Ontarians continued to expect the judicial system to incarcerate sex criminals, if only to get them off the streets. Occasionally news reports focused on lenient sentences handed down for men convicted of sexual assault, and experts were sometimes held accountable. For example, around the time Susan Cadieux was found frozen in the snow, twenty-eight-year-old William Backshall of St Catharine's was caught molesting two girls, aged seven and eight. The judge agreed with the expert psychiatric witness who claimed that Backshall's sex problem was cured by 'not drinking alcohol,' and gave him a suspended sentence.[100] Shortly after, the *Globe and Mail* reported on a similar case in which a man found guilty of molesting three boys aged six, seven, and eight was only fined because, the magistrate argued, prison would do little good. He advised the perpetrator to 'move from the district as soon as possible.'[101]

Readers were outraged by these judgements, and in letters to the provincial and federal governments as well as to local and national newspapers, parents demanded that sexual assaults against children be taken more seriously.[102] Individual citizens, local councils of women, Home and School organizations, and county councils across Ontario wrote to the attorney general and the minister of health complaining about the light and suspended sentences handed down in child sexual assault cases. The owner of a Hamilton construction company described how the local postman attempted to sexually assault his five-year-old daughter. The perpetrator pled guilty and in return received a suspended sentence. 'This struck me as being a very peculiar way to deal with a person who might easily have killed the child, or damaged her physically and certainly mentally for the rest of her life.'[103] The Dufferin Home and

School Association denounced the judgements in two recent trials involving sexual offences against children as 'ridiculous.' In the first instance, the judge ordered the offender to leave town, and in the second, the magistrate released the offender because he showed remorse for his actions.[104] 'What we women and children need is protection from the judges,' complained a *Toronto Telegram* reader.[105] While most everyone agreed that mental health treatment was part of the solution, increasingly the public viewed the judicial system as part of the problem.

Mainstream Ontario press coverage of lenient sentences was usually brief, and did not include editorial or investigative embellishment. In contrast, Toronto's tabloid *Justice Weekly* provided readers with the 'shocking details' of sex crime trials in the local women's and police courts. Yet contrary to what we might expect from a scandal sheet, stories and editorials strove to enrage readers by focusing on the outrageously light or suspended sentences perpetrators received. Laziness and inexperience were the culprits, the editor claimed. Magistrates were only able to impose a maximum sentence of six months in prison. For a longer conviction, the trial had to be transferred to a higher court, but prosecutors rarely bothered to pursue this course of action since it required trial preparation.[106] The editor also blamed Ontario's attorney general for sending young and inexperienced prosecutors to the Toronto Police Court where cases of sexual assault were often heard.[107] As a result, men who forced children to engage in sexual acts received little more than a slap on the wrist. *Justice Weekly* argued that because mainstream dailies deemed stories of sexual assault trials unfit for print, women and children remained ignorant of the 'dangers that lurk on Toronto Streets,' and offenders continue to freely roam public walkways and reoffend.[108]

Justice Weekly persistently opposed pathological interpretations of sexual deviancy and instead blamed a corrupt legal and political system for failing to deal with sex crimes in a serious manner. Highly suspicious of 'mental health' experts, editorials repeatedly challenged Dr Kenneth Gray or anyone else to provide evidence that even one sex criminal had been 'cured.' The paper's journalists characterized sex criminals as vicious cowards, not victims of a disease. Ron Kenyon advised PAL to ignore the tabloids, but *Justice Weekly* did not ignore PAL; the editor complained that their journalists were persistently shut out of league meetings. He insisted that court reporters from any of Toronto's three tabloids could tell PAL more about sex criminals than could any medical doctor.

PAL did eventually take up the editor's suggestion that they visit the courts to discover for themselves the kind of 'beasts' on whose behalf they advocated. PAL members were horrified by what they witnessed in courtroom trials, but instead of joining the tabloid chorus demanding stiffer sentences for convicted sex criminals, leaguers focused on the low rate of victims reporting sexual assault. As members learned, sex crime may have been a feature story, but the stigma attached to sexual assault remained as entrenched as ever, and many parents were disinclined to press charges. No doubt parents were equally discouraged by reports of inconsequential sentences, making the embarrassment and humiliation of going public seem hardly worth it. In 1954 the *Miami Herald* asked its readers if they would press charges if their child had been 'molested by a sex pervert.' Of the 1200 replies they received, a full third claimed that they would not.[109] Three years later, PAL surveyed 364 of its own members and discovered that among the 75 who indicated at least one family member had been sexually assaulted, only 26 reported the incident to the police.[110] PAL and other parent activist groups tried to change social attitudes by insisting that reporting incidences to the authorities was a civic duty. By remaining silent, parents allowed sex deviants to roam the streets, free to commit more assaults against other children. It is difficult to know how successful such campaigns were, but it does demonstrate that in the 1950s, a vigorous effort was undertaken to strip away the shame that prevented so many from pressing criminal charges, and to tie sex crime reporting to responsible citizenship.

Finally, while I have argued that the media was instrumental in popularizing modern sexology, it is also clear that Ontario newspaper readers did not always accept news stories in the ways the media framed them.[111] As I showed at the beginning of the chapter, the murder of two immigrant women in 1954 sent journalists scrambling to find new narratives to frame the story when readers rejected a variety of traditional tropes. Readers once again revolted in 1956. Just days after the death of five-year-old Susan Cadieux, fourteen-year-old Linda Lampkin, a girl who took dance lessons, was 'popular with the boys,' and belonged to a girl gang named the Four Hustlers and wore an embroidered jacket that said so, was murdered by the married man she was reputedly dating.[112] After her body was found at the side of Commissioners Road near Toronto's industrial lakeshore, the *Toronto Daily Star* printed four large portrait photos of Lampkin. In the top two, she appears as a typical young woman. In sharp contrast, the bottom two show her bare-shouldered and wearing a dark shade of lipstick, thus inviting readers to see her as a sexually precocious teen who looked for trouble and found it.[113] The public immediately rejected the *Tely's* spin on Lampkin's murder. They insisted that her death was as tragic as that of five-year-old Susan Cadieux and eight-year-old Judy Carter. Indeed, her murder elicited as many hundreds of telephone calls and letters demanding government action as did the earlier slayings.[114] Moreover, her captured and convicted murderer, Robert Fitton, confirmed what psychiatrists and PAL were saying all along: sex criminals were 'apt to be quiet, married, mild-mannered pillars of the community.'[115] Fitton was a young, Anglo-Canadian married man with two small children, a wife, and dreams of home ownership.[116]

Linda Lampkin was the last victim of the 'wave' of sex crimes in Ontario in the 1950s. As the decade came to a close, parents appeared weary of experts' increasingly audacious pronouncements. Tired of being blamed for the most heinous crimes against young and innocent children, parents turned their frustration against the very experts they once championed. In an angry response to a *Toronto Telegram* article by sex crime researcher John Rich, one female reader grumbled, 'He doesn't call [sex criminals] maniacs but poor, timid, pathetic, immature men – and of course he blames the mothers.'[117] The constant stream of criticism aimed at the average parent was wearing thin, and the experts were getting far too big for their professional britches. In 1961, for example, a panel of speakers from Toronto's Outpatient Forensic Clinic argued that 'many parents were not qualified, or were unlikely, to give their children frank, sound training nor to set good examples.'[118] Disenchantment crystallized in a massive survey undertaken by the CFHSPTA. In 1957 the leadership looked to record 'the experience, judgement and hopes of people who are often silent and yet who should be competent to speak for themselves – the parents.' The author lamented that social scientists had shed much new light on child development over the last quarter century but the role of wisdom was 'lost in knowledge.'[119] Clearly the mood among Canadian parents was shifting, and the experts needed to modify their message if they hoped to enjoy the continued support of their audience.

The baby boom generation was also growing up. As the 1950s rolled on, vulnerable children grew into troublesome teenagers, creating a whole new set of problems with which parents had to contend.[120] The public and media appetite for groups like the Parents' Action League dissipated, and media coverage of the sex crime problem dropped off. In a 1963 issue of *Maclean's*, journalist Robert Fulford described how Leopold Dion, a repeat offender out on parole, sexually assaulted and murdered four young boys. Fulford blamed the crime on the failure of the federal corrections system to live up to the promises made in the previous decade; treatment had yet to be made available for sex offenders in federal institutions. Ten years earlier, revelations such as these prompted massive letter-writing campaigns, a royal commission, and resolutions from organized labour and social service agencies, but in 1963 they fell on deaf ears. Ontario's preoccupation with sex crime had run out of steam, not to be revived on such a grand scale until the 1977 sex slaying of shoeshine boy Emmanuel Jacques in Toronto. In 1977 the police did not hesitate to publicly declare that they were rounding up homosexuals, and this news was well-received in many quarters. Interestingly, as an open assault against the gay community unfolded, so too did debates about the meaning of sexual violence re-emerge. Within five years, the federal government sponsored a national study on sexual assaults against children and youth in Canada. The way complainants were treated in the courts, and the need for meaningful sentences for perpetrators of sexual assault were once again on the national political and public agenda, only this time the discussion was informed by second-wave feminist analysis.[121] Few were likely aware that the cycle was repeating itself.

PAL was founded on two of the most ubiquitous pieces of misleading information that fuelled postwar anxiety about sex crime: that violent sexual assaults against children were on the increase, and that there were large communities of dangerous sexual deviants openly congregating in public city spaces. In Toronto, the 1955 disappearance of eight-year-old Judy Carter was wrongly assumed to be sexually motivated. The Toronto police responded by raiding bars and other public places where male homosexuals were known to congregate, and experts pronounced novel solutions, which, with the help of PAL and Ontario's dailies, enjoyed widespread public support. On the face of it, the events in postwar Ontario appear to be a moral panic in its classic form. However, by paying closer attention to the groups that supported expert intervention, and by looking at the way the public responded to the media and experts alike, it is clear that concern about the sexual assault of children was much more complex. Led by parent-citizen activists, public discussions about sex crime marked a transition in the way Canadians thought about the nature of sexuality and desire, about norms and deviations, and about children and adults. In a process greatly assisted by parents of the baby boom generation, by organizations representing their middle-class familial interests, by professional and lay advocates of the mental health approach, and by the federal and provincial governments, which financed and promoted the mental health movement, the 'modern' scientific approach to understanding and talking about sex assumed cultural dominance. Displacing religious and classic criminological as well as biological explanations for sexual assault, the panic over attacks on children facilitated a paradigmatic shift that changed the way Canadians would think about human sexual behaviour in the latter half of the twentieth century. Canadian mothers saw the problem of the 'stranger in our midst' in liberal, humanitarian terms. Drawing on the socio-political ideology promoted by the United Nation's World Health Organization and Education, Social, and Cultural Organization, Canadian sex deviants were considered in need of compassionate understanding, not judgement and opprobrium.

As a political lobby group, PAL's success in achieving at least one of its primary goals cannot be understated. The Toronto Outpatient Forensic Clinic, an arm of the Toronto Psychiatric Hospital, put Toronto and Canada on the forensic sexology map. Though psychiatric interpretations of deviant sexual behaviour in Canadian criminal court trials can be traced back to the end of the nineteenth century, the field was only in its toddler stage in the 1950s. Despite its small size, the clinic made its mark on the international scene with its innovative research and treatment programs. When the TPH folded and was reborn as the Clarke Institute in the mid-1960s, the Outpatient Forensic Clinic moved in and evolved into the present-day Clinical Sexology program, which includes a nationally recognized phallometric testing facility and gender reassignment clinic. Without PAL, the Centre for Addiction and Mental Health (CAMH) would not enjoy the reputation it has today as a leading-edge sex and gender research institute.

Initially championed by the network of parent-teacher and Home and School associations in the interwar period, the mental health movement enjoyed much greater exposure in the postwar decades. Intelligent approaches to parenting were not only accepted by the PAL leadership, but were promoted in their lectures, media reports, and published literature. However, we would be wrong to assume that the league membership's middle-class pedigree and its focus on the family meant that it was culturally conservative. Indeed, compared to the current emphasis on long-term sentences and sex offender registries, PAL's vision appears radically progressive. Additionally, to reduce league members, and the expansive web of local women's councils and parent-teacher organizations who supported them, to mere foot soldiers marching in the service of Ontario's medical elite is to obscure how the mental health movement was an expression of the interests and ideals of the postwar Anglo-Canadian middle class. The opening of the Outpatient Forensic Clinic was a remarkable political victory for grass-roots activism, and benefited not only the career aspirations of sex researchers, but, in the minds of its lay advocates, benefited society as a whole. Not only would sex deviants be cured, their future victims would be spared.

Though the 1950s focus on sex crime did little to improve the way victims of sexual assault were treated by the courts, and, in fact, did little to affect the way the courts treated sex offenders, what did revolutionize the issue for PAL was the new information psychiatrists were feeding them. In addition to the claim that the home was where sex abnormalities took root, statistics revealed that sexual offenders were more likely than not to be known to the victims. In contrast to the popular image of the stranger luring unsuspecting children and teens with offers of car rides and candy, experts in the 1950s repeatedly pointed out that family members, community leaders, and other people in positions of trust were more often the perpetrators of sex crimes against children. Moreover, experts also 'discovered' that boys were often victims of sexual molestation as well. A key part of PAL's work was visiting with parent, church, and community organizations to lecture on the problem of sex crime. Breaking through silence and debunking mythology were at the core of PAL's agenda, and they spoke with a frankness that shocked some of their audiences. As a group of 'just housewives,' PAL demonstrated that talking openly about human sexuality, including sexual violence, was not only acceptable, but was every parent's civic duty. Moreover, as did first-wave feminists before them, and second-wave feminists after them, PAL successfully constructed sexual assaults against children as a public as well as a private issue.

If parents didn't already have the language to continue the conversation outside school gymnasiums and church basements, PAL provided them with the language in clear and understandable terms. From fetishism to fellatio, the league's publication taught readers the language of sexual deviation. However, they also exploited the popular image of the sex criminal in the title and on the cover of their published pamphlet, 'The Strange One.' Despite persistent claims to the contrary, 'stranger danger' continued to define the sex crime problem throughout the postwar era, leaving the sanctity of the family and its network of respectable community organizations unblemished by the stain of sexual deviancy.

The decision of experts to exclude incest from public discourse about sexual danger and deviancy supports what other historians have argued about the construction of the sexual psychopath: by emphasizing 'stranger danger,' experts characterized the problem of sexual violence as a threat that existed in the public, not private, world. Modern sexology idealized the middle-class heterosexual family and stigmatized those who lived outside its normalizing influence. The decision to frame the Parents' Action League in familial rather than gendered terms may be partly explained by the absence of an organized women's movement, but it also demonstrates how in the 1950s social problems were often articulated through the rubric of civic activism and in accordance with the perceived needs of the modern family. Since medical experts understood sex crime as the product of unhealthy parenting resulting in abnormal personality development, it comes as little surprise that neither PAL nor the experts who advised them placed sexual assault within the wider social context of unequal gender or power relations. Gender was the bedrock on which healthy families and healthy children were built, and masculine and feminine ideals were regarded as the source of stability, not inequality.

Perhaps if PAL went to the courts before they went to the couch, they would have been less inclined to advocate medical treatment, but Canada's middle class was more interested in generating understanding across differences rather than trying to explain them. Just as the United Nations sought to promote mental and emotional wellness as an atomic war preventative, PAL sought to use the science of the mind to stop future attacks on children. In the 1950s, retribution and punishment were artefacts of an earlier, less rational age. Though little attention was paid to victims of sexual assault, the knowledge that aggressors were usually known to the victim, that sex crimes were grossly underreported, that recidivism rates for sex criminals was among the lowest of any crime category, and that only a very small percentage of sex offenders were 'psychopathic' was as much a part of expert discourse then as it is now. The league played a critical role in popularizing and sustaining a pathological construction of sex offenders by ensuring that research into 'sex deviants' continued long after the sex crime panic passed.

There is much to learn from the Parents' Action League. Its story adds to the growing body of literature that disproves the perception that women were politically inactive in the postwar period. It reveals how postwar sexual anxiety was about much more than anti-homosexual witch hunts. The public engaged in a vigorous public conversation about everyday heterosexual sexual assault, particularly against children. PAL was also instrumental in making the reporting of sexual assault a matter of civic duty, thus helping to reduce, to some extent, the social shame attached to being sexually victimized. With massive support from the middle class, these conversations led to the creation of sex offender treatment programs in Ontario. The crisis that began with the disappearance of Judy Carter is now long over, but the legacy of these historical developments remains with us today. As I argue in more detail in the conclusion, few new advances have been made in treating sex offenders in the sixty years since Canada's criminal sexual psychopath law was passed. Indeed, virtually no studies have demonstrated success in reducing rates of recidivism among sex offenders through medical or psychiatric treatment. Nevertheless, Canadians continue to maintain at least some faith in medicine and mental health solutions to 'curing' sex offenders of their deviant desires.

chapter three

Surveying Sex: The Royal Commission on the Criminal Law Relating to Criminal Sexual Psychopaths

From Mackenzie King's early twentieth-century investigation into the relationship between labour and capital, to the 1960s report on bilingualism and biculturalism, royal commissions have played a key role in shaping twentieth-century Canadian political and cultural life. However, most often they are extremely costly ventures that result in no significant policy changes at all. When leading civil-rights advocate Chief Justice James Chalmers McRuer was appointed to lead the Royal Commission on the Criminal Law Relating to Criminal Sexual Psychopaths (hereafter referred to as the commission) in 1954, he was determined to produce a report that would contribute to the growing body of international literature on sexual deviancy and the law. Though he cautioned against turning the hearings into a 'Kinsey' investigation, there is no doubt that the 1948 publication of American sex researcher Alfred Kinsey's *Sexual Behavior in the Human Male* contributed significantly to the high level of public and political tolerance for state-sponsored investigations into its citizens' sexual practices. Concomitantly, widespread parental anxiety over sexual assaults against children made forthright dialogue about sex not just respectable, but necessary. Chief Justice McRuer may not have wanted to collect detailed information about the sexual practices of everyday Canadians, but he did want to produce a state-of-the-art document that advanced the field of forensic sexology.

In their quest to determine how the criminal sexual psychopath law could better regulate sex crime in Canada, the commissioners allowed for a wide range of testimony, almost all of it 'expert,' on a variety of sexual practices. Talking about sex, especially within the context of sexual danger and exploitation, was not new; feminists, social purity activists, and mental health experts had a long-standing dialogue with both the public and the government concerning sexual danger. The royal commission, however, shifted the discursive ground upon which public discussions of sexuality took place. Contained by the language of science, experts for the first time abandoned euphemisms and spoke directly and publicly about very specific sexual practices, including masturbation and oral and anal sex. The hearings of the commission greatly contributed to the normalization of frank discussions about sex.

The post–Second World War era was imbued with a spirit of optimistic exploration along new avenues of scientific research in general, and into mental health issues in particular. The decades of research already undertaken, and especially the very well-publicized work of Alfred Kinsey, led to an expansion of the definition of acceptable or 'normal' sexual activities. However, this shift from morality to science, from natural to normal, represented a new type of regulation rather than the deregulation of sexual practices. In the territorial struggle for control over who should properly regulate sexual behaviour, there was not a *divestment* of authority over sex but rather a *transfer* of authority. By claiming professional jurisdiction, psychiatrists and psychologists asserted their roles as the architects and regulators of 'norms,' a concept that provided the scientific basis for the regulation of sexual morality in much the same way eugenics had provided a scientific basis for the regulation of race.[1] Though in their final report the commissioners upheld the primacy of legal professionals in courtroom trials, the commission effectively entrenched mental health professionals as authoritative interpreters and regulators of sexual and gender behaviour and norms.

Male homosexuality served as a reference point for many of the discussions that took place. This was partly because homosexuality was what medical experts thought they knew the most about, but it was also because homosexuality was the ground upon which experts distinguished between sexually deviant behaviour that was merely abnormal and that which should be subject to criminal sanction. Like Kinsey himself, psychiatrists and psychologists argued that the law should concern itself only with those acts causing harm. Morality, they claimed, is no longer the province of judges. What was once considered sinful and immoral behaviour were recast as mental health problems best handled by medical experts. Adults who engaged in sexual acts with adults of the same sex, for example, needed counselling, not incarceration. Only when these acts involved minors or non-consenting adults should the police, and the courts, intervene. The argument for limiting criminal regulation of sexuality to harm-causing acts included examples of sado-masochism and other consensual but 'perverted' sex acts, but male homosexuality served as the prime example of the type of sexual practice that was deviant, but not harmful. Although it would be more than a decade before same sex acts between persons over the age of twenty-one were de-criminalized, male homosexuality represented the grey area between morality and criminality and clearly marked out a terrain that properly belonged to health, not legal, professionals. Consequently, homosexuality served as one of the main themes of the hearings as the commission made its way from Halifax to Victoria.

This chapter looks at both the practical and the ideological issues that shaped and plagued the post–Second World War rise of modern sexological thought, its integration with criminal law, and ultimately the extension of its cultural authority in Canada. I begin with a brief overview of some of the practical problems that confronted legal and medical authorities as they struggled with a law that pleased neither group. Next, I explore the intellectual and conceptual basis of sexological thought by examining the way homosexuality and the sexual victimization of female children, two key areas of discussion, were characterized, and how these claims were contested by other experts. It appears that the commissioners had no qualms with the idea that the law should limit itself to regulating sex acts that caused harm and, thus, constituted a danger to society. However, as this chapter shows, harm (and its counterpart, safety) is a socially constructed concept. I conclude the chapter with an examination of the way women did and did not figure into these conversations as victims of sex crime and as witnesses during the hearings. Modern sex knowledge was based less on experience than it was on particular sets of beliefs about behavioural development. The diversity of opinion and experience evident during the commission's hearings, and the lack of any evidence to support mental health treatment as an effective remedy, was subsumed by a blind faith in scientific solutions.

On 29 March 1954, the three appointed commissioners met in Ottawa for the first time. Chief Justice James Chalmers McRuer took his seat, and, turning to his fellow appointee, the Quebec City-based psychiatrist Gustave Desrochers, asked, 'So, exactly what is a criminal sexual psychopath?' Desrochers replied: 'That is a legal definition, not a medical one. We do not know exactly what is a sexual psychopath.'[2] Both the question and the answer reveal a great deal about why the law was so little used, but they also indicate that the commissioners' task was not to be an easy one. In conducting the inquiry, the three commissioners (McRuer and

Desrochers were joined by Ontario County Court Judge Helen Kinnear) travelled across Canada, holding public hearings in each of the provincial capitals as well as in Montreal and Vancouver. They received submissions from four major interest groups: medical and mental health experts, practitioners of the law and law enforcement agents, social service agencies, and women's groups. In total, the commission received fifty-two briefs, and more than one hundred witnesses gave evidence orally. Medical doctors and psychiatrists accounted for almost half of the witnesses. Other participants included lawyers, judges, academics and myriad social service agencies, women's groups, volunteer organizations, and parent-teacher associations.[3] When the commissioners finally sat down to write their report, they had almost two thousand pages of evidence to consider. By the time they submitted their final report, everyday Canadians were much more familiar with the language of sexual deviancy, though no one would be any more certain of just what a sexual psychopath was.

According to the original 1948 law, a criminal sexual psychopath 'means a person who, by course of misconduct in sexual matters, has shown a lack of power to control his sexual impulses and who as a result is likely to attack or otherwise inflict injury, pain or other evil on any person.'[4] The offences that fell under the legislation at the time the commission began its hearings were rape, sexual intercourse with a female under fourteen, indecent assault on a female, buggery or bestiality, indecent assault, assault by male on male with intent to commit buggery, and gross acts of indecency (often, but by no means exclusively, used in cases involving consensual sex between two male adults). Persons charged with an attempt to commit any of these offences were also included.

By the end of the 1950s, twenty-nine American states had also adopted sexual psychopath legislation, but the law did not operate the same way everywhere. In some states, people who faced criminal sexual psychopath charges were dealt with as mentally ill patients, and were civilly committed to a psychiatric facility for treatment. In others, the successfully convicted were first sentenced to treatment, and once deemed 'cured,' were sent on to serve the original prison sentence for the crime. A third approach required the prosecution to submit an application to have a sex offender declared a sexual psychopath after a guilty verdict was rendered, but before a sentence was passed. It was this approach that Canada adopted. The minimum evidential requirement was the testimony of two psychiatrists, at least one of whom was nominated by the attorney general. If the application was successful, the minimum sentencing requirement was for a term of not less than two years in respect of the offence for which he was convicted and, additionally, a sentence of preventive detention.[5] In Canada, a term of two years or more meant that those convicted served the sentence in a federal penitentiary.

Preventive detention was introduced in Canada in 1948 solely for the purpose of enabling the penal system to keep in custody criminal sexual psychopaths and 'habitual criminals,' both of whom were judged to be recidivists. In order to ensure that those sentenced to preventive detention were not forgotten, the law stipulated that the minister of justice review such cases at least once every three years.[6] The idea behind preventative detention was that prison did not bring about reformation for recidivists and that some other form of treatment was required, but the federal government did not include treatment provisions in the law. Thus, in contrast to some American states, treatment for criminal sexual psychopaths in Canada was not mandatory, and the government was not legally obliged to provide it.

For most psychiatrists, the whole notion of psychopathy was dubious, and sexual psychopathy was even less satisfying.[7] Many called psychopathy a 'wastebasket category' into which everything that falls outside of the norm is tossed.[8] The majority of Canadian experts were loath to support its use as a medical diagnosis, and many were doubtful of the merits of isolating sex criminals as a treatment group.[9] Dr George Herbert Stevenson, one of the few Canadian doctors with practical experience treating sex criminals, was especially critical of the law. Though in favour of psychiatric treatment, he opposed giving precedence to one group over another.[10]

Legal experts also had reservations, though for different reasons. Officially, the Canadian Bar Association supported greater cooperation between law enforcement agencies and medical experts, but individual judges and lawyers could be either ignorant about or hostile to psychiatric interventions in the legal process.[11] Even among those who were well informed, there was no shortage of scepticism about mixing the two practices.[12] For example, Dr Kenneth Gray, an expert in medico-legal jurisprudence, suggested that if a convicted offender reveals previous sex offences in therapy, the psychiatrist should be able to seek preventive detention under criminal sexual psychopath legislation; he seemed unable to appreciate that it would be akin to information obtained under duress. Moreover, he had no qualms about breaching professional confidence in the interests of public safety. Lawyers and judges felt quite differently about procedural integrity, and concluded that psychiatrists were 'wandering into pastures, the way through which they do not understand at all,' as Crown Prosecutor Thomas Grantham Morris put it. The commissioners appear to have taken these professional tensions in stride: McRuer responded, 'We will give the psychiatrists a chance to give their opinion of the legal profession later on.'[13]

McRuer could afford to have a little fun during the commission's hearings, but in the courtroom the opinions of legal experts mattered most. While the law required the testimony of two psychiatrists in order to have a convicted sex offender declared a criminal sexual psychopath, it fell to the judge to rule either in favour of or against the Crown's application. Even when a judge accepted the idea that some people harboured sexual tendencies that deviated from the norm, be they learned or biological, few judges were willing to accept the argument that a person lacked the power to control his sex impulses, the key to the definition of a criminal sexual psychopath. Illustrating this problem, Ontario's Attorney General Kelso Roberts cited a case in which a trial judge found a man charged with multiple offences against children not to be a criminal sexual psychopath. His actions, the judge argued, 'showed cunning, planning, resourcefulness and preparation [thus] he could not be said to show "a *lack* of *power* to *control* his sexual impulses."'[14] Queen's Counsel Mr Dansereau cited a recent Montreal case in which a group of four men repeatedly trapped women in cabs and raped them. 'We never considered them as habitual criminals because it was their first time in court, and we never considered them as insane. They were just "wise guys"; that is all they were.'[15] Rather than seek a treatment solution, Dansereau vigorously pursued the death penalty. Most witnesses who worked in either law enforcement or as prosecutors agreed that the typical perpetrator of a sex crime put a good deal of forethought into his actions.

Psychiatric expertise in the area of sexual deviation was hard to come by in Canada in the mid-1950s, but the few psychiatrists who came to the hearings with practical experience were the most likely to agree with Dansereau and others like him. For example, Dr John Senn, a psychiatrist since 1925 and the medical superintendent of the Ontario Hospital in Hamilton, complained that local judges had gotten into the habit of sending all men charged with sex crimes to his hospital for thirty days of pretrial observation. Senn saw little difference between their actions and 'those who would patronize a brothel: it is a calculated risk.' According to him, sexual offences were well-planned crimes, and their perpetrators had no desire to control their sexual impulses.[16] Indeed, many psychiatrists thought the whole idea of 'lack of control' to be unscientific.[17] As one Vancouver practitioner put it, 'it is the old bugbear, is it non-controllable or is [it] uncontrolled? I do not see how the greatest doctors in the world could look into a man's mind and say, this man could not control the impulse, or could control it but did not.'[18] Criminal sexual psychopath laws only made sense if the former were true, but since it was impossible to determine whether perpetrators of sex crimes failed to control or lacked control of their sex impulses,, medical doctors with substantial experience assessing or treating sex criminals were not in favour of the law. Few Canadian experts actually had first-hand experience treating sexual deviation or sex offenders, however, and it was they who persistently claimed that, with sufficient funding, it was only a matter of time before a successful program of treatment was discovered. Ultimately their optimistic prognosis carried the day.

In practice, the convergence of law and psychiatry made for an uneasy marriage.[19] The purpose of the law is to determine whether the accused possesses a guilty mind, known as *mens rea*, with respect to the commission of the crime he or she is charged with. Psychiatry, on the other hand, is never interested in examining a single event in isolation, but positions itself as a medical science based on an understanding of the whole person.[20] From a medical point of view, if a sex offender is a sexual psychopath, he is mentally ill and should not be treated as a criminal. Psychiatrists may have been extremely critical of the terms and definitions provided by the law, but despite the cynicism of medical practitioners like Senn, the majority held to the view that sex offenders posed a mental health problem, and were best dealt with by psychiatrists, even if in conjunction with the courts and prison system.

For the purposes of getting an offender into treatment, many medical experts accepted the legislation, faulty though it was, with the hope that it would furnish them with the opportunity to conduct new research into sexual deviation. But the law could not set aside its need to adhere strictly to the definition provided in section 661 of the Criminal Code. Convicted sex offenders could only be declared a criminal sexual psychopath if the judge was convinced that the accused had shown evidence of a 'lack of power to control' his sexual urges. Because of their independence from the political process that brought the law into existence, judges were much more inclined to look critically upon Crown applications to have a convicted sex criminal tried as a criminal sexual psychopath than were psychiatrists. The troubling lack of clarity about psychopathy, combined with a good deal of confusion about the procedure for hearing these cases, meant that few judges were impressed with the law, and even fewer were persuaded by the testimony of psychiatrists.[21] For their part, psychiatrists were willing to accept such a flawed model because they stood to gain tremendous ground in expanding the application of their professional services. Judges had no such motivation and, indeed, some may have resented the incursion of mental health experts in their courtrooms. Though they had neither the power nor the authority to determine the content of the Criminal Code, judges and magistrates had the power to interpret it. Given that some judges were unwilling to accept sexual psychopathy as an explanatory concept, and that not all psychiatrists were willing to testify with certainty that an individual lacked the power to control his actions, it is clear why by 1956 there were only nineteen sex offenders successfully prosecuted under Canada's sexual psychopath law.[22]

A recent study of sex crime laws in the State of New Jersey suggests another reason why the law was so little used. According to historian Simon Cole, one of the main determinants of the degree to which sexual psychopath statutes were implemented was the availability of treatment programs.[23] Perhaps the lack of treatment facilities in Canada had a similar dampening effect. Throughout the commission's hearings, witness after witness complained that there were no treatment services available in Canada. Federal penitentiaries in British Columbia, Saskatchewan, and Manitoba each employed one psychiatrist who served on a part-time basis. One psychiatrist, also working part-time, was shared by Kingston's Prison for Women, the prison for men, and Collins Bay, which had a combined population of approximately 1500.[24] No psychiatrists were on staff at Quebec's only federal prison, St Vincent de Paul, which in the mid-1950s held three of Canada's nineteen criminal sexual psychopath inmates, or at Dorchester, the penitentiary that served all of the Maritime provinces.[25]

To place criminal sexual psychopaths in federal institutions and not provide treatment was regarded by both legal and medical witnesses as a violation of the principal of the law. Mr N. Boris, a Crown prosecutor in Quebec, drew a less than subtle comparison to Nazi Germany, arguing that long-term imprisonment without treatment 'begins to resemble ... a suggestion to exterminate sex deviates as a measure of social hygiene. Extermination, I am sure, is not acceptable to democratic countries.'[26] Maxwell Cohen, also a member of the Quebec bar, insisted 'Canadian penal policy cannot have it both ways; it cannot, on the one hand, attempt to define a new type of offender who shall be given a new type of penalty, with the aim ultimately of treating him in a special category and yet not to provide the facilities for that treatment.'[27] Most witnesses agreed that an indefinite sentence with no treatment provisions was a particularly cruel punishment, leaving inmates with little hope for their eventual release.

Despite these seemingly insurmountable difficulties, the royal commission proceeded with its investigation into deviant sexuality, the law, and psychiatry. As the first question McRuer put to Desrochers suggests, there was much to be learned about psychiatry's potential contribution to the sex crime problem. Before the commissioners could begin to consider how the law might be improved, they needed clarity on sexual psychopathy itself. Much of the conversation during the public hearings concerned the complexities of human sexuality and the science of sexual deviancy. It is to these discussions that we now turn.

Mental health experts spent much of the post–Second World War period defining and clarifying sex and gender norms, a process historian Mona Gleason calls 'normalizing the ideal.' Her examination of psychology and the family in post–Second World War Canada describes psychologists' 'normalizing strategies of comparing, differentiating, hierarchizing, homogenizing and excluding' as 'technologies of normalcy' in which the normal was conflated with the socially acceptable.[28] In a separate study of heterosexuality and Canada's postwar youth, sociologist Mary Louise Adams argues that the ability to 'lay claim to a definition of normality was a crucial marker of postwar social belonging. To be marked as sexually "abnormal" in any way was to throw into question the possibility of achieving or maintaining status as an adult, as a "responsible citizen," as a valued contributor to the social whole.'[29] Both Gleason and Adams demonstrate how the predominant discursive construction of normal sex and gender roles was based on the science of mental health. Psychologists, psychiatrists, and other professionals vigorously promoted their visions of normalcy through the media, schools, courts, mental health clinics, and other regulatory and voluntary outlets.

The debate over sexual norms was greatly facilitated by Alfred Kinsey's 1948 *Sexual Behavior in the Human Male*.[30] His massive survey of the sexual habits of American men was the largest ever conducted in the United States, and it showed that the sexual activities of Americans were much more varied than was commonly thought. Kinsey used this information to argue against the scientific scaffolding that was being erected around conventional moral values and beliefs, and in 1949 he and his research associates publicly denounced the entire notion of sexual 'norms' as sophistic. Modern sex laws were grounded in religious and cultural tradition, they argued, and while prohibitions against forms of behaviour that 'do damage to the bodies of other persons' should be considered assault and battery, scientists had no training in the business of social custom, religious and cultural taboos, and morality, which were the root of legal prohibitions regulating 'unnatural' sexual activities.[31] For Kinsey and his research team, 'sex norms' are simply 'the price ... society demands of those who wish to share the advantages of belonging to an organized group.'[32]

Most Canadian mental health professionals recognized the culturally and historically variable nature of perceptions around normative sexual practices.[33] Sometimes this led to some rather extraordinary claims: social worker John Arnott argued against including incest under the sexual psychopath laws because, he explained, in societies such as the Incas it was a revered practice.[34] More typically, however, medical doctors explained that the range of 'sexual expression' was wider than was once believed, and doctors were redrawing the lines around what constituted acceptable behaviour. Dr D. Ewen Cameron, for example, described how, when he first began to practice psychiatry in the mid-1920s, it was not uncommon to treat anxious patients of both sexes who were concerned about masturbation. Up until at least the First World War, experts warned that 'the solitary vice' led to infertility, blindness, and insanity. However, Cameron told the commission, 'now that we know masturbation is a practically universal phenomenon ... there are very few people I ever see who are concerned about it at all.'[35] Psychiatrists had also 'discovered' that married couples had a much longer and more varied sex life than was previously assumed. Not only were married Canadians continuing to enjoy sex well beyond their reproductive years, but they were also engaging in oral and anal sex without showing any evidence of physical, mental, or moral damage to either partner. 'It may be repugnant to a widely held view of decorum and aesthetics,' Cameron argued, 'but [it] is certainly not a matter of pathology.'[36] He felt confident that it was only a matter of time before other forms of sexual activity enjoyed the same level of acceptance.

While few had as much experience treating sex problems as Cameron, almost all psychiatrists agreed that sex crimes were committed by people from 'all walks of life.'[37] This was a significant departure from earlier beliefs, which located sexual immorality in poor and immigrant neighbourhoods. Cameron's testimony reflected the wholesale abandonment of eugenic and other biological theories that attributed criminal and pathological behaviour to inferior races and classes.[38] Residue of older ideas concerning class degeneracy left its mark on the hearings: Dr R.R. Maclean of Saskatchewan told the commission that incest was most often the result of 'special home circumstances and conditions, namely crowding in the home and poor morals.'[39] But Maclean was the exception. No matter when or where they trained and began practicing their profession, most mental health experts in the 1950s dismissed poverty as a cause of sexual deviancy or crime, and paid virtually no attention to those other early-twentieth-century sources of immorality – racial inferiority and immigration.

However, while social and economic class were no longer seen as determinants of the aetiology of sex deviation, class was widely used to legitimize certain sexual practices. Psychiatrists emphasized that people were having sex in ways never imagined (or at least not openly discussed), and, more important, that the upper and middle classes were also participating in 'abnormal' sexual practices. For example, Vancouver psychiatrist Dr Douglas Earl Alcorn explained to the commissioners that 'the practice of whipping is by no means limited ... to people we think of as inferior or deteriorated. Some of these people are extremely brilliant and are actually outstanding people in the community.' Through a patient he learned of a club of sadists, some of whose members he was able to read up on in Who's Who – 'people qualified for that on the basis of their public service.'[40] Clearly, the Kinsey study and similar research endeavours were casting new light on old questions about the boundaries of normal human sexuality. This was indeed one of the great ironies of the 1950s: the effort to provide definitions of what constituted normal behaviour facilitated public and professional dialogues that recognized, validated, and to a large extent normalized sex beyond a reproductive function. By recognizing (hetero)sexual pleasure, a wider range of activities was legitimized.

Another activity popular among men 'from all walks of life' was same-sex sex. Homosexuality emerged as a central point of reference throughout the commission's hearings, especially when it sat in Montreal, Toronto, and Vancouver, Canada's three largest urban centres. Indeed, despite the fact that the public's attention was squarely focussed on sexual assaults against female children, homosexuality was the single most discussed criminal sexual act.[41] Interestingly, buggery and gross indecency, the two criminal charges for sexual acts between men, were initially excluded from section 661 of the Criminal Code, and were added only in 1953. However, while this addition was likely a reflection of the federal government's response to the conflation of homosexuality with cold war security issues in the United States, homosexuality itself was not perceived to be a menace in Canada the same way it was in the United States. In cities like Boise, Idaho, little to no distinction was made between male homosexuals and child rapists.[42] In Canada, however, psychiatrists, the media, and the general public were often – though not always – careful to distinguish between consenting sex between adult males in private and deviant sexual behaviour. Where in the United States only a minority of psychiatric experts seem to have advocated for the decriminalization of homosexuality, in Canada the opposite was true.

The difference between American and Canadian psychiatrists' opinions regarding homosexuality and the criminal law raises important questions about the peculiar sexual politics that characterized the post–Second World War cultural landscape. Popular representations of the male homosexual underwent significant changes in the 1950s, and took on an enormous symbolic weight. Historians have identified three main factors at play: the deployment of homosexuality as a political red herring in the United States; the expansion and increased visibility of public lesbian and gay communities; the changing medical model of homosexuality from gender inversion to sexual deviancy, and the consequent linking of homosexuality with other forms of sexual 'perversion' including transvestism, exhibitionism, rape, and pedophilia. Together these factors created a new and dangerous sexual archetype, the 'stranger in our midst.'

In 1950 the U.S. Senate Appropriations Committee learned that most of the ninety-one employees who had recently been dismissed from the civil service were fired because they were homosexual. Republican senators pounced on the opportunity to discredit President Truman's administration as 'soft' on degeneracy. According to legal historian William N. Eskridge, 'National Republican Party Chairman Guy Gabrielson sent several thousand Republican party workers a newsletter, alerting them to the new "homosexual angle" in Washington: "sexual perverts ... have infiltrated our Government in recent years," he warned, and then stated they were perhaps "as dangerous as the actual Communists." Eager to fend off Republican charges, the Truman Administration stepped up its investigations.'[43] From that meeting forward, Republican senators made homosexuality, more commonly referred to as 'sexual perversion,' an issue of national concern, and forced the resignation and firing of virtually thousands of government employees.[44] It is difficult to accurately measure the impact these events had on the sex crime problem in Canada, but the 1953 addition of gross indecency and buggery to the list of offences that fell under criminal sexual psychopath legislation is a clear indication that the American Congressional 'witch hunt' for homosexuals influenced official Canadian policy.[45]

Numerous historical studies have documented how a post–Second World War sex crime panic affected homosexual men in particular by linking homosexuality with other forms of dangerous sexual behaviour, particularly pedophilia.[46] In the interwar period, sex scientists abandoned the early twentieth-century concept of gender inversion (male/female variation) in favour of the new model of sexual deviancy (normal/abnormal).[47] The nuances of this model did not often survive the translation from textbook to popular press, and media representations of dangerous 'sex degenerates' included homosexual men whose public displays of sex and gender 'abnormality' were considered an expression of sexual psychopathy. The changing medical model, combined with heightened anxieties about sex crime fuelled by the media, critically shaped the way people came to think about, and fear, homosexuality. Both the pre–Second World War images of homosexuality as gender inversion and the post–Second World War images of homosexuality as deviancy existed side by side in popular culture.[48] In Canadian and American local papers, cross-dressing male and female homosexuals were usually depicted as pathetic and comical, and perhaps even as a public nuisance, but certainly not as violent or dangerous. As the medical model of sexual deviancy became more and more ubiquitous in the late 1940s and early 50s, the male homosexual was increasingly viewed as a (hetero)sexual menace and pedophilic predator. Lesbians also felt the effects of the changing medical meanings attached to homosexuality, but were not commonly viewed as a threat to children. Though considered predatory toward heterosexual adult women, lesbians 'never come to public attention' explained one medical witness to the commission. Public sex might have happened sporadically, but gay women did not generally congregate in parks, lavatories, or other public places and, as women, they were not so easily conflated with sexually violent predators, a decidedly masculine construct.[49]

The greater visibility of homosexual men and women made them vulnerable targets in the ongoing effort to, in the language of the time, fight sex crime and eliminate sexual deviancy. In the years following the Second World War, most major North American cities witnessed the creation of new, and in some cases the expansion of existing, homosexual 'haunts.'[50] Openly congregating in restaurants, bars, city parks, and hotels made gay men easy targets for the police who were anxious to appear to be doing something about the sex crime problem. The mass arrests in urban parks, bars, and restaurants, and local media coverage that typically described these actions as 'rounding up known sex deviates' popularized the misconception that homosexual men were part of a well-organized society of sexual predators who posed a threat to women and children.

Psychiatrists repeatedly challenged the idea that homosexual men were dangerous, and argued that, like exhibitionism and 'Peeping Tomism,' homosexuality harmed only the men that engaged in it. Quebec psychiatrist Bruno Cormier and his colleague Justin Ciale argued 'though they may create annoyance and conflicts for the offenders and the milieu in which they commit their offences, they present more often than otherwise no really great danger. Such offences are not to be considered similar to offences that involve bodily harm such as sadistic acts.'[51] Dr MacLeod concurred: 'They are offensive to the public or repulsive in their behaviour but they are not necessarily dangerous.'[52] Some social service agencies, such as the British Columbia John Howard Society, argued homosexuality 'and other socially distasteful, rather than socially dangerous, conduct' should be dealt with more leniently.[53]

While psychiatrists agreed that public sex was a problem, some used the hearings to denounce the heavy-handed tactics that local police forces used against urban homosexuals. During a private session with the commission, respected Quebec criminologist Reverend Noel Mailloux reported that homosexuals are 'very often ... despised and treated with contempt, and often the way the police talk to them it is just as if they were the very dust of humanity, and it is an extremely poor way to handle such cases. I have seen worse than that, and this I would like to leave off the record, if you please.'[54] The chief psychiatrist for the Department of Reform Institutions in Ontario, Frank H. van Nostrand, was asked his opinion of Montreal's 1954 'aggressive police campaign' to clean up the mountain and other prime cruising and social meeting spots.[55] Though not generally sympathetic to homosexuals, van Nostrand insisted that 'they were not violent people,' and that 'after their haunts were found out,' they simply 'moved off to some other place.' He dismissed police tactics as accomplishing little more than 'a certain tidying up.'[56] In fact, mass arrests of homosexuals were denounced by even the most hard-nosed proponents of old-fashioned methods of punishing criminals, who were less concerned about the human rights and dignity of the men targeted by the police than the unnecessary strain such actions placed on medical, psychiatric, psychological, and social work professionals who were expected to provide assessment and treatment services. Psychiatric facilities were becoming a dumping ground for those caught up in police sweeps in the United States as well. In 1952 Dr E. Kelleher, the director of the Chicago Psychiatric Institute, complained that the police, acting under pressure from the media and various public organizations, conducted a campaign to clean up North Clark Street. On one particular night, forty-two suspected homosexuals were dropped on his institute's doorstep, overloading the staff with work that they were neither interested in nor had the proper resources to cope with.[57]

Virtually every mental health expert agreed that sex between adult men did not cause harm, but the experts also maintained that it was a sickness requiring treatment. Even Dr D. Ewen Cameron, Canada's greatest champion of America's best-known opponent of the criminalization of homosexuality, Dr Alfred Kinsey, favoured medical intervention. Borrowing a page from Kinsey's 1948 tome, Cameron testified that 33 per cent of men engage in at least one homosexual act in their lifetime, yet only 7 per cent become exclusively homosexual. It is unfair to send a man off to prison for what might be a one-time act, he argued, and as for the others, why send them to prison when there is no treatment or help available? 'Humanity has many unhappy occurrences on its records, but certainly incarceration of the homosexual man in a prison with no contacts save other men, where *he is given no treatment to rectify his condition* and where he is kept, not until a predetermined period of time has elapsed, certainly ranks high among those things in which we can take little pride.'[58] For Cameron, the real offence was that homosexuals were being thrown in jail but were not being offered any treatment to cure their disorder.

The experts remained adamant that sexual deviation was a medical, not a criminal, problem, but they were also forced to admit that it was a disease without a cure, yet. By the 1950s, the few who already had treatment programs running were cynical as to whether they could bring about a heterosexual orientation in homosexual men. But while only the most sanguine held out any hope for a cure, more and more experts were turning to behaviour therapies to teach homosexuals to conduct their lives in socially appropriate ways. During the commissioners' research visit to New Jersey's Menlo Park Clinic, where sexual psychopaths were sent for assessment and treatment, Director Ralph Brancale explained, 'we do not attempt to change ... the deep-seated homosexualist ... all we are interested in the lifelong homosexual is that he is able to contain himself and sublimate his own sexual activities and channels so that it does not make him publicly offensive.'[59] Vancouver's Dr Alcorn echoed this view, describing homosexuality not as a disease but a 'defect of taste. One could perhaps not speak of curing them any more than one could speak of curing a person who liked Bach or Stravinsky.'[60] Alcorn's method of treating homosexuality, exhibitionism, voyeurism, and 'occasionally playing with children' consisted of teaching their practitioners how to 'live with their peculiar tastes, to teach them the dangers that they may encounter in allowing tensions to develop, to avoid those tensions which arise and which create the setting in which most of these offences occur.'[61] If mental health experts could not teach some one to *be* normal, then they hoped they could teach him to at least *act* normal.

Private sex was one thing, but public behaviour remained cause for concern. Cruising in parks, making out in the bushes, congregating in clubs, and having sex in public washrooms had long been considered inappropriate behaviour for any person, male or female, but in the 1950s, the gay male cruising practices took on new meaning.[62] Given the social, economic, and familial consequences of being discovered in homosexual 'haunts,' homosexual men's repeated visits to such places appeared compulsive, irrational, and consequently provided a direct link to the criminal sexual psychopath model. Viewed through the lens of the postwar middle-class heterosexual family, men (and exhibitionists) who had sex in public places appeared both out of control and dangerous.[63] Canadian psychiatrists agreed that in such instances homosexuality constituted a social nuisance, and sex between men should continue to be subject to criminal, as well as medical, regulation.[64]

Some witnesses defended male homosexuals on the grounds that many made important contributions to Western civilization. Even Minister of Justice Stuart S. Garson, responding to the rising level of hysteria surrounding the commission of sex crimes, took up this angle during a House of Commons debate. 'The picture is not all bad,' he reassured his fellow MPs. 'If one goes back through the history of music and literature and the arts one will find that some of the greatest masterpieces in these fields have been achieved by sex deviates to whom we are in fact greatly indebted for what they have created and handed down to their fellow man.'[65] But during the commission hearings, Toronto Police Chief Constable John Chisholm dismissed such characterizations outright, calling this line of reasoning 'a dangerous trend and an insult to the intelligence of the masses.'[66] A Saskatchewan member of the Canadian Mental Health Association similarly described homosexuals' 'tendency to acquaint their behaviour with the achievement of high intellectual and cultural achievements' as a means to seduce 'susceptible and impressionable persons.'[67] Attempts to normalize homosexuality by associating its practitioners with the middle and cultured classes failed dismally, demonstrating that to be middle class in the 1950s did not just mean having a car, a house, and a good-paying corporate job. It also meant being married with children, signalling not only material success but also healthy and positive sexual and social adjustment. Oral and anal sex in marriage might be 'normal,' but similar sexual acts between two men were certainly not. Though the science of sex paid a good deal of attention to parsing individual acts from ambiguous concepts of immorality, the issue was never just what kind of sex, but with whom.

One lone witness objected to the pathologization of homosexuality. Axel Otto Olsen appeared before the commission as a private citizen without connection to any group or profession. Unprotected by the armour of science, and vulnerable to public scrutiny, Olsen requested and received a private hearing, though his comments were transcribed into the official record. He argued that sexual relations between men over the age of sixteen should be of no concern to the state. Perhaps Olsen was encouraged by similar arguments then being made in Britain, where the government-appointed Committee on Homosexuality and Prostitution proved amenable to recommending the removal of sexual activity between men from the purview of the criminal law. However, while the English committee drew on the testimony of a number of homosexual men to challenge some of the myths and misconceptions about male homosexual behaviour, there was no effort on the part of the commission in Canada to seek out the views of homosexual men. This is partly because of the different directives the two commissions were given. However, it is also because the Canadian commissioners were not convinced that male homosexuality did not constitute a menace to society.

If the commission were to support a law that distinguished between harm-causing behaviours and those that were merely morally distasteful, witnesses who supported the continued criminalization of homosexuality would have to persuade the commission that homosexuality *was* indeed harmful. This goal was achieved by linking homosexuality with pedophilia. Men who congregated in parks, restaurants, and theatres at night posed little threat to children, but the Toronto police chief suggested otherwise. 'Homosexuality is a constant problem for the Police in large centres,' he argued at the Toronto hearings, 'and if the Police adopt a laissez-faire attitude toward such individuals, city parks, intended for the relaxation of women and children and youth recreation purposes, will become rendezvous for homosexuals.' Concern over the way

public park space was being used extends almost back to when they were
first created. Completed in 1877, Mont Royal Park was the subject of very
similar complaints not twenty years after it opened. Then, the local bour-
geoisie complained that the park was overrun with prostitutes, vaga-
bonds, flâneurs, and unmarried couples.[68] Parks were intended to serve
as an antidote to the pollution created by industrial factories, the germ-
and disease-ridden urban slums, and the immorality spawned by com-
mercial leisure activities. Grand landscapes like Montreal's Mont Royal,
Toronto's High Park, and Vancouver's Stanley Park were meant to promote individual well-being by combining healthful and leisure pursuits.
Poverty, filth, and sex had no place in city parks.

Struggles over park usage were microcosmic versions of wider contests
between defenders of middle-class familial morality and those whose
lives challenged conventional social mores. How after-dark 'cruising'
interfered with the daytime use of Mont Royal was never explicitly stated,
but Queen's Counsel J. Fournier defended the Montreal police drive to
'clean up' the mountain on the grounds that ten years earlier a boy was
murdered there.[69] What Fournier implied, Police Chief Chisholm made
explicit. From Chisholm's vantage point, Toronto parks were in danger
of becoming recruiting grounds for homosexuals.[70] We might expect
nothing less than a law-and-order response from a chief of police, but
Reverend Noel Mailloux, Quebec's leading proponent of positive penology, also argued that homosexuals were dangerous because 'they constantly recruit new members ... younger boys, usually around eighteen –
sixteen, seventeen, eighteen to twenty.'[71] Sexual cruising among men in
Canada's urban green spaces posed no threat to their daytime users, but
the symbolic value of parks as places of bucolic retreat for urban families
tightened the link between male homosexuality, sexual danger, and
pedophilia.

In the sexological configuration of homosexuality, pedophilia served
as cause and effect. For example, throughout the course of the hearings
homosexuality was repeatedly linked to the sexual exploitation and ruin
of youths. Dr John Nelson Senn, the medical superintendent at Ontario
Hospital in Hamilton, told the commission that the majority of adult
homosexuals claim 'their homosexuality stems from an assault when a
boy. You cannot believe them all but you can believe quite a few of them,
and I do feel that if we are ever going to stop homosexuality that is where
it has to be stopped.'[72] A precursor to the modern-day construction of
the sexual abuser whose actions are often attributed to his own history of
victimization, the homosexual was trapped in a victim-perpetrator hall of

mirrors, illustrating the tension between the postwar construct of sex deviants as the objects of pity *and* fear.

Representatives of social service agencies who served the needs of children and adolescents were the most vocal proponents of maintaining and even strengthening legal sanctions against homosexual sex acts. The British Columbia Psychiatric Division of the Social Welfare Branch described 'homosexuality generally and pedophilic homosexuality in particular' as a great concern of their department. In their view, treatment had not achieved meaningful results, and they recommended maximum-security incarceration instead.[73] Though no one confused the adult heterosexual male with the adult pedophile, most were unable to make the same clear distinction with homosexual men.

This conflation is easier to comprehend given the developmental model of sexuality popularized by child psychologists and other experts. According to historian Stephen Robertson, the concept of psychosexual development had been gradually taking shape since the late nineteenth-century. However, it was not until the popularization of the notion of sexual psychopathy in the post–Second World War period that biological explanations for sexuality were eclipsed by theories of personality development that highlighted parental and familial relations during childhood over hereditary factors in shaping sexuality. Sexual psychopathy was premised on the assumption that the 'normal' adult male was able to contain his sexual impulses within the bounds of prevailing social and legal conventions. By the 1950s, those lacking this skill were regarded as sexually immature; they did not possess full and proper sex knowledge or a healthy sex attitude. The homosexual (both male and female) was also described as sexually immature, but for different reasons. Along with the 'dirty old man,' whom experts described as having regressed to a pre-adult sexual level, the male homosexual similarly was regarded as a sexual predator who failed to achieve full heterosexual maturity.[74] According to this logical formulation, homosexual men were unable to control their sexual urges and often sought adolescent sexual partners. Consequently, male homosexuality came to be regarded as a serious threat to children's sexual safety.

If sexual advances toward or assaults on adolescent boys were considered a grave danger, it is odd that there were virtually no explicit discussions concerning those particular offences, short of the occasional inference or outright claim that homosexual men were *ipso facto* pedophiles. However, the commissioners did spend time exploring the problem of sexual assaults against female children, the offence that galvanized public demands for criminal sexual psychopath legislation in the first place. These discussions centred on two main concerns: the problem of prosecution and the question of harm.

Laying charges and taking a case to trial was a major ordeal for children and their parents. In Canada and the United States alike, postwar experts estimated that only a minority of cases of sexual assault were ever brought to trial, and even fewer were successfully prosecuted. The greatest single problem with respect to prosecuting adults who assaulted children under the age of fourteen was that, according to the Canada Evidence Act, the uncorroborated evidence of 'a child of tender years' was not admissible in court.[75] Indeed, members of the Vancouver City Police Department identified the difficulty of securing evidence acceptable to the courts as the most significant barrier to the prosecution of pedophiles, arguing that the criminal sexual psychopath is 'cunning enough to get his victim in circumstances where little or no corroborative evidence is available.'[76] Ontario's attorney general agreed. 'The law provides that the unsworn evidence of a child of tender years, who is too young to appreciate the nature of an oath, may be given, but cannot be acted upon unless such evidence is corroborated by other evidence implicating the accused.' When all the court has is the testimony of the child victim, even if that testimony is corroborated by another child, 'the Court has no alternative but to dismiss the charge.'[77] One of the reasons why judges were not inclined to accept the notion that some sex offenders lacked the power to control their sexual impulses was that most perpetrators took steps to ensure that they were not caught.[78] For this reason, the Provincial Council of Women of Ontario regarded the sexual assault of minors as 'a fertile field for those who might be sexual psychopaths.'[79]

The problem with evidence was compounded by a dismissive attitude toward children's claims of sexual assault. Because children were considered imaginative, suggestible, and incapable of distinguishing fact from fiction, female minors faced a kind of double jeopardy in the courtroom.[80] According to Ovilia Pelletier, detective-inspector in charge of the Preventive Bureau of the City of Montreal, 'little girls imagine offences and sometimes there is a series of complaints of which 70 per cent of them are unfounded.'[81] Ontario Attorney-General Kelso Roberts claimed that 'young children are frequently prone to invent untrue occurrences or may give erroneous and exaggerated interpretations to innocent gestures, words or conduct of an adult,' and that there 'is the possibility of a plan of blackmail lurking in the background of some of these cases on the part of parents.'[82] The opinions of Pelletier and Roberts, the former involved in criminal investigations and the latter with prosecuting them, typify the level of scepticism characteristic of expert views of child sexual assault.

Ironically, the other significant barrier to prosecuting sex crimes against minors was the Juvenile Delinquents Act and the family courts that administered it. Early twentieth-century responses to the special needs of children in the criminal justice system, whether as victims or perpetrators of crime, resulted in the creation of family courts. Originally intended to provide an atmosphere of informality where the media was locked out and social workers rather than prosecutors were the first to interview children, it had become evident by the 1950s that the family court was doing a better job sheltering the perpetrators than protecting the victims of sexual assault. Forensic psychiatrist Dr Kenneth G. Gray argued that the parents of victims were most likely to choose family court where evidence is taken *in camera* over police court where trials are 'published to the world.'[83] Additionally, argued Constable M. Leach of the London Police Department, it is much easier to secure a conviction in Juvenile Court than it is in police court.[84] For this reason, sex offenders whose victims were under the age of fourteen were usually charged with contributing to juvenile delinquency, a catch-all infraction that covered everything from 'telling the child to tell lies and to steal to doing the gravest sexual outrages.'[85] Moreover, sentences were much more lenient under the Juvenile Delinquents Act. Maximum penalties were rarely invoked, and often no charges were ever laid.[86] As for repeat offenders, a conviction under the Juvenile Delinquents Act was a summary conviction, not an indictable offence, so it could not be brought under criminal sexual psychopath legislation. Family court judges were only authorized to hear summary convictions and were not permitted to transfer charges from their court to a higher court, even in cases where they thought the defendant posed a considerable risk to the community.[87] According to J.D. Atcheson, the chief psychologist of the Metropolitan Toronto Juvenile and Family Court, crimes of a sexual nature charged in an adult court were taken much more seriously, and had greater social consequences, than a charge of contributing to juvenile delinquency.'[88] He recommended that juvenile court judges be given the power to transfer a case to an ordinary court. Given that public demand and support for a criminal sexual psychopath law was driven by the desire to deal more effectively with sex crimes against children, it is astounding that the court that heard the majority of child sexual assault cases could not make any use of it.

Even so, a good percentage of child victims of sexual assault never made it anywhere near the Family Court or any other court. Parents' outrage against an attacker could easily be outweighed by their concern that exposing their child as a victim of a sexual attack would subject her or him to the stares of neighbours and ostracism by peers. Karen Dubinsky's study of sexual assault in rural Ontario describes the years from 1880 to 1929 as a transitional period during which the courts came to be used more frequently in settling disputes and seeking retribution for sex-related crimes.[89] In the post–Second World War era, it appears the transition was still underway, though more specifically with respect to offences against children. In 1948 the *Montreal Standard* reported that the parents of an eleven-year-old girl who had been raped, became pregnant, and contracted venereal disease would only lay a charge of indecent assault. It was not for lack of evidence that the victim's parents chose this lesser charge; an adult had witnessed the assault. The parents cited the 'unhappy publicity that would accompany the case' as the deterrent.[90]

Part of the impact of the sex crime panic was to shift public opinion in favour of formal and public prosecution of sex offenders, in spite of the stigma attached to being the victim of a sexual assault. Referring again to late nineteenth- and early twentieth-century Ontario, Dubinsky shows how fear of sexual assault 'seemed to revolve around public disgrace and community disapproval. Fears about moral standing eclipsed concerns about physical safety.'[91] Pre–Second World War ideas about sexual assault tended to regard its victims as corrupted by the attack, ideas reflected in the charge of contributing to juvenile delinquency. The belief that sexual assaults made children delinquent was expressed by Montreal Police Inspector Ovilia Pelletier. He argued that 'children cannot defend themselves like the adults and that there always remains in the child something which sometimes is difficult to remove. Now this little child could teach to friends, class mates, those things which would have been done to him, and there also is the danger that the adult's illness should transmit itself from child to child and should create a certain problem for us.'[92]

Though Pelletier's ideas about sexual abnormalities being contagious would have made any modern medical man grimace, he at least reaffirmed the view that sexual assault harmed children. In the 1950s, most experts talked about sexual assault upon children in terms of the emotional and developmental damage it would cause, and though an awareness of physical harm was implicit in such descriptions, this aspect of sexual assault was not articulated. In order to impress upon the commissioners the seriousness of sexual assaults on children, for example, Dr John Senn claimed that an 'impression is left with children which remains with them indefinitely.'[93] Even exposure to an exhibitionist 'might be rather ominous,' argued Dr William Griffith Black.[94] Senn, Black, and others validated parents' claims that sexual assaults against children needed to be treated very seriously.

Finally, most perpetrators of sexual assault were known to the victim, a fact which certainly must have influenced parents' decisions to prose- cute. I.M. Thomson of the Recreation Directors' Federation of Ontario told the commission he was concerned about the offender who commits assaults within recreation organizations, particularly one who has 'lead- ership qualifications' and who 'rises in an organization and has the trust and support of the organization.'[95] (Ironically, Thomson urged greater family participation in recreational organizations in order to combat sex- ual deviancy.) Dr Edward Turner, the director of a clinical outpatient program for the treatment of sex deviation in Toronto, claimed that families sometimes avoided prosecuting other family members on sex charges by forcing them to undergo treatment.[96] By avoiding the humil- iation and pain of a criminal trial, families could protect their reputation and perhaps the employment status of a male breadwinner, while at the same time feeling that they were taking effective measures to deal with the problem.

Since the beginning of the twentieth-century, social service and other experts have been well aware that most perpetrators of sexual assaults against children are known to the victim, yet the public continued to imagine sex offenders as strangers, not family members or trusted neigh- bours.[97] Critics of the sexual psychopath laws regularly cited research by American criminologist Paul Tappan, which showed that of 324 murders of women, 102 were killed by their own husbands, 37 by fathers or other close relatives, and 49 by lovers or suitors. Only 136 were murdered by someone outside of these three groups.[98] John Howard Society represen- tative A.M. Kirkpatrick submitted a table showing that of seventy-four local cases of sexual assault on a child, only fourteen involved a stranger. The commission's own research, based on RCMP files, also indicated a surprisingly high ratio of known offender versus non-known offender assaults.[99] Even these numbers likely underestimated the degree to which sexual assault was committed by known offenders. According to Kirkpatrick, people are much more likely to report stranger assaults over those committed by a known offender, thus magnifying the perception of 'stranger danger.'[100]

Edward George Potter, the executive director of the Society for the Protection of Women and Children of Montreal (SPWC), had first-hand experience with the way the law worked to shelter perpetrators of intra-familial sexual assault. Potter insisted that only by looking at the victims could we escape the polarized positions that characterized the sex crime debate. At one end of the spectrum, he claimed, is the view expressed in the House of Commons that 'we must be ruthless with these men'; on the other end are those opposed to any judicial measures 'lest [the offenders'] feelings of hostility be increased while voluntary medical and social work efforts are being attempted.' Yet Potter was dismayed that the same compassion shown offenders was rarely expressed for the victims 'of sadistic and sexual outrages, or for the close relatives and friends of such victims.' We would do well to attend to feelings of hostility aroused in the victims and their families, he argued.[101]

The SPWC's greatest concern involved cases of incest, which Potter claimed judicial authorities took few measures to address, despite the repeated pleas of his organization. In the first of two examples, Potter described how the Montreal SPWC became involved with a family where the father was forcing his three daughters to have sexual relations with him. The SPWC arranged to have the children removed from the home and placed with foster parents, but no charges were laid against the father. Subsequently the father attempted suicide, was hospitalized, and was placed under police watch. The watch was discontinued, however, when his condition was downgraded, and he was transferred to another hospital, indicating that the 'watch' had more to do with his suicide attempt than with an effort to protect his children. On the day he was dis-charged from hospital, he made a number of threatening phone calls to the foster mother, who contacted the SPWC, who in turn implored the hospital not to release him. The hospital ignored the request, and the father proceeded to the foster home where he shot and killed the foster mother. 'Only at that point was this man brought under police and legal control,' Potter said.[102]

Potter's frustrated testimony is a poignant reminder of how the police and the courts, the two arms of the state most able to take decisive action against perpetrators of sexual assault and physical violence, were often reluctant to intervene in family matters. According to American histo-rian Linda Gordon's study of family violence, incest is only brought out into the open when women's groups challenge the myth of the family as a sanctuary of safety and security.[103] British and American feminists' efforts to expose incest as a serious social problem in the late nineteenth-

century may well have contributed to the 1890 introduction of new legislation and harsher penalties for the crime in the Criminal Code of Canada,[104] but while many early feminists considered incest to be at least in
part a problem of patriarchal authority, incest nonetheless quickly became associated with disease and immorality, both of which were most
often attributed to poverty and race or ethnic 'otherness.' In the 1950s,
neither poverty nor race was acceptable as a causal explanation for sex
crime or sexual deviancy, but the refusal to include incest as an offence
that could trigger a criminal sexual psychopath hearing reveals how the
family (and its problems) continued to function as a uniquely private
matter. Despite evidence that showed children were most likely to be
assaulted by either a family member or someone known to the family,
the public perception of 'stranger danger' persisted.[105]

During the commission's hearings, almost every medical witness was
asked whether incest should be included among the crimes that fell under
the sexual psychopath law. It was not always clear whether the question or
the answer referred to sexual relations between siblings or between a parent and child, but on the few occasions when it was clear, experts felt that
only parent–child cases should be prosecuted.[106] Dr Ewen Cameron
thought that father–daughter incest 'would be very disruptive to [the victim's] personality and to her future relations with other men. I would
regard it as quite a serious thing, as serious as I would a homosexual situation.' But this did not mean that incest should be included under criminal sexual psychopath legislation.[107] Montreal's Dr Alistair MacLeod
explained that while as a citizen he could see its value in maintaining
moral standards, 'as a psychiatrist I would have to say that I do not see that
such people are dangerous to society ... It is a matter peculiar to that relationship, rather than a man who is a danger to the public.'[108]

Though no one suggested or implied that incest was acceptable, the
commissioners concluded that the danger was contained within the family, unique to the father-daughter relationship, and thus should not be
subject to criminal sexual psychopath legislation.[109] Clearly, though old
interpretive paradigms like poverty and race were being replaced by
modern measures of normal and deviant behaviour, the sanctity of the
family and the focus on public versus private danger remained firmly
intact.[110]

Sexual assaults against women were similarly unchallenged by the new
mental health model. For example, the chief of the Toronto Police
Force was concerned that women's reports of sexual assault were viewed
with scepticism. Chisholm complained to the commission that 'there is

in the minds of many intelligent people a fixed idea that [rape] cannot be committed without some degree of acquiescence on the part of the victim. This,' he continued, 'is a very unfair attitude to adopt ... Many rape cases are just on the borderline of murder.'[111] Though it was not always the case that a female rape victim had her rights championed by law enforcement agents and judges, no one in a position of authority would deny justice to a woman who was the victim of an attack. The problem was, however, that much like children, women had to first convince the authorities that she had been attacked. 'This will make you laugh,' Queens Counsel J. Fournier promised the commissioners. He recounted the story of a 'girl' of 'about 26' who recently tried to lay a criminal complaint. She claimed she was raped three times in two hours. 'I told her, "Are you serious?" I said, "You did not resist?" She said, "I did not resist because he was too tall and I was too weak and I thought to myself I would be better to accede than to resist." She wanted to bring a complaint of having been raped three times in two hours. So we have not to take that too seriously.'[112]

In the 1950s, abnormal sexual acts were constructed as pathological, and as was the case with incest, virtually no attention was paid to gender or, for that matter, patriarchy. Because the construction of the problem focused exclusively on the assailant and not the victim, victims of sex crime hardly registered at all. Not surprisingly then, prevailing attitudes about male sexual attacks on women over the age of fourteen remained largely intact. For example, asked if he would consider rape an abnormal act, Dr Louis Bourgoin explained that psychiatric assessments were not based on the act, but on the subject's personality. Sexual assault 'has its social importance, but from the psychiatric point of view, it is not so much the offence which is important, as it is the one who commits [the] offence.'[113] The commission asked Dr D. Ewen Cameron whether men who rape were all sexual psychopaths, or if some were simply 'ruthless, selfish, aggressive men who take advantage of others such as one finds in the business world.' Cameron agreed with the analogy, explaining that a man who rapes might either lack sex control, or he might possess an 'attitude towards women in general ... of a primitive, acquisitive male.'[114] Postwar forensic sexology had normalized the male desire to possess women. Men needed only to keep their methods of acquisition in line with acceptable social limits. Thus, the criminal sexual psychopath construct did not seek to uproot the tree of male sexuality, it only trimmed its atypical branches. Because mental health experts took little interest in the more mundane conflicts that occurred between 'normal' adults, rape involving adult female victims was excluded from postwar theories about sexual assault.

Adult women did figure into the hearings of the royal commission, just not as one might have expected. As a political force, women across Canada (organized through local and provincial councils, the umbrella National Council of Women, as well as parent-teacher and Home and School associations) were responsible for generating the public pressure that forced the government to implement sexual psychopath legislation in the first place. When it became clear that the law was not having an impact, the troops were rallied for another round of petitioning and letter writing, calling for an investigation into the matter, and leading ultimately to the creation of the commission. But unlike earlier generations of women who put sex on the political agenda, women in the 1950s did not come to the table with a critique of sexual danger that grew out of an independent analysis of women's and children's needs in a male-dominated society. Instead, the majority advocated for mental health treatment alternatives to prison. At the commission hearings, most women's and parent-teacher groups attended with their official medical advisor in tow.

Ironically, while it was women who made sex crime and its treatment a central social and political issue in the 1950s, the experts they promoted held parents, and especially mothers, responsible for causing sexual abnormalities in the first place. As we saw in chapter 2, mental health experts drew a direct line from parenting practices to all aspects of their children's sexual behaviour.[115] It was a theme that emerged during the commission hearings. The president of the Canadian Mental Health Association, J.D. Griffin, argued that the common denominator among all aggressive offenders is 'maternal deprivation of some sort, and by maternal deprivation I mean the lack of a warm, protecting and supporting mother love.' But, he added, 'I would say in parenthesis that [love and affection] is best given in a situation where there is father affection, too, as a total family group.' Though Griffin was very cautious in making this statement, even pointing out that sex crimes are committed by those who do not fall into this group, he suggested that it was possible that 'we ought to [be] discourag[ing] mothers from working, for instance, during this crucial period.'[116] The United Church of Canada agreed. Though they had nothing substantive to offer on the criminal law relating to the criminal sexual psychopath, the United Church saw the hearings as an opportunity to express its concern 'about the detrimental influence of the increasing employment of mothers outside of their homes.'[117] That they did so is a very clear measure of just how thoroughly entrenched was the belief that mothers were primarily and perhaps ultimately responsible for their children's psychosexual development. As if that were not enough, a number of critics charged women with inflaming the sex crime problem by constantly bringing attention to it. In this way the debate was sexed: male doctors and female advocates had different roles to play in solving the sex crime problem.

But the debate was also gendered. The very same women who demanded a scientific approach to the problem were characterized and subsequently denounced as hysterical and panicky, while the male experts they promoted were viewed as reasoned and rational. Ontario's Dr Frank van Nostrand suggested that the 'publicity and hysteria' surrounding sex crimes 'initiates thoughts which are latent in unstable individuals.'[118] Toronto Chief Constable Chisholm told the commission to warn parents not to take 'any hysterical approach to the problem,' but to be a more active presence in their children's lives.[119] Suddenly, women found themselves on the defensive. When Mrs. W.R. Walton, the national vice-president of the Imperial Order Daughters of the Empire (IODE), submitted the resolutions of the 957 delegates representing 32,000 members 'from Yukon to Newfoundland' she felt compelled to insist, 'we have no wish to be emotional or to add to the hysteria that is going around, and we have made no suggestions specifically because we thought that others better qualified than ourselves could do that, but it was just to let you know that there was this concern existent right across the country.'[120] Similarly, Mrs. Kerr, president of the Ontario Provincial Council of Women, defended her organization's brief by insisting, 'our submission is not the result of recent newspaper publicity at all; [our study] has been going on for a considerable length of time. We are not a panicky group.'[121]

The construction of the masculine expert as objective and authoritative and of the feminine as irrational and hysterical was felt across the country, not just at the royal commission hearings. At least one small group of women rejected these terms, preferring instead to assert their maternal authority and goading men to take forceful action against sex criminals. In a 1956 letter to Ontario's attorney general, five women from the semi-rural town of Whitby instructed the premier of Ontario to 'heed the rumblings of our anger as i will surely break into a mighty roar. we are disgusted with all this "Mamly Pamly" coddling of "Sex Perverts." they are a menace and the way most of us feel right now consider the "Lash" should be used; failing that "The *Death Penalty*" our children must be protected.'[122] Another mother writing in the same year also insisted that she be heard, though she made her demands in less colourful terms. After describing an attempt made to lure her seven-year-old daughter into a car, she wrote, 'I trust that this letter will not be disregarded as just another emotional mother blowing off steam. Perhaps I am emotional,' she continued, 'but I feel I have sufficient reason to be. We do pay for protection, and we are free to vote, and we do have freedom of speech.' Women's freedom of speech, however, was undermined by the royal commission's resistance to give due consideration to the personal experiences and opinions of non-expert witnesses appearing before them. Instead, the commission accepted their testimony and submissions, and, when representatives of women's and parents' groups brought along a medical adviser, questioned him.[123]

Mothers were to blame for not providing their children with proper role modelling and for failing to provide them with a sound sex education, but an improper response to sexual assaults against children was one of the most common criticisms levelled against parents during the commission hearings. Mental health experts argued that parental reactions could be more harmful than the sexual assault itself. Like American expert Paul Tappan, Canadian doctors, psychologists, and social workers argued that the effects of sexual assaults on children were grossly exaggerated, and that the level of trauma 'is almost always a product of cultural and individual responses rather than because of the intrinsic emotional value of the experience itself.'[124] Initially, parent organizations uncritically accepted these claims. After a series of roundtable conferences, for example, the British Columbia Parent-Teacher Association advised members that 'the parent attitude had a stronger effect on a child than the actual incident of molestation ... Parents should avoid emotional reactions which might impress the incident unduly on the child's mind. Parents should not over respond to an assault, that sometimes this is more traumatic than the actual assault.'[125] Before the decade was over, parents began to take a more circumspect view of expert advice, but initially, at least, they shouldered the burden of raising children who would not turn into deviants, of protecting their children from deviants already out there, and of responding appropriately should their child be assaulted.

After months of public hearings and four years of intermittent research, McRuer, Kinnear, and Desrochers completed their report in 1958, but it was not tabled in the House of Commons until 1959. As is typical of periods of heightened anxiety about sex crime, public and parliamentary interest in the issue eventually began to wane. As the baby boomers grew from small vulnerable children into troublesome teenagers, juvenile delinquency and illicit drug use eclipsed fears concerning the sexual molestation of children.[126] Unlike Britain's controversial 1957 *Report of the Departmental Committee on Homosexual Offences and Prostitution* (better known as the Wolfenden Report), which advocated for the decriminalization of homosexual sex between consenting adults over the age of twenty-one, the final report of the commission was strikingly conservative, and contained nothing controversial enough to reignite debate on the issue. Moreover, neither the federal government nor the opposition were in any hurry to see the modest recommendations implemented.

On the whole, the *Report of the Royal Commission on the Criminal Law Relating to Criminal Sexual Psychopaths* maintained the status quo with respect to both the relationship between the law and psychiatry, and the application of criminal sexual psychopath legislation. The only consistent position taken was against the erosion of the authority of the court in the face of advancing psychiatric expertise about criminal behaviour: virtually every proposal that granted more power to psychiatrists in the disposition of sex crime cases was strongly opposed on the grounds that it would diminish important protections that the law afforded the accused and the convicted. Only two recommendations were of any significance with respect to the Criminal Code of Canada. First, the commission argued in favour of eliminating wording that undermined the application of the law, namely that 'criminal sexual psychopath' be changed to 'dangerous sexual offender,' and that 'lack of power to control' be changed to 'failure to control.' With these modifications, which were adopted in 1961, the law could capture those who planned and plotted their assaults as opposed to only those who might be considered mentally ill, lacking 'normal' cognitive and containment skills.[127] Most important, although the commission did not recommend any changes to the requirement that two psychiatrists testify in a hearing to determine whether a man found guilty should be sentenced to an indeterminate term, the successful application to have a man declared a criminal sexual psychopath was no longer dependent on the vagaries of psychopathy or on the opinions of psychiatrists. Instead, the law required only that the Crown must convince the court of the probability that the accused might reoffend.

Probabilities, however, have more to do with crystal-ball gazing and less with science. In the postwar cultural imagination, sex offenders were by nature recidivists, but this image was not supported by the numbers the commission had at its disposal. Citing RCMP and Statistics Canada figures, as well as a handful of American studies, the report pointed out that as a group, sex offenders had the lowest rates of recidivism, and when homosexuals and second offences that were not sex-related were excluded, recidivism rates were almost inconsequential. Moreover, the commission found there had been no increase in the number of sex crimes committed, and no change in the rate or severity of conviction.[128] Such were the findings of virtually every similar study undertaken in the United States. The belief that there was an epidemic of sex-related crimes was, as Saskatchewan's Dr Lucy put it, the result of 'a somewhat morbid public interest no doubt stimulated and titillated by an unscrupulous and sensation mongering press.'[129] That, combined with the over-selling of psychiatry and a false belief in its ability to cure sex deviants, amounted to a disproportionate level of social anxiety over what was essentially a marginal phenomenon. As many Canadian and American police officers repeatedly pointed out, children were almost three hundred times more likely to be killed by an automobile than by a violent assault.

Crime statistics were not well or consistently kept in this period. Moreover, the media attention and parent activism around the issue may well have resulted in a rise in the number of reported cases. But even if the rates of sexual assault had remained stable, that did not mean that all was well. Despite the testimony of a number of witnesses who argued that the police and the courts were failing victims of sexual assault, the commission did not use the opportunity to discuss ways in which sexual assault cases could be better managed. Nor did they suggest that the law be scrapped. Though the commissioners argued that the concept of preventive detention and punitive detention was illogical, that the failure to provide treatment 'is definitely wrong and in large measure defeats the purpose of the law,' and that there was no justification for differentiating sexual psychopaths from other psychopathic offenders, the commissioners concluded that the principle of the law was right.[130] Though they argued that there were very few repeat sex offenders, the commissioners believed that the state should have the power to detain offenders in prison until they were deemed safe to return to society.

The final report supported psychiatric treatment of sexual deviation, but it rejected psychiatrists' arguments for the decriminalization of homosexuality. Despite experts' insistence that the law had no business regulating morality and that the state should concern itself with harm-causing behaviour alone, and though Britain's Wolfenden Report called for the decriminalization of homosexuality in that country, the McRuer commission evaded the controversy by claiming that it was not their place to call for the decriminalization of anything. That may be, but the commissioners made no recommendation to remove sex between consenting adults of the same sex from the purview of criminal sexual psychopath legislation. While on the one hand they argued that the law should not be used against those charged with consensual homosexual sex, and claimed that it never had been, they nevertheless felt it prudent to leave it open to the court's discretion rather than to block the court from laying criminal sexual psychopath charges in such cases.[131] The commissioners supported their position by quoting Toronto Police Chief Chisholm, who argued that homosexuals recruited youths into their fraternity. Commissioners thus cemented the link between the homosexual, the sexual predator, and the pedophile. By suggesting that homosexual acts included the potential for harm to others, the commission could preserve the traditional role of the law in regulating morals while appearing to apply modern 'scientific' standards.[132]

Equally astonishing to the modern reader is the commission's refusal to include incest as one of the crimes that could trigger a criminal sexual psychopath hearing. Most witnesses agreed that incest had serious consequences and should be covered by the sexual psychopath legislation, yet the commissioners decided against its inclusion. Remarkably, the report claimed that 'there were no specific cases brought to our attention in which ... the punitive provisions of the criminal law were not sufficient to protect society,' despite the compelling evidence to the contrary given by a member of the Montreal Society for the Protection of Women and Children. This decision clearly demonstrates that the tendency of the law to be applied to strangers versus offenders known to the victims was neither an accident nor a mere tendency, but was a fundamental part of the postwar construction of sexual danger and the sexual psychopath. Although psychiatrists urged a reassessment of sex crime based solely on a measure of harm, old ideas about the dangers of the public and the safety of the private clouded the commissioners' ability to shape new laws based on statistical claims about who was assaulting whom. Despite evidence that showed most perpetrators of sex crimes were known to the victim, and were often family members, the family continued to symbolize refuge from danger.

Criminal sexual psychopath legislation was a response to sexual assaults committed against children, so it is not surprising that the legislation was directed toward offenders whose victims were under the age of fourteen. In response to testimony about the problems created by the

Juvenile Delinquents Act, the commission noted that twenty-three of the offenders currently serving indeterminate sentences as criminal sexual psychopaths would not be doing so had they been tried under the Juvenile Delinquents Act, and recommended that all offences that fell under the provision should be heard in the criminal court, not in a juvenile and family court. They argued that existing criminal code provisions provided judges with the necessary tools to ensure a courtroom free from the prying eyes of the public and the press, but they failed to address how the absence of social workers and other support staff might make the experience more intimidating and emotionally taxing for child witnesses. Indeed, the commissioners' belief in the rightness of the existing structure of Canada's legal system was unshakable. They flatly rejected any suggestion that the unsworn evidence of children should be accepted. The need to protect the accused, they argued, outweighed the potential benefit to the victim. In other words, so long as there was no corroborating evidence in a case involving a person younger than fourteen, the law would provide no inroad for those seeking justice and no hope for formal retribution or punishment.

The most obvious missing piece of the sexual psychopath puzzle was the absence of treatment programs, facilities, and staff in federal penitentiaries, a fact that was not overlooked in the final report. The report quoted extensively from expert testimony that described a lack of knowledge about and treatment methods for dealing with sex offenders. Nevertheless, the commission concluded that 'a positive attitude toward the problem is of great importance ... We are convinced that with custodial care must go definite progressive methods of the application of all known helpful means of treatment and the development of new means. These we must leave to the medical profession.' Yet without treatment, they argued, the only justification for criminal sexual psychopath legislation was segregation from society. Echoing the findings of a decade of research into the problem of sex crime, the royal commission recommended that the government support the creation of a joint federal-provincial board of researchers, clinical treatment programs, and more education in the area of human sexuality. Though the federal government's culpability was made clear, the tone and language of the report was reserved, and the recommendations soft-pedalled. Little wonder that the report sat unclaimed by the House for a full year, and that its recommendations were implemented piecemeal, if at all.

When the government set out to undertake a study of criminal sexual psychopath legislation, it produced a survey of ideas about the regulation of human sexuality in postwar Canada. Taking many of their cues from pre–Second World War European sexologists as well as from contemporary American studies in the field, Canada's medical, psychiatric, and psychological experts asserted their authority as regulators of deviant sexual behaviour by proposing a new paradigm for the organization of sex laws: the criminal code should regulate harm-causing behaviour such as rape and sexual assault, and mental health experts should play a central role in the rehabilitation of offenders. Persons convicted of crimes that do not cause harm but that are merely an affront to morality should not be treated punitively but as victims of a mental health problem.

One of the most important ways in which psychiatrists and other professionals advanced this argument was through the example of homosexuality, a 'problem' behaviour that did not in and of itself bring physical or psychological harm to its participants. Though the linking of homosexuality with sexual psychopathy and deviancy ultimately led to waves of increased surveillance and regulation of urban homosexual public spaces, most Canadian and some American psychiatrists were opposed to punitive measures and instead advocated the decriminalization of consensual homosexual relations. However, even the most modern expert advocated treatment for homosexual men, illustrating that psychiatrists were not simply seeking to liberate but were competing to regulate.

The construction of the sexual psychopath ultimately propped up the myth of stranger danger and insulated the family – not from sexual assault, as the legislation's supporters had hoped – but from the scrutiny of the law and the punishment of the criminal justice system.[133] Indeed, as Philip Girard has shown, the 1969 report of the Canadian Committee on Corrections reviewed the legislation and found that one in four child sex offenders made victims of family members or relatives, but only one out of every fifteen offenders in the same category was sentenced under the criminal sexual psychopath or, after 1961, the dangerous sexual offender law. 'In other words,' Girard writes, 'the dangerous sexual offender category was reserved for those who fit the public's stereotype of the "sex deviate" or child molester: the unattached man, the outsider.'[134]

The heightened concern over sex crime after the Second World War has been described as the product of anxiety about transforming idealized masculinity from the fearless male soldier into the domesticated breadwinner. The sexual psychopath has also been described as yet another cultural trope used to cajole women into staying at home, lest one of their own children become the next victim. While these are meaningful ways to help understand the cultural context in which sexual psychopathy was popularized, and partly accounts for the disproportionate attention paid to sex crime in contrast to other social problems, it does not attend to the simple fact that sexual assaults against children were a real problem with a meaningful impact, one for which parents, women's groups, church councils, and other citizens looked to the state for help. The royal commission gave witnesses and the letter-writing public the opportunity to reveal the ways that the criminal justice system failed to work in favour of victims, and exposed some of the most egregious aspects of the law's failure to take action against abusers, particularly when abusers were family members. Though the criminal sexual psychopath was problematic even for psychiatrists and other mental health experts, the Royal Commission on the Criminal Law Relating to Criminal Sexual Psychopaths nevertheless provided those working directly with child victims the opportunity to reveal how the criminal justice system was failing the people it purported to serve.

The mid-century construction of the criminal sexual psychopath continues to shape the way we think today: male homosexuality is still linked with pedophilia, and sex offenders whose victims are children are still thought of as psychologically and emotionally immature, afflicted by a character disorder that prevents them from 'normal' sexual expression, and worse still, that compels them to continuously seek out new victims. The gay rights movement and even the social networks that predated it enabled gay men to resist the construction of homosexuality as a disease in need of a cure, and to challenge the way mental health experts characterized them as a group. However, as one psychiatrist pointed out during the commission hearings, other sex offenders did not have the same social group support through which they might counter claims about their criminal and sexual histories. This is not to say that men (or women) who have sex with children, by consent or coercion, should be regarded as a sexual minority group on par with homosexuals. Nor is this to deny that sexual assault is a serious problem that causes real harm to its victims. My point here is that the sex offender is a construction: grounded in pre–Second World War studies of homosexuality, tainted as they were by mid-century heterosexist ideas about what constituted maturity and normalcy, and what constituted danger and harm. If we are to renew our efforts to understand why people choose to seek out sex with, or coerce sex from, children, we must be prepared to think differently about both victims and perpetrators of sexual violence.[135] In the last decades of the twentieth century, feminist critiques of patriarchy, sexism, racism, classism, and ageism developed new critical analyses of the material and discursive meanings of sexual conflict, and changed the way we respond to it in our courts, prisons, and education and health care systems. But most of these efforts have focused on victims of assault or victims of racist sexual politics (or both). We need also to cast a critical eye on the meanings attached to offenders.

Finally, the commission's report would have disappointed critics that prompted its birth, but it did help push the court of public opinion to favour consequential sentencing in sexual assault cases. Though the criminal sexual psychopath legislation and, later, dangerous sexual offender legislation were little used, judges were encouraged to treat these matters more seriously, and to apply harsher penalties in child sexual assault cases. As I explore in greater detail in chapter 4, criminal sexual psychopath legislation did provide some opportunities to vigorously pursue experiments in treatments for sex offenders. In Europe, Denmark led the way at the controversial institution in Herstedvester; in the United States, California provided generous funding for its free-standing program for imprisoned sex offenders; and in Canada, Ontario led the way with the Guelph Reformatory's Neuro-Psychiatric Clinic, and later its special segregation unit for sex offenders and sex deviates (homosexuals). However, Canada's federal government lagged far behind, despite the recommendations of the commission. Only in the early 1990s did the federal government, under pressure from the populist Reform Party, increase the number of treatment spaces for sex offenders serving time in federal penitentiaries from 200 to 1,800.[136]

PART TWO

Practices

chapter four

The Mad and the Bad: Treating Sexual Deviation

'Experiment is ... superior to precedent,' American sexologist Benjamin Karpman proclaimed in 1948. 'Old methods are readily abandoned, to give way to newer methods.'[1] Indeed, at war's end medical and psychiatric experts had all but renounced somatic solutions to sexological problems in favour of increasingly popular theories of personality and ego development. Drawing on the work of people like G. Stanley Hall in the United States, Sigmund Freud in Europe, and George Stevenson in Canada, postwar sexologists elaborated on the role of culture, society, and especially the family in shaping the sexual self. Not one of the experts knew how to best translate these theories into treatment. Experiment was not just superior to precedent. In the atomic age, it was the only way forward.

Despite the absence of any evidence suggesting that psychiatrists could 'cure' sex deviation, court and prison clinics dedicated to that purpose opened up in Ontario and across the United States from the late 1940s onward. The Neuro-Psychiatric Clinic at the Guelph Reformatory, Menlo Park in New Jersey, Waupun in Wisconsin, Patuxent in Maryland, and Norwalk in California were just a few of the institutions that aimed to provide services to a population so recently identified that almost nothing was known about them. This impressive expansion of forensic sexology was not the result of either an explosion of medical interest in sexual deviation research or of advances in psychiatry, psychology, or any other field of medical science or mental health. In fact, treating 'the mad and the bad,' people whose crimes were attributed to mental instability, aberration, or illness, was one of the least appealing fields of psychiatric work, and sex deviants were the least palatable among them.[2] The development and diffusion of forensic sexology in the 1950s and 60s was largely driven by public pressure on provincial, state, and federal governments to provide medical and psychiatric treatment for sex offenders.

Criminal sexual psychopath legislation was only one manifestation of this widespread cultural trend. After the Second World War, sex deviation treatment programs emerged throughout the British Commonwealth, including in England, New Zealand, and Australia, yet none of these countries adopted a sexual psychopath law. Furthermore, adopting criminal sexual psychopath legislation did not always lead to the creation of sex criminal treatment programs. For example, while the law typically required that judicial determinations of sexual psychopathy be informed by a psychiatric assessment of the patient, thereby creating a demand for consultants who could speak to matters of sexual pathology, criminal sexual psychopath laws did not oblige the state to provide treatment. While Canada's law held that criminal sexual psychopaths should be incarcerated in a federal prison until deemed cured by a psychiatrist, the penitentiary system did not offer a sex offender treatment program until the mid-1970s. Therefore, in Canada, as in some American states, the law had only a minimal impact on the growth of forensic sexology.

The situation in Canada illustrates this point well. Convicted sex criminals who were successfully charged under criminal sexual psychopath (1948–61) and dangerous sex offender (1961–77) legislation were a responsibility of the federal government. Yet it was the province of Ontario that became an international leader in research and treatment on sexual deviation. In the mid-1950s, Premier Leslie Frost's Conservative government established a hospital-based clinic mandated to assess men charged with, and treat men convicted for, minor sex offences. It also created a prison-based treatment program for men serving time in provincial reformatories, even though the province was not responsible for prisoners convicted under the sexual psychopath law. As we saw in chapter 2, the Toronto Psychiatric Hospital's Outpatient Forensic Clinic, which specialized in the treatment of sexual deviation, was established as a direct result of public pressure from everyday Ontario citizens, not because Frost himself was a champion of mental health treatment programs. Thus, local activism and grassroots support for what was widely considered an innovative, progressive, modern, and humane approach to an age-old problem, and not the 1948 federal legislation, was responsible for expanding forensic sexology in Canada.

Treatment for sex criminals expanded throughout the British Commonwealth in two directions after the Second World War. Services were offered either in hospital-based medical clinics, or in prisons and penitentiaries. Though fuelled by the same set of public demands, the institutional setting profoundly affected how treatment was delivered. For this reason, I examine Ontario's hospital and prison programs separately. This chapter focuses on the ten-year history of Toronto's Outpatient Forensic Clinic. Established in 1956 as a unit in the Ontario Department of Health's Mental Health Division, the clinic was part of the Toronto Psychiatric Hospital (TPH), a teaching hospital affiliated with the University of Toronto. There were few clinics like it. Most forensic sexology services elsewhere were offered through existing psychiatric units, typically only on an in-patient basis, and provided only diagnosis for pre-sentence hearings. The clinic's mandate went much further and included a robust and innovative treatment and research program.

News of the clinic spread quickly throughout the Metropolitan Toronto area, and intake numbers climbed steadily. Between 1956 and 1966, staff interviewed approximately 1,500 men (and perhaps a few women) who were subsequently classified as sex deviants.[3] When the TPH officially closed its doors in 1966, more than 60 per cent of the clinic's patients were being treated for homosexuality, pedophilia, or exhibitionism. Only a third were there as the result of a court order. A probation officer, a social service or community agency, a church official, a psychiatrist or doctor, or a family member referred the other two-thirds, or patients came of their own volition, evidence that psychiatric treatment for sexual deviation was more than just a punishment. It took less than a decade for the whole concept of sexual deviation, and mental health treatment as its solution, to achieve widespread acceptance.

None of this brought clinic staff any closer to finding an effective treatment for sexual deviation, however. Despite enjoying a high level of public support, the intellectual freedom to determine their own course, and the ideal treatment setting, staff failed to 'cure' or even curb homosexual, exhibitionistic, or pedophilic practices among their patients, notwithstanding early claims to the contrary. In this chapter, I explore how frustration with poor progress using psychoanalysis and psychotherapy led treatment experts to experiment with a variety of increasingly invasive methods that were intended to facilitate, not replace, a psychotherapeutic approach. Convinced that therapy failed because patients were either unable or unwilling to push past emotional and psychological barriers, treatment experts introduced sodium amytal, LSD, and other consciousness-altering drugs to help conquer patient resistance. Often mistakenly described as aversion therapy, such attempts to facilitate psychotherapy unwittingly served as the thin edge of the wedge that made the more radical interventionist techniques used in behaviour modification therapy more palatable.

Distinguishing what was intended to facilitate psychotherapy from the aversion and behaviour modification therapies may appear to some to be a hair-splitting exercise, but if we are to begin to understand how a popular grassroots movement that favoured humane and compassionate alternatives to imprisonment for sex offenders led to what appears to be cruel and unusual experiments, then it is critical that we understand the nature of and the intention behind various treatment practices. For example, historians of the medicalization of homosexuality often begin with the assumption that treating homosexuality is repressive and sexually conservative. Indeed, traditional accounts of this period generally maintain that liberal experts like biologist and sex researcher Alfred Kinsey and psychologist Evelyn Hooker stood apart from their colleagues by openly challenging the prevailing system of sexual morality, particularly with respect to the treatment of homosexuality.

But the story turns out to be rather more complicated. Many forensic sexologists became 'sexual liberals,' and espoused modern, progressive views. Kinsey had an enormous impact on many forensic sexologists who eventually developed a hybrid approach to treating sexual deviation that combined his theories of human sexual behaviour with Freudian concepts. Alongside their American colleagues, staff at the Forensic Clinic came to view homosexuals as victims of public opinion and prejudice. As in California, where some forensic sexologists allied themselves with the emerging homophile movement and openly spoke out against the social and legal persecution of homosexuals, Canada's first known gay rights group regarded the clinical staff as allies, not enemies. Working at the intersection between medicine and the law, a significant number of forensic sexologists agreed that only behaviours causing harm should be criminalized. Acts that merely offended the moral sensibilities of the public, they believed, should not be subject to legal – or for that matter medical – regulation. The law should be concerned with protecting citizens from danger, and medicine with healing them from illness. Morality had no place in either realm.

The flip side of sexology's progressive liberalism and permissive stance toward human sexual behaviour is significantly less appealing. Sexual assault against young girls, which is what fuelled the drive for sexual psychopath laws and treatment programs in the first place, was under-theorized and minimized throughout this period. Indeed, experts believed that many young female victims of sexual assault were not damaged physically, emotionally, or psychologically and they continued to locate pathology in the victim's family.[4] Moreover, the Forensic Clinic's studies drew on both Freud and Kinsey to give scientific legitimacy to the popular view that young girls who were assaulted were willing participants. If we were to limit our examination to the treatment of homosexuality, the history of the clinic might offer us the comfort of knowing there were more sexual liberals than were once thought. But the purpose of history is never to make us comfortable. Instead, my goal is to deepen our understanding of the foundation upon which forensic sexology is built. Homosexuality was an important area of public concern and a target for medical treatment, but it was only a part of the whole. The larger social concern was sexual danger, and we cannot afford to ignore ideas about pedophiles, exhibitionists, or victims of sexual assault.

In order to place research and programs at the Forensic Clinic within the wider North American context in which they developed, this chapter examines programs undertaken outside Ontario, including Norwalk in California, Quebec psychiatrist Bruno Cormier's therapeutic community at Clinton Prison in Dannemora, New York, and psychiatrist Anthony Marcus's research with sex offenders in a federal British Columbia prison. The chapter begins, however, with a brief overview of the various forms of medical intervention used to treat sex and morals offenders in the early twentieth century, when eugenics was in its heyday. As we shall see, the convergence of medicine, psychiatry, and the law in dealing with sex 'perversion' and 'immorality' began more than half a century earlier, but ideas about the nature of sexual behaviour, the methods of treatment, and the tremendously high level of public support for medical alternatives in the 1950s all indicate that the postwar era was a period of significant change in the history of the pathologization of sex.

Using medical science and psychiatry to control, regulate, and punish sex crimes, which included morals offences, was certainly not new in the post–Second World War era.[5] During the interwar period, both sterilization and vasectomy were widely considered to serve both therapeutic and prophylactic purposes.[6] In the United States, thirty-two states had eugenic sterilization laws in place before the Second World War, and by 1938, 25,403 'surgical treatments' had been recorded.[7] Switzerland, Germany, Denmark, Norway, Finland, and New Zealand adopted similar legislation that allowed for the sterilization of exhibitionists, rapists, homosexuals, and those who committed 'crimes against the morals of minors, boys and girls.' In all cases, the decision to sterilize was based on

psychiatric testimony. The Swiss, Danish, and Finnish used the law mini-
mally; the Swiss recorded 6 instances, the Danes 63, and the Fins 9. But
Germans documented 1,116 castrations between 1933 and 1936. Marie
Kopp, an American medical doctor and advocate of castration, wrote of
the Germans' zeal with approval. She recommended greater availability
of sterilization to treat 'abnormal persons' and lifelong imprisonment for
those 'not amenable to treatments.'[8]

The idea that sterilization could eliminate crime and immorality in
future generations was a product of eugenics, a purportedly scientific theory that linked human behaviour to biological heredity. Positive eugenics
encouraged procreation among the white middle and upper classes. Negative eugenics discouraged reproduction among those deemed to have
weak or immoral constitutions. In Canada, support for sterilization was
high among the educated middle classes, particularly as a means to control sex perversion. Though Canadian experts knew it did not eliminate
or even reduce the male sex drive, they believed that by eliminating the
ability to reproduce, they could eradicate immoral defectives for future
generations.[9]

Initially, reports of sex crimes against children after the Second World
War led to a revival of support for compulsory sterilization. For example,
an Ontario farmer wrote to the minister of the Department of Reform,
Major John Foote, to explain how 'any stock breeder' knows a castrated
animal can be 'turned loose among any female without the slightest danger of trouble' and 'those who attack children or make brutal attacks on
women sexually should get the knife.'[10] Foote agreed that in some cases
it seemed that castration was the only possible solution. But, he added
regretfully, 'it looks as though there will be a tremendous lot of opposition to amending the Criminal Code to make this possible.'[11]

He was right. During the late 1940s and through the 1950s, hundreds
of citizens demanded that sex criminals be castrated, but by that time
most Canadian doctors abjured eugenic sterilization.[12] Historians have
attributed the postwar renunciation of eugenics as a theory, and of certain invasive medical procedures as a practice, to the horrible revelations
of Nazi medical experiments.[13] While gruesome testimony at the Nurem-
berg trials doubtless had an impact, Canadian doctors rejected castration and sterilization based on local data that showed castration had not
reduced immorality or the number of sex crimes committed. Furthermore, some medical experts believed castration could actually aggravate
a disturbed sex deviant.[14] Thus, the search for new treatment methods
was underway.

In the 1950s, a number of North American, European, and Scandinavian doctors experimented with hormone (estrogen) injections, electroconvulsive therapy (ECT), castration, and lobotomy (also known as leucotomy) for treating sexual deviation.[15] A thorough examination of psychiatric hospital records in Canada has yet to be undertaken, but in Ontario at least, psychopaths, homosexuals, and other sex deviants were formally excluded from the eligible pool of candidates for leucotomy.[16] Virtually all psychiatrists and medical doctors who testified before the Royal Commission on the Criminal Law Relating to Criminal Sexual Psychopaths rejected lobotomy, and only one spoke in favour of U.S. experiments with chemical castration.[17] Not one would advocate the surgical castration used at Denmark's controversial Herstedvester Prison, where the director of psychiatry firmly believed in its effectiveness as a tool to help sex offenders overcome or gain control of their 'impulses.'[18] According to the commissioners' final report, psychiatrists from one end of the country to the other generally felt that the whole concept of castration violated Canadian views of civil rights.[19]

Psychotherapy was by far the fastest growing approach to treating deviancy.[20] More than a repudiation of eugenics, it reflected a fundamental shift in thinking about the aetiology of human behaviour. What was once thought to be caused by heredity and biology was now seen as the consequence of social and environmental processes. After the war, most North American psychiatrists argued that every person was born with the potential to be social or antisocial, normal or psychopathic. As California's leading forensic sexologist Karl Bowman bluntly put it, all men have the capacity to become 'sadistic sex killer[s] or ... emotionally mature, respected citizen[s].'[21] Life experience alone determined what one became.

The combined popularity of Freudian psychoanalysis, particularly among psychiatrists, and the child development theories of G. Stanley Hall and George Stevenson, especially among psychologists, meant that most postwar experts focused exclusively on early childhood experiences to explain sexual deviancy. Mental health experts believed that helping patients resolve the hidden traumatic experiences at the root of their behaviour could eliminate sexual deviancy and would thus eliminate the sex crimes deviants commit. In other words, psychiatrists would fix what parents had broken.[22]

Postwar sexology was built on Freud's theory of child sexual development. Briefly, Freud held that from birth to age five, children passed through four phases of sexual development: oral, anal, phallic, and finally, what seemed to be the source of most problems for men, the Oedipus complex (Freud called the female version of this stage the Electra complex, though he was never confident that it adequately explained women's sexuality). The Oedipus complex occurred at age five, when male children experience a deep love of the opposite sex parent and a hatred of the same sex parent. Boys seek to supplant their fathers, but fear their fathers will castrate them as punishment. Male children successfully resolve this conflict by emulating, and therefore identifying with, the father. After a long period of sexual latency that follows, children go on to become heterosexual adolescents who live comfortably within contemporary social and cultural conventions that include sexual mores, and seek sexual pleasure in conventional monogamous marriages.

Thus, according to Freud, adult heterosexuality was mature sexuality. Deviations from the norm either in practice (fetishes, exhibitionism) or object choice (children, members of the same sex) were regarded as expressions of infantile or immature sexuality, but these were merely symptoms of a deeper neurosis caused by the failure to smoothly transition from one stage of development to the next. A psychoanalytic approach to treating sexual deviation involved resolving the deeper conflict that produced the behaviour, not treating the behaviour itself.[23] In the immediate postwar era, almost all acts considered deviant were explained by an unresolved Oedipus complex, which was consistently attributed to growing up with an overbearing mother and a weak or absent father. Best known as an explanation for homosexuality, the Oedipus complex was also used to explain exhibitionism, pedophilia, and other deviations from an adult heterosexual norm.

Freud's theory fit well with postwar gender anxieties. 'Finding a place for father' in a world where it was commonly understood that women were not going to simply return to the domestic hearth was both a social imperative and a cultural problem.[24] Psychoanalysis gave scientific legitimacy to the mother- and wife-blaming that characterized the baby boom era, while at the same time propping up male authority by linking mental health and normative masculinity to mastery over women.

It was also a theory in search of a practice. In the early 1950s, psychotherapy (not psychoanalysis, an even more specialized form of therapy) was still considered a novel method of treatment. The Department of Reform Institution's Chief Psychologist F.H. Potts described it as 'educating the individual as to the nature, development and possible effects of aberrated sexual behaviour and redirecting his attitudes from fear and shame to confidence and courage adequate to make a satisfactory social adjustment.'[25] Exactly how one might 'redirect' attitudes was still something of a mystery, and defining 'satisfactory social adjustment' was, of course, entirely subjective. As so many sex experts complained, far too many treatment sessions were tarnished by psychiatrists' own moral sensibilities. Developing a scientific approach to sexual deviancy was undermined by everything from therapists' aversion to the actual patient to the use of subjective moral standards to determine what constituted 'normal' behaviour.

Sex researcher Alfred Kinsey proved to be extremely influential on this point. Kinsey's approach to sexuality was distinctly different from Freud's, yet many postwar sexologists combined Freudian theory and Kinsey's methodology. For example, Kinsey's massive surveys of human sexual behaviour served as a guiding light for postwar sexologists, particularly the staff at the Forensic Clinic in Toronto, who abandoned the traditional case study approach altogether. By subjecting their data to quantitative scrutiny, they believed they overcame the danger of moral interpretation that so clearly shaped the work of their predecessors (and contemporaries). However, their commitment to deviancy as a medical concept and to psychotherapy and psychoanalysis as methods of understanding and treating its aetiology blinded them to the moral judgements written into Freud's theories of sexual development. Furthermore, the theoretical and treatment approach that forensic sexologists like Mohr and Turner forged focused on offenders, not victims, and in so doing reproduced and reinforced a masculine heterosexual norm that was built on an unlikely combination of psychoanalytic and postwar liberal scientific approaches to understanding sexual assault.

Of particular significance were the emphasis on heterosexual coitus as 'mature' and 'normal,' the construction of normative masculine heterosexuality as aggressive and dominant, and the failure to critically examine the subtleties of power and coercion in cases of sexual assault. One thing they left unchallenged was the view held by mental health experts, magistrates, and judges (but not the general public) that in many cases children were not harmed by sexual assault. If their quantitative research is to be trusted, the Forensic Clinic staff's position may be partly explained by the fact that most sexual assaults involving children did not include physical violence, and in cases of heterosexual pedophilia did not typically involve vaginal penetration.[26] Their research showed that most instances were limited to exposing and/or touching genitalia, and in some cases digital- or oral-genital stimulation. Physical violence was extremely rare. Victims did not necessarily show signs of bruising, bleeding, or vaginal tearing, for example. Their research also showed that the dangerous stranger was less of a threat than was popularly believed. In their study, family members accounted for one-quarter of the perpetrators; just over half were neighbours or well acquainted with the victim through another close association. Only about one-fifth were strangers, making it less surprising that Forensic Clinic staff found force and coercion hardly ever played a part.

Some victims were regarded as active or complicit participants in the sexual acts in question, a claim that was given scientific legitimacy by the Forensic Clinic's research data and analysis. A major study of heterosexual pedophilia found that in most instances the age of the victims overlapped with the age at which Kinsey found girls engaging in 'early sexual explorations.' While research associate Hans Mohr and clinic director R. Edward Turner recognized that the legal system needed to treat child victims with greater care, their research findings implied that girls in this age group were receptive to the sexual advances of the adult offender. It did not occur to Mohr or Turner that their analysis might work in the other direction: offenders carefully exploited a nascent sexual curiosity, a phenomenon that today is referred to as 'grooming.' Similarly, the fact that most of the offenders they studied knew their victims and that almost none of the reported incidents involved intercourse but were limited to showing and touching, led Mohr and Turner to paint a picture that looked more like a sexual incident or event (however inappropriate or morally wrong) rather than a sexual assault with potentially traumatizing effects for the victim. Indeed, they concluded that 'the total situation in which the [pedophilic] act occurs suggests that there is a factor of mutuality between the child and adult.'[27] Ironically, the damage in these cases was psychological, an area these experts were presumably most qualified to study and explore, and yet the general view was that children were more likely to be traumatized by an overreaction on the part of the parents rather than by the actual assault.

Psychoanalysis was the main treatment method of choice at the TPH's out-patient Forensic Clinic. The clinic's approach was in keeping with trends in the United States and Britain, but the TPH clinic was unique in the world of forensic sexology in a number of ways. This was the closest Canada came to creating the ideal treatment environment that postwar experts insisted was essential if any hope of a cure was to be found. It serviced a stable group of patients in a hospital-like environment dedicated solely to their treatment; it employed a multidisciplinary treatment team composed of psychiatrists, psychologists, and social workers to deliver programs and devise research projects; it offered research support that facilitated the development of new programs, experimentation in treatment approaches, and comprehensive empirical studies of the patient population, and staff were professionally rewarded for keeping abreast of the literature and publishing their own research results. The clinic's facilities were modest, but patient participation was generally stable, staff relations were amicable, teaching and consulting responsibilities kept the clinicians vitality buoyant, and the research program was quite productive. From its opening in 1956 until it was absorbed by the new Clark Institute for Psychiatry in 1966, Forensic Clinic staff made significant contributions to the literature on sex offending and sexual deviation, much of it produced collaboratively.

The majority of the clinic's 'sex deviant' patients fell into one of three treatment groups: homosexuality, pedophilia, and exhibitionism. Patients received individual psychotherapy and were assigned to a weekly group therapy meeting organized according to their deviant type. In contrast to other treatment and research experts, the Forensic Clinic staff never collapsed homosexuals with pedophiles, something they complained other sexologists often did.[28] Each deviation appeared equally concerning when approached as a mental health problem, but when evaluated from a forensic perspective, clear distinctions were made between harm-causing behaviour (pedophilia), 'nuisance' behaviour (exhibitionism), and behaviour that was merely a deviation from the norm (homosexuality). A variety of people sought treatment for other sexual issues, among them Catholic priests hoping to learn how to sublimate their sexual desires, but their numbers and needs were never great enough to require more than individual counselling. A very small minority of patient referrals were turned away, usually because their sexual behaviour was not considered the result of a disorder, or because they were below normal intelligence and therefore, it was believed, unable to benefit from psychotherapy.

Interestingly, the majority of court referrals were exhibitionists and pedophiles, yet male homosexuals constituted the largest single group of sex deviant patients. Of these, 80 per cent were voluntary patients, meaning that they were there of their own volition or because they were referred to the clinic by a family member, a parole officer, a social service agency, or a medical doctor.[29] Exhibitionists and pedophiles, in contrast, were almost always there as the result of a court order or a parole condition. The few 'voluntary' cases usually came as the result of family pressure. Anxious to avoid the criminal justice system, families sometimes avoided laying criminal charges and instead pressured fathers, husbands, uncles, and cousins caught having sex with another family member to seek treatment. Over time, the Forensic Clinic became much more than a resource for the courts. It was also a resource for members of the broader community who sometimes took matters into their own hands.[30]

As a forensic unit, the clinic was always situated at the crossroads of law and psychiatry. The criminological categorization of sexual acts did not often fit with psychiatry's classifications of mental disorders, so staff quickly developed their own working definition of sexual deviation to help them bridge the gap.[31] Following Freud, they defined a sexual act as deviant when the final gratification was derived from non-coital acts, or, in the case of masturbation, for example, when the act interfered with 'normal' coital relations. Thus, the courts might charge a man with indecent exposure if he was caught undressed in a park (or in a parked car) while initiating consensual sex with an adult woman. In this case, the act itself was normal, unless of course the person in question was only able to achieve orgasm in a public place, in which case it was deviant. But in neither case was the person an exhibitionist. A true exhibitionist, by Mohr and Turner's definition, gained his 'final sexual gratification' from exposing his genitals in public. Therefore, indecent exposure might be a 'sex crime' and it might be morally offensive, but it was not always an expression of sexual deviation.

The approach taken by Forensic Clinic staff straddled the line between the postwar sexual liberalism most closely associated with sex researcher Alfred Kinsey, and the more conservative adherence to sex and gender normativity that historians have linked to postwar domestic retrenchment. For example, the working definition of sexual deviation clearly reinforced a heterosexual norm. However, clinic staff found this troubling precisely because it depended on a norm for its definition. Echoing Kinsey, they pointed out that norms could be defined statistically, culturally, socially, or legally, and concluded that any attempt to define a norm was more subjective than objective. By the 1960s, staff abandoned trying to 'label' their patients according to diagnostic categories and focused instead on the social context in which their patients' problematic sexual activities occurred.[32]

By drawing on Kinsey's view of sexuality as natural and variable, clinic staff believed they had left morality out of the picture and advanced a genuinely scientific, or at least medical, model for understanding and treating sexual deviations. They separated sexual problems, which they defined as issues related to the patient's own moral code, from sexual deviations, which they considered scientifically abnormal. When patients sought advice about masturbation or oral sex, acts modern sexologists did not consider abnormal as a prelude to intercourse, they were told that the problem was an individual struggle with moral and spiritual values, and were advised to seek religious counsel.

The clinic's liberal approach also extended to homosexuality. In the 1950s and 1960s, many gay and bisexual men sought treatment in the hope that they might live a fully heterosexual life. Others came looking for something quite different. Some sought help dealing with depression and anxiety that stemmed from their intimate relationships (for example, dealing with the loss of a partner), and the clinic was one of the few places gay men felt they could safely reveal their homosexuality.[33] Others hoped to learn how to control their sexual desires so that they could resist the temptation to seek out sex in public places where they were vulnerable to arrest. In these cases, treatment was at least in part patient-driven. Homosexual patients were helped to achieve the goals they set, not goals set by the staff.[34] This permissive approach was facilitated by the treatment team, who regarded homosexuality as tragic or perhaps as a social problem, but certainly not as a social threat.

Indeed, by the late 1950s, a growing number of experts were convinced that while homosexuality was a deviation from the existing norm, it was not a mental illness and was not even something that needed to be 'corrected.' At many of the clinics established to treat men convicted under criminal sexual psychopath laws, staff became critics of both the law and of the pathologization of homosexuality.[35] American homophile groups like the Mattachine Society and the Daughters of Bilitis courted those critics willing to openly express their views, regarding them as allies in the movement toward, to use the language of the period, a 'better understanding of the homosexual and his problems.' For example, at a 1959 Mattachine Society conference on Homosexuality and Mental Health, Dr. Trent Bessant, a psychologist at the Metropolitan State Hospital in Norwalk, California, where criminal sexual psychopaths were treated, unequivocally stated that the mental stresses homosexuals experienced were caused by social and cultural prejudice, not by homosexuality itself.[36] The audience broke out in applause. Significantly, this event came two years after the publication of psychologist Evelyn Hooker's study of male homosexuals, in which she famously challenged the pathologization of homosexuality. Hooker was in the audience for Bessant's presentation, and when asked by one of the panellists whether she believed homosexuality was a mental illness, would only say that in her *personal* opinion 'she had a very tentative "no" in mind.' Forensic sexologists laid the groundwork for the campaign to remove homosexuality from the American Psychiatric Association's *Diagnostic and Statistical Manual of Mental Disorders* well before Hooker committed herself to taking a clear position against its pathologization.[37]

Staff at the TPH's Forensic Clinic never took on the role of legal or psychiatric reform activists (at least not publicly), but their 'sympathetic attitude' was enough to make them allies of the nascent homophile movement in Canada. In 1964 members of the Vancouver-based Association for Social Knowledge, one of the country's first gay organizations, invited Director R. Edward Turner to speak with them about the clinic's work, and subsequently lobbied their provincial government for a similar treatment program in Vancouver.[38] Given the association's commitment to creating a social, intellectual, and political space for exploring and developing a better understanding and acceptance of homosexuality, it seems likely that they imagined such a clinic as a positive space for gays and lesbians.

A progressive attitude toward homosexuality did not mean that experts finally rejected Freudian theory. Throughout this period, Turner, the clinic's director; Paitich, the staff psychologist; and Mohr, the full-time research associate, remained wedded to psychoanalysis. They maintained that male homosexuality was produced by a combination of dominating mothers who stood between their sons and normal sex and gender development, and weak or absent fathers who failed to provide the necessary masculine heterosexual role model.[39] However, here again they combined a Freudian view of sex and gender development with Kinsey's model of variable sexual experience. Turner and Mohr argued that experts should abandon the idea of exclusive homosexuality and 'absolute cure' and instead 'think in terms of the homosexual-heterosexual balance and what tips the scale in terms of actual behaviour.'[40] Using the Kinsey scale, which posited that there were few exclusive homosexuals or heterosexuals, Paitich, Turner, and Mohr reasoned that everyone had the potential to move from one end of the spectrum to the other. Seen this way, the job of the therapist shifted from exposing and resolving the Oedipus conflict to simply encouraging some, and discouraging other, sexual activities. As we shall see, when experts began losing faith in psychotherapy, the treatment model shifted away from uncovering hidden childhood conflicts toward changing present-day behaviour through the use of behaviour modification therapy.

Dominating mothers and weak or absent fathers were also used to explain the two other major deviations that consumed the clinic's work: exhibitionism and pedophilia. This is particularly noteworthy, since the clinic treated each of the deviations as discrete groups and in so doing found differences among them, yet they continued to adhere to a single causal model. For example, heterosexual pedophiles and homosexual pedophiles showed very different patterns of offending behaviour.

Heterosexual pedophiles were most likely to have known the victim, chose girls between the ages of six and twelve, and rarely sought orgasm. Patients also described experiencing feelings of shame concerning their actions. Because the nature of the sexual activity was non-coital, treatment staff concluded that it resembled child sex play, thus confirming it as an expression of 'immature' sexuality in the Freudian sense of the term. Patients in this group married later than the average Canadian male, which was taken as further evidence of their immaturity. Studies of their criminal history suggested that of the three groups, these patients were the least likely to reoffend, leading Mohr and Turner to conclude that in most cases heterosexual pedophilia was 'transient' and 'situational,' usually caused by marital breakdown and loneliness.[41]

In contrast, homosexual pedophiles typically sought out boys between the ages of twelve and fourteen (clinical staff did not consider sexual activity with a person over fourteen to be pedophilic), were very likely to reoffend, and in most cases sought and achieved orgasm. As a rule, they did not express feelings of shame for having sex with minors. Because the type of sexual activity they engaged in was no different than the kinds of sexual activity adult homosexuals engaged in with each other, staff did not regard it as 'immature' sexuality, which is striking since, according to classic psychoanalytic theory, homosexuality of any kind is immature. Turner and Mohr also concluded that homosexual pedophiles were more like heterosexual pedophiles than they were like homosexuals, thus setting themselves apart from a number of leading U.S. experts who characterized all male homosexuals as actual or potential pedophiles.

Exhibitionism proved much more difficult to understand, since the final sexual gratification did not involve physical contact with another person. Turner and Mohr rejected earlier sexological reports that attributed the practice to moral depravity, epilepsy, and mental disease, and instead saw it as a compulsive behaviour intended to cause an emotional reaction in a (usually adult female) stranger, although exactly what reaction was desired was never clear. Patients claimed that their objective was to attract a woman's interest with the hope of having sexual relations, but staff were convinced that they were actually quite fearful of women and that to be approached after exposing was the worst possible outcome for the exhibitionist.[42]

Solving the mystery of exhibitionism meant focusing on when and why men exposed their genitals in public to strangers. Quantitative analysis showed that of the three treatment groups, exhibitionists were the most likely to reoffend and were the only group whose behaviour seemed to be compulsive. It also revealed that most began exposing during puberty or while they were in their early to mid-twenties, periods that Turner and Mohr linked to the development of masculine identity, heterosexual relationships, and sexual and social confidence. In puberty, they argued, 'the patient is usually engaged in a struggle of freeing himself from a mother who has endangered his masculinity.' If he does not successfully gain control over his masculinity, he is doomed to continue to suffer from feelings of inferiority. The man who begins offending in his mid-twenties is acting out stresses created during courtship and early married life, when he finds himself 'attracted and bound to a female whom, never the less, he experiences as threatening and frustrating.'[43] They concluded that exposing was driven by the patient's need to prove his masculinity. Because he was fearful of women, normal social intercourse was problematic; eliciting a reaction by exposing the penis from a distance bolstered his flagging sense of manhood. This seemed to fit with exhibitionists' own reports that they were most satisfied when women reacted with horror, revulsion, or even fear, and least satisfied when they were ignored, laughed at, or ridiculed. It also reveals how both patient and therapist linked masculinity with male sexual dominance and female sexual subordination.

As far as the Forensic Clinic staff was concerned, heterosexual men who grew up with an overbearing mother and an absent or weak father recreated similar patterns in their married life. In fact, according to staff psychologist Daniel Paitich, a dominating wife provided the 'vital clue' to both the heterosexual pedophile and the exhibitionist's 'condition.'[44] Both exhibitionists and pedophiles suffered from underdeveloped masculinity. Exhibitionists therefore exposed to women out of a need to prove their masculinity, which they were unable to do at home because of either an overbearing mother or an overbearing wife who thwarted their ability to express mastery over their domain, a decidedly masculine trait that was essential to a healthy heterosexual life. Pedophiles similarly suffered from the stifling effects of an overbearing mother. For them, pre-pubescent girls were the preferred sexual object choice since girls lacked the maternal qualities that adult women possessed and that reminded them of their mothers, which invoked feelings of inferiority and inadequacy. According to Turner, Mohr, and other postwar forensic sexologists, one important aspect of treatment for exhibitionism and heterosexual pedophilia was to help the men who engaged in such behaviour to strengthen their masculinity by becoming more assertive at home.[45]

Mohr and Turner were careful not to blame wives for their husbands' actions, but they did see the wife's behaviour as 'co-relational,' meaning that her patterns of relating to her husband aggravated his 'condition' by elevating the stresses that led the husband to offend.[46] Treatment staff held that marrying dominating women exacerbated men's feelings of inadequacy and failed masculinity. So significant was this dynamic that the clinic ran group therapy for the wives of exhibitionists whom staff believed actively sabotaged their husbands' treatment. Exhibitionistic patients frequently claimed that they missed group therapy meetings because their wives committed them to other social or practical engagements. Assuming that staff was savvy to typical patient excuses for absenteeism, one might speculate that some wives were not terribly pleased to find themselves subjected to assertions of masculine authority at home.

Despite the 'ideal' treatment and research conditions, the Forensic Clinic could claim few successes with their patients. According to virtually all reports, the model psychotherapy candidate was intelligent and self-motivated. However, a study undertaken in the TPH's in-patient Forensic Unit showed that patients ordered into treatment were resentful, antisocial, suspicious, and would rather 'just forget the whole thing.'[47] Reticence was a serious obstacle, since individual and group therapy required full and willing cooperation. However, even among those patients who continued well after their mandatory treatment period had ended, and among homosexuals who were by far the most motivated and willing patients, the results were disappointing. The failure to produce meaningful changes in sexual behaviour threatened the future of sexology and had to have been enormously frustrating for individual practitioners.

By the end of the 1950s, it was clear that psychoanalysis was good for diagnosing sexual deviancy, but not terribly useful for treating it. Years of individual and group therapy sessions had no impact on patients' sexual choices. Some blamed this on patients' defence mechanisms and began experimenting with a variety of methods to break down resistance. Hypnosis was tried, but pharmaceuticals proved easier to administer and required no special training for doctors. Sodium amytal, widely used by Canadian military doctors during the Second World War, was known for its ability to 'produce an "easily controlled hypnotic state."'[48] Injected intravenously, it made patients drowsy and produced a 'lowered state of consciousness' during which time 'inhibitory processes are released, rapport is often produced and suppressed conflictual material is brought into consciousness.'[49] As Maritime psychiatrist Dr Menzies explained, 'once that needle gets in the vein, why, you get co-operation.'[50] Psychiatrists at the Forensic Clinic and elsewhere used the drug to conduct 'intensive psychiatric interviews.'[51]

Another popular pharmaceutical was D-lysergic acid diethylamide (LSD). Invented in 1938, Sandoz Laboratories distributed it free of charge to scientists interested in exploring its therapeutic potential, and it was quickly adapted as a psychotherapeutic aid for the treatment of sex deviation. In a 1961 article in the *Canadian Psychiatric Association Journal,* J.R. Ball and Jean J. Armstrong describe an experiment at England's Royal Victoria Infirmary at Newcastle upon Tyne involving ten voluntary, out-patient subjects, six of whom were described as homosexual (one female, five males), one as transsexualist, and another as transvestist (two are not indicated).[52] Participants were given the drug to facilitate a single session of psychoanalysis, and while it certainly had a brief consciousness-altering effect, Ball and Armstrong reported no lasting change in the patient's sexual behaviour and concluded that treatment with LSD will 'probably ... often fail.' Despite this, they recommended it be adopted as 'one extra weapon in our armoury,' demonstrating just how utterly desperate some experts had become. When the TPH's Forensic Clinic hired Ball in the early 1960s, he continued to experiment with LSD.

Pharmaceuticals were intended to facilitate psychotherapy, not replace it. As Jonathan Metzel points out in his study of women and psychopharmacology in America, historians have erroneously characterized the postwar popularity of drugs to treat a variety of neurotic and depressive conditions as a step away from the psychoanalytic paradigm and a return to a biological model.[53] In fact, drugs were prescribed (and advertised) to treat symptoms and conditions that were given shape and meaning through psychoanalytic frames. Forcing patients to take a hallucinogenic drug readily conjures up images of the mad doctor, but psychiatrists like Ball are better understood as frustrated Freudians.

Eventually some of the younger staff began experimenting with aversion therapy, but not without controversy. Known as operant conditioning (now called systematic desensitization), psychotherapist Joseph Wolpe championed it in his 1958 classic *Psychotherapy by Reciprocal Inhibition.* The method of treatment involved the slow and careful introduction of an anxiety-causing stimulus that was to be used as a means to overcome 'irrational' or disturbing anxiety responses.[54] Chief Psychologist H.C. Hutchison and Staff Psychologist I.K. Bond were probably the first in Canada to apply Wolpe's methods for the treatment of sex deviation. In

1959 the clinic's director reluctantly allowed them to attempt the treatment with a homosexual and an exhibitionist, both of whom were considered 'intractable, very severe cases.'[55] Wolpe himself was keen to learn of their progress and corresponded with the project leaders.[56] Bond and Hutchinson triumphantly published a positive result in the case of the exhibitionist, who later reoffended.[57] They immediately began planning a new experiment, this time employing aversion therapy to treat a pedophile who was rejected for psychotherapy because of his low scores on intelligence testing.[58]

The use of conditioning was controversial, and divided the clinic's otherwise amicable staff into opponents, who preferred to stay the course with psychotherapy, and proponents, who were anxious to achieve success with all of the clinic's referrals.[59] Indeed, in 'helping' patients resolve hidden conflicts, experts were driven by frustration with the failure of psychotherapy, but restrained by the personal and professional views of the treatment team. For example, the clinic's director reluctantly approved Ball's experiments with LSD, and even then on a very limited basis. In a prison setting, however, where consent was always mediated by coercion and where the treatment paradigm was subordinated to the disciplinary regimen, there existed an enormous potential for abuse.[60] The next chapter shows the very different ways treatment for sex criminals was, and was not, applied inside Ontario's prison system. Aversion therapy is also explored in greater detail.

The treatment of sex crime as a mental health problem received public support and official sanction in Ontario, but the Forensic Clinic never came close to achieving its goal. Indeed, of all the sex deviant treatment programs that operated in the postwar period, not a single one could claim success in reducing recidivism. Though many treatment experts hastily pronounced positive results within months of the end of a program of treatment, a series of comprehensive longitudinal studies confirmed that, in most cases, sex offenders who received treatment of any kind did not have a lower incidence of recidivism and in some cases had an even higher rate than untreated populations.[61] Studies of the Forensic Clinic's patient population revealed that homosexual pedophiles were most likely to seek out sexual activity with a stranger, while heterosexual pedophiles were most likely to pursue a female child known to them.[62] First-time sex offenders were the least likely of all criminals to reoffend, but the more one offended, the greater the likelihood he would continue to reoffend. However, as researchers lamented in their own time, no matter how accurate the profile they were able to create of different types of sex offenders, it did nothing to prevent sex crime from happening.

Nevertheless, as a form of knowledge and power over the field of sexuality, forensic sexology was a complete success. From the time the clinic opened in 1956 until it was absorbed by the new Clarke Institute of Psychiatry a decade later, the director reported increasing numbers of patients who sought treatment on their own initiative. Voluntary patients believed they had a sexual abnormality that could be, and should be, treated.[63] The annual rise in the number of voluntary patients is a testament to how everyday people absorbed the postwar construction of pathological sexuality by becoming self-regulating citizens.

In Toronto and elsewhere, a significant number of forensic sexologists became critical of sex norms in general, and in the way homosexuals were vilified and marginalized in mainstream society in particular. Bringing psychiatric and psychological expertise to bear on matters of law and criminal regulation led many forensic sexologists to ask important questions about how the law acted as a moral regulator. A 'sympathetic' approach was hardly revolutionary, but to offer compassionate understanding to homosexuals, exhibitionists, pedophiles, and other reviled sex deviants led them to cast a critical eye on the sexual politics of their own time. Influenced by Alfred Kinsey's studies in human sexual behaviour, they practised, if not championed, an unusual brand of sexual liberalism. Tolerant of variation and critical of essentialism, they nevertheless continued to adhere to Freudian and other models of behavioural development that located adult sexual behaviour in childhood family relations.

Neither Freud nor Kinsey could open their eyes to the way women and children figured into the equation, including the ways victims of sexual assault were harmed by certain sexual offences. Indeed, Kinsey's findings were used to support the pre–Second World War contention that victims of sexual assault were sexually precocious and even willing partners. Not until the 1970s and 1980s did feminists successfully challenge sexist, patriarchal assumptions that shaped the way women and children were treated in the courts, by police officers, and by the helping professions. Insisting that morality had no place in either the law or medicine may have laid the foundation for the delisting of homosexuality as a disease, but forensic sexology continued to perpetuate a model of sexuality that equated normative male desire with mastery over women. It may have been a compassionate and sympathetic approach to dealing with sex offenders, but the assumptions about masculinity and sexuality that informed postwar sexology demonstrate a remarkable blindness to the ways gender and power shaped so many of the sexual encounters that brought their patients to them.

chapter five

Sex Deviant Treatment in Ontario Prisons

In the 1950s, treatment experts agreed that the prison environment was the least likely place for any kind of psychotherapy to be successfully undertaken. In Ontario, the Department of Reform Institutions' own research and treatment policy statement conceded that the conflict between the need to protect society from the criminal, and the desire to effect the reformation and rehabilitation of the prisoner, made it 'impossible to achieve the maximum rehabilitation in the presence of maximum security.'[1] As Justin Ciale, the psychologist at Quebec's federal penitentiary St Vincent de Paul, explained, it is impossible to help an inmate work toward normal socialization in such an abnormal social environment. Therapy in prison, he continued, is thwarted by the 'serious personality modifications' caused by emotional starvation and deprivation of liberty. The antisocial and non-compliant attitude of most prisoners, the 'defiant, authoritarian and oftentimes suspicious atmosphere' of the prison, and the greater need to help an inmate adjust to the prison environment meant that it was unlikely treatment staff would ever come close to addressing the behaviour that brought him to prison.[2] If the government was serious about shifting from a punitive model to a therapeutic one, he argued, it would have to reconsider the entire structure of the penal system. Employing a handful of psychiatrists was not going to do the trick.

In 1948 the House of Commons passed criminal sexual psychopath legislation into law. As was shown in earlier chapters, this was a direct result of the efforts of English Canadian parents who embraced the mental health movement's promise of solving long-standing social problems. As it turned out, however, the federal government was not at all serious about shifting away from the traditional punitive model. Indeed, as the

1938 *Report of the Royal Commission to Investigate the Penal System of Canada* revealed, basic living conditions in Canada's federal prison system were extremely poor. Despite its long list of recommendations, Ottawa's efforts to provide even the most basic medical services for inmates continued to move at a snail's pace. Criminal sexual psychopath legislation, which allowed for the indeterminate sentencing of sex criminals until deemed cured by a psychiatrist, was passed by a unanimous vote in the House of Commons in 1948, but it was not until the mid-1970s that the federal government created a treatment program for sex offenders.[3] Some inmates convicted under the legislation received individual counselling from the prison psychiatrist, and the psychiatrist at British Columbia's federal penitentiary ran his own individual and group therapy sessions for that institution's dangerous sexual offenders. But as a confidential memo from the solicitor general to all penitentiary wardens noted, 'in general our institutions are not equipped to carry out intensive observation and diagnosis [for sex and violent offenders].'[4] A 1973 Committee on Sexual and Dangerous Sexual Offenders, appointed by the commissioner of penitentiaries, described current treatment efforts as 'limited and inadequate.'[5] At the federal level, the dream of turning prisons into therapeutic communities never came close to being realized.

In Canada, people sentenced to periods of incarceration for anything less than two years serve their time in provincial, not federal, institutions. The provinces were therefore never responsible for men found to be criminal sexual psychopaths or dangerous sex offenders. However, provincial governments were responsible for men charged with a wide variety of sex crimes, and they were also subject to public pressure to provide these offenders with treatment. In contrast to Ottawa's general indifference to the mental and physical health of its prisoners, treatment programs for sexual deviation fit well with the goals and ideals of the 'Ontario Plan,' an ambitious project introduced by the Ontario Department of Reform Institutions (DRI) in 1947. Officially, its objective was to transform the province's military-style custodial institutions into hospital-like treatment facilities where inmates could get the help they needed in adjusting to the demands of everyday life.[6] The goals of the Ontario Plan were never achieved, but significant efforts were made toward treating recidivist populations, that included alcoholics, drug addicts, and sex criminals.

In the early 1950s, convicted criminals serving time in an Ontario reformatory who were also alcoholics and drug addicts were selected to participate in programs located in a well-appointed treatment facility in the small town of Mimico, near Toronto. The clinic was inspired by progressive reform activists who favoured compassionate medicine over punitive imprisonment, but staff at the Alex G. Brown Memorial Clinic quickly learned that upper-level administrators, including the DRI's deputy minister, Colonel Hedley Basher, and its chief of psychiatry and neurology, Dr Frank van Nostrand, both veterans of the Second World War, were openly hostile toward any program that departed from traditional military-style rule and discipline.[7] Efforts to run a treatment program for sexual deviation were stymied for the same reason, but sex offender treatment programs faced an additional challenge: when they were finally put in place in the mid-1950s, they came to be used as a tool to manage what was called the prison sex problem.

Beginning in 1955, men found guilty of a sex offence in Ontario were sent to the Neuro-Psychiatric Clinic (NPC) at the Ontario Reformatory in Guelph, a minimum-security institution. By 1957, however, the DRI's chief psychiatrist, Dr van Nostrand, orchestrated the diversion of most 'sex deviates' to a newly created wing at the Millbrook Reformatory, where the day-to-day experience of serving time was intentionally punitive and treatment was practically non-existent. The majority of the inmates sent to the 'sex pervert' wing were convicted of offences involving children under the age of fourteen and were therefore considered pedophiles. Men convicted of incest were included in this group. The remainder were those identified as homosexual by the prison administration and were sent to Millbrook regardless of the nature of the offence that brought them into the prison system. Officially, the purpose of the wing was to create a place where sex criminals could be treated, but DRI records clearly demonstrate that the real purpose was to improve prison discipline. Either way, neither group was offered meaningful treatment. Experts in the know denounced Millbrook as a 'storage bin' for problem inmates. What appeared to the average Ontario citizen as 'progress' was looked upon with dismay by advocates of reform.

Using sex offender treatment programs to regulate a prison discipline problem exemplifies the clash of objectives between those who operated prisons and those who sought to treat deviant prisoners. As was shown in chapter 2, public support for sex offender treatment was widespread. 'Soft-pated' psychological approaches, however, were vigorously opposed within prisons and penitentiaries. Though both the custodian and the psychologist essentially wanted the same thing – cooperation, compliance, and voluntary submission – they had starkly opposing ideas about how to procure it and for what end. Mental health experts encountered aggressive resistance at all levels of the DRI, from the deputy minister and prison superintendents all the way down to custodial officers and inmates themselves. Despite the positive assessment that mental health expertise enjoyed in the civilian world, it suffered a wretched fate in Ontario prisons. Mental health approaches to understanding and interacting with prisoners challenged the authority of prison staff by raising fundamental questions about the logic and legitimacy of the prison itself. The mental health approach also demanded a radically different form of human interaction than the existing hierarchy allowed. Mental health experts and their supporters made little headway in penetrating the DRI's military-style culture of discipline and control.

This chapter explores the history of sex offender treatment in Ontario's provincial prison system from the mid-1950s to 1973. Top DRI administrators harnessed political and popular support for the treatment of 'sex deviants' to extend the maintenance of order and control over inmates. Seen through the administrators' eyes, a sex deviation treatment program was an ideal way to deal with the prison sex problem – to segregate homosexuals and men who sought out sex from other men from other inmates. The DRI claimed to offer a distinct program for treating 'sex deviants,' but what the public had demanded was treatment for men who sexually assaulted children.[8] Convinced that pedophilia was on the rise, and that most, if not all, pedophiles were recidivists, English Canadian parents were certain that a mental health approach to solving the problem could bring an end to sexual assault against children. Even though the public would likely have supported treatment for homosexuality, pedophilia was the principal concern. Once treatment was in the hands of the prison administration, however, disciplinary imperatives trumped public sentiment. The history of sex offender treatment in Ontario prisons must be understood in this context.

Establishing a clinic to treat incarcerated sex offenders was one thing. Finding the staff to run it was another. The DRI had tremendous difficulty hiring and keeping qualified staff to run sex criminal treatment programs, in part because there were almost no Canadian psychiatrists or psychologists with experience working in the area of sexual deviation, and precious few who could be enticed into the field. Moreover, economic planning for postwar reconstruction meant that there were plenty of decent jobs to go around. With the growing popularity of industrial psychology, and the high demand for social work services in the expanding welfare state, a DRI offer of low-paying employment in a hostile and occasionally violent work environment in isolated parts of the province was not much of a draw.[9] Even those with a particular interest in working with the criminal population were more likely to take up a position with the Ontario Parole Board, which, under the auspices of the attorney general, paid its social work and psychological staff significantly better wages.

Psychiatrists and psychologists who did accept work in Ontario prisons quickly learned that most of the DRI's upper administration was overwhelmingly hostile toward the provision of mental health treatment services for prisoners. Major John Foote, the minister of the Department of Reforms from 1950 to 1957, was a staunch advocate of the Ontario Plan, but his staff was not. His own deputy minister, Colonel G. Hedley Basher remained steadfast in his refusal to assist psychologists in any way, and regularly undermined their efforts to address some of the institutional problems plaguing inmates.[10] Basher was the superintendent of the Guelph Reformatory when the Ontario Plan was introduced, and he was reprimanded for ignoring psychological reports regarding appropriate work assignments for inmates. He was later promoted to deputy minister, but not because he had a change of heart. According to Donald MacDonald, the outspoken leader of the provincial Co-operative Commonwealth Federation, Basher had a nineteenth-century military management style. The DRI is 'Basher's empire,' he argued, 'and the motto of that empire is "Bash 'em."'[11] Director of Psychiatry and Neurology Dr Frank van Nostrand, whose service as a military doctor during the Second World War clearly influenced his hard-nosed management style, consistently supported Basher's approach.[12]

Hostility was compounded by parsimony. Canada's federal and provincial governments had long been tight-fisted in the administration of prisons, even in times of economic prosperity. Newly recruited psychiatrists quickly realized that individual therapy, the most time-consuming and consequently the most expensive form of treatment, was virtually impossible to provide in an ongoing fashion.[13] In post–Second World War Canada, United States, and Britain, group therapy emerged as an economical alternative. Not only could treatment be provided to an entire group in just a single hour, group therapy sessions could be led by lesser-paid staff, such as psychologists, social workers, and even trained custodial officers.[14]

Group therapy also contributed to building therapeutic communities, the other landmark development in institutional treatment in this period. While practising in British military hospitals during the Second

World War, Maxwell Jones re-imagined the hospital as an organic society where everyone played a role in patients' emotional and social rehabilitation.[15] His model was based on creating planned, structured activities in which every human interaction, including those between patients, had an intrinsic therapeutic value. This way, patients actively participated in their own 'adjustment,' and the therapeutic role that non-medical staff played was recognized and validated. Medical experts who advocated prison reform touted the therapeutic community model as the next, obvious step forward in the way modern society could address criminal behaviour.[16] Indeed, some of the most enthusiastic reformers predicted that by the end of the 1960s, the entire prison system would disappear and be replaced with therapeutic communities. Obviously, this never came to pass, but later we will see how Jones's ideas were applied in two different sex deviant treatment programs, one at the Guelph Reformatory in Ontario and the other at the Metropolitan State Hospital hospital program for sexual psychopaths in Norwalk, California.

The public demand for sex offender treatment in Ontario began in 1947 with the widely reported sexual assault and murder of Arlene Anderson, a young disabled Toronto girl. In response to the public outcry, the Department of Health appointed seven psychiatrists to a Committee on Sex Delinquency with a mandate to explore the possibility of creating a treatment program.[17] Contrary to the commonly held view that psychiatrists were eager to expand their realm of authority and expertise, committee members were sceptical about the initiative. Most felt there were not enough sex offenders in the prison system to warrant such a program. They also pointed out that there was little authoritative data on the issue of treating sexual deviation or even of the benefit of singling out sex criminals as a distinct group. Finally, they concluded that there were no proven methods of treatment.[18] In the end, they would only recommend more research.

Once the question fell into the hands of the Department of Reform Institutions, the sex deviant treatment program was seen from an entirely different perspective. In the spring of 1952, renewed public pressure to provide treatment for incarcerated sexual deviants prompted the minister to assign his department's chief psychologist to investigate the matter. In his report, F.H. Potts supported the idea on the grounds that a separate clinic for sex deviates would allow Guelph Reformatory, the province's largest adult prison, to get rid of its homosexual inmates.[19] Segregating homosexual inmates from the rest of the prison population clearly did nothing to satisfy the public demand for treatment for incarcerated child molesters. Yet none of the administrative records acknowledge that internal uses of such a clinic differed from public desire, suggesting either that Potts and his colleagues considered homosexuals, as 'sex deviants,' appropriate targets for transfer to a clinic, or that they were so well isolated from public scrutiny that consideration of public desire was rarely, if ever, put before the drive to maintain traditional forms of regulation.

Disagreement occurred around defining who the problem homosexuals were. For van Nostrand and many other prison administrators who came of age in the pre–Second World War era, effeminate homosexuals were a major disciplinary problem since, in addition to defying gender norms, they persistently provoked and aroused other men's sexual passions.[20] Potts's thinking was more in line with post–Second World War experts who viewed tough, masculine prisoners who sought out weaker men as sexual partners as the source of the problem. As he explained in his final recommendation, creating a separate clinic where 'homosexuals' could be incarcerated would eliminate the 'grave danger' posed by inmates who 'engage in aberrant sexual activity.' 'Morale generally is likely to be improved if this group is segregated because it is not unusual to find that several, for example homosexuals, may combine forces in any Institution and through intimidation and force make normal boys indulge in abnormal sex practices with them.'[21] Unlike van Nostrand, Potts was less concerned with the 'queens' and 'fairies' who were already kept in a segregated unit than he was with 'wolves' who used real violence, or the mere threat of violence, to coerce other inmates into having sex.[22] Wolves did not consider themselves, nor were they considered by others, to be 'homosexual.' However, in the postwar era, when definitions of sexual identity shifted from gender to the biological sex of one's sexual partners, wolves were increasingly characterized as homosexual. More important, they were also more likely to be considered the root of the 'prison sex problem.' Indeed, Potts's proposal was likely influenced by a psychological report issued only a few months earlier that identified sexual violence as one of inmates' main grievances.[23] Potts believed that by segregating 'wolves,' the department would protect younger inmates from becoming homosexual prey, while at the same time creating an opportunity to conduct research into the treatment of homosexuality.

Perhaps it was confusion and disagreement over who was homosexual and which homosexuals were a disciplinary problem that explains the failure to take any action on Potts's proposal. However, just two years

later, the provincial Select Committee on Problems of Delinquent
Individuals and Custodial Questions spent an entire day discussing sex
criminals and deviant sexual behaviour within the prison system. When
committee members asked DRI Minister Foote about the current procedure for placing men charged with sex crimes, he defended his department's failure to develop a policy on the grounds that there were no
medical treatments known to help sex deviants. A strong supporter of
prison reform, he nevertheless saw no use 'in just herding them into one
place.'[24] Aldwyn B. Stokes, a professor of psychiatry at the University of
Toronto and head psychiatrist at the Toronto Psychiatric Hospital's in-
patient Forensic Unit, countered that the only way for experts to discover effective treatments was to create research opportunities, which
would be provided by clinical programs. 'If we could get an understanding of how far our present treatment measures can assist,' Stokes
explained, 'we would be making some advance.'[25] The committee was
convinced, and in its final report recommended that a detailed study of
sex offenders be made to help guide magistrates in sentencing; that sex
offenders be given indefinite sentences that were not to be determined
until 'curative measures have taken effect'; that a separate close-security
unit, adequately staffed with trained personnel, be established for their
treatment; and that an extensive study should be undertaken to develop
an understanding of the nature of sex deviation and the methods of
dealing with it.[26] Since men who committed sex crimes and men who
had sex with other men inside prison were both considered 'sex deviants,' little or no distinction was made between what the contemporary
reader clearly recognizes as two separate matters.

Two significant initiatives were undertaken toward meeting the committee's recommendations. Plans for two new DRI facilities already
under construction – the first a hospital ward for prisoners diagnosed
with tuberculosis, and the second a maximum-security prison in the
town of Millbrook – were modified to create a separate space for housing
and treating sex deviants. The TB unit was changed to a Neuro-Psychiatric Clinic (NPC), where sexually deviated prisoners were given priority.
Plans for Millbrook, a new facility intended to siphon off the most violent
and non-compliant prisoners from the Guelph Reformatory, were modified to accommodate a special sex deviant wing for prisoners whose sexual aggression toward other inmates made them a disciplinary problem
or threat in a regular reformatory.

At the official opening ceremony in 1955, the DRI proudly boasted
that the NPC was to be more than just a treatment facility. It was also des-

ignated as a research centre, the first of its kind in Canada. Here, all first-time offenders convicted of carnal knowledge, incest, rape, assault with intent to commit rape, indecent assault, indecent exposure, seduction, and buggery were to receive a complete psychological and psychiatric examination as well as treatment.[27] Interestingly, gross indecency, the charge most commonly laid against men caught having sex with men, was not included on this list, reflecting the priorities established by the public, not those of the prison administration. However, case files reveal that homosexual men were patients in the NPC.

Like many postwar sexologists, the one hired to run the NPC embraced psychotherapy. What inmate patients needed, claimed Dr Buckner, was 'insight into the fact that they were individually responsible for their actions, to give them confidence in themselves, and to help them [learn] to cooperate with their fellow beings.' Buckner was an advocate of the therapeutic community; he rejected the hierarchical doctor-patient model and favoured active patient participation in an organized collective of enlightened participants. He aspired to socialize patients out of the prisoner culture of hostility, suspicion, and resistance and into a clinical culture of healing by pairing new patients with established ones who supported and accepted the treatment program. He showed inmates the federal Department of Health and Welfare's series of Mental Mechanisms films to help explain the concept of unconscious motivation and the fundamental drives of human behaviour.[28] Inmates were expected to participate in the day-to-day operation of the clinic, from running the library to producing an in-house newsletter and participating in and even leading group therapy sessions.

Buckner was soon frustrated with the lack of progress among his patients, and he was not alone. As we saw in chapter 4, treatment in a medical facility, even when conducted on an out-patient basis with voluntary patients, was unsuccessful. Prison psychiatrists and psychologists across Canada and the United States felt they suffered additional obstacles. They complained that prisoners were hostile to psychotherapy, that they refused to take responsibility for their actions, and that they suspected treatment would be used against them.[29] Even in the NPC's hospital-like setting, Buckner struggled against patient resistance.

To overcome this, selected inmates were treated twice weekly with CO_2. Carbon dioxide therapy was popularized in the 1950s and used to treat a variety of disorders, including anxiety states, phobias, obsessive-compulsive neurosis, and depression, all of which were seen as being at the root of homosexuality.[30] With a 'controlled' application of carbon dioxide, subjects were immediately robbed of oxygen, inciting a panic state. Once oxygen was returned to the lungs, patients frequently experienced a violent outburst. The theory was that these outbursts of aggression broke though protective mechanisms and rendered a patient more open to exploring repressed emotions through the preferred method of treatment, psychotherapy.

Author and ex-inmate Roger Caron was one of the 'hostile' inmates Buckner treated this way. Caron 'volunteered' as an alternative to receiving the strap for an earlier infraction.[31] As described in his prison memoir, *Go-Boy!*, he was escorted into a small room where, without warning or explanation, he was placed in a full-length canvas sack 'with a heavy-duty zipper running from head to foot.' The sack was strapped to the table. A mask was clamped over his mouth and nose. Caron was instantly unable to breathe; he panicked, 'thinking that the doctor goofed.' He described a 'buzzing sound as if my brain were being invaded by wasps'; he 'felt a surge of super human strength,' the faces in the room appeared 'hairy,' and the room started to spin. 'I was being engulfed by a wave as thick and dark as molasses, a wave that was carrying me off into a shadowy world full of lurking horrors, a universe of flashing lights and buzzing sounds, sounds that were getting louder and louder until I was being consumed.' Once the mask was removed, Caron 'felt an intense anger and began thrashing about.' He endured seven treatments in three weeks and finally quit.[32] It is not known whether Buckner used CO_2 with his sexually deviated patients, but it was considered an appropriate and effective treatment in such cases.[33]

The DRI appeared unconcerned with the goings-on at the NPC until Buckner violated government protocol by inviting a CBC radio journalist to witness a CO_2 treatment without first gaining the department's permission. Bucker defended himself on the grounds that just a short time earlier the minister insisted that any journalist was free to visit and report on any prison at any time. Van Nostrand retorted that Buckner's actions violated a number of regulations, including the obligation to protect inmates' identities. Shortly thereafter, the administration received a letter from an ex-prisoner who claimed that he was forced to participate in group therapy with other sex offenders. The group was led by two prisoners who demanded that he reveal details about his sexual relationship with his wife, something that he refused to do. Permitting inmates to run group therapy was in keeping with the therapeutic community ideal. However, staff members confirmed that Buckner had allowed two inmates to exert authority over other patients.[34] Department officials rarely paid attention to prisoners' complaints, but when inmates provided van Nostrand with the ammunition he needed to shut down the NPC, he proved an enthusiastic listener. Van Nostrand declared group therapy to be problematic in a prison setting, particularly for those convicted of sex offences. An inmate might reveal other crimes for which he had not been charged, he explained, and emotionally vulnerable participants might reveal personal details or information that could be used for personal gain by less ethical participants.[35] Though van Nostrand was never a champion of therapeutic treatment for prisoners, it is true that confidentiality was a significant problem for inmates involved in group therapy and led some to refuse to participate.[36]

It was also of some concern that the two inmates accused of dominating the NPC program were homosexual. Taking his cues from Maxwell Jones, Buckner adopted a liberal attitude toward homosexuality, but prison administrations were of a different mind on the matter.[37] DRI superintendents ran prisons like boot camp, relying on a military-style regimen to maintain control over inmates and public confidence in the prison system. The slightest appearance of institutional laxity was instant fodder for political point-making in the House of Commons. Although the DRI's most persistent public critics – the CCF and Stuart Jaffray of the University of Toronto School of Social Work – usually attacked the department for not taking the treatment ideal far enough, it is unlikely that even they would countenance giving homosexuals 'free reign.'

Buckner's group therapy sessions also violated one of the longest-standing practices in Canadian and American prisons: keeping younger inmates away from the corrupting influence of adult prisoners, especially if the older prisoner was known to engage in homosexual practices. Participants reportedly included some 'seasoned sex offenders, past middle-age, and some young first offenders,' leading van Nostrand to conclude that 'these sessions should have never been tolerated!'[38] Even more worrisome was the dormitory-style housing all NPC patients shared. In a memo to the deputy minister, van Nostrand complained that the Ontario Training School boys who shared some of the adult prison facilities were 'forced or permitted to associate with hardened incorrigible sexual deviates whose conversation appears to centre around abnormal sexual practices.'[39]

Despite van Nostrand's complaints, Buckner refused to change the way he ran the NPC and continued to openly violate orders from the Guelph superintendent and even from van Nostrand, claiming a proprietary right to run the clinic as he saw fit. In 1957 the DRI began accepting inmates at its new, maximum-security prison in Millbrook, Ontario, where the segregated treatment facility that experts had long recommended was in place. Most sex deviants were to be transferred to Millbrook, and Buckner was offered the opportunity to go with them. However, given that Buckner was frequently criticized for devoting too much time to his private practice in town at the expense of the NPC, van Nostrand correctly anticipated that Buckner would turn down the offer and resign.

With the transfer of sex deviants and the forced resignation of Buckner, van Nostrand saw an opportunity to scale back the NPC program. The DRI's head psychologist and the remaining NPC staff argued that mandatory assessments for all inmates convicted of a sex offence used up precious few resources and robbed seriously mentally disturbed patients of much-needed care.[40] Although the NPC continued to assess and recommend treatment for a handful of men serving time on sex-related charges, Potts dramatically reduced the original 1955 list of offences meriting a full assessment by eliminating those charged with rape, which he viewed as a violent crime, not a crime of sexual deviation; carnal knowledge, a charge that was erroneously believed to be used in cases of non-coercive sexual activity, most often between a male sixteen years of age or slightly older and an adolescent female fifteen years or younger; and seduction, perceived as a crime of sexual betrayal, not assault. Significantly, the new list identified the sexual act rather than the criminal charge and expanded to include inmates who were discovered to have engaged in any of the listed sex acts, regardless of the charge that brought them to prison. Those acts included having sexual relations with a person of the same sex, a person of the opposite sex who had not obtained puberty, an animal, one's own children, or having engaged in exhibitionism. Such men were to be examined by a staff psychologist. Notably, men who engaged in sex with other men were first on the list.[41]

The DRI's new policy was created in consultation with the Toronto Psychiatric Hospital's Forensic Clinic and clearly reflects the clinic's own working definition of what constituted sexual deviancy. Defined as 'an act performed for sexual gratification other than sexual intercourse with an adult of the opposite sex,' sexually deviant acts were further divided into two groups: the first included those who made a normal object choice but engaged in sexual acts that were abnormal. These included sadism, masochism, exhibitionism, and voyeurism. The second group included those who made 'abnormal object choices'; examples included homosexuality, pedophilia, transvestism, fetishism, and bestiality.[42] Rape and other forms of sexual assault where adult (or adult-like) women were victims were not considered deviant unless the accompanying violence was deemed 'sadistic.' There was no clear demarcation showing where this threshold might be, but presumably physical violence that was superfluous to the act of forcible vaginal penetration qualified as such.

Using this model, the DRI removed men convicted of heterosexual crimes involving victims over the age of fourteen from its list of treatment candidates, thus emphasizing how 'normal' heterosexual assaults were seen as crimes of male aggression, not of sexual violence. As a result the rise of forensic sexology contributed to the decreased visibility of rape and other forms of assault against women as a socio-sexual problem. Changes to the sex deviant policy, particularly with respect to same-sex sex, also brought the program more squarely in line with the department's disciplinary objectives.

The narrowing of the treatment mandate was of no concern to Dr G.S. Burton, Buckner's replacement. Likely hand-picked by van Nostrand, Burton did not favour of any sort of treatment at all. 'Too much therapy would not be wise for the kind of inmate we are largely dealing with,' he argued. Inmates would simply learn the language and methods of modern psychotherapy and 'bandy these about, but would not really be changed in their personality.'[43] By 1960, staff agreed that the clinic did little more than provide a diagnosis, and no further attempts were made to build up a treatment program.[44]

Had Buckner been given the funding and the support enjoyed by treatment staff in California, his program might well have come to resemble that offered to sex offenders in the Metropolitan State Hospital in Norwalk, the Haight-Ashbury of the treatment movement. Norwalk is worth examining, since it gives us a glimmer of just where such a program might have gone under different circumstances. Indeed, Buckner was likely attuned to developments across the United States, and certainly would have kept abreast of the research reports that resulted.

In 1950 Norwalk became one of two California state hospitals assigned to establish a separate unit to accommodate sex offenders for ninety-day pre-trial observation and to provide treatment as well as conduct research on sex deviation. Robert E. Wyers, the superintendent and medical director, was determined to have 'more than just an eyewash treatment program.' He hired new staff and emptied out a small ward in anticipation of an estimated sixty to eighty patients. Within three years, Norwalk was home to over four hundred convicted sex offenders.[45]

With hospital care as its model, the Norwalk philosophy was founded on a spirit of non-hierarchical voluntarism. 'We do not force treatment,' Wyers explained to a mixed crowd of staff, patients, and prominent citizens from the local community, 'lest the professional staff become another authority ... for you to reject and to resent.' It established an Emotional Security Program (ESP), a self-governing patient board that helped determine the pace and scope of the program, contributed to shaping policy, assisted with new arrivals' integration into the program, and boosted patient morale on the floor. Like Buckner, Norwalk staff knew that once a group of patients was entrenched in a program, they would set its tone and reinforce it by socializing new participants. ESP was therefore a critical element in the overall scheme. It kept patients together as a cohesive group, helped foster 'proper attitudes,' and helped 'sell' therapy to unmotivated patients. In short, it strove to combat the culture of resistance by creating and reinforcing a culture of participation.

But Norwalk's controversial position vis-à-vis sexual matters was what really made the program one of a kind. First, the sex offender ward employed female staff, a practice almost unheard of in the early 1950s. Women were excluded from working directly with male prisoners for a number of reasons, one of them being that inmates might become sexually aroused by their mere presence.[46] Integrating female staff was a fundamental part of the alternative vision proponents of the therapeutic community brought to the field of corrections and forensic sexology. Hiring women was part of a carefully planned strategy to 'heterosexualize' carceral institutions, thus creating a more 'normal' social environment. Bruno Cormier, one of Quebec's most prominent forensic psychiatrists, also employed female treatment experts at the therapeutic community he established at Clinton Prison in Dannemora, New York.[47] However, both of these programs were exceptional. By and large, women were excluded from the intellectual and practical development of forensic sexology.[48]

Norwalk was purposely permissive in its structure. Its director believed that therapeutic gains could not be made without meaningful opportunities for sexual expression. Patients were permitted to engage in sexual activities with each other and were encouraged to speak openly about them. Staff estimates of homosexual activity varied widely, from 90 per cent to hardly at all, but most guessed that between 30 and 50 per cent of patients engaged in some form of sexual contact.[49] Staff approved of same-sex intimacy because, they believed, it provided an opportunity for men to discuss and gain insight into their emotions.

Norwalk staff was also cognizant of the need for heterosexual contact, especially if they felt that an inmate's orientation was toward women. Thus, physical contact between visitors and patients was encouraged, and on visiting days couples freely roamed the ward. Couples were also allowed privacy in patients' rooms, although only heavy petting was officially sanctioned. One social worker argued that the ward should have a 'sex room' where inmates and their visitors could have intercourse, but, she lamented, 'this is not possible in our culture.'[50] Some felt that patients without a wife or 'sweetheart' should be provided with prostitutes. Only this way would inmate-patients learn to put into practice the normative sexual values their therapeutic peers tried to promote.[51]

While it is unlikely that the California state budget would afford the services of local prostitutes, the institution did find other ways to create opportunities for heterosocial contact. Recreational therapy was a standard part of institutional programming at hospitals for the mentally ill. Dances, hairdressing services, and, for women, beauty classes were made available in an effort to help raise self-esteem and try to normalize institutional life.[52] Aided by a group of volunteer housewives from the local community, weekly dances were added to the Norwalk program. Female volunteers gave dance lessons to the men in the sex offender program, and female dance partners were recruited from the psychotic ward. The dances were regarded as an ideal opportunity for sex offender patients to learn social skills and 'put into operation some of the insights gained in psychotherapy.'[53] According to one staff psychiatrist, dances provided a needed sexual outlet, and 'helped keep the institution heterosexual.'[54] If staff members conceived of any possible benefit for the invited guests, they failed to mention what it was, but the shortcomings of the program were impossible to ignore. Staff actively encouraged mild petting between the sexual psychopaths and the psychotic female patients, and secretly arranged 'private visits' between them. Even the hospital minister maintained a permissive stance, explaining to a Kinsey Institute researcher that he would 'wink at it if it is not exploitative.' However, at least two of the female wards became pregnant, and the superintendent quickly intervened, putting an end to these practices.[55]

Canadian psychiatrist and psychoanalyst Bruno Cormier's therapeutic community at Clinton Prison in New York also tried to put into practice the ideas Maxwell Jones and his proponents advanced concerning sexuality.[56] At Dannemora, homosexuality was considered part of 'the prison landscape,' and treatment staff similarly battled against the stigmatization of sex offenders. There were no facilities to allow for conjugal visits, but Cormier supported the concept and allowed inmates and their visitors to engage in physical touching in the visiting room.

Unlike Norwalk, however, female members of the Dannemora treatment team were highly critical of some of the more 'liberal' attitudes the program promoted. For example, they argued that using women to sexually gratify male prisoners as a way to manage homosexuality was 'simplistic.' Therapist Lydia Keitner claimed that inmates would continue their negative patterns of behaviour in their relationships with women without ever having to change. Moreover, she directly challenged the ethics of providing women to service inmates sexually. From where would these women come, she asked, and how could we allow them to engage in relationships with men we know are abusive and destructive? Keitner and her female colleagues were also circumspect about the notion that female employees 'heterosexualized' the prison environment, pointing out that a variety of sexual tensions coursed through the program, including those between male treatment staff and inmates.[57] Their criticism highlighted one of the fundamental assumptions of the psychotherapeutic paradigm: that the therapist was a living embodiment of 'normativity.' As the women at Clinton Prison pointed out, male therapists failed to openly acknowledge and account for the ways that their own ideas, thoughts, sexual fantasies, and 'impulses' shaped the therapeutic relationship. Female staffs' critiques of male therapists' permissive approach appear to have been ignored.

Buckner's short-lived program at the NPC was the closest Ontario came to transforming the prison into a therapeutic environment, and to treating sex offenders as more mentally disturbed than criminally motivated. In this respect, the 1957 transfer of 'sex deviants' from Guelph to the newly opened maximum-security facility in Millbrook was a giant step backward for the prison reform movement.[58] Touted by the DRI as the first North American facility for psychopathic inmates, Millbrook was intended to house the 'tougher and meaner breed of inmates' that guards complained were overrunning the Guelph Reformatory and corrupting young, first-time offenders.[59] Officials claimed that the province's most incorrigible inmates were to be reformed by the new prison's highly regimented and strictly controlled environment, in which treatment, not punishment, would be the guiding spirit. However, it was precisely the opposite. By the mid-1960s, critics denounced Millbrook as Ontario's Alcatraz.

Intended to house the province's most violent prisoners, Millbrook was an extremely punitive environment. Situated on one hundred acres of bucolic Ontario countryside, the prison buildings were immured in a twenty-foot concrete wall. Eight glass-enclosed towers housed guards who were on watch twenty-four hours a day. According to the sentencing guide for magistrates, an inmate was 'lodged in a single cell bare of anything but a matressless [sic] steel bunk, bedding, and flush-to-wall-button wash-basin and toilet; with a frosted bullet-proof glass window set in masonry and solid flush-with-wall door. The atmosphere of the place is chill, clean, silent, and self-revealing.'[60] Though each cell had a window, it was too high to look through, and prisoners were forbidden to stand on their beds to do so.[61] In an effort to prevent organized protests and riots, there were no dining facilities where inmates could gather. Meals were delivered through a small opening at the bottom of cell doors and consumed alone. In a letter to his father, one inmate wrote, 'You read about the place a while back how tough it is. You either resolve to a zombie state of mind or go out of it completely whether that is the intention or not. All I can say it is a survival of the fittest this is mentally.'[62] Indeed, a year earlier Millbrook's consultant psychiatrist, F.E. Webb, expressed grave concern over the growing number of inmates showing signs of severe emotional and psychological damage. At least one Group II (sex deviant) inmate was sent to the nearby psychiatric hospital in Penetanguishene. Webb anticipated that it was only a matter of time before more would follow.[63]

A major aspect of the disciplinary regime at Millbrook was the Progressive Stage System, which aimed on the one hand to force compliance with prison regulations through the withdrawal of sensory stimulation, and on the other hand to reward compliance by incrementally introducing the pleasures of food, human contact, and leisurely pursuits. Upon arrival, inmates spent sixteen days on a 'special diet' without letters, visitors, opportunities to exercise, and with only a Bible to read.[64] At Stage 2, inmates were permitted regular meals, one non-fiction book, tobacco, forty-five minutes of recreation, and one thirty minute visit from a family member each week. The best-behaved inmates entered Stage 3, where they were granted library privileges, one letter out to family, one movie a week, and the opportunity to take a correspondence course.[65] Initially, all inmates entered at Stage 1, but staff pointed out that Group II (sex deviants) and Group III (drug addicts) were not sent there for punishment, and therefore should not be forced to endure two weeks of what amounted to solitary confinement. Soon thereafter, the policy was changed so that Groups II and III entered at Stage 2. It was a slight improvement, but they still had to 'earn' their way to Stage 3.

Despite promises that Millbrook would be a laboratory for the treatment of sexual deviation, the reality was that the warehousing of homosexuals, sexual predators within the inmate population, and men charged with crimes of sexual violence and the sexual assault of children violated every tenet of the treatment ideal. First, Millbrook made no distinction between male homosexuals, male sexual predators within the prison system, and men incarcerated for sex crimes. While it is true that male homosexuality was medically and popularly regarded as a sexual deviation, public demands for prison treatment programs grew out of a concern over sex crimes against children and, to a lesser extent, women. Most would have agreed that homosexuals should have the opportunity to receive treatment, but pedophiles were the primary object of concern. Second, placing sex 'deviants' of any kind in a maximum-security facility was diametrically opposed to the fundamental belief that perpetrators of sex crimes needed psychological help, not punishment. Sending them to a maximum-security prison for the 'disturbers and disturbed' is 'really a terrible way to deal with this type of offender,' complained Helen Kinnear, one of the three commissioners who studied and reported on Canada's criminal sexual psychopath legislation. '[The commissioners] would think that was discriminating against the sex offender as compared with other offenders.'[66] Some experts simply protested against the inclusion of homosexuals in the Millbrook program. For example, W.T. McGrath, a leader in Ontario's prison reform movement, complained that the criminal justice system was being used to enforce a moral order that 'made criminals out of otherwise normal people.' Learning to see that most homosexuals are 'in no way dangerous' would solve the problem of homosexuality in prison, he argued. It would reduce the number of homosexuals committed to prisons and would 'remove the need to plan for these special types of inmates.'[67]

DRI officials were unfazed by their critics. In fact, Frank van Nostrand acknowledged that there was no plan to treat Millbrook's homosexual prisoners and that the policies were intended only 'to remove them as a disturbance factor.'[68] Officially, the primary objective of Millbrook's 'sex deviate' unit was the 'complete segregation of some of the sexual perverts ... for the protection of other inmates,' but even this was a gross abuse of the purpose of treatment programs for convicted sex offenders. As far as the supporting public was concerned, treatment was intended to facilitate safe release of sex criminals into the community, not to provide inmates with protection from sexual predation within the institution.[69] Yet this is precisely how van Nostrand justified the sex deviate unit. Providing treatment was never an imperative.

Emboldened by the 1958 retirement of van Nostrand and the hiring of long-time reform activist J.D. Atcheson as director of treatment services, Millbrook's treatment staff, its pastor, and its pro-reform Superintendent R.H. Paterson appealed to the deputy minister to move forward with a sex deviant treatment program.[70] Concerned that some staff treated homosexual inmates poorly and that non-homosexual Group II inmates were distressed by the 'constant sex talk' among homosexuals, Millbrook staff pressed Basher to allow the two groups to be separated from each other. They claimed that homosexuals showed 'a higher incidence of major personality disorder, or potential mental illness,' and that they 'present less criminal tendencies' than other Group II (sex deviant) inmates. If homosexuals could be separated, staff that had a strong dislike of homosexuals would not have to work among them. They recommended hiring 'Custodial Staff who are manly, well-adjusted types and who have some understanding and acceptance of their charges' to work with them exclusively.[71]

The suggestion that homosexuals would benefit from appropriate role models whose gender presentation fit the masculine ideal demonstrates the enduring link between gender and sexuality in the 1950s and was consistent with popular theories of developmental psychology, now widely considered oppressive. However, DRI records clearly demonstrate that Paterson's advocacy on behalf of Group II inmates was intended to ease the extremely punitive and hostile conditions homosexual inmates were forced to endure. At that time, there were a total of forty-four Group II (sex deviant) inmates, almost half of whom were labelled homosexual (often based on prison activity, not criminal conviction). Surprisingly, the deputy minister approved the request and hired two new guards to work in a special wing created for homosexual inmates. Custodial staff were given the option to refuse work in that section.[72]

Millbrook had an even worse track record for providing treatment than did the Guelph Reformatory. Millbrook's first consultant psychiatrist F.E. Webb prescribed narcotics to the 'sex deviant' population to 'jump start' the therapeutic process, and just before retiring in the early 1960s began to administer ECT to those willing to volunteer for the treatment.[73] Based on the few surviving case files, it is clear that he administered both sodium pentothal (popularly known as 'truth serum') and shock therapy to make patients 'more accessible to psychotherapy.' As we saw in chapter 4, both types of treatment were becoming a popular aid to facilitate psychotherapy.[74] However, at least one file suggests that ECT may also have been used punitively. In February 1958, 'Norman,' a French-Canadian prisoner in an Ontario facility, was cited for 'doing his hair in a feminine way' and was docked seven days good conduct remission.[75] One month later, Officer Woodly reported the same prisoner for 'biting his lips and rubbing his cheeks to make them red and also plucking his eyebrows.' This time Norman was sentenced to three days in solitary confinement on a rationed diet. On 1 April he received yet another misconduct report for 'failing to achieve the required standard in conduct and industry for 5 weeks,' and lost yet another five days of good conduct. Two weeks later Norman was admitted to the prison hospital for a course of ECT. He received a total of six treatments and was released back into the prison. It is impossible to conclude with certainty that his refusal to conform to institutional masculine ideals and the disciplinary regime resulted in his receiving ECT, but given the absence of any other documented explanation – medical or otherwise – it seems reasonable to assume that his persistent effort to feminize his appearance was the problem in need of treatment.[76]

Despite ongoing requests from the superintendent to create a therapeutic community, Webb's ECT experiment was the last significant venture in treating the sex criminal and homosexual population at Millbrook. Yet, over the next four years, the Group II population almost doubled from forty-four to eighty-three. In 1962 the few remaining members of the treatment staff unanimously agreed that a program for sex offenders could not be carried out at that institution and that other alternatives should be pursued.[77] Potts cited Millbrook's remote location as one of the reasons quality staff were difficult to attract and retain. Other obstacles to building up a program included conflict with the prison administration, lack of flexibility, and the architecture of the building itself.[78] The abandonment of treatment was abetted by Webb's successor, B.A. Kelly, who maintained that 'incarceration is a useful thing' for Group II inmates and that most sex offenders were not amenable to treatment. Even among those who were, Kelly insisted that treatment in an outpatient setting was most suitable, since 'sincere motivations for changed sexual behaviour can only be assessed by a patient's willingness to keep appointments.'[79]

In 1957 Minister Major John Foote, the DRI's most important reform advocate, retired. In the six years that followed, the DRI portfolio changed hands five times. J.D. Atcheson, an outspoken activist for criminal justice reform and former head psychiatrist of the Toronto Family and Juvenile Court, was hired as the director of research and treatment services the year Foote left, but could do little to keep the Ontario Plan vision alive. In 1958 he complained to the minister that inmates were being transferred to Millbrook simply to keep the marker plant running at full capacity, to no avail.[80] A year later, following a series of articles in the *Toronto Daily Star* and the *Toronto Telegram* denouncing the continued use of the strap to administer punishment for rules infractions, ministry staff held a special meeting on the issue, but because of Atcheson's known opposition to corporal punishment, he was not invited to attend.[81] In light of the negative publicity, Ontario Premier Leslie Frost approved its continued use only at Millbrook. Alarmed by reports that inmates were actually requesting transfers to Millbrook, Frost warned his deputy minister to 'Keep Millbrook tough,' and custodial officers were told to keep their distance from inmates.[82] Millbrook's pro-reform superintendent resigned in disgust.[83]

By 1963 Millbrook's skeletal treatment team of two part-time consulting psychiatrists could no longer provide even a general counselling service for inmates. Staff agreed that the maximum-security needs of Group I inmates, the 'troublemakers,' clashed with the therapeutic needs of Group II inmates, and the clinical program never got beyond conducting intake assessments.[84] R.R. Ross, the supervising psychologist for the region, reported that treatment services would 'henceforth be extremely limited in scope,' and that because of the shortage of staff, 'there is little room for optimism about future expansion.' Ross recommended that the department transfer to a custodial officer many of the duties that normally fell to the social worker and psychologist, such as general counselling, psychological testing, and intake interviewing.[85] Various political appointments and public promises during the late 1950s and 1960s kept afloat the illusion of the DRI as a therapeutic haven, and magistrates continued to assume homosexuals and others charged with sex crimes would receive treatment in prison. However, insiders regarded Millbrook as little more than a 'storage bin' for problem inmates.[86] In 1965 two inmates tried to draw public attention to the poor conditions at the prison by hoarding their lighter fluid rations and lighting a fire. Guards anonymously met with journalists to describe the appalling conditions inmates were forced to endure. The opposition party called Millbrook the 'Alcatraz of Ontario,' and demanded its closure.[87]

The problem was not limited to Millbrook. The treatment sham exploded in 1961 when all but two of the staff at Toronto's Juvenile and Family Court quit after the government imposed new and highly punitive policies on the clinical management of the court's clients.[88] Later that same year, eight staff members at the Alex G. Brown Memorial

Clinic resigned *en masse*. The DRI claimed the problem was budget cuts, but according to Stuart Jaffary, increasingly rigid custodial regulations and practices were creating insurmountable obstacles for professional staff who were operating treatment programs in the clinic. 'Despite its name,' Jaffary argued, 'they got little indication that the therapeutic program was really the primary purpose of the clinic.'[89] The only hope for saving the system was for the DRI to take concrete steps toward resolving the conflict between punishment and treatment. 'Does the institution exist for the man, or the man for the institution?' he asked. 'If the former, it will have to have a full complement of treatment services, and use them. If the latter, all you need is a rockpile and a treadmill.' As it stands, the pretence of 'treatment,' he concluded, gives a show of humanity with one hand and keeps a firm hold on the inmate population with the other.[90]

By 1961 the director of treatment services, director of psychiatry, and director of social work positions in the Department of Reform Institutions were vacant. F.H. Potts, the first psychologist hired by the department, was the only mental health administrator remaining on staff. Minister George Calvin Wardrope announced that he was retreating from the 'idea that every offender, given the proper treatment and assignment, could be successfully molded into a useful citizen. Penologically speaking,' he concluded, 'the pendulum is swinging nearer to where it should [be].'[91] Allan Grossman revived the rhetoric of rehabilitation while he served as minister from 1963 to 1971, but the DRI continued to function in much the same manner as it had since the Second World War, if not earlier.

As the only province to respond to public pressure and provide treatment for incarcerated sex criminals, Ontario must have appeared progressive indeed. Appearances, however, were deceiving. Unfortunately, Ontario was not unique in this regard. The conflict between the postwar treatment ideal and the military-style disciplinary regime played out wherever treatment staff were hired. Guy Richmond, a psychiatrist at the British Columbia federal prison, lamented that prison doctors were forced to render unto Caesar, not Hippocrates.[92] According to another British Columbia psychiatrist who undertook a study of sex offenders in prison, 'the real power structure in the institution is mainly concerned with custody, with keeping the inmates in line, in order, and above all, *inside* ... This is not an environment in which the principals of reform and rehabilitation can even exist and to say otherwise would be a mockery.'[93] Showing predictable restraint, the 1969 report of the Canadian Committee on Corrections concluded that the relationship between prison services and treatment professionals in the federal system was an uneasy alliance of opposing ideologies, the latter lacking the support of the former.[94]

As for the Group II program, top administrators would concede only that Millbrook's remote location and the nature of the work undermined any chance of success. In 1962 Potts concluded that the only solution was to continue to court outside help by building bridges between reformatories and faculties of psychiatry, psychology, and social work. In the meantime, he recommended that a sex deviant treatment program be set up at the Alex G. Brown Memorial Clinic (AGBMC), where the DRI ran a pre-release treatment program for alcoholics and drug addicts. There, he argued, research into the effective treatment of homosexuals, who constituted approximately 25 per cent of the Millbrook Group II population and who posed the greatest discipline problem for prison administrators, could be set up.[95]

If the use of mental health treatment as a means to control prison discipline can be taken as a measure of the clash of ideologies, Potts's last proposal is a clear indication that nothing had changed. Sex between inmates remained the primary concern. The public demand for treatment for pedophiles, exhibitionists, and other sex criminals who were considered a serious danger to the public was of no interest to the Department of Reform Institutions.

This would likely have been the end of the early history of sex offender treatment in Ontario, were it not for Richard Steffy, an Ontario native recently returned from graduate school in Illinois. Steffy approached the DRI with a proposal to treat pedophiles with a combination of psychoanalysis and aversion therapy.[96] With funding from the newly formed Ontario Mental Health Foundation in hand, he was quickly given the green light.[97] Unaware of the recent controversy at the AGBMC, he saw his first pedophile offenders in 1965 at the Mimico Clinic. Inmates arrived at this home-like minimum-security facility (nicknamed 'finishing school') for the last four months of their sentences so that they might gain control over their addictions or disorders and thus avoid reoffending.[98] External funding meant Steffy was less likely to be pressured to use treatment as a disciplinary measure, and insulated his program from the parsimonious policies of the DRI.

Aversion therapy enjoyed something of a renaissance in the 1960s.[99] First used to treat sexual deviation in 1935, it was popularized in the postwar era by followers of Hungarian-born psychoanalyst Sandor Rado. He, along with Irving Bieber and Charles Socarides, viewed homosexuality as an anxiety response to heterosexuality resulting from unhealthy parental relationships. If an anxiety response was learned, they argued, then so could it be unlearned. Immortalized in Stanley Kubrick's 1971 film *A Clockwork Orange*, the treatment involved introducing a noxious stimulus such as nausea, vomiting, or electric shock when the patient experienced the inappropriate or deviant sexual response.[100] Kubrick's character was convicted for violently raping an adult woman and therefore would not have been considered a candidate for sex deviation treatment in postwar Ontario. Nevertheless, Steffy's program operated along similar lines. Pedophiles were presented with images of prepubescent boys, or girls, or both, depending on the sex of their victims. The image was accompanied by an electric shock with the aim of rewiring the pleasure response and replacing it with a painful one. Images of an appropriate sexual object choice, in this case adult women, were also shown, but without an accompanying shock.[101]

The behaviour being treated was still pathologized through a psychoanalytic frame, but aversion therapy differed from Webb's experiments with ECT and sodium pentothal in that it was not intended to facilitate psychotherapy. Though Steffy offered talk therapy as well, aversion therapy was a treatment in its own right, based on non-psychoanalytic principles about human behaviour and desire. Aversion therapy's growing popularity reflected a re-emerging interest in the body, but this time focused on neural pathways, not genes or hormones.[102] The failure of psychotherapy combined with a renewed interest in somatic solutions led experts to argue that while sexual behaviour was the outcome of a developmental process, it became hard-wired into the brain and could not be treated by talk therapy alone, if at all. A number of American programs explored similar treatments. At Atascadero and Vacaville in California, for example, treatment staff experimented with succinylcholine, an anxiety-producing drug that causes instant paralysis of all muscles, including those linked to the cardiovascular system.[103] Inmates undergoing behaviour modification were administered the drug and kept alive through the use of machines.

Richard Steffy's pedophile program was the first and probably the only Canadian sex offender program to employ aversion therapy as the central treatment modality. Conscious of the problems associated with providing treatment as part of a prison term, he permitted inmate-patients a choice between the full program of ECT shock treatments combined with talk therapy, only talk therapy, or only shock. Ninety-three per cent of the program participants chose to undergo the combination treatment, demonstrating a remarkable willingness to be 'cured.' According to Steffy, pedophiles who were selected to participate in the Mimico program were 'relieved to be offered more than just talk,' though given the lack of treatment services at Millbrook, it is difficult to determine where they might have received even that.[104]

Experiments with aversion therapy were cut short by the rising tide of protest launched by a new generation of journalists, psychiatrists, and psychologists who denounced it as a violation of prisoners' rights, and as cruel and unusual punishment.[105] In a special issue of the journal *Psychiatric Opinion*, Phyllis J. Lundy and Peter R. Breggin used the sex offender and sex deviant treatment programs at Patuxent Institution in Maryland as an example of how drug and aversion therapies were employed as tools of institutional control and oppression.[106] There is no such thing as voluntary consent in a prison setting, they argued. 'In therapeutically oriented facilities in which psychiatrists have the most control, prisoners are most likely to lose their human rights.' The public was horrified, and growing criticism of ECT and aversion therapy prompted Steffy to abandon his work at the AGBMC.[107] His departure marked the end of an era in Ontario corrections.

Given that there was no effective treatment for sexual deviation, does it matter that the Ontario Department of Reform Institutions, or the federal government, for that matter, failed to offer a robust therapeutic program? Should we not be relieved that there were fewer, not more, opportunities to administer ECT, CO_2, and 'truth serum' to prisoners undergoing 'treatment'? Perhaps, but the material in this chapter raises a number of important historical and contemporary concerns that deserve consideration.

First, the early history of sex offender treatment in Canadian prisons demonstrates how seemingly progressive reform projects can take horribly regressive turns. For men found by the courts to be criminal sexual psychopaths or dangerous sex offenders, the promise of treatment and a cure sometimes amounted to a life sentence in a federal prison with little or no hope of parole.[108] For example, when in 1952 a criminal court judge found George L. Tilley, who had violently sexually assaulted a female prostitute and a twelve-year-old girl, to be a criminal sexual psychopath, the judge expressed what most of the English Canadian public believed: that by sending Tilley to prison for an indefinite period, he was acting 'humanely and wisely' by ensuring that Tilley would be treated for his condition.[109] For many of the men sentenced under this novel piece of legislation, treatment was never made available. When a sex offender treatment program was finally created for federal inmates in the mid-1970s, many were denied admittance on the grounds that the years they had spent in prison rendered them beyond reform. None of the advocates of sexual psychopath legislation and sex offender treatment could ever have imagined that their efforts to change the way society approached the problem of sexual assault would have this result.

The history of sex offender treatment in Canada is more than just a matter of federal neglect. In Ontario's provincial prison system, parsimony was compounded by outright hostility toward the Ontario Plan, the DRI's scheme to modernize and humanize its reformatories by offering its inmates a mental health approach to rehabilitation. The dream of creating a therapeutic culture was harnessed to serve a different set of interests and objectives – despite almost a decade of leadership by a pro-reform minister, top administrators, including the deputy minister, maintained the military culture of prison management and ultimately pushed Millbrook's pro-reform superintendent and virtually all the treatment staff at the Alex G. Brown Memorial Clinic to resign. From the post–Second World War beginnings of the era of mental health reform to its demise in the early 1970s, both treatment staff and official policy were subordinated to the militaristic management of Ontario prisons. According to Deputy Minister Colonel Basher and Chief Psychiatrist Frank van Nostrand, the real sex problem was the prison sex problem. Although other types of sex criminals were singled out for transfer to Millbrook, policy changes regarding the selection of candidates reflected the administrators' primary concern with prison discipline.

Prison experiments treating sexual deviation further illustrate how postwar sexology's permissive stance toward the expression of sexual desire, including homosexual desire, was in some ways both liberal and progressive. However, its underlying heterosexist and patriarchal assumptions meant that postwar forensic sexologists' ideas about treating male sexual deviancy could veer in rather disturbing directions. Buckner's willingness to allow two patients to take control of the Neuro-Psychiatric Clinic's therapy group was only the tip of the iceberg. In offender treatment programs in places like Norwalk and Dannemora – the first offered in a hospital setting and the second in a prison – a sexually permissive environment, intended to undermine moral prohibitions in favour of a more Kinsey-influenced understanding of the naturalness of sexual expression, created and even encouraged exploitative conditions in which women were regarded as mere outlets for male (hetero)sexual pleasure. The tolerant attitude toward homosexuality among some forensic sexologists is noteworthy, especially among experts working in the United States where anxiety about male homosexuality registered at a significantly higher pitch than Canada, but we must not end our critical assessment there. Toleration of homosexuality was liberal and progressive in the postwar era, but this particular brand of liberal permissiveness was deeply embedded in heterosexualist, patriarchal thinking that both privileged and naturalized male sexual desire. Attempts to encourage heterosexual development were undertaken with no consideration for the experiences or desires of the women such measures depended on. With the significant exception of the women who worked at Dannemora, postwar forensic sexologists did not readily grasp how structured inequalities shaped heterosexual relations and male sexual privilege. Our assessment of postwar sexology must examine its approach to heterosexuality as well as to homosexuality.

Almost as soon as criminal sexual psychopath laws and the treatment programs they engendered were created, they were critiqued by leading forensic psychiatrists across Canada and the United States.[110] In Canada, professional misgivings were articulated during the hearings of the Royal Commission on the Criminal Law Relating to Criminal Sexual Psychopaths, and Parliament responded by redefining repeat (or expected to repeat) sex criminals as 'dangerous sexual offenders.' In 1977 the designation was changed once again to 'dangerous offender,' bringing us back to what psychiatrists suggested all along: that sex criminals should not be singled out, and should be treated as any other criminal who suffered from mental health problems. In practice, however, sex offenders continued to be singled out in society, in prison, and under the law.[111]

Few have faith in medicine's ability to 'cure' sex offenders, yet the construction of a criminal sexual psychopath remains more or less intact. According to Canadian criminologist Jacqueline Faubert, experts for the prosecution continue to characterize sex offenders according to the same criteria: they harbour a '"substantial element of hatefulness towards women" and "mother figures."' They are 'typically angry and impulsive yet cunning and glib.'[112] Yet in dangerous offender hearings, she argues, 'expert discussions about reoffence risk and the protection of the community through risk management have replaced dialogue about treatment and rehabilitation. Contributing to this anti-therapeutic focus was the growing expert perception that any reformative investment in a certain type of offender, such as the psychopath or the pedophile, was futile.'[113] Currently, inmates who have been designated as dangerous offenders are the *least* likely to receive treatment. With few resources to go around, those about to be released are given top priority. Sex offenders serving an indefinite sentence rarely make their way up the list.

More support for meaningful health care services of all types would tremendously benefit the approximately 32,100 men and women serving time in Canadian prisons.[114] However, my argument is not that sex deviation programs should have been or should now be better funded. Rather, it is that the entire foundation upon which the modern conception of the repeat sex offender rests is a social construction based on hopes, dreams, and ideals that were, from the beginning, subject to intense criticism by legal, medical, and psychiatric experts alike. Sex offending is a serious social problem, but the modern construction of the sex offender hinders rather than promotes understanding of the nature of human sexual behaviour. The justification for the in-definite incarceration of men who commit sex crimes is based on a legal construct that no longer exists. If indeterminate sentencing is to continue, a new justification must be found. From the vantage point offered us by history, it is clear that we need to go much further than rethinking the law. We must re-evaluate our most basic beliefs and as-sumptions about the nature of sexual offending, and about those who commit such offences.

Compulsory Heterosexuality and the Limits of Forensic Sexology

In the 1950s, most of the public anxiety about and news media coverage of sex crime concerned sexual assaults against female children, but because sex between men was a sex crime as well as a form of 'sex deviation,' discussions about pedophilia often segued into talk about sex between adult men. During government commission hearings and public inquiries, as well as in the news media, conversations easily glided from child molestation to homosexuality. As we saw in chapter 3, the ambiguity of the term 'sexual deviation' allowed for the increased policing and regulation of male homosexuality, even though the primary public concern was about men who repeatedly sexually assaulted female children. Thus, for example, when a child sexual assault case hit the front page of the papers, the Metropolitan Toronto Police raided gay bars, and the next day local papers reported that authorities were 'rounding up all known sex deviates' for questioning. Similarly, as was shown in the last chapter, when the Ontario government supported the creation of a sex offender treatment program for the province's inmate population, the deputy minister of the Department of Reform Institutions (DRI) and his director of neuropsychiatry used the initiative to regulate sexual activity among inmates. What the Ontario public demanded was that pedophiles receive treatment for their disease, not that sex between prisoners be more carefully policed. However, since the public was largely unaware of the details of the DRI's programs, because sex between men was considered a form of sexual deviation, and since once inside the prison, mental health experts in the 1950s and 60s became concerned about the effects the institution had on sexuality and masculinity, the 'prison sex problem,' as it was called, became a major focus of discussion and concern. The ambiguity and expansiveness of the term 'sexual deviate' made this slippage possible.

This chapter further explores the progressive and conservative tensions that shaped postwar forensic sexology by examining how the 'prison sex problem' was constructed, articulated, and reconstructed in the postwar era. A study of the logic of sexologists' responses further highlights the field's permissive approach to human sexual behaviour as well as its conceptual limitations with respect to the role of gender and power in organizing sexual and social relations. Specifically, enduring patriarchal and heterosexist assumptions about masculinity and sexuality left modern forensic sexologists incapable of addressing the role that gender, sexual violence, and coercion played in shaping sexual relations. Indeed, as long as victims were adults of the opposite sex, sexologists considered the act 'normal.' Experts did not deny that violence and coercion existed, or that it should be punished by the state. It was simply a matter of propriety. In such cases, the crime was an act of violence, not sexual deviation, and therefore was not a mental health issue. As the material in this chapter shows, however, forensic sexologists and other mental health experts who worked inside the prison were surrounded by a culture of sexual coercion that provided plenty of evidence that sexual behaviour was more complicated than their own models allowed. Heterosexism, androcentrism, and a preoccupation with sexual 'outlets' prevented postwar forensic sexologists from developing a theory of sexuality that could account for sexual violence and gender oppression.

Inside prisons in Ontario and elsewhere, sex was part of an elaborate hierarchical social structure that organized inmates into distinct social groups. Mediated by a range of variables including age, physical stature, past prison experience, race, and ethnicity, prison sex culture was structured around a tough working-class masculinity that was defined in large part by the naturalization of male entitlement to sexual gratification. Grounded in earlier ideological systems that defined normative masculinity as sexually aggressive, men in prison who took an insertive role in the sex act were not considered sexually aberrant. As is sometimes the case in 'normal' heterosexual relations, wolves' relations with younger men – known as 'punks,' 'kids,' and 'lambs' – were structured by a combination of negotiation and coercion, and on the threat of violence and the exploitation of sexual shame. Though the feminized partners of sexual aggressors were able to exercise some agency, it was an agency seriously constrained by what Adrienne Rich describes as a system of compulsory heterosexuality.[1]

In her groundbreaking 1982 article, 'Compulsory Heterosexuality and Lesbian Existence,' Rich laments the tendency to describe female heterosexuality as a natural, inevitable choice. In fact, she argues, heterosexuality is a political institution, the 'beachhead of male dominance,' a 'many-layered lie.' 'We are confronting not a simple maintenance of inequality and property possession,' she writes, 'but a pervasive cluster of forces, ranging from physical brutality to control of consciousness.'[2] Indeed, because women and men live in a state of economic, social, and psychological inequality, it is impossible to speak of heterosexuality as a choice for women, especially in light of the threat of physical and sexual violence. Citing feminist legal theorist Catharine MacKinnon, Rich wonders to what extent 'the institution of heterosexuality has defined force as a normal part of "the preliminaries. Never is it asked whether, under conditions of male supremacy, the notion of 'consent' has any meaning."'[3] It is the absence of choice, she concludes, that 'women will remain dependent upon the chance or luck of particular relationships and will have no collective power to determine the meaning and place of sexuality in their lives.'[4]

Ironically, compulsory heterosexuality also shaped male prison sex culture. Despite the absence of biological women, conventional forms of masculine and feminine identities and social roles were reproduced in postwar Ontario male prisons. If we replace Rich's pursuit of a theory of women's sexuality and instead understand heterosexuality as a system organized according to gender rather than sex, we deepen our understanding of the social and conceptual limitations of forensic sexology and mental health solutions to 'sex problems.' As we shall see, inside the prison, compulsory heterosexuality was sustained by guards, administrators, prisoners, and experts who all assumed that for manly men sex was necessary, assertive, and dominant. Sustaining this view depended not on the systemic oppression of women – there were none – but on a remarkable indifference to anyone who occupied a feminine or feminized 'role.'

Gender was central to the way medical experts, prison administrators, and inmates themselves organized and understood bodies, desires, and pleasures. With remarkable consistency, the distribution of power among inmates was produced and reproduced through sexual activities that were almost always expressed in masculine and feminine terms.[5] Throughout the twentieth century, most inmates housed in Ontario prisons adhered to some version of a 'wolf-punk-fairy' sex system grounded in heterosexist, patriarchal, and familial constructions of masculinity and femininity that were accepted, legitimized, and perpetuated by inmates, their keepers, and medical professionals. In other words, gender as an expression of relations of power was ever-present, even when women were not.

This chapter begins with a brief overview of the way homosexual activity in prison was organized, understood, and managed by administrators and medical experts in the pre–Second World War era, and shows how the postwar shift from sexual perversion to sexual deviation and from gender performance to biological sex, in combination with the popularity of Kinsey's insistence on the natural need for sexual 'outlets,' and increasing critical attention toward masculinity transformed the way experts thought about prison sex culture. Drawing on modern sexology, prison psychiatrists and other treatment experts responded to the problem in a number of surprising ways, the most lasting being their attempts to heterosexualize the institution. These efforts failed dismally, but they illuminate some of the more problematic aspects of the modern sexological model of human sexuality, particularly with respect to sexual violence and assault.

The inability to connect gender, sexuality, and violence was a major flaw in modern sexology. As we shall see, some mental health experts, particularly psychologists, began formulating a critique of masculinity and sexual aggression in Western culture. However, these ideas were never fully developed. When the 'prison sex problem' was exposed to the public as an epidemic of violence in the late 1960s, it was expressed in the language of social justice and civil rights, not mental health. It would be another half decade before feminist critics argued that sexual violence was both sexual *and* violent.

An equally well-known feature of prison culture is that sex offenders are so reviled by other inmates that they typically serve their sentences in protective custody. Using evidence from an early 1970s study of sex criminals incarcerated in British Columbia, and a 1971 prison riot in Kingston, Ontario, this chapter explores the social status of incarcerated sex offenders within the prison social system, focusing particularly on the way prison sex culture and the status of the sex offender contributed to expressions of masculinity upon which social (and economic) power rested. However natural the shunning of a sex offender may seem, the 'diddler' (slang for a child molester) is a social construction, a by-product of the postwar 'discovery' of recidivism among pedophiles, and the mental health construction of the sexual deviant as a distinct sexual type. To the general public, this meant that unless treated for his deviation, a man who sought out sex with children would continue to do so for the rest of his sexual life. In other words, what was once treated as a solitary criminal act was now regarded as a deeply rooted mental condition. What began as a campaign to re-integrate sex offenders into mainstream society through compassionate care and mental health treatment ended in their total segregation in prison, and vilification in public life. 'Diddlers' became one of the most reviled, and consequently one of the most vulnerable and endangered, social groups within North American prisons and had to be provided with constant protection.

Evidence of everyday life in prison is hard to come by, and that of prison sex culture even more so. First-hand accounts of 'life behind bars' often include some reference to sexual activity, but usually only in passing. Institutional records contain fragments of evidence, but officials rarely broached the subject directly, because admitting that sex occurred in prison was to admit failure to maintain control over prisoners. Even inmates caught having sex were often charged with a non-identifying infraction, thus making disciplinary records of limited use. Consequently, this chapter casts a wider net than the previous chapters. Canadian sources are supplemented by U.S. materials that include medical studies of sex in prison, a Philadelphia investigation into complaints of sexual assault in its jails and prisons, and a collection of notes and letters exchanged between inmates (and confiscated by prison staff) in various American prisons.[6] Although there were undoubtedly important differences between Canadian and U.S. prisons, these sources demonstrate an overwhelming uniformity in prison sex culture.

Historians who write about marginal social groups are often forced to work creatively with sources, but methodological innovation raises important interpretive questions. Does the organization of sexual relationships in the state of Indiana bear any relationship to male sexual relations in Millbrook, Ontario? Can an Alabama inmate's destructive response to the release of his lover tell us anything about love and loss in Guelph, Ontario? Were sex offenders vilified in Canada in the same way they were in the United States? Given the history of the racialization of crime and practices of segregation in America, can any meaningful comparison be drawn between these institutions and Ontario's racially and ethnically homogeneous reformatories?

After reading a wide cross section of sources that extend from the beginning of the twentieth century to the end, and from almost every region in the United States, including the South, as well as from Ontario and British Columbia, I am struck by the overwhelming continuity in prison sexual culture across time *and* space. This is made less remarkable by well-documented evidence that demonstrates similar continuities in other sexual subcultures, such as postwar butch and fem lesbian culture, for example. For these reasons, I am convinced that the general picture is accurate, and I leave the important task of further refining the history of inmate sexual cultures to future researchers.

As former U.S. federal prison inspector Joseph Fishman put it, sex in prison was shrouded in a 'passive conspiracy of silence.'[7] In his 1934 exposé on sex in New York's prison system, Fishman claimed that on the inside homosexuality was an open secret, but prison officials did their best to keep the matter from leaking out into the public arena for 'political reasons.' Fear of public criticism and of the potential political damage that revelations about homosexual activity would bring ensured that prison officials remained silent on the matter. Indeed, it was a political scandal that prompted Fishman to go public with his own insider's report.[8] In 1934, New York City's newly elected mayor, Fiorello La-Guardia, and political appointee, Austin H. MacCormick, made good on their campaign promise to clean up the city by conducting a highly publicized raid of Welfare Island, the New York City jail. According to George Chauncey, the prison's 'sex pervert' population was singled out for special attention and quickly came to symbolize 'the depths to which the prison had sunk.'[9] Both the *New York Herald Tribune* and the *Daily Mirror* offered detailed descriptions of the effeminate occupants of the homosexual segregation unit who reportedly were permitted tremendous liberties in their style of dress and conduct and were also granted freedom of movement around the island complex.[10] The warden and his deputy were publicly lambasted for neglect of moral duty, and MacCormick proposed a 'get tough' style clean-up program.[11]

However unwelcome these events may have been on Welfare Island, the media coverage cleared a path for more open dialogue among prison administrators about managing homosexual activity in male institutions. Samuel Kahn, another major figure in New York's prison administration, followed Fishman's gambit with *Homosexuality and Mentality*, a book based on a study he conducted ten years earlier while serving as a prison psychiatrist.[12] In the 1940s, prison wardens and superintendents of both men's and women's institutions began speaking openly about the problem at conferences, in professional journals, and in other, more public, venues.[13] Most wardens and superintendents understood, approached, and handled the issue in a remarkably similar fashion, a coincidence made less remarkable by the fact that most twentieth-century prisons operated like military boot camps.[14]

Prisons did not – and still do not – permit sexual activity among inmates, but punishment for sexual activity was doled out inconsistently.

In 1933, a year before the Welfare Island exposé, Dr Oswald Withrow claimed that inside Canada's maximum-security federal penitentiary in Kingston, Ontario, 'filching a piece of pie might be a heinous crime; homosexuality would probably be treated lightly or passed over altogether.'[15] Harvey Blackstock's autobiographical account of life in and out of various Canadian prisons in the 1930s, 40s, and 50s tells a different story. He recounts one incident in Prince Albert, BC, where two inmates were found together in a cell. The usual punishment for such an infraction was 'the paddle,' a piece of thick leather punctured with holes attached to a handle used to strike the back, buttocks, and legs, but the prison warden only charged one of the two with being away from his place of work, and Blackstock received three days in solitary confinement. Blackstock claimed that the warden purposefully created an atmosphere of distrust and fear by meting out different sentences for the same offence.[16] That punishment was used in a manipulative manner is supported by the events surrounding a riot at Guelph Reformatory in 1952. Despite the fact that 'sexual perversion is so prevalent during both normal and abnormal times,' a disproportionately high number of the inmates who received corporal punishment in the fallout after the riot were charged with 'indecent act (homosexual practices)' and given the strap.[17]

The strap at Guelph was a piece of leather three inches wide, three-eights of an inch thick, and fifteen inches long. It was used to punish a wide range of activities, including any attempt to commit sodomy 'and other unmentionable crimes of like character' since at least 1934.[18] Inmates were stripped naked and strapped face-forward to a wall to prevent them from identifying the person who administered the punishment.[19] Even the toughest prisoners readily admitted that being hit with the strap was excruciatingly painful and utterly humiliating.

Some found solitary confinement worse. In Ontario's federal penitentiary at Kingston, twelve cells in the basement were reserved for recalcitrant prisoners. An inmate's clothes were removed upon entering, and he was issued a baby doll outfit with wool socks. At 6 p.m. he was provided with three blankets, and at 6 a.m. they were taken away. Nourishment consisted of bread and water. Roger Caron described the cell as a 'brick cocoon': he could touch both walls at the same time. A single bright light burned around the clock, and the toilet consisted of a hole in the floor 'that gurgled and flushed once every sixty seconds.'[20] Close confinement was regularly used to punish men for having sexual relations with other men, but inmates could also be punished for speaking openly about sexual abuses. One Guelph inmate was thrown into close confinement for three days – for his own protection, the guards assured him – after he revealed that some inmates knew the reformatory chaplain to be a 'sex pervert.'[21]

The degree to which sexual activity was punished varied from institution to institution, but all imposed at least some restrictions on inmates in an effort to reduce its frequency. At the Second Annual (American) Superintendents' Conference in 1945, 'various methods of dealing with sex problems in institutions were described,' reported the Ontario Department of Reform Institutions' Dr Heaslip. 'It was emphasized that discussion and talk about sex activities tended to intensify the problem and it should be dealt with quietly.'[22] The Victorian assumption that sex was a dormant force awakened by the right stimulus translated as 'thinking about sex inevitably led to it.' Thus, with the exception of family members, male prisoners were prevented from having contact with women lest they become sexually aroused. Mixed-sex institutions were almost completely phased out by the time of the Second World War. Partitions were placed between prisoners and visitors to prevent physical contact. In many institutions, female employees were restricted to clerical work, where they were well away from the general inmate population, and where pin-up posters and other images of the opposite sex were prohibited.[23]

It was not only the opposite sex that threatened to spark the sexual longings of inmates. The 'sight and smell of naked bodies' created sexual stimulation, noted American sexologist Benjamin Karpman. Where it was economically possible, dormitories were eliminated or reduced.[24] The military lockstep, a march that required men to follow one behind the other, with the right hand resting on the shoulder of the man in front, the left hand swinging, and 'the toe of one man practically touching the heel of another,' was abolished in U.S. federal prisons based on the premise that close contact was potentially arousing. Inmates were prohibited from entering other men's cells, and physical contact of any sort was discouraged unless it was on the sports field.[25]

The shower was another common trouble spot. In the mid-1950s, staff at the Guelph Reformatory complained that the steam was so thick that inmates could not be properly monitored. Within months, an improved exhaust system was installed.[26] Further advances included a shower facility built in the shape of a horseshoe. Prisoners handed in their clothes upon entering and walked through a series of stations that allowed them to wet down, soap up, and rinse off. They were expected to keep in constant motion until they reached the exit where fresh towels and a clean set of clothes were provided.[27] Nicknamed 'the carwash,' the shower facility was operated by guards posted on an elevated platform.

But more than the lockstep, the dormitories, and the showers put together, prison officials before the Second World War considered the greatest sex stimulant to be the 'fairy.' According to U.S. historian George Chauncey, 'like most men and women,' gay men 'also sought to engender their bodies in ways that approximated the ideal gender types of their cultural group.' Clothing and behavioural cues indicated one's sexual preference. Gay men and fairies used 'unconventional styles in personal grooming to signal their anomalous gender status. "Plucked eyebrows, rouged lips, powdered face, and marcelled, blondined hair" were the essential attributes of the fairy, one straight observer noted in 1933, successfully summarizing the characteristics that at least two generations of New Yorkers have used to identify such men.'[28] Familiarity with gay or fairy style extended well beyond New York. Just a 'mincing walk' and lilting voice were indications of 'the classic homosexual,' easily identifiable even to a small-town Ontario prison guard in the 1950s.[29] Many others also tweezed their eyebrows, bleached their hair, and used cosmetics to enhance their femininity, but in prison fairies had a difficult time sustaining their cultural style and went to tremendous lengths to acquire needed goods. There, classroom chalk doubled as face powder; laundry room bleach lightened hair; hospital tweezers plucked eyebrows; cell bar grime doubled as eyeshadow; and tomato can labels from the kitchen were soaked in water to make rouge.[30]

Prisoners seeking contraband material were forced to become highly inventive, and fairies were no different. The desire to procure beauty products was well known among the staff, of course, and could sometimes interfere with real medical needs. Some of the most difficult items to procure were creams and oils, usually only available in medical supply chests. In 1962 an African-American imprisoned at Ontario's Millbrook Reformatory repeatedly requested shaving salve for a skin condition, claiming that without it 'it is next to impossible to shave.' Each time the doctor refused his request. Though by all reports a model prisoner, the doctor insisted 'this "man" is a confirmed passive homosexual who wants to be beautiful.'[31] The superintendent accepted the doctor's explanation, and the medication was never provided.

Though fairy style was never officially sanctioned, there existed a certain level of acceptance of those inmates who insisted on feminizing their behaviour. No doubt this was because the majority of prisoners and custodians were from the working classes. In his study of homosexual cultures in pre–Second World War New York City, Chauncey discovered that fairies were tolerated in much of working-class society: 'He was so obviously a "third-sexer," a different species of human being that his very effeminacy served to confirm rather than threaten the masculinity of other men, particularly since it often exaggerated the conventions of deference and gender difference between men and women. The fairies reaffirmed the conventions of gender even as they violated them: they behaved as no man should but as any man might wish a woman would.'[32] Based on his 1920s study of imprisoned fairies in New York State, psychiatrist Samuel Kahn described the 'true' homosexual as 'not just one who is in love with a member of his own sex,' but who 'has an emotional makeup of the opposite sex so that he could attract his own sex.' Kahn specifically excluded those capable of loving the opposite sex.[33] For him, fairies were in a class of their own, a distinct sex 'entitled to the same rights as women.'[34] After the Second World War, many prisoners and guards continued to treat fairies as women. 'So well has inmate culture created the concept of "broad" that it is accepted as if it were real,' wrote Edwin Johnson in 1971. 'It is more than a theatrical performance, it is an actual life situation.'[35]

It was the fairy's womanly ways that early sexologists pinpointed as the main source of trouble. Their 'feminine carriage, gestures and mannerism,' observed Fishman, 'tends to keep aglow the fire of sex in even the most heterosexual of the prisoners.'[36] Consequently, one of the strategies that wardens and superintendents in North America used to control the sex problem was to isolate effeminate men from the main adult male prison population. Known variously as Lover's Lane, Queen's Row, and, at the Guelph Reformatory in Ontario, Gunzil's Alley, special wings or cell blocks were typically reserved for these types of prisoners.[37] Singling out effeminate men – a practice that effectively reinforced and reified their difference – reflected early twentieth-century popular cultural and, increasingly, medical perceptions of the relationship of gender to sexuality, which held that only effeminate men were 'true' homosexuals.[38] Segregating them was both punitive and protective; the practice was intended to stop them from inflaming the passions of men, and to protect them from men's passions. Obviously, because they were fewer in number, it was easiest to remove them from the general population than it was to 'remove' the males that sought them out.

While it is clear that fairies were made to bear the burden of men's sexual desire, many valued the protection that segregation provided. Camping it up and appearing as 'swish' as possible when first admitted to an institution practically guaranteed a prisoner a cell in segregation where he would be protected from the threat of sexual assault by a wolf.[39] At the Guelph Reformatory, fairies commingled with the rest of the prison population throughout the day, and were separated 'only during the darkness of a picture show' and when they were in their own cells.[40] However, some prisons kept fairies segregated around the clock, something that only became possible to implement in Ontario with the opening of the Millbrook Reformatory in 1956. In these instances, virtually every aspect of their daily lives was conducted apart from the general inmate population. Segregated prisoners took their meals, attended religious services, and used the exercise yard separately from the rest of the inmate population. They slept one to a cell and had much less freedom than did other prisoners. Inmates in segregated units usually had less time outside of their cell block, and less time outdoors.[41] In such instances, segregation offered a small amount of protection but at a significant price.

By the 1960s, the media began to report that fairies and queens were sometimes the targets of abuse. In 1965 the leader of Ontario's provincial opposition party launched an official investigation into rumours that 'sex perverts' were forced to wear baby doll pyjamas at Millbrook.[42] The accusation could not be proved, and the investigation was closed, but there was no shortage of examples of cruel treatment meted out to Millbrook's effeminate inmates. Only two months earlier, the *Peterborough Examiner* described how an effeminate inmate in Group II (sex deviant) segregation was forced to parade up and down the cell block while a guard repeatedly demanded that he 'walk like a man.'[43]

Most treatment experts were horrified by the way prisons treated their inmates, and were particularly critical of the unofficial policy of sexual repression.[44] By the 1930s, medical professionals agreed that sublimation over the long term was neither healthy nor possible.[45] The sex urge is 'too elemental and instinctive to be completely controlled by confinement,' explained American sex expert Benjamin Karpman in 1948. Celibacy is rare, he continued, and can only be achieved by those who 'have other diversions and stimulants.'[46] Four years later, Albert R. Virgin, the Ontario Department of Reform Institution's director of rehabilitation, explained that this prescription was not to be confused with older ideas about simply wearing a man down: 'I do not know whether working with a wheel-barrow, or a pick and shovel, is a cure for sexual tendencies or not. I do not think so. We have heard from time immemorial about hard 'slogging' work as a cure for the sex urge. Maybe that is so. But I think a full occupation is the main thing in connection with men of that type.'[47] Unfortunately, one of the major problems for prison management was a sorry lack of things for inmates to do. Labour unions who successfully argued that prison labour was unfair competition, and staunch defenders of the prison as a punitive, not reformative, institution, ensured that during most of the twentieth century inmates were likely to serve the majority of their time with little or nothing to occupy them.[48] Fresh air and exercise were severely limited, reading materials were often unavailable, inaccessible, or worn out from overuse, and letter writing was restricted and censored, as were visits from family and friends.

For all of these reasons, many experts viewed sexual activity between prisoners as normal. 'All environments in which large masses of men congregate – navy, army, concentration camps and prisons, lend themselves to homosexuality,' declared Samuel Kahn, a New York prison psychiatrist. This standpoint remained intact after – and may even have been boosted by – the Second World War. Despite vigorous attempts to eliminate homosexuals from the ranks of the military during the early 1940s, the high instance of homosexual activity led many to concede that in certain settings it was impossible to eradicate.[49] For example, Dr Aldwyn B. Stokes, a leading medical and psychiatric expert in Canada, explained that prison 'merely illustrates that the homosexual way of satisfying sex impulses is because, in most people, circumstances bring it out. That was evident in some of the prisoner-of-war camps, and other places of that kind ... There is a tendency there which finds its expression when the sexes are aggregated. It was true in the women's barracks during the war, and it is an expression of sex deprivation.'[50] American doctors and psychiatrists made the same arguments. For example, the authors of a 1952 article on the treatment of homosexuality in prison wrote, 'those who have served in the Navy will recall the saying, "Any old port in a storm."'[51]

So widely accepted was this phenomenon that at least three U.S. treatment experts focused their attention on prisoners who did *not* want to have sex. In a 1951 article that attempted to dispel the myth that prisons 'make' homosexuals, Robert Linder conceded that confinement did have certain 'regressive effects.' However, he argued, 'homoeroticism, a function of heterosexual starvation,' should be distinguished from the 'integrated and patterned attitudes characteristic of homosexuality.'[52] In other words, there were homosexual acts and then there were homosexuals.[53] Finally, Linder argued that while all prisoners experienced some type of mental breakdown as a result of confinement, the most common mental disturbance found in prisons was the 'acute panic episode' during which one's 'natural' defences against homosexuality began to crumble.

One of the earliest medical experiments in prison related to homosexual activity was not, as one might have expected, aimed at curing homosexuality or gender inversion, but rather focused on the treatment of homosexual panic.[54] Like Linder, Sing Sing prison psychiatrists Bernard C. Glueck Jr and Russell H. Dinerstein diagnosed inmates who reported fear of homosexual contact with 'homosexual panic state,' and they set out to cure them with one of the newest psychiatric treatments available: insulin shock. Discovered by accident, insulin coma therapy was first used in a psychiatric context in Vienna in 1933. By 1937 insulin coma wards were established in Canada and the United States. Regularly employed during the Second World War, this treatment was used to 'break down the vicious circle of anxiety and loss of weight' associated with panic states.[55] Psychiatrists were unable to explain how the treatment worked, but were satisfied that 'putting patients into repeated comatose states seemed to improve their condition.' Dinerstein and Glueck noted that the combination of rest, sedation, and sub-coma insulin therapy resulted in 'a marked decrease in the physiological components of anxiety, a greater degree of manageability and a feeling of well-being.'[56] Their experiment is remarkable in a number of ways, the most obvious being its intention to help men overcome their fear of homosexual sex. It lucidly illustrates how treatment in prison was driven by economic, not sexual, concerns. In addition to keeping the problem out of public and political view, in-house treatment allowed the administration to save on the cost of transferring inmates to a psychiatric institution. Despite the many pronouncements on the evils of homosexuality peculiar to this period, the moral cost of sex between men was apparently judged to be less expensive than the financial burden imposed by providing medical refuge to inmates paralysed by their fear of it.

These examples clearly illustrate how psychiatric and psychological theories about human sexuality and gender normativity sometimes worked in concert with an institutional push to produce prisoner manageability.[57] Indeed, as we saw in the previous chapter, medical measures in places like Millbrook could be used to bring about institutional conformity, and were equally, if not more, punishing than traditional prison techniques. But some experts proved quite content with 'tradition.' In

1939 American prison doctors J.G. Wilson and M.J. Pescor suggested that 'known homosexuals ... be thrown in with men who are known to be aggressively heterosexual, and ... that the authorities turn a blind eye if physical mischance befall them if they are assaulted by those who may resent their advances.'[58] Contemporary legal actions against American state authorities indicate that, in the United States at least, this practice is still widespread.[59]

After the Second World War, most experts supported the continued segregation of fairies, but not because fairies were to be treated like women. Ontario's Department of Reform Institutions' director of neurology and psychiatry, Frank van Nostrand, used the sex deviant treatment program as a way to remove homosexuals 'as a disturbance factor.'[60] Experts defended such policy initiatives on the grounds that it was a mental health measure aimed at protecting impressionable young inmates from the influence of homosexuals. Officially, at least, van Nostrand expressed the hope that treatment for homosexuals would be initiated, but he did nothing to assist the few who were hired to do the job. Moreover, some of those hired proved willing to put treatment in the service of discipline. Shortly after Millbrook opened, consulting psychiatrist F.E. Webb initiated an experimental program for homosexuals who 'volunteered' to receive electric shock treatments, but as we saw in chapter 5, the experience of one such volunteer suggests that medical 'help' was wielded as a punitive and regulatory device against inmates who failed to conform to masculine ideals in dress and conduct.[61] As the staff at the Toronto Psychiatric Hospital's Forensic Clinic complained, medical professionals who treated sexual deviation were not always guided by psychoanalytic and 'scientific' principles.

In prison settings, medical treatment was also withheld in order to exact compliance. Throughout the postwar era, fairies were denied medical supplies that authorities suspected were for 'beauty purposes,' and later, transgender inmates were similarly denied treatment. For example, in 1973 T.S., an inmate serving time at Millbrook, insisted on being treated as a woman. However, the presiding physician withheld her medication and hormone treatments, and prison staff was instructed to refer to her as a male 'on all occasions.' Although not a fairy, T.S. responded as many fairies did: by refusing to capitulate. According to one prison report, she refused to leave her cell 'unless he was provided with his dress.'[62] Fairies (some of whom would later be identified – self or otherwise – as transsexual) persistently refused treatment aimed at curing their deviation, and repeatedly insisted that it was society, not themselves, that needed changing. As one probation officer put it, 'the ordinary homosexual is more inclined to shun the idea of treatment – preferring to remain in his demi-mode.'[63] Though it is difficult to gain an accurate sense of how often and for how long fairies maintained this oppositional stance, given the various forms of punishment that were used to enforce complicity, the consultant psychiatrist who replaced F.E. Webb regarded 'confirmed homosexuals' as the worst treatment prospects.[64]

So long as fairies were considered 'true' homosexuals, men who sought them out as sexual partners were not considered abnormal either by their peers, by fairies, by prison officials, or by medical doctors. From the beginning of the twentieth century through to the end, masculine-looking and -acting men who exhibited a preference for sex with fairies earned a moniker of their own: 'wolves.' As historians George Chauncey and Peter Boag have shown, a wolf-punk-fairy culture organized and gave shape to pre–Second World War urban and rural male sexual relationships. This culture was reproduced in Canadian and American prisons with two important differences: first, as a distinct 'gay' identity emerged after the Second World War, wolf-punk-fairy culture became less dominant as a system of socio-sexual organization. For reasons that will become clear, however, in prison the wolf-punk-fairy system has remained largely intact. Second, while many punks were drawn into sexual relations with wolves as a means of economic survival, there was clearly an element of choice, whereas in prison punks were more typically coerced.

In prison, wolves unable to access inmates who willingly assumed a feminine role readily forced smaller, weaker, and more timid inmates to do so. New inmates were called 'fish,' a moniker with etymological roots in early twentieth century male homosexual slang – 'fish' was originally a derogatory word for a woman.[65] If a fish was young and especially if he was attractive, wolves sought him out as a sexual partner. 'He needn't be a homosexual nor necessarily is the kid, who with his adolescent smile, his unsophisticated manners, soft skin and aesthetic proportions, embodies the female,' explained Roger Caron, an inmate with experience in a number of Ontario institutions. Like prison staff and postwar forensic sexologists, prisoners understood the wolf as a 'normal' heterosexual man. The wolf used his sexual partner – a biological male – as he would a woman.

When a wolf used a fish for sexual pleasure, the fish became a 'punk.' In early twentieth-century urban gay cultures, street punks were not gender inverts, and therefore not identified as true homosexuals in the way fairies and pansies were. But punks were willing to have sex with men, usually for money. Inside prisons, punks were likewise part of an exchange economy, but not by their own choosing. 'A punk is neither a wise kid nor a small time hood,' explained one inmate, 'he is a kid that has been made, made many times in the past, and that can be made now with no difficulty whatsoever. He is what, if he were a girl, would be known as a pig. Sometimes he is actually a prostitute.'[66] Although prison punks were not entirely without agency, the wolves were able to exercise a much greater degree of physical and psychological control over other inmates in prison than they could on the streets, and conversely, punks a much lesser degree. With the exception of close confinement, there was nowhere to escape.

Breaking from their predecessors who were largely preoccupied with the prison fairy, post–Second World War experts identified the wolf as the problem inmate. During a 1952 review of Ontario's reformatories and training schools, investigators questioned Director of Rehabilitation A.R. Virgin on the problem of effeminate inmates. 'We have seen them running around with their sideburns down to here (indicating), and swinging their hips. What can we do with them?' asked the chairman. 'Segregate him at night,' replied Virgin, 'and try to keep him under supervision.' But, he added, they are 'not nearly as dangerous as the aggressive homosexuals ... those are the ones we have to watch.'[67] Yet Virgin and his colleagues continued to dismiss or deny the seriousness of the problem in their day-to-day work. Following a riot at the Guelph Reformatory in the same year, three psychologists were sent in to conduct extensive interviews with inmates to determine the sources of discontent. This was one of the few examples of the Ontario Plan put into action, and it produced interesting results. In their final report to the DRI, the psychologists identified the sexual assault of inmates by other inmates as a key source of discontent among the population. They recommended that known homosexuals be segregated, though in this case they meant wolves, not fairies. 'Until this is done,' they concluded, 'inmates will have to go through the terrifying and revolting experience of having to comply with the wishes of sexual perverts who overpower them by force.' Both A.R. Virgin and G. Hedley Basher, the deputy minister, dismissed sex perversion as a factor in the riot, though Basher admitted that sexual coercion was a problem they needed to address nonetheless.[68]

Despite the growing concern about acts of sexual aggression perpetrated by manly prisoners, when Millbrook opened to accept Guelph's problem inmates, van Nostrand continued to single out effeminate inmates for transfer. 'It must be clearly understood that they will include only actual Homo Sexuals [fairies] and not those caught at some indecent act with another prisoner [wolves and punks] or those charged with such by the Courts.'[69] However, superintendents of other Ontario prisons disregarded the directive and continued to transfer wolves to Millbrook, forcing van Nostrand to admit that while these inmates were once 'only petty annoyances,' they were now widely considered 'major trouble-makers.'[70] Millbrook had little choice but to accept them, and van Nostrand prepared a new directive to reflect the population change. Those who have had 'homosexual experiences in which he takes the "male role" but whose *preferred* sex object is a woman' should be classified as a Group I (discipline problem) inmate.[71]

So long as they appeared to take the 'male role,' wolves were treated as a discipline problem, not a sex deviant problem. Indeed, they were never incorporated into any medical theories of sexuality. Instead, the wolf was understood exclusively in gendered terms that assumed masculinity as inherently heterosexual and naturally dominant, two important qualities that the prison environment reputedly thwarted. For sexologists, aggressive homosexuals were not sex deviants; they simply lacked the appropriate sexual outlets. Developments in Ontario were echoed elsewhere. When called to the nearby Terre Haute Federal Prison to assist with managing the sex problem there, Kinsey Institute researcher Wardell Pomeroy explained to Indiana prison officials, 'the usual way a man asserts his masculinity is to have heterosexual sex.' If an inmate 'can create a fiction with a person who appears to be feminine, it helps him assert his lost manliness.'[72]

Remarkably, Pomeroy, van Nostrand, and a host of others gave virtually no consideration to the prison punk despite the fact that, throughout the twentieth century, it was the victimization and corruption of young men by older, hardened prisoners that preoccupied prison reformers. Indeed, those who were bold, desperate, or stupid enough to complain about sexual assault were hard pressed to find a sympathetic ear. Prisoners were considered untrustworthy, a stigma that worked in favour of the wardens and superintendents who were keen to avoid negative publicity. Inmates had no one to whom they could confide or complain; the few who attempted to seek redress or protection from sexual violence had their complaints quickly dismissed by prison authorities as fabricated lies. Administrators did not hesitate to mobilize their resources, including medical and treatment staff, to silence complainants. For example, as per DRI procedure, after a 1945 riot at the Guelph Reformatory, an investigator set up interviews with prisoners interested in filing a grievance. Of the twenty-three complaints submitted, Dr Heaslip, the prison superintendent, dismissed eleven on the grounds that the complainant was either a 'moron' (a formal diagnosis), 'psychopathic,' or 'borderline' personality. Two examples are especially illuminating. One inmate reported 'the bullies are stealing tobacco and desserts, and suggested that the victims should be protected by placing them by themselves and that inmates should have someone to confide in other than the Superintendent and Sergeant.' Heaslip responded to the report: 'Recidivist and psychopathic personality. No further comment.' An inmate from C-3, the section reserved for 'perverts,' told the investigator that for the previous two months the guards refused to take him and others in his block out for exercise. Heaslip wrote, 'a psychiatric patient in the army and is under treatment. Suffers from hallucinations and has had corporal punishment here for gross indecency and will be transferred to Ontario Hospital [as a psychiatric patient] if necessary.' The threat of psychiatric treatment, either in the prison hospital or by means of a transfer to a mental hospital, was real for all prisoners, but was of special concern for homosexuals, and had been since at least the 1920s.[73]

Heaslip's dismissive tactics were employed by his successors as well. In 1954 one inmate's family physician was horrified to see his patient return home from the Guelph Reformatory in a 'starved and beaten condition.' The inmate claimed he had been gang-raped repeatedly, especially in the shower area. A year later, a physician at an Ontario hospital made a written enquiry to the Department of Reform Institutions concerning a patient who described the brutal treatment he endured at Guelph. In both cases, Deputy Minister G. Hedley Basher went to great lengths to describe the many risks inherent in running a prison, and managed to convince both physicians that the complaints are 'not in keeping with the facts and grossly exaggerated' and, moreover, that the inmate had engaged in homosexual activity and was trying to 'justify his own unnatural behaviour.'[74] Victims of sexual assault and those who were punished for engaging in consensual sex – in addition to the non-homosexual sex offender population, which was routinely harassed, assaulted, abused, and isolated – had no channel through which they might gain a fair hearing.

A small sign of change occurred in 1965, when an inmate at Kingston Penitentiary, Canada's oldest federal prison, was allowed to send a brief to the Joint House Senate Committee on Penitentiaries, whose task it was to explore problems and propose reforms in the federal prison system.

Given how tightly prison wardens controlled information, his input was likely solicited by a member of Parliament or by someone of similar stature. In his submission, the writer described how young offenders are

> preyed upon by those individuals with homosexual tendencies in an effort to satisfy their own abnormal desires, which is in itself very detrimental to the youths whether they become involved with these individuals or not. In the past two years I have seen many youths come into the institution who have been turned from decent kids who made a mistake into tough young punks who will most likely be in trouble for the rest of their lives, by the older men who took them under their wing when they first entered the institution and need someone to help them to get adjusted to prison life.[75]

Attached to his submission was a psychiatrist's report characterizing the author as a 'skilled manipulator.' It also indicated that he had attempted suicide and was being treated for depression. Just as the Ontario deputy minister and the superintendents at the Guelph Reformatory had done in the previous decade, Kingston Penitentiary's administration did everything in its power to undermine the writer's claims, and it appears to have worked. His complaints were dismissed.

And yet sex was everywhere, or at least so it seemed. As American ex-prisoner Edwin Johnson put it, all inmates fall into one of three categories: 'those who do, those who watch, and those who observe and occasionally participate.'[76] Just how much sex was going on in male prisons is impossible to ascertain. By the mid-1950s, most prison staff estimated that anywhere from 25 to 35 per cent of the inmate population engaged in sexual activity of some sort, but there is little reason to think these estimates were accurate. In the 1960s, staff at California's sex offender treatment unit in Norwalk permitted homosexual activity, and inmates were actively encouraged to talk openly about their experiences. Estimates of the number of inmates engaging in homosexual activity ranged from as low as 10 per cent to as high as 90 per cent.[77] The tremendous disparity in staff perceptions well illustrates the difficulty in trying to ascertain the level of sexual activity in prisons, hospitals, or, for that matter, anywhere. Nevertheless, in the 1950s and 60s, most Canadian (and American) prisoners and treatment staff were confident that there was 'a great deal of sex play among the Inmates.'[78]

After the Second World War, prison superintendents and wardens were more likely to admit that sex occurred, but they denied that it was coercive and placed the blame on inmates, not on the administration.

For example, an American warden insisted that the fault lay with older inmates who convinced the younger ones that sex between men in prison was 'perfectly normal.' What young inmates needed, he argued, was sex counselling to inform them otherwise.[79] In the post–Second World War era, sex education was widely regarded as one of the most important weapons in the fight against sexual deviation.[80] Prison psychologists and social workers often interpreted sexually deviant behaviour, including incest, as a knowledge problem. Sex education was sometimes the only thing prescribed to help bring an inmate's behaviour patterns in line with social norms. However, to suggest that young punks were engaging in sexual activities with older, stronger prisoners because they were misinformed about what was normal and what was not demonstrates either a remarkable level of ignorance or an inability or refusal to challenge male sexual privilege, even when that privilege was at the expense of the sexual 'rights' of other male inmates.

For some mental health experts, interest in the psychology of masculinity eventually led to an increasing curiosity in the link between manliness and violence as a social problem. Canadian psychologist F.R. Wake's 1959 study of cruelty among institutionalized boys is an excellent example of this trend.[81] Wake posited that delinquency was the natural by-product of a society that inculcated and rewarded male aggression. 'The growing boy,' Wake claimed, 'learns that aggressive behaviour is a requirement if he wishes to feel, and to be seen as a man.'[82] Though young men were also taught the limits of acceptable aggressive behaviour, Wake suggested that we should not be surprised to discover that while the majority might learn to live within the bounds of convention, some would fail to live up to the masculine ideal, while others would tend to over-perform. In a modified version of the Kinsey scales, Wake suggested that delinquency studies should abandon the focus on finding a single cause of criminal behaviour and look at delinquency across a scale. For example, delinquency varied in degree, he argued, 'such as the theft of a few pennies from a church to robbing a bank and from tentatively suggesting sexual intimacy with a like-aged female to raping a three year old child.'[83] Society must either decide that 'upholding the present concept of masculinity is not worth the price' and should 'devalue the characteristic of aggression' or it should 'concentrate on teaching better methods of control.'[84] Wake chose the latter.[85] Whether the issue was aggression, sexual activity, or a combination of both, most postwar sexologists and mental health experts failed or perhaps simply refused to re-evaluate certain masculine rights and privileges. Even when the element of harm seemed unavoidable, experts like Wake voted in favour of improving mechanisms of control and containment, and in the case of abnormal sex, creating appropriate outlets for the expression of normative masculinity.

Little wonder that the mental health experts' solution to the prison sex problem was the conjugal visit. It was an idea that received scientific support from an unexpected quarter: the Kinsey Institute for Sex Research. When Terre Haute officials called upon its sex research staff for help in 1962, Wardell Pomeroy responded by convincing officials that the repressive approach was based on 'myth and folklore, not fact.'[86] Like the staff at Toronto's Forensic Clinic, he used Kinsey's findings of human sexual variability to argue against the notion of a 'fixed' sexual identity and to recast heterosexual and homosexual behaviour as socially and culturally malleable. Kinsey himself opposed attempts to 'normalize' sexual practices, but Pomeroy and others drew on his theories to explore ways to correct 'variant' sex behaviour. Pomeroy argued that persistent efforts to eliminate sex in prison had failed because sex cannot be repressed. He explained how homosexual men who tried to change their sexual identity by simply refraining from same-sex sex became tense, nervous, and upset. On the other hand, those who replaced it with a 'positive program toward heterosexual adjustment,' such as dating the opposite sex, could 'make their way down the Kinsey scale [i.e., from an almost exclusively homosexual 5 toward an almost exclusively heterosexual 2] and achieve near full heterosexual adjustment.'[87] The problem, Pomeroy claimed, was that in prison there is no opportunity to develop heterosexual relationships, so such programs were impossible to implement.

Pomeroy encouraged prison officials to find ways to redirect inmates' attention toward heterosexual attachments. Citing the example of a girls' reformatory that allowed its wards to go out on dates with boys so as to permit 'normal' heterosexual development, he advocated the system of home visits that had been implemented in some Scandinavian countries. Unlike conjugal visits that benefited only married men, who constituted less than a third of the total inmate population, home visits allowed *all* men a day pass. This, Pomeroy argued, would enable both single heterosexual and homosexual men opportunities for sexual contact.

Such proposals were not new, but with the rise of mental health and modern sexology, they were more warmly received than they had been in earlier decades.[88] In 1965 Arnold Peters, an NDP member of Ontario's provincial Parliament, suggested that the DRI hire prostitutes to pleasure male prisoners. Prostitution is normal in society, he insisted, citing a 'cat house' that had existed in Kirkland Lake for twenty years. 'There were a lot of single miners,' Peters explained. 'It's better than having them raping your daughters.' He also recommended organized periodic visits by female prisoners to 'cut down on homosexuality.'[89] Reverend John Griffin, a United Church minister and graduate student in psychology, urged the government to allow wives and prostitutes to visit men in prison 'as an alternative to sex with other males ... Many fights were over homosexual rights to new prisoners,' he said.[90] That fall, the federal commissioner of penitentiaries, A.J. MacLeod, reported that he was allowing seventy-two-hour passes for men to return home to visit their wives and families, and to mow the lawn. According to a report in the *Toronto Telegram*, he felt it helped eliminate homosexuality.[91] The 1969 report of the Canadian Committee on Corrections agreed that prison was conducive to homosexual behaviour, and that many inmates did not consider homosexuality in prison abnormal. Using the language of mental health expertise, it argued, 'for the mature prisoner with a history of reasonably adequate heterosexual functioning outside prison, adaptation to the heterosexual deprivation of prison is generally reversible. On his release he usually finds opportunity for heterosexual relationships to which he can adjust. For the immature, or the sexually inadequate, however, the homosexual emphasis of prison life frequently integrates into his habit pattern a practice of deviance or sexual malfunction which is difficult to reverse when he is released.'[92] Permitting sexual contact between male inmates and their female spouses was not an acknowledgment of prisoners 'sexual rights.' Rather, the state deployed the wives of inmates as a deviance-distractor, a calming mechanism, and a management tool. Small home-like cabins began dotting the corrections landscape in the 1970s.[93]

By the 1960s, creating more opportunities for heterosocial contact seemed like a good idea for all inmates. Department of Reform Institutions Minister Allan Grossman described how home economics students from MacDonald Institute for Domestic Science at Guelph were attending organized dances at the nearby Brampton Ontario Training Centre for 'reformable' young offenders.[94] Inmates would develop 'adequate social relationships and healthy attitudes towards members of the opposite sex,' he argued. But it wasn't to stop there. The DRI was also exploring the possibility of opening co-ed training schools for delinquents.[95]

Proposals like these highlight how in the postwar era sexologists were blind to the ways human sexual behaviour was embedded in systems of power, and that, as Joan Scott famously put it, gender is a primary way of signifying relationships within a given system.[96] The idea that manly, apparently heterosexual, men simply needed an appropriate sex outlet was naive and simplistic. The conjugal visit did not bring an end to prison sex culture, and co-ed facilities would most certainly have been a disaster. The final section of this chapter takes a closer look at the way masculinity, intimacy, and sexuality were woven into the fabric of post-war prison culture to see what many forensic sexologists could not.

Intra-inmate violence of any kind has always been grossly underreported, in part because for prisoners the ability to endure hardship boosts one's status and prestige among other inmates. Roger Caron's immersion in prison-tough masculinity upon entering the Ontario Reformatory in Guelph at the age of sixteen began with a grim determination to conceal his fear. He quickly learned that, when under attack, calling a guard was considered 'unmanly.'[97] Prisoners who received the strap might 'beg for mercy,' and those who managed to maintain their composure gained the respect of other inmates. Conversely, those who lied about enduring the punishment without 'breaking' were 'contemptible cowards.'[98]

Prisoners who were raped quickly learned to submit in silence. Fellow inmates enforced their complicity even when the assailant was a staff member. In a case cited earlier, a young inmate learned that the prison's Anglican minister was known as a 'sex pervert.' Two inmates explained how they submitted to masturbation with the minister in the hope that his good favour would get them an early parole. When the inmate reported this information to a guard, he was immediately placed in solitary confinement. Even in cases involving sexual coercion, 'ratting' to the authorities was not condoned by most inmates, and made one a target of violence and abuse. While it is possible that the prison superintendent wanted to silence him, placing him in solitary confinement likely *was* for his protection from other inmates.

Similarly, in 1973 Dan, also a young inmate at Guelph, escaped from the prison after his dorm captain laughed off his complaint about a guard's sexual advances. The dorm captain also told him to keep his mouth shut. When Dan was captured some days later, he reported to the staff exactly what had transpired. A prison guard attempted to have sexual relations with him in the kitchen. As a sexual assault survivor, he was overcome with tremendous fear and managed to escape the guard's advances. Later, however, the guard told him that he would arrange to bring him over to his house to do some repair work for a few days. The inmate knew what was in store and decided he would rather escape than endure three days of coerced sex. Upon his capture, the prison administration was certain he would be brutally beaten by the other inmates for 'squealing,' and they transferred him to another institution.[99] Reporting sexual violence was not a viable option.

But not all sex in prison was coercive. Once acculturated to prison sex culture and their own role within it, intimidated, coerced, and raped punks often went on to form emotionally meaningful relationships with wolves, relationships that closely resembled traditional heterosexual ones. Many postwar experts, especially psychologists and sociologists who were more inclined to situate sex within a larger cultural system, viewed these relationships empathically. Sensory deprivation, colloquially known as 'prison stupor,' was widely considered a serious psychological problem.[100] It was well known that emotional isolation and loneliness led many prisoners to engage in self-mutilation, for example.[101] Gresham Sykes, a leading post–Second World War sociologist, laid out what he described as the five 'pains of imprisonment.' Lack of heterosexual outlets was one of them, and he and others regarded sex among male inmates as a way to ease those pains. One sociologist described sex between inmates as 'a substitute for baseball and marriage and movies and bragging and friendship and success, a substitute for anything and everything that makes life worthwhile.'[102]

While it is true that relationships in prison could not be extricated from the coercive context in which they took shape, it is nevertheless true that some sexual and domestic relationships evolved into emotionally satisfying ones. Roger Caron characterized close monogamous relationships that included physical affection and emotional intimacy as a 'marriage of convenience':

> The wolf will protect his sweet kid with his life and an intimacy and friendship so loyal as to defy belief can spring up between the two whom society has rejected as losers. They feel that it's just the two of them against the prison jungle and they help each other to survive and share each other's loneliness and hopes for the future. The kid's ol' man will make all sorts of sacrifices in order to provide the boy with little gifts and extra food. More than anything else he will make very certain that the kid stays out of trouble.[103]

Letters written between such couples in the 1950s reveal that wolves, punks, and fairies articulated their feelings of love, affection, need, and

desire in remarkably conventional ways. They expressed emotions and
sentiments common to everyday courting couples.[104] 'My love for you is
not just a pen[itenitary] love it is a love that I am proud of and one that
I know I'll always carry in my heart out side in the free world or in the
pen,' wrote one prisoner. 'Your not filling in for someone else while I am
in the joint.'[105] 'Male' partners described and defended their emotional
commitments:

> *You're not just another woman to me. Damn whether you are or have been a whore or*
> *what not in your life* ... Baby I really don't know what or how to say it to make
> myself plainer except to say that *I love you I want you and J I need you.* I have
> never in my life released myself to a woman the way I have on you J simply
> because I never felt this way about it with them.[106]

As in other same-sex cultures, couples in prison sometimes organized
a formal marriage ceremony complete with a marriage licence, and lived
in a conventional domestic fashion.[107] Astonished to learn that an inmate
'claimed he was "married" to a man and seemed very happy with the situation and even proud of the fact,' the superintendent at Guelph Reformatory immediately recommended his/her transfer to the maximum-
security unit at Millbrook Reformatory. Even though s/he was kept in
continual segregation with fifteen other 'active homosexuals,' the superintendent felt 'this type of inmate could be a very poor influence on the
impressionable teen-aged inmate.'[108] Perhaps the superintendent was
simply unaware of just how common such relationships were. According
to Roger Caron, most guards left couples alone because such relationships have 'a steadying effect.'[109] Psychiatrist Guy Richmond's experience
as the doctor at British Columbia's Oakalla Prison supports Caron's
claim. In Richmond's published memoirs, he describes three separate
instances in which inmates attempted suicide – two were successful – in
response to the loss of or separation from a partner.[110] Long before Richmond or Caron published their first-hand accounts, Alabama sociologist
Malcolm M. Moos documented a case in which the prison transferred
one of two inmates who had fallen in love. The one left behind expressed
his grief and rage by destroying $400 worth of machinery in the wool
mill.[111] In fact, it was common knowledge among inmates that violence,
sometimes directed outward and other times inward, was often one person's way of responding to being separated from his lover.

There was little a wolf could do if the administration decided to separate him from his lover, but as a group wolves exercised considerable social power. This is particularly well demonstrated by the fact that the wolf-punk-fairy system continued to survive virtually intact in the postwar era, and indeed to the present day. While it is true that similar gendered and sexualized identities exist in present-day gay male cultures through-out Canada and the United States, in the second half of the twentieth century men who took a masculine role were not considered heterosex-ual as they had been before the Second World War. This was, of course, largely due to the popularization of mental health ideas about human sexuality. Experts' claim that the only criterion for defining homosexu-ality and heterosexuality was the biological sex of those engaged in a sex-ual act meant that even though some men may have continued to think of themselves as heterosexual, others were less likely to agree. Moreover, in spite of the severing of sexual identity from gender performance in popular medical discourse, homosexuality continued to be linked to effeminacy. Consequently, having sex with another man diminished one's masculinity.

Wolves' resistance against the administrations' attempts to label them homosexual, and against the meanings attributed to same-sex sex in the civilian world from whence the prison population came and would return, stemmed from wolves' particular investment in a configuration of masculinity, sexuality, and power defined through gender role, not biology. Modern sexology's emphasis on the biological sex rather than on the gender attributes as determinative of a sexual 'orientation' made sense to a society attempting to forge separate but equal roles for men and women. Inside prison, however, pre–Second World War working- and street-class masculinity prevailed. Aided by a military-style disciplin-ary regime that continued to see effeminate men as 'true' homosexuals and that naturalized sexual aggression and violence among men, prison sex culture continued to organize *itself* according to the values and meanings of an erotic system that no longer worked for the mass middle class, but continued to work well for those who wielded the most social power inside the prison.

The threat modern sexology posed to the manly men who sustained the wolf-punk-fairy system may well have contributed to one of the things that did appear to change in Ontario prisons' social hierarchy. It is com-monly understood that in Canadian and American prisons, 'diddlers' – men known to have or merely rumoured to have had sex with children – sink to the bottom of the prison barrel. Administrators maintain that the only way to protect them from physical injury is to keep them separate from other inmates. That pedophiles and other sex criminals are seen as loathsome miscreants within the prison appears at first to be a natural expression of a ubiquitous cultural sentiment, but according to historian Phillip Jenkins, sex criminals were only defined as a distinct group in the late nineteenth century.[112] Evidence suggests that within Canadian prisons the 'diddler' either emerged or became a member of a more distinct and endangered social group in the post–Second World War era.

Two important historical developments point toward the causal factors at work in creating these important changes. The first was the construction and popularization of the sex deviant as a social and criminal type, combined with the creation of sexual psychopath laws and internal treatment programs that treated sex offenders as a distinct group; this solidified diddlers' status as outsiders. Interestingly, this outcome was anticipated by many medical and other mental health experts who opposed criminal sexual psychopath legislation in the 1940s and 50s. As early as 1952, junior DRI psychologists expressed grave concern over the practice of segregating certain types of inmates from the larger population, arguing that this only led the main inmate body to treat them with ridicule and even violence.[113] During the 1950s hearings of the Royal Commission on the Criminal Law Relating to Criminal Sexual Psychopaths, experts feared that any attempt to single out sex criminals for treatment would only further stigmatize and isolate a population they hoped to integrate into 'normal' society. According to mental health principles, normal society depended on the total integration of all citizens, not on the isolation or segregation of problem groups. Experts correctly anticipated that the differential treatment of sex deviants would only worsen an already difficult situation. By singling out sex offenders for treatment, by assigning them to particular cell blocks, and by creating new clinics to treat them, diddlers emerged as a distinct social group within the prison's existing social hierarchy.

The second likely factor was new pressure on wolves to affirm their masculinity in light of their sexual activities with other males. As we have seen, in the postwar era men who engaged in sexual activity with other men, regardless of gender identity, were cast as deviant, their masculinity questioned rather than confirmed by their sexual activities.[114] Given this shift in the outside world, and the persistence of the wolf-punk-fairy culture inside prison, it is possible that violent assaults against inmates who victimized children became a new, or at least a more prominent, way to assert a tough heterosexual masculine identity, and thus a means to establish or confirm one's authority and respectability within the prison setting. In other words, diddlers were ideal victims of the kind of brutal physical and verbal violence that affirmed wolves' status as manly, powerful, and fearsome. The social marginalization of pedophiles created the target, the demand that men 'protect' women and children served to make the assault of a pedophile not only an act of physical and psychological domination, but also an expression of familial heterosexuality.

One of the first studies to document the experiences of incarcerated sex offenders was undertaken in the late 1960s by Dr Anthony Marcus, an assistant professor in the Department of Psychiatry at the University of British Columbia. Motivated by his participation in a number of parole hearings for dangerous sexual offenders, Marcus assembled a multidisciplinary research team that set out to better understand the 'lifestyle' of the sex offender in and out of prison.[115] Inmates were frustrated with the legal system, the treatment process, and their status as 'social pariah' within the prison community where 'even as a number you are nothing.'[116] As one dangerous sex offender explained, the police, probation officers, lawyers, and other 'defining agents' were 'disgust[ed] that they have to speak to me, and the sooner they can be rid of me and do some symbolic hand-washing, the better.'"[117] Judges and magistrates indicated during the sentencing process that sex offenders would receive some type of treatment, but once in prison, offenders found that psychological or psychiatric services were not generally available. 'The sex offenders sense that they are being left to rot for a long period of time in confinement,' Marcus argued. 'Even with a superabundance of good will, they find "rehabilitation" an empty word.'[118] Those who had engaged in some form of treatment claimed that therapists got more out of the interaction than they did, and that therapists manipulated treatment outcomes for their own professional gain.[119] Most were disappointed with therapies they were offered, and as a result were unmotivated to participate in 'milksop measures to improve ... institutional conformity, or isolated research schemes, conducted by outsiders for their own aggrandisement, using them as guinea pigs.'[120] Finally, they described how they lived on the social margins of the prison. Subject to constant verbal and physical assaults from inmates and sometimes guards, many were forced to seek refuge in solitary confinement or to escape altogether by committing suicide.

The solutions Marcus proposed were familiar. He called for a specialized facility resembling a hospital rather than a prison; for shared decision-making powers between inmates and treatment staff; for the positive use of peer pressure; for greater personal responsibility on the part of inmate-participants for their actions, growth, and development, and for staff to role-model appropriate behaviour rather than impose controls to force compliance.[121] Inmate-participants should have greater mobility within the institution, more intensive and meaningful interaction with staff, and more heterosocial contact.

In addition to the usual critique of dangerous sex offender legislation, Marcus's study also examined offenders' parole hearings. His research concluded that the hearings were riddled with misguided and ill-informed sociological and psychological assessments of what constituted 'reform.' Prisoners often engaged in all kinds of deviant, 'antisocial' behaviour, including homosexual sex, which parole boards interpreted as 'poor adjustment.' Marcus argued that parole boards failed to consider the unique pressures placed upon sex offenders within a prison community. Based on discussions with his group, he argued that maintaining one's dignity over a long period of time in a maximum-security setting 'required personal rules of adaptation that did not necessarily conform to those the institution would wish him to have ... Facultative homosexuality in the prison setting may be an appropriate adjustment response to increased sexual tension.'[122] For most professionals, inmates who had sex with other men had failed to develop normative sexual habits. This interpretation had a negative impact on dangerous sex offenders' application for parole. For Marcus, however, sex between inmates was a logical adaptation to the existing environment. He argued that inmates probably knew a good deal more about 'satisfactory social adjustment' and the 'adaptive function' than did any expert.

Masculinity was the social field upon which the sexual systems that organized men into wolves, punks, and fairies, and that made diddlers a distinct, despised, and endangered social group intersected, a fact that was graphically illustrated during the final hours of one of the most horrifically violent events in the history of Canadian prisons. Dubbed 'Bloody Sunday,' 18 April 1971 was the last day of a four-day-long riot at Kingston Penitentiary (KP), Canada's most notorious, and oldest, federal prison. The riot was started by six men as a protest against the lack of rehabilitation services and the KP population's impending transfer to a newly built maximum-security prison where inmates would be subject to video surveillance. Led by Billy Knight, the organizers easily captured five guards as hostages and subsequently gained complete control of the penitentiary. On the third day of the takeover, while Knight was in a meeting negotiating the conditions of their surrender, a small group of inmates led by David Shepley took control of the riot. Shepley and his group insisted that no one would be surrendering. Although almost all of the six hundred plus inmates were anxious to bring the occupation to an end, fear of Shepley and his followers ensured compliance. The protest swiftly moved in an entirely new direction.[123]

According to Roger Caron, Shepley and his group were eager to flex their muscle by committing acts of physical violence. After a failed bid to gain access to the five hostages who were under the protection of a group of inmates, they turned their attention to the prisoners in 1-D, a protective custody unit that housed informers and sex offenders who were collectively known in KP as 'the undesirables.' The media had already expressed fear of just such an action. To reassure the public, Toronto journalist Henry Champ was allowed to tour 1-D and speak to some of the undesirables. He 'was visibly shaken by the experience.'[124] Indeed, once Shepley was in control, the 'undesirables' were in grave danger. On 18 April, Shepley and his group dragged 1-D inmates from their cells, tied and chained them to wooden chairs, covered their heads, and placed them in a circle under the main prison dome. Shepley called upon everyone to witness and show approval for the mock trial that followed.

Two successful attempts were made to have diddlers released from the circle. In one case, a wolf stepped forward to save his 'sweet kid,' and in the other a 'young and popular homosexual' successfully defended his wolf, demonstrating the significance as well as the emotional intensity of intimate relationships between prisoners. The remaining twelve were subjected to hours of physical assault that began with each person's nose being broken and continued with repeated kicks and iron bar blows to the head, legs, arms, and ribs.[125] As Ralph Lake, who was serving an indefinite sentence as a dangerous sex offender and who survived the circle, put it, 'there was a lot of hostility in the general population' toward sex offenders.[126] In the end, two of the 'undesirables' died as a result of the beatings. Both were believed to have committed crimes against children.[127]

Committing acts of violence against those deemed appropriate targets was a sure way to enhance one's status in the prison hierarchy. According to eyewitness accounts, most inmates kept as much distance as possible from the violence in the main dome. Many reported that watching and hearing the beatings made them feel extremely ill, but fear of retaliation from Shepley's group kept them from completely withdrawing. However, two who joined in on the beatings were 'sweet kids' who, according to Caron, saw the assault as an 'opportunity to create a macho image ... In an effort to upstage the seasoned psychos, they added extra little touches of cruelty, like violently twisting the bleeding noses to see if they were truly broken, which brought forth anguished screams from their victims.'[128] Melodrama aside, Caron's account reveals how violence served purposes that extended well beyond the regulation of 'undesirables.' As sociologist Fred Desroches explained, 'convicts gain status and deference through the use of violence,' and the child molester is 'a legitimized target of aggressive inmates.'[129] The parallel between Desroches's explanation for prisoner violence and Pomeroy's earlier explanation for sex between inmates – that 'the usual way a man asserts his masculinity is to have heterosexual sex,' and that an inmate will 'create a fiction with a person who appears to be feminine' to help 'him assert his lost manliness' – should not be overlooked. Authority is established through certain types of masculine performances that feature displays of physical strength and, in this case, socially sanctioned acts of cruelty. Masculinity is what linked the marginalization of sex offenders and prison sex culture to the social organization of power.[130] The relationship between masculine authority, prison sex culture, and the marginalization of diddlers hinges on the range of assumptions about normative male heterosexuality as aggressive and dominant, as well as protective.

Initial media reports of the 1971 riot at Kingston claimed that prisoners were raping other prisoners with abandon. Whether or not this was true and to what degree are hard to ascertain, but the coverage reflected an important shift in public discourse about prisoners that occurred at the end of the 1960s as the result of a well-publicized U.S. study of the problem. In 1968 the Philadelphia District Attorney's Office decided to investigate a complaint by a man who claimed he was sexually assaulted within moments of arriving at a detention centre for a pretrial evaluation. In his final report, Chief Assistant District Attorney Alan J. Davis concluded that Philadelphia prisons suffered an 'epidemic' of physical violence, intimidation, and sexual assault. Prison staff and the warden admitted that every new inmate of slight build will be approached within two or three days of admission, and that those who do not seek the protection of a wolf would be gang-raped.[131] One inmate reported that he screamed for over an hour while he was gang-raped, and the guards did not come to his aid. All told, the investigators interviewed 3304 inmates who had been in the system between June of 1966 and June of 1968. They estimated that 2000 assaults took place. In that time period, only 156 were documented, only 64 were mentioned in the prison records, and only 40 of those resulted in internal discipline against the aggressor.

The Philadelphia report described a typical setup in which a new inmate was offered food, cigarettes, blades, or candy.[132] Another method was to involve him in gambling. Sex was demanded in return for the 'gift' or to repay the debt. The report accused staff of being quick to label these sexual encounters as consensual. Moreover, Davis and his investigators found that the staff actively facilitated wolves' access to fish and punks. Requests by a wolf for a fish or a punk to be assigned to his cell were typically approved in order to maintain order among the prison population. Since wolves were one of the most influential social groups in prison, and because they benefited most from the social and economic organization of inmates, most of their conflicts were with other prisoners, not with the prison authorities. Consequently, wolves were least likely to organize mass protests, and indeed were more likely to discourage or even undermine them. Supplying wolves with desirable inmates helped keep the peace, and made discipline and order that much easier to maintain.

Most striking to Davis was the fact that the 'typical sexual aggressor does not consider himself homosexual, or even to have engaged in homosexual acts. This seems to be based upon his startlingly primitive view of sexual relationships,' he continued, 'one that defines as male whichever partner is aggressive and as homosexual whichever partner is passive.' Davis interpreted inmate expressions 'such as "fight or fuck," "we're gonna make a girl out of you" and "we're gonna take your manhood"' as primordial practices of conquest.[133] Echoing Wardell Pomeroy, Davis viewed rape as the 'primary and only way to maintain one's masculine identity,' but unlike mental health and sex experts, he maintained that sexual assault in prison was an expression of anger and aggression, not sexual deprivation.[134] This was an important distinction. Late 1960s social and political concern over institutionalized forms of oppression and victimization forced attention to turn to the *victims* of violence as well as its perpetrators. What was once considered an adaptive deviation of the normal sex drive was recast as an act of organized violence.

No longer would a permissive attitude toward sex in prison be tolerated, or so one might have thought. Over the next two decades, a handful of researchers published article and book-length studies documenting sexual violence in prison, but the long-term effect was to normalize prison rape as part of the price of 'doing crime.'[135] Furthermore, Davis's revelations that pedophiles were subject to the worst kind of physical and sexual abuse and had to be kept in protective custody became a way for some members of the public to feel assured that such offenders were getting the treatment the state could not and would not sanction, but which they believed sex offenders deserved. When Toronto sex offender Paul Bernardo was convicted of the sexual assault and murder of two teenage women in the 1990s, for example, it was not uncommon for people to suggest that he be taken out of protective custody so that the general inmate population could administer some rough justice. Member of Parliament Stockwell Day, then Alberta's provincial treasurer, made a similar remark about Clifford Olsen, another well-known Canadian serial murderer and sex offender.[136]

Conjugal visiting is one of the lasting legacies of the postwar era's enthusiastic embrace of mental health approaches to solving the sex crime problem. Though a far cry from what reformers had in mind when they called for sex criminal treatment programs, the logic that informs conjugal visiting nevertheless reveals the two sides of postwar liberal sexology. The claim that prisoners need (and should have) a 'sex outlet' reflects the progressive, 'pro-sex stance' held by Kinsey and his followers.[137] But sexologists' suggestions went much further and included proposals to provide sexual services for inmates, and even to create co-ed institutions so that male prisoners could enjoy 'normal' heterosocial relations. All of these proposals were based on a series of unexamined beliefs: that masculinity was given shape and meaning through sexual and social relations with women (or feminized men), that male sexual desire and activity was natural and should not be repressed, and that women were a secondary consideration, if they were considered at all. Clearly sexual permissiveness was complicated by liberal forensic sexologists' failure to recognize and account for the ways sex was embedded in gendered social hierarchies that unfolded in the context of coercion, violence, and oppression. It seems that prison sex culture's use of traditional masculine and feminine codes made the matter less, not more, visible to the sexologists who tried to address the prison sex problem. Despite attempts at objectivity, many unexamined and unspoken assumptions about male and female relations informed the scientific-psychoanalytic approach favoured by many modern sexologists.

The other lasting legacy of the postwar project to treat rather than punish sex criminals was the construction of the 'diddler' as a specific sexual type. As Canadian and American experts debated the merits of criminal sexual psychopath legislation, critics of the law cautioned against singling out sex criminals. In addition to seeing no useful purpose in separating sex offenders from any other inmates who might benefit from psychiatric help, critics feared that doing so would further isolate and marginalize an already stigmatized segment of the population. They were right.

It could have been otherwise. Sexual offenders were fully integrated into Quebec psychiatrist Bruno Cormier's treatment program in Dannemora, New York, for example. However, Cormier's inmate-participants were quick to point out that the moment they were back in a prison, they would have little choice but to adhere to 'the inmate code.' Despite learning that sex offenders are 'just like everyone else,' they knew that inside a regular prison, 'diddlers' were a class of their own. As we have seen, treatment specialists hired to deliver therapeutic programs to cure inmates of sexual deviancy first singled out men charged with sex crimes as a unique type of prisoner who needed 'special' care. Inmate culture adapted accordingly, and won the tacit approval of the public.

Postwar Ontario male prison culture reminds us that sex is never just about sex. The complicated intersection between meanings on the ground and meanings literally in the tower, and between those with formal and those with informal power, all converge in the prison setting. Systems of power 'make sense' to those who enforce them. The wolf-punk-fairy triad worked well for the prison wolves who used sex to exert control over other prisoners while at the same time enhancing their status as manly heterosexuals. It also worked for the fairies, who, given the prison's refusal to protect them from physical harm, were allowed the freedom to retain their identities as fairies, pansies, and queens, and to take refuge from those who would harm them, by serving their time in segregation. Punks, who enjoyed almost no protection whatsoever, were perhaps its greatest victims.

This story also reminds us that theories of sexuality must begin with an understanding of the various ways sex accrues meaning and is given expression through gender. Other critical points of difference, especially race and ethnicity, but also age and class, need to be taken into account, something that the limited scope of this study combined with the racial and ethnic homogeneity of Ontario's prison population in this period did not permit. My hope is that future scholars will build on, revise, and refine this initial exploration into an unexplored but essential part of our past, but my suspicion is that in the inevitable process of sharpening our insights into the way power operates, it will remain true that, as Joan Scott pointed out, gender is one of the primary ways of signifying relations of power. It isn't the only one, but its persistent enunciation in everyday life – including in all-male prisons – reminds us not to lose sight of the fact that what we are seeking to expose is not gender itself, but how masculinity and femininity are implicated in the organization of systems of power.

Conclusion

In 2007 the popular magazine *Scientific American Mind* published a five-page review of current research on sex offender treatment. Readers learned that some experts view child sex offending as the product of a psychological disorder, while others hunt for biological explanations. In London, England, for example, researchers have found that men who were raised in violent homes, who were victims of parental neglect, and who were sexually assaulted as children are, as adults, most likely to sexually assault children. At the University of New Hampshire, sociologist David Finkelhor identified lack of education and self-esteem, as well as 'deep-seated sexual anxiety' and 'a general lack of [sexual] inhibition,' as key characteristics of the modern day pedophile. From the University of Toronto's Faculty of Medicine, we learn that childhood brain trauma and attention deficit hyperactivity disorder may be related to the inability to develop normal sexual habits, while research undertaken at the Johns Hopkins School of Medicine shows a potential genetic link. Fred Berlin's work indicates 'higher rates of pedophilia are found among members of pedophiles' immediate families than among the families of non-pedophiles.'[1]

There are two ways to respond to this remarkably disparate range of research opinion. If we take an optimistic view, we might be comforted in knowing that contemporary forensic sexologists remain determined to do whatever it takes to get at the root cause of pedophilic sex offending behaviour so that they might develop more effective treatments to deal with this serious social problem. If we view the current state of research and treatment cynically, we might conclude that, after more than half a century of research in the soft and hard sciences, we are no closer to finding a 'cure' than we were when criminal sexual psychopath legislation was first introduced. We might agree with leading Canadian mental health expert Cyril Greenland and the American Group for the Advancement of Psychiatry who both concluded in the 1970s that the experiment with criminal sexual psychopath legislation had failed. If we side with the optimists, the only course is to support the scientific search for cause and cure. If, however, we side with the cynics, it seems the only solution is to incarcerate sex offenders for as long as we possibly can.

Contemporary analyses of sex offender treatment program outcomes give no cause for optimism, yet many of those working in the now well-established field of sex offender treatment and research refuse to concede defeat. For example, psychiatrists still consider repeat and violent sex offenders one of the hardest populations to treat. These offenders reportedly tend to deny responsibility for their crimes, they are marginalized within the prison setting, and they are heterogeneous in their therapeutic needs. Moreover, studies of treatment program outcomes show that treatment has had a marginal impact on recidivism rates. Yet most sex offender treatment providers cling to the notion that with more effort will come better results.[2] Others defend their work on the grounds that the social and economic costs of even one offender not reoffending is recuperated.[3] However, some studies show that sex offender populations who received treatment have a higher rate of reoffending than those who did not receive treatment, suggesting that there is real reason to abandon this project entirely.[4] Sixty years after Canada's introduction of legislation that would pave the way for 'some experimentation' into the psychotherapeutic treatment of sex offenders, it is clear that experts are no closer to finding a solution.

In sharp contrast to the unwavering determination shared by many forensic sexologists, the general public has lost faith in treatment programs for offenders. For example, in the 1960s protesters carried signs demanding 'Psychotherapy not Cyanide,' protesters at the beginning of the twenty-first century called on police to 'Get the Pedophiles Out.'[5] Inspired by the *News of the World's* anti-pedophile 'name-and-shame' campaign, residents of Paulsgrove, a neighbourhood in Portsmouth, England, organized a very public campaign in August 2000 to force a released sex offender out of their area.[6] Images of adults and even children wielding signs demanding the offender's removal made international news. Two months later, Canadian Peter Whitmore, who had served a sentence for sexually assaulting children while working as a professional babysitter, was released into an Etobicoke, Ontario, community where he was enrolled in a Circle of Support and Accountability group.

Begun by a member of the Hamilton, Ontario, Mennonite community in 1994, Circles of Support provide a supportive community to help sex offenders reintegrate into society while holding them accountable for their past and present actions.[7] Etobicoke residents were unimpressed and used vigilante tactics similar to those used in Paulsgrove to force Whitmore to move. Their plan worked.[8] In 2007 similar neighbourhood campaigns were organized to drive Paul Callow, known as the 'balcony rapist,' out of his halfway house in Surrey, British Columbia. He moved to his sister's home in the neighbouring community of New Westminster, where subsequent attempts to force him to move failed yet again.

Postwar faith in scientific, medical, and mental health research to solve the most serious social and political problems, and the compassionate approach that groups like Parents Action League encouraged in society's handling of sex offenders came to an end in the late 1960s. The antipsychiatry movement in combination with the mid-1970s shift to the political right marked the beginning of a new era in public attitudes toward crime and criminals. The treatment approach fell out of public and political favour, and American and Canadian citizens demanded community protection. Community protection seeks to address the problem of sexual assaults against children by placing restrictions on the movements of registered sex offenders. Proponents of community protection demand longer sentences for sex crimes, the creation of sex offender registries, the close monitoring of released sex offenders with the use of global positioning devices, and in the United States the use of local ordinances restricting where convicted sex offenders can live. Indeed, at least fifteen states have passed laws that impose restrictions on where registered sex offenders can reside, and at least one developer has capitalized on the trend by building a subdivision that bars registered sex offenders from ownership.[9] Some state legislatures are trying to go even further. In 2005 the Ohio State Assembly introduced a bill requiring that registered sex offenders use a pink licence plate, but criticism from Mary Kay Cosmetics and breast cancer research advocates resulted in its defeat. Presently Ohio and Alabama are now considering a bright green plate.[10] In the 1950s, building better communities meant reaching out to 'strangers in our midst.' By the 1990s, it meant driving them out.

In the United States, these laws and ordinances – and there are many of them – have had extraordinary consequences. A 2007 report by Human Rights Watch illustrates how the same problems that arose with sexual psychopath laws occur with present day sex offender laws, namely that these laws emphasize stranger danger when in fact only 14 per cent of reported victims of sexual assault were victimized by strangers. According to the U.S. Bureau of Justice Statistics' 2005 survey of crime victimization, 'sexual assault victims under the age of 18 at the time of the crime knew their abusers in nine out of 10 cases: the abusers were family members in 34 per cent of cases, and acquaintances in another 59 per cent of cases. When the sexual assault victim was under six years old, almost half (49 per cent) of the offenders were family members.'[11]

What is new is how these laws turn minor incidents into major crimes. Human Rights Watch cites one case in which an adolescent male who engaged in sex with his younger girlfriend was declared a sex offender, and will have to register with local law enforcement for the rest of his life. They also report the case of another teenager who exposed himself to a group of girls on their way to gym class. After being labelled a sex offender, he committed suicide.[12] Restrictions against registered offenders are sometimes extraordinary. In 2005 Florida banned sex offenders under state supervision from entering hurricane shelters.[13] Two years later, the media reported on five registered sex offenders who were living under the Julia Tuttle Causeway in Florida's Miami-Dade county. They had been placed there by State Corrections because the men were unable to secure housing, but a parole officer needed to be able to check in on them each night.[14]

In Canada, advocates of the victims' rights and community protection models received a major boost after a 1993 Ontario coroner's inquest into the 1988 sexual assault and murder of Christopher Stephenson by Joseph Fredericks, a violent pedophile who was out on mandatory supervision at the time of the offence. The first recommendation was the enactment of community protection legislation modelled after Washington State's Sexually Violent Predators Act. The inquest also called for mandatory registration of sex offenders with the police and for the amendment of the definition of a serious harm offence to include any sexual offence against a child.[15] In 2000 Ontario became the first province to create a sex offender registry. In January the Ontario Progressive Conservatives introduced Christopher's Law, which made it a crime for anyone charged with a sex-related offence to fail to maintain a current listing of their address with the local police force.[16] In 2004 the Conservative Party of Canada created a national registry as part of its effort to 'make Canadians safer in their homes and in their streets.'[17]

Sex offender registries are new, but the laws that are aimed at dealing with repeat violent sex offenders are not. Present day laws are, however, used in quite a different manner than was intended by their mid-century architects. As we saw, the original 1948 'criminal sexual psychopath' law was changed to a 'dangerous sex offender' law in 1961. In 1977 'dangerous sex offender' was eliminated from the Criminal Code, but violent sex offenders are now subject to Canada's 'dangerous offender' law, which carries an indeterminate sentence, as did earlier versions of the law. Although the word 'sex' was removed, the law is still used largely for sex offenders. As of 2007, 80 per cent of all dangerous offenders had at least one current conviction for a sexual offence.[18] In 1997 yet another category was created: the 'long-term offender.' The long-term offender category is applied in cases where the convicted sex criminal is deemed likely to reoffend, but where it appears that there is a 'reasonable possibility of eventual control of the risk in the community.'[19] It also allows for long-term community surveillance, usually for a period of ten years. Currently, 75 per cent of the 425 offenders with long-term supervision orders have at least one current conviction for a sexual offence.[20]

The long-term offender law does what the criminal sexual psychopath and dangerous sex offender laws used to do: it allows the state to maintain control over a convicted sex offender for a period of time longer than the Criminal Code allows. Canada's dangerous offender law, on the other hand, is used when psychiatrists either fail to convince a judge or simply do not believe that a convicted sex offender can be treated successfully. In other words, a law that was introduced as the result of a public movement that believed sex offending was a medical problem, not a criminal one, and that sex offenders should be treated with compassion and provided with access to modern treatment methods is now used for precisely the opposite purpose. Dangerous sex offenders are those whom the system has no hope of reforming, and who, it is argued, will always be a risk to the community. Significantly, there has never been a public debate or discussion about this transition in the purpose and intent of the law. There should be.

Corrections Canada remains officially committed to providing treatment for sex offenders, which has only been offered on a voluntary basis since the passage of the *Canadian Charter of Rights and Freedoms* in 1982. Although there is renewed interest in biomedical explanations for sexually deviant behaviour, a modernized version of postwar behavioural therapy remains the treatment of choice in Canada. At clinics and in prisons where sex offender treatment is offered, cognitive-behaviour therapy distinguishes itself from its predecessor by attempting to restructure the way a person thinks rather than redirect his or her sexual interests. Part of that process, according to one of its key proponents, involves

offender accountability and responsibility as a necessary precondition
for an effective therapeutic experience, a standard that formalizes·the
long-standing recognition that an offender is not a good therapy prospect unless he engages in the process voluntarily. Though the methods
are somewhat different, the goals of contemporary treatment programs
for sex offenders have changed little since the 1940s. Psychiatrists are still
trying to 'increase the feeling of moral sensitivity' by 'inspiring lively feelings of guilt,' the prescription handed out by the head of the Canadian
Mental Health Association, J.D. Griffin, in 1947.

Feminist critiques of human sexual relations inform many contemporary sex offender treatment programs. Misogyny, for example, is directly
addressed in therapy. Offenders are encouraged to recognize and come
to terms with feelings of hostility they may harbour toward women.
Other beliefs, or what treatment experts refer to as 'cognitive distor-
tions,' that characterize offenders' justification of their behaviour
include the claim that children initiate and enjoy sexual activity with the
offender, that fondling does not constitute sexual abuse, and that a
woman's manner of dress is an indication of her sexual availability. Cog-
nitive-behavioural techniques like cognitive restructuring involve using
role-playing, role modelling, and creating feelings of empathy for the
victim in order to challenge unacceptable or outmoded values, both conservative and common, and replacing them with what are considered to
be more appropriate and adaptive ones.[21]

Release from prison depends on the ability to demonstrate that one is
no longer a danger to the public, and Canada's National Parole Board is
guided by experts' assessments of an applicant's demonstrated progress
through a range of treatment programs. The process is self-perpetuating.
Gaining admission to and successfully completing a treatment program
requires that sex offenders understand themselves, their motivations,
and the content and nature of their sexual desire according to whatever
psychiatric models of human sexuality they are presented with. As this
study has shown, sexological and psychiatric interpretations of human
sexual behaviour are highly subjective, shaped by prevailing views of normative sex and gender roles as well as changing historical definitions of
harm and deviancy. This is not to argue in favour of cultural relativism, as
did John Arnott in his testimony to the Royal Commission on the Criminal Law Relating to Criminal Sexual Psychopaths when he suggested that
incest should be excluded from the law because it was a revered practice
among the Incas. Rather, it is to borrow from the insights of transgender
theorists who represent a very different medicalized community, but one

that stands in an equally dependant relationship to psychiatric knowledge about sexuality and gender. Transgendered people who wish access to hormones and sex reassignment surgery, for example, are forced to accept a psychiatric diagnosis of gender 'dysphoria,' which reinforces a two-gender system by requiring patients to describe themselves as one gender born into the body of the other.[22] As Kate Bornstein points out, sex and gender identities are much more complex than the binary system allows.[23] It is entirely reasonable to suggest that the same constraints apply to pedophiles and other sex offenders who are similarly obliged to accept the assumption that they have failed to control their sex impulses.[24] As I have shown, this construction is rooted in an interpretation of consensual homosexual behaviour among adult men who refused, and therefore failed, to control their desire for sex with other men, and who also therefore failed to live in accordance with prevailing socio-sexual moral standards. But the roots are so deep, they are hidden from contemporary practitioners.

Many repeat sex offenders describe their behaviour in ways that conform to this model, but recent research by criminologist Dany Lacombe shows that it is only by conforming to the given narrative that incarcerated offenders can make their way through prison treatment programs.[25] In the inter- and postwar era, many homosexuals embraced the medical construction of homosexuality largely because it was the most sympathetic representation of same-sex sexual attraction and desire available. Transgendered people adopted it for similar reasons, motivated at least in part by the fact that it was the only way to access medical services. For pedophiles in treatment, the situation is much the same.

Sex offenders must accept whatever model of sexuality their therapists operate from. Currently, treatment experts are moving toward an orientation model that posits that, like homosexuals, pedophiles are 'sexually oriented' toward children. Just as the staff at the Outpatient Forensic Clinic concluded with respect to homosexuality, present-day thinking is that a pedophile's sexual orientation cannot be changed; the goal then is to teach them to live according to the social mores of their times. This is a frustrating development. The suggestion that there is a fixed sexual orientation has always been contested, and has been rejected by lesbian, gay, queer, and transgender activists and theorists since the days of gay liberation. It once again reinforces a heterosexual norm, and locates the problem of sexual assault and violence within the individual and, in the behavioural sciences, within his family, and ignores the way sex, gender, and power are linked in the broader social and cultural context.

The orientation model has been adopted by boy- and girl-lover activists who characterize themselves as an oppressed minority in much the same way as some gay rights activists have. Presently the public perception is that the Internet is responsible for the emergence of a pedophile 'community,' but activist groups have been around since at least the 1970s. A pedophile rights movement evolved alongside, and in some cases within, the gay liberation movement. For example, the Pedophile Information Exchange was founded in the United Kingdom in 1974; and its members had links to the Gay Liberation Front. Members of the North American Man Boy Love Association, founded in 1978, regard themselves as a part of the gay liberation movement.[26] The Netherlands has perhaps the longest history of organized pedophile action groups.[27] In 2006 the PNVD Party, a Dutch acronym for Brotherly Love, Freedom, and Diversity, had its official launch. Its main platform was to lower the age of consent from sixteen to twelve years of age.[28]

Historians of sexuality have shown how the pathological construction of the homosexual created a whole new regulatory regime that oppressed lesbians, gay men, and others who resided on the margins of sex and gender. At the same time, however, the modern concept of the homosexual also facilitated the mobilization of important social justice and sexual rights movements. Sexologists are now talking about pedophilia as a type of sexual orientation. By insisting that pedophilia is a legitimate and recognized sexual identity, twenty-first century boy- and girl-lovers are currently using this medical construct to argue that as long as they do not break any laws, the state should stop interfering in their lives. It is beyond the scope of this book to engage the complex issues and contentious history of the pro-pedophile movement or its relationship to the lesbian and gay communities, but these developments need to be considered in light of the longer history of sexual deviancy. The issue of pedophilia, of man-boy love, of girl-lovers, and of sexual exploitation, coercion, and assault should not be left to the field of medicine and criminology alone. These contemporary issues can and should be reconsidered in light of the theoretical and empirical contributions made by those working in the now very expansive field of sexuality studies.

Reacquainting ourselves with the historical origins of dangerous offender legislation allows us a more thoughtful reflection on the way the broader issue of sex offending is framed and understood in the present day. For example, the post–Second World War entrenchment of sexology was much more than the triumph of the modern expert over

Victorian morality. It legitimated the cultural values and social aspirations of a generation of parents for whom the threat of atomic war was an inescapable and horrifying reality. The science of sex provided an illusory sense of stability and security at a time when deviations from an increasingly narrowly defined heterosexual norm were viewed with various combinations of concern, suspicion, and fear. Middle-class parents heartily endorsed the extension of psychology and psychiatry into the prison and judicial systems so that treatment experts might re-parent boys gone wrong. By linking sexual safety with national and even international well-being, groups like PAL and the Canadian Federation of Home and School and Parent-Teacher Associations made child victims and adult perpetrators of sexual violence a matter of public concern, and sought political support for what they perceived as progressive and humane remedies by demanding sex offender treatment services be written into the expanding welfare state.

The results in the immediate postwar period were contradictory and have not been well understood by historians. Specifically, the policing of gay men increased, thus intensifying the repression of male homosexuality in particular, and sexual deviancy in general. Sexual psychopath legislation drew medical experts into the process of regulating sexuality. Frustrated by the Criminal Code's punitive approach to a wide range of sex crimes, liberal progressive forensic sexologists helped to force the debate on the role of the state in regulating homosexual and other types of deviant but harmless sexual activity, thus helping to pave the way for the decriminalization of homosexuality in Canada and the United Kingdom. Historians have overemphasized the role of Alfred Kinsey and Evelyn Hooker, who, to be sure, were key figures in this shift. However, they were only the most famous. Many lesser-known psychiatrists and psychologists, such as the staff at Toronto's Outpatient Forensic Clinic, advocated a liberal progressive model of human sexuality that challenged the right of the state to regulate morality by insisting that only harm-causing behaviour should be subject to criminal prosecution.[29]

Alfred Kinsey has been given a great deal of credit for mainstreaming sex talk in the postwar period, but in Canada, at least, parent groups made talking about sex a civic duty and, indeed, a matter of national significance. The expansion of sex talk was in some ways liberating, but in other ways simply functioned as a different form of moral regulation. Just as the 1945 return of soldiers liberated women to the kitchen, the expansion of modern sex discourse liberated homosexuals to the therapist's couch. For some, the couch was much more comfortable than a prison cell, but for others it was just a different kind of horror. The complex results of the process of pathologizing sexuality remind us yet again that history does not march ever forward on the path to liberation.

The link between homosexuality and pedophilia persists in the minds of many, but homosexual men are not the targets they once were. As a society, however, we are no less anxious about pedophilia, and a history of the emergence of the dangerous sexual offender reveals that the present-day construction of pedophiles as amoral recidivists who have no interest in treatment is grounded in pre– and post–Second World War medical assessments of homosexual men, many of whom were unashamed of their 'deviant' desires and who risked their families, jobs, and reputations for the opportunity to participate in urban gay cultural life. Viewed through the eyes of middle-class heterosexual experts, those risks made no logical sense.[30] As experts saw it, the homosexual and transsexual men studied by medical doctors and mental health experts during the interwar era lacked the ability, or desire (experts weren't sure which), to resist the impulse to reoffend. Sexual psychopathy, which was first used to account for the behaviour of prostitutes, was the best available explanation. Although sexual psychopathy has been largely abandoned as a medical diagnosis, its past resonates clearly in both contemporary definitions of pedophilia and cultural anxieties about sexual predators.[31]

Part of the construction of the sex offender as intractable rests on the assumption that sex offenders do not take responsibility for their crimes and lack empathy for their victims. These characteristics were first 'discovered' by early and mid-twentieth-century sexologists, and continue to characterize sex offenders whose victims are strangers, even though the types of criminal sexual behaviour at issue are quite distinct from those that formed the basis of the early findings. However, neither of these qualities is unique to this particular criminal constituency. Many people refuse to take responsibility for their crimes, and many of the men who committed sex crimes were very anxious to have access to treatment that would help them deal with their inappropriate desires. In a 1977 letter to the Kinsey Institute's research associate Paul Gebhard, a confessed child sex offender who was serving time under his state's sexual psychopath law asked for advice on how to stop fantasizing about young boys since, he explained, the treatment he received had had no effect. (Gebhard advised him to slowly introduce mature women into his fantasies and 'try to adjust himself in that sense.')[32] More recently, Canadian Peter Whitmore, who appears to fit the psychopathic profile quite well, repeated his request for chemical castration after being sentenced for the kidnapping and sexual assault of two boys, one adolescent and one prepubescent. (He had previously agreed to it when released from prison in 2005, but the parole service was unable to find a doctor willing to provide the necessary drugs.) Whitmore attempted suicide twice: first during the standoff with the police when he and the two boys he had kidnapped were finally located, and then when he was in the Regina Correctional Centre.[33] While it does seem likely that Whitmore will reoffend, it also appears that he experiences remorse, which suggests at least some capacity for empathy. The point is that the sexual psychopath designation and its modern incarnations, both as medical categories and social ideas, limit us in our ability to think about these sorts of social problems.

None of this is to say that we should not be concerned about repeat sex offenders or to suggest that the psychopath is a mere construction. Clearly, persistent sex offenders who seem immune to the consequences of their actions, either for themselves or their victims, are of serious concern. But as Michael Petrunik points out, the tendency to forge new legislation in response to these exceptional cases amounts to little more than a 'symbolic attempt to appease community outrage over sensationalized but relatively infrequent incidents of predatory violence against children than a demonstrably effective instrumental effort to reduce the incidence of serious harm to the community.'[34] Indeterminate sentences might be the only plausible solution for hard core offenders, but special legislation has a number of ill effects that include the ineffective distribution of funds to programs that serve a very small proportion of the offender population and divert attention away from the more common type of sexual assault: that which occurs in families and by perpetrators known to the victims.

The organized women's movement drew attention to intra-familial sexual assault and challenged the way Canadian and American criminal justice systems dealt with sex crime and assault against women in general. Feminists' critique of the way women were treated as little more than receptacles for male lust converged with other victims' rights advocates' concerns and so gained a wider audience.[35] In Canada, for example, the controversial 1984 *Report of the Committee on Sexual Offences against Children and Youth* claimed that more than half of Canadian women and one-third of Canadian men reported experiencing some form of unwanted sexual activity. Women's groups and feminist intellectuals argued that all sex crimes were crimes of violence, not the product of a deviated or overblown male sexual drive.[36] The point was made most effectively by emphasizing the traumatic impact sexual assault had on its victims, countering some of the myths perpetuated by medical science that held women, and even children, partly – if not wholly – responsible for sexual assaults against them.

Attention to the impact of sexual assault on victims filled an important vacuum in the way the sex crime problem was taken up, but other equally important critical insights have been overlooked, namely that deviancy-based models focus on the 'abnormal' sex offender to the exclusion of garden-variety rapists, and that sexual assault mirrors wider social issues regarding the sexualization of women's bodies and social inequality between men and women. Feminist concern for the victims of sexual assault coincided with the more conservative community-protection movement already under way. As was the case with the alignment of anti-pornography feminists and pro-censorship conservatives in the same period, the right-of-centre 'law and order' agenda converged with feminists' demands for more meaningful sentencing of those who physically and sexually assaulted women and children. Unfortunately, those seeking harsher sentences for sex offenders did not share feminist concerns about contemporary sexual relations. Demands for a critical engagement with structures of patriarchal power and oppressive gender ideologies were eclipsed by calls for longer and more rigid periods of incarceration.

I hope to have accomplished a number of things with this book. I hope to have shown that the history of sexuality has fashioned tools that have great utility for understanding the present as well as the past. I also hope to have convinced readers that moving beyond the homosexual subject to engage some of the more discomforting categories of sexual deviancy allows us an opportunity to contribute to some of the more concerning issues in contemporary sexual politics today. I have also tried to show that the postwar era was one in which a strong impulse toward progressive reform dominated, and that women played an active role, but not in ways traditionally recognized as 'women's activism.' Finally, and most important, I hope this study will encourage a serious reconsideration of the way we think about, treat, and deal with sex offending in Canada and elsewhere. We need a new model to counter the current one that informs sex offender treatment, and I hope that the questions raised here will encourage us to begin to imagine what that model might look like.

Notes

Introduction

1 After working with Winnipeg's immigrant population, Woodsworth retracted his position and instead championed a Canadian national identity based on diversity. J.S. Woodsworth, *Strangers within Our Gates, or Coming Canadians* (1909).

2 Interestingly, in Britain the 'stranger in our midst' continued to refer to immigrants. Chris Waters, '"Dark Strangers in Our Midst": Discourses of Race and Nation in Britain, 1947–1963,' *Journal of British Studies* 36, no. 2 (1997): 207–38.

3 In 1951, children under 19 years of age accounted for 38.5 per cent of the Canadian population. K. Phyllis Burns, 'What's Happening to Canada's Children?' in *Social Problems: A Canadian Profile*, ed. Richard Laskin (New York: McGraw-Hill Company of Canada, 1964), 316. See also Doug Owram, *Born at the Right Time: A History of the Baby Boom Generation* (Toronto: University of Toronto Press, 1996); Veronica Strong-Boag, 'Home Dreams: Women and the Suburban Experiment in Canada, 1945–60,' *Canadian Historical Review* 4 (1991): 471–504; Peter S. Li, *The Making of Postwar Canada* (Toronto: Oxford University Press, 1996).

4 Two of the earliest critical responses were Edwin H. Sutherland's 'The Diffusion of Sex Psychopath Laws,' *American Journal of Sociology* 56 (1950): 142–8 and Paul Tappan's *The Habitual Sex Offender: Report and Recommendations of the Commission on the Habitual Sex Offender* (Trenton, NJ: New Jersey Commission on the Habitual Sex Offender, 1950).

5 Group for the Advancement of Psychiatry, *Psychiatry and Sex Psychopath Legislation: The 30s to the 80s* (New York: Group for the Advancement of Psychiatry, 1977), vol. 9.

6 Estelle Freedman, '"Uncontrolled Desires": The Response to the Sexual Psychopath, 1920–1960,' in *Passion and Power: Sexuality in History*, ed. Kathy Peiss and Christina Simmons (Philadelphia: Temple University Press, 1989), 199–225. Rob Champagne, 'Psychopaths and Perverts: The Canadian Royal Commission on the Criminal Law Relating to Criminal Sexual Psychopaths, 1954–1958,' *Canadian Lesbian and Gay History Network Newsletter* 2 (September 1986): 7–9; Gary Kinsman, *The Regulation of Desire: Homo and Hetero Sexualities*, 2nd ed. (Montreal: Black Rose Books, 1996). See also Kinsman's '"Inverts," "Psychopaths" and "Normal" Men: Historical Sociological Perspectives on Gay and Heterosexual Masculinities,' in *Men and Masculinities: A Critical Anthology*, ed. Tony Haddad (Toronto: Canadian Scholars' Press, 1993), 3–35.

7 See, for example, Jennifer Terry, *An American Obsession: Science, Medicine and Homosexuality in Modern Society* (Chicago: University of Chicago Press, 1999); Henry Minton, *Departing from Deviance: A History of Homosexual Rights and Emancipatory Science in America* (Chicago: The University of Chicago Press, 2002); Joanne Meyerowitz, *How Sex Changed: A History of Transsexuality in the United States* (Cambridge, MA: Harvard University Press, 2002).

8 Philip Jenkins, *Moral Panic: Changing Concepts of the Child Molester in Modern America* (New Haven, CT: Yale University Press, 1998), 61. See also Fred Fejes, 'Murder, Perversion, and Moral Panic: The 1954 Media Campaign against Miami's Homosexuals and the Discourse of Civic Betterment,' *Journal of the History of Sexuality* 9, no. 3 (July 2000): 305–47.

9 The historical literature in this area is vast. In Canada, see especially Gary Kinsman and Patrizia Gentile, *In the Interests of the State: The Anti-gay, Anti-lesbian National Security Campaign in Canada: A Preliminary Research Report* (Sudbury: Laurentian University, 1998); Daniel Robinson and David Kimmel, 'The Queer Career of Homosexual Security Vetting in Cold-War Canada,' *Canadian Historical Review*, 75, no. 3 (September 1994): 319–45. For the United States, see especially Allen Berube, *Coming Out Under Fire: The History of Gay Men and Women in World War Two* (New York: Free Press, 1990); Martin Duberman, *Cures: A Gay Man's Odyssey* (New York: Dutton, 1991); Elizabeth Lapovsky Kennedy and Madeline Davis, *Boots of Leather, Slippers of Gold: The History of a Lesbian Community* (New York: Routledge, 1993).

10 It is impossible to write the history of homosexuality without addressing its pathologization. Some of the key literature that makes this process a central focus include Terry, *An American Obsession*; Minton, *Departing from Deviance*, Ronald Bayer, *Homosexuality and American Psychiatry: The Politics of Diagnosis* (New York: Basic Books, 1981); Janice M. Irvine, *Disorders of Desire: Sex and*

Gender in Modern American Sexology (Philadelphia: Temple University Press, 1990). In Canada, see Gary Kinsman, *Regulation of Desire*, and Mary Lousie Adams, *The Trouble with Normal: Postwar Youth and the Making of Heterosexuality* (Toronto: University of Toronto Press, 1997).

11 John Gerassi, *The Boys of Boise: Furor, Vice and Folly in an American City* (New York: Collier Books, 1966; Seattle: University of Washington Press, 2001).

12 At least one other person known to have been designated a criminal sexual psychopath as the result of sex acts committed with another adult male was Francis Sanders. The circumstances of his arrest are not clear, but the Criminal Court Cases report from his 1969 appeal suggest that he was involved in an ongoing relationship with another adult male. Sanders was charged with one count of 'gross indecency' and subsequently found to be a criminal sexual psychopath. In 1965 he launched the first of three known appeals against his conviction. The judge who heard the appeal stated that Sanders did not fit the legal definition of a dangerous sexual offender, but, because the appeal did not question the finding of sexual psychopathy, he had no authority to rule on that issue; thus, he could not overturn the dangerous sexual offender designation. By this time, Sanders had served eleven years in prison. His release date is unknown. *Regina v. Sanders* (1965) [1966] 2 C.C.C. (N.S.) 345 (B.C.S.C).

13 Kinsman, *Regulation of Desire*, 259–64.

14 RG 73, Records of the Solicitor General, acc. 1982-83-105, box 15, file 85-4, 'Sex Offenders,' Gays Ottawa, Letter, 12 Dec. 1974; RG 73, acc. 1980-81/039, box 64, file 8-24-1 National Gay Rights Coalition, Letter, 12 May 1976.

15 For a Canadian example, see Kinsman, *Regulation of Desire*, 148–287. For the United States, see Neil Miller, *Sex Crime Panic: A Journey to the Paranoid Heart of the 1950s* (New York: Alyson Books, 2002); and Fejes, 'Murder, Perversion, and Moral Panic.'

16 Bayer, *Homosexuality and American Psychiatry.*

17 On the origins of the dangerous offender and the concomitant rise of the clinical model, see Michel Foucault, 'About the Concept of the "Dangerous Individual" in 19th-Century Legal Psychiatry,' *International Journal of Law and Psychiatry* 1 (January 1978): 1–19. For a historical overview of the emergence of the clinical model in Canada, see Michael Petrunik, 'Models of Dangerousness: A Cross Jurisdictional Review of Dangerousness Legislation and Practice' (Policy Branch, Ministry of the Solicitor General of Canada, 1994).

18 *Time Magazine* (21 March 1960): 18. See also Eric Cummins, *The Rise and Fall of California's Radical Prison Movement* (Stanford, CA: Stanford University Press, 1994), 18.

19 Hans Mohr, 'A la Recherche,' in *Breaking the Chains: Bruno M. Cormier and the McGill University Clinic in Forensic Psychiatry*, ed. Renée Fugère and Ingrid Thompson-Cooper (Westmount, QC: Robert Davies Multimedia Publishing, 1998), 150.

20 Mona Gleason, *Normalizing the Ideal: Psychology, Schooling, and the Family in Postwar Canada* (Toronto: University of Toronto Press, 1999).

21 See the work of Thomas S. Szasz, including *The Age of Madness: The History of Involuntary Mental Hospitalization, Presented in Selected Texts* (Garden City, NY: Anchor Books, 1973) and *The Manufacture of Madness: A Comparative Study of the Inquisition and the Mental Health Movement* (New York: Harper & Row, 1970).

22 Nicholas N. Kittrie, *The Right to Be Different: Deviance and Enforced Therapy* (Baltimore: Johns Hopkins University Press, 1971).

23 *A Clockwork Orange*, prod. and dir. Stanley Kubrick, 1971. Film. Anthony Burgess, *A Clockwork Orange* (New York: Norton, 1962).

24 Philip Jenkins, *Moral Panic: Changing Concepts of the Child Molester in Modern America* (New Haven, CT: Yale University Press, 1998), 217.

25 Canadian historian Valerie J. Korinek, for example, demonstrates quite clearly that the dominant view of women in the postwar era in U.S. historiography is unsustainable in Canada. *Roughing It in the Suburbs: Reading Chatelaine Magazine in the Fifties and Sixties* (Toronto: University of Toronto Press, 2000).

26 Bruno Cormier and Siebert P. Simons, 'The Problem of the Dangerous Sexual Offender,' in *Social Deviance in Canada*, ed. W.E. Mann (Toronto: Copp Clark, 1971), 343.

1 Criminal Sexual Psychopathy

1 Archives of Ontario (hereafter AO), RG 10-107-0-224, Letter to the minister of health, 17 April 1947.

2 Library and Archives Canada (hereafter LAC), RG 73, vol. 70, file 1-16-15, pt 1, Medical Services for Sex Offenders.

3 *Corpus Juris*, vol. 32 (New York: American Law Book, 1923), 600–1; Simon N. Verdun-Jones and Russell Smandych, 'Catch-22 in the Nineteenth Century: The Evolution of Therapeutic Confinement for the Criminally Insane in Canada, 1840–1900,' in *Criminal Justice History*, vol. 2 (New York: Crime and Justice History Group and John Gay Press, 1981); James E. Moran, *Committed to the State Asylum: Insanity and Society in Nineteenth Century Quebec and Ontario* (Montreal: McGill-Queen's University Press, 2001).

4 Verdun-Jones and Smandych, 'Catch-22,' 85.

5 Roy Porter, *The Greatest Benefit to Mankind: A Medical History of Humanity* (New York: W.W. Norton, 1997), 501.
6 Alex K. Gigeroff, *Sexual Deviations in the Criminal Law: Homosexual, Exhibitionistic, and Pedophilic Offences in Canada* (Toronto: University of Toronto Press, 1968), vii.
7 Enrico Ferri, *Criminal Sociology,* xlii (Boston: Little, Brown, 1917), cited in Nicholas N. Kittrie, *The Right to Be Different: Deviance and Enforced Therapy* (Baltimore: Johns Hopkins University Press, 1971), 173–4.
8 Kittrie, *The Right to Be Different,* 173–4.
9 Mariana Valverde, *Diseases of the Will: Alcohol and the Dilemmas of Freedom* (New York: Cambridge University Press, 1998).
10 Kittrie, *The Right to Be Different,* 112, 178–9.
11 Lorne Stewart, *The History of the Juvenile and Family Court of Toronto* (Toronto, 1971), 16–19.
12 James Cowles Prichard, cited in Paul Gebhard, John H. Gagnon, Wardell B. Pomeroy, and Cornelia V. Christianson, *Sex Offenders* (New York: Harper and Row and Paul B. Hoeber Medical Books, 1965), 845. See also Elizabeth Lunbeck, *The Psychiatric Persuasion: Knowledge, Gender, and Power in Modern America* (Princeton, NJ: Princeton University Press, 1994), 65–71.
13 Philip Jenkins, *Moral Panic: Changing Concepts of the Child Molester in Modern America* (New Haven, CT: Yale University Press, 1998), 39; see also Anne Meis Knupfer, '"To Become Good, Self-Supporting Women": The State Industrial School for Delinquent Girls at Geneva, Illinois, 1900–1935,' *Journal of the History of Sexuality* 9, no. 4 (October 2000): 420–46.
14 Estelle Freedman, '"Uncontrolled Desires": The Response to the Sexual Psychopath, 1920–1960,' in *Passion and Power: Sexuality in History,* ed. Kathy Peiss and Christina Simmons (Philadelphia: Temple University Press, 1989), 199–225.
15 George Chauncey Jr, *Gay New York: Gender, Urban Culture and the Making of the Gay Male World, 1890–1940* (New York: Basic Books, 1994), 334.
16 Jennifer Terry, *An American Obsession: Science, Medicine and Homosexuality in Modern Society* (Chicago: University of Chicago Press, 1999), 271.
17 Cited in Terry, *An American Obsession,* 129.
18 Kittrie, *The Right to Be Different,* 179.
19 Group for the Advancement of Psychiatry, *Psychiatry and Sex Psychopath Legislation: The 30s to the 80s,* vol. 9 (New York: Group for the Advancement of Psychiatry, 1977), 862.
20 Freedman, 'Uncontrolled Desires,' 202–5. For a complete historical account and analysis of American studies in sexuality in the 1930s, see Terry, *An American Obsession,* 120–267.

21 Jenkins, *Moral Panic*, 55–6; Freedman, 'Uncontrolled Desires,' 206; Terry, *An American Obsession*, 271–2.

22 A.J. Kilgour, 'Sex Delinquency: A Review of 100 Court Cases Referred to the Toronto Psychiatric Hospital,' *Ontario Journal of Neuro-Psychiatry* (September 1933): 34.

23 Cyril Greenland, 'Is There a Future of Human Sexuality?' In *Sexual Behaviour in Canada: Patterns and Problems*, ed. Benjamin Schlesinger (Toronto: University of Toronto Press, 1977), 279–90; Michael Bliss, '"Pure Books on Avoided Subjects": Pre-Freudian Sexual Ideas in Canada,' *Historical Papers* (1970): 99. Workman's report was subsequently reprinted in two American texts; see Bliss, n. 33.

24 For a detailed study of Krafft-Ebing, see Harry Oosterhuis, *Stepchildren of Nature: Krafft-Ebing, Psychiatry and the Making of Sexual Identity* (Chicago: University of Chicago Press, 2000).

25 Alex Gigeroff, 'The Evolution of Canadian Law with Respect to Exhibitionism, Homosexuality and Pedophilia,' in *Research Conference on Delinquency and Criminology, Proceedings / 4e Colloque de Recherche sur la Delinquance et la Criminalite, Montreal 1964* (Ottawa: Societe de Criminologie du Quebec, avec la collaboration de l'Institute Philippe Pinel, 1965), 299–308.

26 Harry Oosterhuis, 'Richard von Krafft-Ebing's "Step-Children of Nature": Psychiatry and the Making of Homosexual Identity,' in *Science and Homosexualities*, ed. Vernon A. Rosario (New York: Routledge, 1997), 80.

27 Lunbeck, *The Psychiatric Persuasion*, 49–54.

28 Angus McLaren, *Our Own Master Race: Eugenics in Canada* (Toronto: McClelland and Stewart, 1990).

29 Kilgour, 'Sex Delinquency,' 50.

30 For an important exception, see Katharine Bement Davis, *Factors in the Sex Lives of Twenty-Two Hundred Women* (New York: Harper and Brothers, 1929).

31 Steven Maynard, 'On the Case of the Case: The Emergence of the Homosexual as a Case History in Early Twentieth-Century Ontario,' in *On the Case: Explorations in Social History*, ed. Franca Iacovetta and Wendy Mitchinson (Toronto: University of Toronto Press, 1998), 65–87.

32 Kilgour, 'Sex Delinquency,' 49.

33 Canada, Parliament, House of Commons, *Debates*, 3 July 1947, H.C. Green.

34 LAC, RG 33/131, acc. 83-84/253, 'Report of the Organization Meeting, Ottawa, 29 and 30 March 1954,' 45.

35 LAC, RG 29, Department of National Health and Welfare, vol. 345, file 436-6-5, 'Mental Health: Diagnosis and Treatment of Sex Offenders,' Letter from R.E. Curran, Legal Advisor, 19 November 1947.

36 House of Commons, *Debates*, 3 July 1947, 5033.

37 LAC, RG 29, vol. 314, file 435-6-2, pt. 2, 'Meetings of the Advisory Committee on Mental Health 1947,' from the Minutes First Federal-Provincial Council of Mental Health Directors, 10–11 October 1946.

38 LAC, RG 29, vol. 310, file 435-5-27, pt. 1, Charles Stogdill to AD Simmons, 30 June 1950.

39 AO, RG 10-107-0-931, Canadian Psychiatric Association 1954–55, 'Canada's Mental Health: Monthly Roundup of News Items from the Mental Health Division, Department of National Health and Welfare, Ottawa,' no. 10 (September 1954).

40 LAC, RG 29, vol. 314, file 435-6-2, pt. 2, Meetings of the Advisory Committee on Mental Health, 1947, 'Minutes. First Federal-Provincial Conference of Mental Health Directors,' 10–11 October 1946.

41 Ibid.

42 LAC, RG 29-29, 'General Departmental, 1950–1974,' Advisory Committee on Mental Health, 1946–1966, vols. 1418–19.

43 Cameron and the Allan Memorial Institute were later incriminated for human rights abuses involving mind-control experiments. The program was funded by the United States' CIA. See Anne Collins, *In the Sleep Room: The Story of the CIA Brainwashing Experiments in Canada* (Toronto: Lester and Dennys, 1988).

44 LAC, RG 29, Department of National Health and Welfare, vol. 322, file 435-7-12, pt. 1, Mental Health Division, Canadian Mental Health Association, Committee on Psychiatric Services of Scientific Planning Council, 1954–1957, 'Survey of Psychiatric Service in Saskatchewan' n.d. [1954?].

45 This was no less true in the United States. See Group for the Advancement of Psychiatry, 'The Public Relations Problem of Psychiatry,' *Report* 5 (April 1948): 6–7.

46 *Hamilton Spectator*, editorial, 30 September 1948.

47 LAC, RG 29, vol. 121, file 190-3-8, Radio Publicity, re: Mental Health, 1946–1952, Chas. A. Roberts, Mental Health Division to Dr B.D.B. Layton, Assistant to the Director, Health Services.

48 LAC, RG 29, vol. 109, file 180-18-1, Education and Information, Mental Health Services, 1953–1958, C.W. Gilchrist to C. Stogdill, Re: Proposed Guide for Improving Relations Between Regional Psychiatric Societies and the Press, 5 January 1949.

49 LAC, RG 29, National Health and Welfare, vol. 314, file 435-6-2, pt. 2, Meetings of the Advisory Committee on Mental Health, 1947, 'Minutes. First Federal-Provincial Conference of Mental Health Directors,' 10–11 October 1946, 4.

50 LAC, RG 29, vol. 190, file 180-18-1, Philip C. Perry, 'Public Education in Mental Health,' 7 November 1949.

51 LAC, RG 29, National Health and Welfare, vol. 315, file 435-6-2, pt. 2, Meetings of the Advisory Committee on Mental Health, 'Resolutions, 1948.'

52 Terry Copp and Bill McAndrew, *Battle Exhaustion: Soldiers and Psychiatrists in the Canadian Army, 1939–1945* (Montreal and Kingston: McGill-Queen's University Press, 1990), 7–8.

53 Mary J. Wright and C. Roger Myers, eds., *The History of Academic Psychology* (Toronto: C.J. Hogrefe, 1982), 26.

54 Ibid., n. 15. Emphasis in original.

55 Archives of Ontario (hereafter AO), RG 10-107-0-784, Committee on the Sex Offender, 'Interim Report,' unpublished photocopy (Toronto: Canadian Penal Association, June 1948), 1.

56 Though it was psychiatrists and other mental health experts who propagated this idea, cold war historians of women and the family have pointed to Philip Wylie's *Generation of Vipers* (New York: Rinehart, 1942) as one of the most egregious examples of this line of thinking. See Elaine Tyler May, *Homeward Bound: American Families in the Cold War Era* (New York: Basic Books, 1988), 74–5.

57 Committee on the Sex Offender, 'Interim Report,' 5.

58 On the emergence of a developmental model, see Stephen Robertson, 'Separating the Men from the Boys: Masculinity, Psychosexual Development, and Sex Crime in the United States, 1930s–1960s,' *Journal of the History of Medicine and Allied Sciences* 56, no. 1 (January 2001): 3–35.

59 Committee on the Sex Offender, 'Interim Report,' 6.

60 Terry, *An American Obsession*, 163–8.

61 Committee on the Sex Offender, 'Interim Report,' 9. For a critique of that claim, see Johann Mohr, 'The Contribution of Research to the Selection of Appropriate Alternatives for Sexual Offenders,' *Criminal Law Quarterly* 4 (January 1962): 317–28.

62 Committee on the Sex Offender, 'Interim Report,' 9. Alfred Kinsey, Wardell B. Pomeroy, Clyde E. Martin, and Paul H. Gebhard, *Sexual Behavior in the Human Male* (Philadelphia: W.B. Saunders, 1948).

63 Committee on the Sex Offender, 'Interim Report,' 9–10.

64 LAC, RG 29, vol. 345, file 436-6-5, Mental Health, Diagnosis and Treatment of Sex Offenders, 'The (New York City) Mayors Committee Reports on the Study of Sexual Offences.' The Mental Health Division of the Department of Health kept a copy of the committee's findings on file.

65 Committee on the Sex Offender, 'Interim Report,' 11.

66 See also Canadian psychologist J.D. Ketchum's 'Prude Is Father to the Pervert,' *Maclean's*, 15 January 1948, 9, 42–4.

67 For the impact of the Kinsey reports in Canada, see Mary Louise Adams, *The Trouble with Normal: Postwar Youth and the Making of Heterosexuality* (Toronto: University of Toronto Press, 1997), 35–8.

68 Committee on the Sex Offender, 'Interim Report,' 18.

69 Ibid., 26. Like-minded psychologists agreed that the Kinsey reports were a clarion call for a 'moral renaissance.' See Kinsey Institute Archives (hereafter KIA), Correspondence Files, Frank Caprio to Alfred Kinsey, 14 August 1953.

70 Committee on the Sex Offender, 'Interim Report,' 27.

71 Ibid., 20.

72 'Resolutions from the 1950 Convention,' *Canadian Home and School* 10, no. 1 (September 1950): 24.

73 KIA, Correspondence Files, J.D.M. Griffin to Alfred Kinsey, 29 November 1947.

74 Philip Girard, 'Gays and Lesbians and the Legal Process since 1945,' 83, cited in Gary Kinsman, *The Regulation of Desire: Homo and Hetero Sexualities*, 2nd ed. (Montreal: Black Rose Books, 1996), 183, 209 n159. See also House of Commons, *Debates*, 14 June 1948, 5203.

75 Reg Whitaker and Gary Marcuse, *Cold War Canada: The Making of a National Insecurity State, 1945–1957* (Toronto: University of Toronto Press, 1994); Robert Bothwell, *The Big Chill: Canada and the Cold War* (Toronto: Irwin Publishing, 1998); Douglas Owram, *Born at the Right Time: A History of the Baby Boom Generation* (Toronto: University of Toronto Press, 1996).

76 LAC, RG 13, vol. 2837, file 155002, Revision of the Criminal Code, 'Summary of Objections and Representations Made to the Special Committee on Bill 93,' clause 661.

77 LAC, RG 29, vol. 345, file 436-6-5, Department of Health and Welfare, Mental Health, 'Diagnosis and Treatment of Sex Offenders.'

2 Social Citizenship and Sexual Danger

1 *Toronto Telegram*, 28 February 1955, 1, 2, 3.

2 *Toronto Daily Star*, 10 April 1955, 3.

3 Stanley Cohen, *Folk Devils and Moral Panics: The Creation of Mods and Rockers* (London: MacGibbon and Kee, 1972); Jeffrey Weeks, *Sex, Politics and Society* (London: Longmans, 1981), 14.

4 Stanley Cohen, *Folk Devils and Moral Panics: The Creation of Mods and Rockers*, 3rd ed. (New York: Routledge, 2002), 9.

5 Mary Louise Adams, *The Trouble with Normal: Postwar Youth and the Making of Heterosexuality* (Toronto: University of Toronto Press, 1997), 56; Estelle Freedman, '"Uncontrolled Desires": The Response to the Sexual Psychopath, 1920–1960,' in *Passion and Power: Sexuality in History*, ed. Kathy Peiss and Christina Simmons (Philadelphia: Temple University Press, 1989), 199–225; George Chauncey Jr, 'The Postwar Sex Crime Panic,' in *True Stories from the American Past*, ed. William Graebner (New York: McGraw-Hill, 1993), 160–78.

6 Gary Kinsman, *The Regulation of Desire: Homo and Hetero Sexualities*, 2nd ed. (Montreal: Black Rose Books, 1996); Rob Champagne, 'Psychopaths and Perverts: The Canadian Royal Commission on the Criminal Law Relating to Criminal Sexual Psychopaths, 1954–1958,' *Canadian Lesbian and Gay History Network Newsletter* 2 (September 1986): 7–9. For the United States, see Philip Jenkins, *Moral Panic: Changing Concepts of the Child Molester in Modern America* (New Haven, CT: Yale University Press, 1998); Chauncey, 'The Postwar Sex Crime Panic'; and Estelle Freedman, '"Uncontrolled Desires": The Response to the Sexual Psychopath, 1920–1960,' in *Passion and Power: Sexuality in History*, ed. Kathy Peiss and Christina Simmons (Philadelphia: Temple University Press, 1989), 199–225.

7 Reva Gerstein is the only female mental health expert I encountered. Women were much more likely to be found in the social workers' ranks. See Lorraine M. Williams, 'Setting Up Social Work at the Forensic Clinic,' in *TPH: History and Memories of the Toronto Psychiatric Hospital, 1925–1966*, ed. Edward Shorter (Toronto: Wall and Emerson, 1996), 253–7; James H. Capshew, *Psychologists on the March: Science, Practice and Professional Identity in America, 1929–1969* (New York: Cambridge University Press, 1999), 21–32, and chapter 3.

8 Kari Delhi, 'Women and Class: The Social Organization of Mother Relations to Schools in Toronto, 1915–1940' (PhD diss., Ontario Institute for Studies in Education, 1988).

9 Mona Gleason, *Normalizing the Ideal: Psychology, Schooling and the Family in Postwar Canada* (Toronto: University of Toronto Press, 1999). See also John R. Seeley, R. Alexander Sim, and Elizabeth W. Loosley, *Crestwood Heights: A Study of the Culture of Suburban Life* (New York: Basic Books, 1956.)

10 See Julie Guard, 'Canadian Citizens or Dangerous Foreign Women? Canada's Radical Consumer Movement, 1947–50,' in *Sisters or Strangers? Immigrant, Ethnic, and Racialized Women in Canadian History*, ed. Marlene Epp, F. Iacovetta, and F. Swyripa (Toronto: University of Toronto Press, 2004), 161–89; Magda Fahrni, 'Counting the Costs of Living: Gender, Citizenship, and a Politics of Prices in 1940s Montreal,' *Canadian Historical Review* 83, no. 4 (December 2002): 483–504; Susan Prentice, 'Workers, Mothers, Reds:

Toronto's Postwar Daycare Fight,' *Studies in Political Economy* 30 (1989): 115–41.

11 For a full analysis of Woodsworth's *Strangers at Our Gates*, see Allen George Mills, *Fool for Christ: The Political Thought of J.S. Woodsworth* (Toronto: University of Toronto Press, 1991), 42–56.

12 A fuller description and analysis of the news coverage of these murders can be found in Elise Chenier, 'Seeing Red: Immigrant Women and Sexual Danger in Toronto's Postwar Daily Newspapers,' *Atlantis: A Women's Studies Journal* 24, no. 2 (spring 2000): 51–60.

13 Dominique Marshall, 'Reconstruction Politics: The Canadian Welfare State and the Formation of Children's Rights, 1940–1950,' in *Family Matters: Papers in Post-Confederation Canadian Family History*, ed. Lori Chambers and Edgar-Andre Montigny (Toronto: Canadian Scholars' Press, 1998), 135–56.

14 Bertha Shvemar, interview by the author, Toronto, 6 December 1998.

15 For a complete list of PAL endorsements, see 'Exhibit 51' in the transcripts of the Hearings of the Royal Commission on the Criminal Law Relating to Criminal Sexual Psychopaths, Osgoode Hall Law Library (hereafter *Transcripts*), 1594–601.

16 Archives of Ontario (hereafter AO), RG 10-107-0-784, Committee on the Sex Offender, 'Interim Report,' unpublished photocopy (Toronto: Canadian Penal Association, June 1948).

17 Bertha Shvemar, personal diary, 30 September 1955.

18 *Toronto Telegram*, 27 January 1956; *Globe and Mail*, 23 January 1956.

19 Shvemar, interview by the author, 1998.

20 Shvemar, interview by the author, 1998. For example, the *Toronto Telegram* paid for the publication of 'The Strange One,' a pamphlet that explained sexual deviation to parents who attended PAL public speaking engagements.

21 The founding members of the Vancouver-based Women's Committee on Radiation Hazards describe the direct media access activist groups enjoyed in the late 1950s and early 60s as instrumental in their success. 'Bomb Ladies,' interview by Kelly Ryan, *Sounds Like Canada*, CBC Radio, 25 July 2005. On Allan Grossman, see Peter Oliver, *Unlikely Tory: The Life and Politics of Allan Grossman* (Toronto: Lester and Orpen Dennys, 1985).

22 AO, RG 10-107-0-784, 'Parents' Action League: Scientific Advisory Committee.'

23 June Callwood, 'The Parents Strike Back against Sex Criminals,' *Maclean's Magazine*, 23 July 1955, 7–9, 48–51; Helen Beattie, 'The Sex Criminals Who Walk Our Streets,' *Canadian Home Journal* (September 1955): 10–11, 66–68.

24 *Toronto Daily Star*, 7 July 1952, 1–5. These developments are examined more fully in chapter 4.

25 Bertha Shvemar, personal diary, 22 September 1955.

26 Ibid., 31 December 1955.

27 Ibid., 3 January 1956.

28 *Toronto Telegram*, 9 January 1956, 1, 3.

29 *Globe and Mail*, 11 January 1956, 2.

30 *Windsor Star*, 13 January 1956, in AO, RG 49, press clippings, MS 755, reel 145, Health, Sex Deviates; detailed notes on the meeting are found in AO, RG 20-15, Ac. 23851, TB 6, Parents Action League of Ontario. Notably the government's director of publicity, John Scott, also attended the meeting.

31 AO, RG 4-2, file 80.1, 'Criminal Sexual Psychopaths and Sex Offenders 1956,' 13 January 1956, mimeograph, Meeting with PAL.

32 In 1966 the Toronto Psychiatric Hospital became the Clarke Institute of Psychiatry, and in the 1990s, the Clarke became the Centre for Addiction and Mental Health. Despite the name and structural changes to the delivery of psychiatric services, the centre remains the Canadian leader in the treatment of sex offenders and people diagnosed with gender identity disorder. Whereas these two groups of people would have been grouped as 'sex deviants' at the Outpatient Forensic Clinic in the 1950s and early 60s, they are currently treated as two distinct medical types and receive treatment from separate departments.

33 *Globe and Mail*, 8 February 1956, 2; AO, RG 64-2, file 283.7, Reform Institutions, 'Mental Health Services,' March–April 1965.

34 Adams, *Trouble with Normal*, 107–35. A late 1950s survey of middle-class parents showed that most felt that sex education was a responsibility belonging to the home, but it also reported a 'growing demand for a more effective partnership in areas of ... sex education.' Canadian Federation of Home and School and Parent-Teacher Associations, *Canadian Family Study 1957–1960* (Toronto: The Federation, 1960): 26, 29.

35 *The Dangerous Stranger*, 1950, Sid Davis Productions. On the history of the National Film Board's role in parent education, see Brian J. Low, *NFB Kids: Portrayals of Children by the National Film Board of Canada, 1939–1989* (Waterloo: Wilfred Laurier University Press, 2002), 121–52; reference to the National Library's possession of Sid Davis's *The Dangerous Stranger* can be found in British Columbia Archives, MS 737, British Columbia Home and School Federation Originals 1946–1971, Minutes of 13 March 1957 meeting of the Executive Committee, 5. Ultimately PAL used Davis's film in their public talks. See 'Parents League Studies Five-Year Gains,' *Globe and Mail*, 1 April 1961, 11.

36 'The Parent Education Bureau – What It Is and What It Does,' Bertha Shvemar, personal papers.

37 Shvemar, interview by the author, 6 December 1998.
38 Ibid. The BCPTA lobbied their attorney general as early as 1955, suggesting that PAL was not unique in looking at issues beyond the medical treatment of sex offenders. British Columbia Archives, MSS 737, BC Home and School Federation fond, box 1, file 1, Board of Directors, Minutes 1950–1957, 15 September 1955.
39 See D. Reifen, 'Protection of Children Involved in Sexual Offences: A New Method of Investigation in Israel,' *Journal of Law, Criminology, and Police Science* 49 (1958): 223–9.
40 John Rich, *Toronto Daily Star*, 23 January 1956; J.D. Atcheson et al., *Incest* (Toronto: The Institute, 1975); Renée Fugère and Ingrid Thompson-Cooper, eds., *Breaking the Chains: Bruno M. Cormier and the McGill University Clinic in Forensic Psychiatry* (Westmount, QC: R. Davies Multimedia Publishing, 1998).
41 Shvemar, interview by the author, 6 December 1998.
42 Shvemar, interview by the author, 6 December 1998.
43 Callwood described PAL as 'militantly hopeful' in 'The Parents Strike Back,' 7. Shvemar described the board as having 'bull dog tenacity' at their 1956 annual meeting. Shvemar, personal papers.
44 'How to Get Father Out to Meetings,' *Canadian Home and School* 10, no. 3 (January 1951): 1. See similar articles in vol. 11, no. 3 (January–February 1952): 19–20; and vol. 12, no. 4 (March–April 1953): 7.
45 When the Local Council of Women, Owen Sound, demanded a meeting with a representative of the Ontario Department of Reform Institutions with regard to a controversial new facility for young female inmates, the director of neurology and psychiatry made arrangements to meet with them personally. AO, RG 20-16, file 143.15, Memo from Dr van Nostrand to Deputy Minister of the Department of Reform Institutions, 26 June 1957; and 'Miscellaneous, Religious Items, Martin Pinker, Chaplains 1957.' See also Barbara Roberts, 'Women's Peace Activism in Canada,' in *Beyond the Vote: Canadian Women in Politics*, ed. Linda Kealey and Joan Sangster (Toronto: University of Toronto Press, 1989), 276–308.
46 Canadian Home and School and Parent-Teacher Federation, *Canadian Family Study, 1957–1960* (Toronto: The Federation, 1960), 28.
47 See Katherine Arnup, *Education for Motherhood: Advice for Mothers in Twentieth-Century Canada* (Toronto: University of Toronto Press, 1994), 32–56.
48 Mrs J.D. Taylor, 'Let's View from the Hill Top,' *Canadian Home and School* 18, no. 1 (October 1958): 30–32.
49 Library and Archives Canada (hereafter LAC), RG 29, Health Services and Promotions Branch, Health Services Directorate, Health Consultants Pro-

gram, vol. 308, file 435-5-8, 'Mental Health Division: Canadian Federation of Home and School, Parent-Teacher Associations, 1944–1954,' 1950 conference, 'Parenthood – A Skill to be Learned.' See also Mrs. John E. Hayes, 'The Place of the PTA in Today's World,' *Canadian Home and School* 9, no. 1 (September 1949): 4–5. Hayes writes, 'this is the most important time in our history to be a parent or a teacher because we are guiding the first generation of children who will face the alternative choice of developing peace over the world or witnessing the destruction of civilization.'

50 Nancy Christie and Michael Gauvreau, 'Introduction,' in *Cultures of Citizenship in Postwar Canada, 1940–1955*, ed. Nancy Christie and Michael Gauvreau (Montreal: McGill-Queen's University Press, 2003), 17.

51 Dean N. Scarfe, 'Youth and Our Changing Concepts,' *Canadian Home and School* 16, no. 1 (October 1956): 20.

52 Parents' Action League, 'You Too Can Curb Sex Crimes,' *Liberty Magazine* (August 1955): 69.

53 Shvemar was also a pharmacist, and though she presented herself as just a housewife, she worked alongside her husband in their jointly owned drug store throughout this period. Shvemar, interview by the author, 6 Dec. 1998.

54 Eugenia Kaledin, *Mothers and More: American Women in the 1950s* (Boston: Twayne Publishers, 1984), 86.

55 Callwood, 'The Parents Strike Back,' 51.

56 Parents' Action League, 'You Too Can Curb Sex Crimes,' 15.

57 Arnup, *Education for Motherhood*, 36.

58 An excellent example is provided by the National Film Board's series 'Ages and Stages.' See especially 'Why Won't Tommy Eat,' directed by Judith Crawley, National Film Board of Canada, 1948.

59 Ironically, it was Shvemar's husband Leslie who suggested they call the organization Parents' Action League. For a fascinating documentary film that anticipates men's more active involvement in the private sphere and women's increased participation in public life, see *Careers and Cradles*, film, directed by Jack Olsen (Toronto: National Film Board of Canada, 1947).

60 Annalee Golz, 'Family Matters: The Canadian Family and the State in the Postwar Period,' *Left History* 1 no. 2 (fall 1993): 9–49. See also Adams, *Trouble with Normal*, 32–35; and Gleason, *Normalizing the Ideal*, 57–62.

61 Ina Van Dyck, 'Should Mothers Be Gainfully Employed? Do Advantages Outweigh the Problems of Two Careers?' *Canadian Home and School* 21, no. 4 (April 1962): 18–19; Valerie J. Korinek, *Roughing It in the Suburbs: Reading Chatelaine Magazine in the Fifties and Sixties* (Toronto: University of Toronto Press, 2000).

62 Golz, 'Family Matters', 15–16.

63 A good example of the persistent call for fathers to get involved in child-rearing is John Nash, 'It's Time Father Got Back in the Family,' *Maclean's Magazine*, 12 May 1956, 28–9, 82–5. Recent studies by Robert Rutherdale confirm that in parts of British Columbia at least, fathers did not live up to the ideal. Robert Rutherdale, 'Fatherhood and the Social Construction of Memory: Breadwinning and Male Parenting on a Job Frontier 1945–1966,' in *Gender and History in Canada*, ed. Joy Parr and Mark Rosenfeld (Toronto: Copp Clark, 1996), 357–75.

64 Philip Wylie, *Generation of Vipers* (New York: Rinehart, 1942).

65 Ted Honderich, 'Home Basic Factor in Sex Perversion Seen Parents' Fault,' *Toronto Star*, 23 January 1956, 2nd ed., 1.

66 John Rich, 'Deviates Vary Widely,' *Toronto Telegram*, 26 January 1956, 1, 28. John Rich's views were widely shared among his contemporaries. It should be noted that in this period, parents were not only held responsible for sexual deviancy but for the full spectrum of 'antisocial' behaviours their children engaged in. Gleason, *Normalizing the Ideal*, 70–2, 86–7.

67 On 'over-mothering' in the Canadian psychological literature, see Gleason, *Normalizing the Ideal*, 62–7.

68 Gleason, *Normalizing the Ideal*, 68–9, 71–2. See also Nash, 'It's Time Father Got Back in the Family.'

69 Alastair MacLeod, 'The Sickness in Our Suburbs,' *Chatelaine*, October 1958, 22–3.

70 P.J. Thomson, 'Response,' *Canadian Psychiatric Association Journal* 9, no. 6 (December 1964): 540–1.

71 Franklin Russell, 'Clinic to Curb Sex Crimes before They Happen,' *Maclean's*, 23 September 1961, 418–24.

72 Manny Escott, 'Clinic that Cures Compulsions,' *Toronto Star*, 4 August 1965, 24.

73 Elaine Tyler May, *Homeward Bound: American Families in the Cold War Era* (New York: Basic Books, 1988), 116–17; Gleason, *Normalizing the Ideal*, 80–118.

74 Jonathan Metzl, '"Mother's Little Helper": The Crisis of Psychoanalysis and the Miltown Resolution,' *Gender and History* 15, no. 2 (August 2003): 240–67.

75 S.R. Laycock, 'Parents Share in Training for Citizenship,' *Canadian Home and School* 12, no. 4 (March–April 1953): 4–6.

76 Jennifer Terry, *An American Obsession: Science, Medicine and Homosexuality in Modern Society* (Chicago: University of Chicago Press, 1999); Paul Robinson, *The Modernization of Sex: Havelock Ellis, Alfred Kinsey, William Masters and Virginia Johnson* (Ithaca: Cornell University Press, 1989).

77 AO, RG 49, press clippings, MS 755, reel 145, 'Health, Sex Deviates,' *The Advertiser* (New Toronto), 24 October 1947.

78 J.D. Ketchum, 'Prude Is Father to the Pervert,' *Maclean's*, 15 January 1948, 9, 42–4.
79 May, *Homeward Bound*, 100–1.
80 J.D. Atcheson, 'The Young Sex Offender,' Parents' Action League Annual Meeting, King Edward Hotel, Toronto, 29 May 1956.
81 'President's address,' Second Annual Meeting of the Parents' Action League, 29 May 1956, Shvemar, personal papers.
82 Ibid.
83 Callwood, 'The Parents Strike Back', 9.
84 Historians have similarly reproduced these assumptions. See Philip Jenkins, *Moral Panic: Changing Concepts of the Child Molester in Modern America* (New Haven, CT: Yale University Press, 1998); John D'Emilio and Estelle B. Freedman, *Intimate Matters: A History of Sexuality in America*, 2nd edition (Chicago: University of Chicago Press, 1998), 280–5. Two Canadian historical sociologists, Mary Louise Adams and Gary Kinsman, have written about PAL specifically. In the first instance, Adams briefly mentions the league in connection with postwar concerns over sex crime and the construction of the sexual psychopath, and she situates the group within the context of an irrational and exaggerated response to local and isolated attacks on children. Though he does not employ a moral panic model, Gary Kinsman situates the group within the context of the growing authority of mental health experts over matters of sexuality. In his more extended examination of the league's activities, Kinsman emphasizes how PAL 'became defined organizationally by the social interests of ... professional experts.' What he fails to see is that the interests of the experts were their interests, and that PAL organized itself accordingly. See Adams, *Trouble with Normal*, 121–3; Kinsman, *Regulation of Desire*, 194–6.
85 AO, RG 10-107-0-931, Canadian Psychiatric Association, 1954–1955.
86 Ibid.
87 'The Strange One: A Report from the Parents' Action League,' pamphlet, printed by the *Toronto Telegram* [1960?], 5.
88 Arnold Hunt, '"Moral Panic" and Moral Language in the Media,' *British Journal of Sociology* 48, no. 4 (December 1997): 634.
89 Chenier, 'Seeing Red,' 51–60.
90 Jenkins, *Moral Panic*, 72.
91 W.C.J. Meredith, 'Law and the Sex Criminal,' *Saturday Night Magazine*, 18 October 1952, 1.
92 Parents' Action League, 'You Too Can Curb Sex Crimes,' 68.
93 A 1963 *Maclean's* story on sex offenders and the lack of treatment programs in prison, for example, failed to generate the response similar stories garnered

in the early to mid-1950s. Robert Fulford, 'What We Can Learn from the Tragic History of a Sex Criminal,' *Maclean's*, 21 September 1961, 24, 46–7.

94 Sidney Katz, 'The Truth about Sex Criminals,' *Maclean's*, 1 July 1947, 12, 46–7; Lotta Dempsey, 'We the People vs. Sex Criminals,' *Chatelaine*, January 1948, 6–7, 50–2.

95 D. Cappon, 'Pervert Not Often Killer,' *Toronto Telegram*, 27 January 1956, 1, 4.

96 Kenneth G. Gray, 'Sexual Deviation: Problem and Treatment,' *Saturday Night Magazine*, 26 November 1955, 9–10. This article provided thumbnail sketches of a wide variety of 'deviations' from the norm, familiarizing readers with terms like 'fetish' and 'sado-masochism.' For the request to order copies for distribution within the Department of Reform Institutions, see AO, RG 20-16-2, file 113.2, 'General Mr Potts and Dr van Nostrand,' Memo to Purchasing Officer, 7 December 1955.

97 'Ask Medical Treatment for Sexual Psychopaths,' *Toronto Telegram*, 18 May 1955, 33.

98 Ron Kenyon, telephone interview by the author, 29 April 1999.

99 Callwood, 'The Parents Strike Back,' 48.

100 'Tiny Girls Assault Verdict Blasted,' *Toronto Telegram*, 10 January 1956, 1–2; AO, RG 49, press clippings, MS 755, reel 145, Health, Sex Deviates, 'Assault Case Here Brings Protests Suspended Sentence Is Indecent,' *St Catharines Standard*, 10 January 1956.

101 'Man, 35, Fined in 3 Assaults, Advised to Move,' *Globe and Mail*, 18 January 1956, 5.

102 AO, RG 4-2, Attorney General, file 71.5, 'Criminal Sexual Psychopaths'; and file 80.1, 'Criminal Sexual Psychopaths and Sex Offenders 1956.'

103 AO, RG 10-107, file 224, 'Sex Criminals 1947–1954,' letter, 10 November 1947.

104 AO, RG 4-2, Attorney General, file 80.1, 'Criminal Sexual Psychopaths and Sex Offenders 1956,' Letter, Dufferin Home and School Association, 13 February 1956.

105 *Toronto Telegram*, 30 March 1955, 5.

106 'Stiffer Penalties Are Asked for Sex Perverts,' *Justice Weekly*, 17 October 1953, 1, 3, 9, 12.

107 *Justice Weekly*, 11 February 1956, 4.

108 *Justice Weekly*, 16 October 1954, 4.

109 Fred Fejes, 'Murder, Perversion, and Moral Panic: The 1954 Media Campaign against Miami's Homosexuals and the Discourse of Civic Betterment,' *Journal of the History of Sexuality* 9, no. 3 (July 2000): 325–6.

110 'President's address,' Parents' Action League of Ontario Annual Meeting,

13 June 1957, Shvemar, personal papers. See also Bernard Oliver Jr, *Sexual Deviation in American Society* (New Haven, CT: College and University Press, 1967): 25–6.

111 Hunt, 'Moral Panic,' 645.

112 'Question Male Trucker, 21, Married with Two Children in Sex Murder of Girl, 14,' *Toronto Daily Star*, 19 January 1956, 1, 2; 'Linda "the Baby" of Dancing Class,' *Toronto Telegram*, 19 January 1956, 1, 4; Phyllis Griffiths, 'The Life Story of Linda Lampkin,' *Toronto Telegram*, 23 January 1956, 1–3.

113 'Young Girl Found Brutally Murdered by Sex Fiend,' *Toronto Daily Star*, 19 January 1956, 5

114 Canada, Parliament, House of Commons, *Debates*, 24 January 1956, 510 (Comments by Ms Aitken of York-Humber); AO, RG 4-2, Attorney General, file 80.1, 'Criminal Sexual Psychopaths and Sex Offenders 1956.'

115 PAL, 'You Too Can Curb Sex Crimes,' *Liberty Magazine* (August 1955): 69.

116 'Linda "the Baby" of Dancing Class,' *Toronto Telegram*, 19 January 1956, 1, 4; Phyllis Griffiths, 'The Life Story of Linda Lampkin,' *Toronto Telegram*, 23 January 1956, 1–3.

117 *Toronto Telegram*, 3 February 1956, 6. It is worth noting that that was only the first insult in the letter. The writer's more important complaint was that Rich claimed that children who were sexually assaulted were 'willing partner[s].' In fact, she blamed psychiatrists for 'creating' sex 'monsters' by counselling parents to tolerate all sorts of bad behaviour so as 'not to frustrate Johnny.'

118 Lex Schrag, 'Doctor Says Horror, Fear of Homosexuality Block Achieving Sexual Maturity,' *Globe and Mail*, 6 February 1961, 4. The panel consisted of R.E. Turner, director of the Outpatient Forensic Clinic, Ed Tutchie, director of the Forensic Inpatient Clinic, Kenneth Gray, an expert in medical jurisprudence and leading advocate of treatment for sex offenders, and J.D. Atcheson, past director of the Toronto Child and Family Court and the Research Division of the Department of Reform Institutions.

119 Canadian Federation of Home and School Parent-Teacher Associations, *Canadian Family Study 1957–60* (Toronto: The Federation, [1960?]), 3–4.

120 There is an enormous body of literature on the social problems and issues that surrounded the baby boom generation in their adolescence. For a general Canadian overview, see Doug Owram, *Born at the Right Time: A History of the Baby Boom Generation* (Toronto: University of Toronto Press, 1996).

121 Committee on Sexual Offences against Children and Youths, *Sexual Offences against Children: Report of the Committee on Sexual Offences Against Children and Youths* (Ottawa: Minister of Supply and Services Canada, 1984).

3 Surveying Sex

1 Psychology as a discipline grew out of moral philosophy, a field of study taught primarily for the benefit of the clergy in nineteenth- and early twentieth-century Canada. In the 1910s and 20s, psychology successfully made the institutional transition from philosophy to science. See Mary J. Wright and C. Roger Myers, eds., *The History of Academic Psychology* (Toronto: C.J. Hogrefe, 1982), 1–15. See also James H. Capshew, *Psychologists on the March: Science, Practice and Professional Identity in America, 1929–1969* (New York: Cambridge University Press, 1999). On the history of eugenics in Canada, see Angus McLaren, *Our Own Master Race: Eugenics In Canada, 1885–1945* (Toronto: McClelland and Stewart, 1990).

2 Library and Archives Canada (hereafter LAC), RG 33/131, acc. 83–84, Royal Commission on the Criminal Law Relating to Criminal Sexual Psychopaths, 'Report of the Organizational Meeting, Ottawa, March 29 and 30, 1954,' 5–6.

3 Canada, *Report of the Royal Commission on the Criminal Law Relating to Criminal Sexual Psychopaths* (Ottawa: Queen's Printer, 1958), 2 (hereafter referred to as *Report*).

4 Ibid., 9–10.

5 Ibid., 6–10.

6 Ibid., 13.

7 See K.G. Gray, 'Psychiatry and the Criminal Code,' *Ontario Journal of Neuro-Psychiatry* 5 (December 1935): 44–53.

8 Transcripts of the Hearings of the Royal Commission on the Criminal Law Relating to Criminal Sexual Psychopaths, Osgoode Hall Law Library (hereafter *Transcripts*), 632, 644.

9 Only one medical doctor supported sexual psychopathy as a medical diagnosis. See testimony of Dr Alastair MacLeod, assistant professor of psychiatry at McGill, and assistant medical director of the Montreal Mental Hygiene Institute, *Transcripts*, 1533–7.

10 *Transcripts*, 579.

11 LAC, RG 13, acc. 89-90/067, vol. 22, file 155002, Revisions of the Criminal Code, Letter from the Deputy Attorney-General, Chairman, Provincial Subcommittee, Canadian Bar Association, Uniformity of Legislation (Criminal Section) to Forsyth, secretary, Criminal Law Section, Canadian Bar Association, Dept of Justice, Ottawa, 10 April 1947.

12 H. Roy Brillinger, 'The Judge and the Psychiatrist – Toward Mutual Understanding,' *Canadian Journal of Corrections* 1, no. 2 (January 1959): 1–9; J.A. Graham, 'Address,' Magistrate's Conference, London, ON, 1959, Archives of

Ontario (hereafter AO), RG 20-16-2, file 163.8, Misc., Visitors, Chaplains, Religious Items, 1958–59.

13 *Transcripts*, 673.

14 Ibid., 1111. Emphasis in original.

15 Ibid., 924.

16 See John Senn's written submission, 'Exhibit 54,' in *Transcripts*, 1609–14, and his oral testimony, *Transcripts*, 1243–5.

17 *Transcripts*, 636, 1686.

18 Ibid., 646.

19 Ibid., 1429.

20 On this point, see A.B. Stokes, AO, RG 49-131, 'Proceedings of the Select Committee Appointed by the Legislative Assembly of the Province of Ontario, to Study and Report upon Problems of Delinquent Individuals and Custodial Questions, and the Place of Reform Institutions Therein,' 28:6481.

21 On confusion about the meaning of psychopathy, see *Transcripts*, 1230. On confusion about the application of the law, see *Transcripts*, 592.

22 Cases are fought and won on interpretations of the wording of the law. For another example of a struggle over the phrasing of a law related to sexual assault, see LAC, RG 13, vol. 2853, file 173600-138(2), Criminal Code Section 138(2), Sexual Offence, which debates whether or not the phrase 'wholly and chiefly to blame' are two incompatible concepts. One judge dismissed a case of assault based on this contention.

23 Simon A. Cole, 'From the Sexual Psychopath Statute to 'Megan's Law': Psychiatric Knowledge in the Diagnosis, Treatment, and Adjudication of Sex Criminals in New Jersey, 1949-1999,' *Journal of the History of Medicine and Allied Sciences* 55 (July 2000): 292–314.

24 *Transcripts*, 1407.

25 Shortly after Major General Gibson, the commissioner of penitentiaries, furnished the commission with these figures, Dr Bruce Cormier was employed to work at St Vincent de Paul two days a week. *Transcripts*, 1041–2. For a more detailed history of psychiatric and psychological services at St Vincent de Paul, see psychologist Justin Ciale's *Tales of St Vincent de Paul Penitentiary* (Toronto: Legas, 1997).

26 *Transcripts*, 1252.

27 Ibid., 1099. For further critiques on this issue, see also 677, 702–3; 1405–15.

28 Mona Gleason, *Normalizing the Ideal: Psychology, Schooling, and the Family in Postwar Canada* (Toronto: University of Toronto Press, 1999), 9, 81; Mary Louise Adams, *The Trouble with Normal: Postwar Youth and the Making of Heterosexuality* (Toronto: University of Toronto Press, 1997), 26.

29 Adams, *Trouble with Normal*, 166–7.

30 Alfred Kinsey, Wardell B. Pomeroy, Clyde E. Martin, and Paul H. Gebhard, *Sexual Behavior in the Human Male* (Philadelphia: W.B. Saunders, 1948). Some historians have argued that the Kinsey reports provoked the debates about what constituted sexually normative behaviour. However, these discussions – and debates – were well under way before the release of the first report, and while Kinsey did serve to galvanize, and to some degree polarize, opinion, the role of his surveys has been overestimated. See Jennifer Terry, *An American Obsession: Science, Medicine and Homosexuality in Modern Society* (Chicago: University of Chicago Press, 1999), 120–58.

31 Alfred Kinsey et al., 'Concepts of Normality and Abnormality in Sexual Behaviour,' in American Psychological Association, *Psychosexual Development in Health and Disease: The Proceedings of the Thirty-Eighth Annual Meeting of the American Psychopathological Association, Held in New York City, June 1948* (New York: Grune and Stratton, 1949), 13–16.

32 Ibid. On the cultural anthropology influence in sexuality studies, see Terry, *An American Obsession*, 163–8.

33 'Exhibit 56,' in *Transcripts*. See Terry, *An American Obsession*, 163–8 for an account of the impact of anthropology on studies into human sexual behaviour.

34 *Transcripts*, 302.

35 Ibid., 829. The irony is that modern-thinking experts pathologized those who preserved 'pre-modern' sexual standards and suggested that they needed therapy to overcome their irrational aversions. See R.S. Rodgers, *Sex and Law in Canada* (Ottawa: Policy Press, 1962).

36 *Transcripts*, 828–30, 1484.

37 Ibid., 692.

38 Carolyn Strange, *Toronto's Girl Problem: The Perils and Pleasures of the City, 1880–1930* (Toronto: University of Toronto Press, 1995), 105–15; Gary Kinsman, *The Regulation of Desire: Homo and Hetero Sexualities*, 2nd ed. (Montreal: Black Rose Books, 1996), 88.

39 *Transcripts*, 500. For a discussion of incest in an earlier period, see Karen Dubinsky, *Improper Advances: Rape and Heterosexual Conflict in Ontario, 1880–1929* (Chicago: University of Chicago Press, 1993), 58–63.

40 *Transcripts*, 620–1. Alcorn's comments were followed by the chairman's question: 'What kind of whipping was it?' For the question and answer, see 621–4.

41 See *Report*. On the public and media panic over sexual assaults against children, and the subsequent police assault on homosexual communities, see Gary Kinsman, 'The Sexual Regulation of Family Relations: The "Public" Construction of Sexual Danger in Canada, 1950–1965,' (paper presented at the History of the Family Conference, Ottawa, 1994); Fred Fejes, 'Murder,

Perversion, and Moral Panic: The 1954 Media Campaign against Miami's Homosexuals and the Discourse of Civic Betterment,' *Journal of the History of Sexuality* 9, no. 3 (July 2000): 305–47; Philip Jenkins, *Moral Panic: Changing Concepts of the Child Molester in Modern America* (New Haven, CT: Yale University Press, 1998).

42 John Gerassi, *The Boys of Boise: Furor, Vice and Folly in an American City* (1966; repr., Seattle: University of Washington Press, 2001).

43 William M. Eskridge Jr, 'Privacy Jurisprudence and the Apartheid of the Closet, 1946–1961,' *Florida State University Law Review* (1997) http://www.law.fsu.edu/journals/lawreview/frames/244/eskrfram.html (accessed 8 June 2001).

44 John D'Emilio, 'The Homosexual Menace: The Politics of Sexuality in Cold War America,' in *Passion and Power, Sexuality in History,* ed. Kathy Peiss and Christina Simmons (Philadelphia: Temple University Press, 1989), 226–40; George Chauncey Jr, 'The Postwar Sex Crime Panic,' in *True Stories from the American Past,* ed. William Graebner (New York: McGraw-Hill, 1993), 160–78; Terry, *An American Obsession,* 329–52.

45 Gary Kinsman, Dieter K. Buse, and Mercedes Steedman, *Whose National Security? Canadian State Surveillance and the Creation of Enemies* (Toronto: Between the Lines Press, 2000).

46 Chauncey, 'The Postwar Sex Crime Panic'; John Marshall, 'Pansies, Perverts and Macho Men: Changing Conceptions of Male Homosexuality,' in *The Making of the Modern Homosexual,* ed. Kenneth Plummer (London: Hutchinson, 1981), 133–54; John D'Emilio, 'The Homosexual Menace,' 226–40; Gary Kinsman, '"Inverts," "Psychopaths" and "Normal" Men: Historical Sociological Perspectives on Gay and Heterosexual Masculinities,' in *Men and Masculinities: A Critical Anthology,* ed. Tony Haddad (Toronto: Canadian Scholars' Press, 1993), 3–35.

47 This was also part of a wider intellectual shift from biology to behaviour. See 'Foreword,' in *Social Deviance in Canada,* ed. W.E. Mann (Toronto: Copp Clark, 1971). In his introduction. Mann notes that theoretically 'Canadians have not widely distinguished themselves' from American scholars of deviance.

48 Eric Setliff, 'Sex Fiends or Swish Kids? Gay Men in Hush Free Press, 1946–1956,' in *Gendered Pasts: Historical Essays in Femininity and Masculinity in Canada,* eds. Kathryn McPherson, Cecilia Morgan, and Nancy M. Forestall (Toronto: Oxford University Press, 1999), 158–78.

49 See *Transcripts,* 1250; Donna Penn, 'The Meanings of Lesbianism in Post War America,' *Gender and History* 3, no. 2 (summer 1991): 190–203.

50 John D'Emilio, *Sexual Politics, Sexual Communities: The Making of a Homosexual*

Minority in the United States, 1940–1970 (Chicago: University of Chicago Press, 1983), 17; Marc Stein, *City of Sisterly & Brotherly Loves: Lesbian and Gay Philadelphia, 1945–1972* (Chicago: University of Chicago Press, 2000).

51 *Transcripts*, 1522.

52 Ibid., 1094.

53 Ibid., 752, see also 680.

54 Ibid., 126.

55 Ibid., 1192–3. Arrests for gross indecency in Montreal jumped from 65 in 1953 to 311 in 1954. *Transcripts*, 978. According to Gary Kinsman, even the 65 arrests in 1953 were abnormally inflated. In that year, Maurice Leznoff's MA thesis on Montreal's gay community garnered media attention that, in turn, aroused public concern and police attention, resulting in an increase in the number of arrests. Kinsman, *Regulation of Desire*, 161–3. Maurice Lenzoff's thesis was 'The Homosexual in Urban Society' (MA thesis, Sociology Department, McGill University, 1954).

56 *Transcripts*, 1192–3. On police sweeps as public housekeeping, see also the Miami Beach police chief, who explained of the 1953 crackdown on homosexuals gathering at the local beach: 'we had no charges we could book them on, but it's just a question of cleaning up a bad situation and letting undesirables know they're not wanted here.' Bureau of Public Information, 'Miami Junks the Constitution,' *ONE* (January 1954), cited in Eskridge, 'Privacy Jurisprudence and the Apartheid of the Closet.'

57 E. Kelleher, 'The Role of Psychiatry in Programs for the Control and Treatment of Sex Offenders' (paper presented at the Institute on the Illinois Penal and Correctional System, 18 May 1952), Kinsey Institute Archives.

58 *Transcripts*, 1485–6. Emphasis added.

59 LAC, RG 33/131, acc. 83-84/253, vol. 2, 'New Jersey Meeting with Royal Commission,' 41.

60 *Transcripts*, 606.

61 Ibid., 608.

62 See Steven Maynard, 'Through a Hole in the Lavatory Wall: Homosexual Subcultures, Police Surveillance, and the Dialectics of Discovery, Toronto, 1890-1930,' *Journal of the History of Sexuality* 5, no. 2 (1994): 207–43. Sarah Schmidt, '"Private" Acts in "Public" Spaces: Parks in Turn-of-the-Century Montreal,' in *Power, Place, and Identity: Historical Studies of Social and Legal Regulation in Quebec*, ed. Tamara Myers, Kate Boyer, Mary Anne Poutanen, and Steven Watt (Montreal: Montreal History Group, 1998), 129–49.

63 On the cultural motif of 'containment' in this era, see Elaine Tyler May, *Homeward Bound: American Families in the Cold War Era* (New York: Basic Books, 1988), 16–36.

64 *Transcripts*, 1004–5.
65 Canada, Parliament, House of Commons, *Debates*, 25 January 1956.
66 'Exhibit 64,' in *Transcripts*, 1648–66.
67 *Transcripts*, 548–9.
68 Schmidt, '"Private" Acts in "Public" Spaces.'
69 See House of Commons, *Debates*, 3 July 1947; 'Exhibit 28, Brief to the Commission from the British-Columbia Parent-Teacher Federation,' in *Transcripts*, 721A–726.
70 *Transcripts*, 1672–3.
71 Ibid., 122.
72 Ibid., 1251–2.
73 Ibid., 789–791.
74 Stephen Robertson, 'Separating the Men from the Boys: Masculinity, Psychosexual Development, and Sex Crime in the United States, 1930s-1960s,' *Journal of the History of Medicine and Allied Sciences* 56, no. 1 (January 2001): 3–35.
75 The term, 'a child of tender years' was used by the commissioners and witnesses to refer to children under fourteen years of age. See *Transcripts*, 761, 1183. See also *Report*, 41.
76 *Transcripts*, 761–2.
77 Ibid., 1124–5. Similarly, a 1936 commission established by the American Bar Association examined the issue of evidence in incest and the molestation of minors and advised the courts to be circumspect about child witnesses whose 'erotic imagination[s]' all too often lead to false charges. Cited in Jenkins, *Moral Panic*, 78.
78 *Transcripts*, 1567–8.
79 Ibid., 1640.
80 Jenkins, *Moral Panic*, 34.
81 *Transcripts*, 894.
82 Ibid., 1568.
83 Ibid., 1210–11.
84 Ibid., 1313.
85 Edward George Potter, executive director of Montreal's Society for the Protection of Women and Children, in *Transcripts*, 948. See also R.E. Turner, 'Treatment of the Sex Offender,' *Criminal Law Quarterly* 3, no. 4 (February 1961): 416–72.
86 *Transcripts*, 1510.
87 Ibid., 1602.
88 Ibid., 1369.
89 Dubinsky, *Improper Advances*, 86–112.

90 Ken Johnstone, 'We Can Do Something about Sex Crimes,' *Montreal Standard*, 10 January 1948, 3, 16–17.

91 Dubinsky, *Improper Advances*, 15.

92 *Transcripts*, 894.

93 Ibid., 1612.

94 Ibid., 637.

95 Ibid., 1474–5. For an example of a similar argument regarding men employed in recreation in interwar Germany, see William Stern, *Jugendliche Zeugen in Sittlichkeitsprozessen: ihre Behandlung und psychologische Begutachtung; ein Kapitel der forensischen Psychologie* [Juvenile Witnesses in Sex Crime Proceedings: Their Treatment and Psychological Assessment] (Leipzig: Quelle & Meyer, 1926).

96 Dr Edward Turner, interview by the author, Toronto, 4 June 1999.

97 Jenkins, *Moral Panic*, 32–3; Angus McLaren, *Twentieth Century Sexuality: A History* (Malden, MA: Blackwell Publishers, 1999), 162.

98 Cited in Michigan, Governor's Study Commission on the Deviated Criminal Sex Offender, *Education, Moral Values, and the Sex Deviate Problems* (Lansing, MI: State of Michigan, 1951).

99 *Report*, 75.

100 *Transcripts*, 1417.

101 Ibid., 1501–11.

102 Ibid., 1500.

103 Linda Gordon, *Heroes of Their Own Lives: The Politics and History of Family Violence, Boston 1880–1960* (London: Virago, 1989), 208.

104 Dorothy E. Chunn, 'Secrets and Lies: The Criminalization of Incest and the (Re)formation of the "Private" in British Columbia, 1890–1940,' *Regulating Lives: Historical Essays on the State, Society, the Individual and the Law*, ed. John McLaren, Robert Menzies, and Dorothy E. Chunn (Vancouver: UBC Press, 2002), 120.

105 This phenomenon is best captured by the production of the highly popular educational film *The Dangerous Stranger*. Sid Davis, who created the film in 1949, explained that he was responding to the recent sexual assault and murder of a local child. The film warns children never to accept rides, candy, or other offers from unknown adults and to avoid playing away from the watchful eyes of familiar adults. None of this advice would have helped the victim who was murdered by the grandfather of a playmate. See Philip Jenkins, 'The Outer Edges: Horror and the Media in the Late 1940s' (2000), online at http://www.personal.psu.edu/faculty/j/p/jpj1/edges.htm.

106 *Transcripts*, 409, 846, 1104, 1370.

107 Ibid., 1212.

108 Ibid., 1096.

109 *Report*, 26.

110 Of course, normal and deviant behaviour is always class- and race-inflected. For a sensitive analysis of how race and ethnicity factored into immigration reception work after the Second World War, see Franca Iacovetta, 'Making "New Canadians": Social Workers, Women, and the Reshaping of Immigrant Families,' in *A Nation of Immigrants: Women, Workers, and Communities in Canadian History, 1840s–1960s*, ed. Franca Iacovetta et al. (Toronto: University of Toronto Press, 1998), 482–513.

111 *Transcripts*, 1673–4.

112 Ibid., 991.

113 Ibid., 806.

114 Ibid., 834–5, 849.

115 Daniel Paitich, 'Attitude toward Parents in Male Homosexuals and Exhibitionists' (PhD diss., University of Toronto, 1964).

116 *Transcripts*, 1225–6.

117 Ibid., 1464.

118 Ibid., 1189.

119 Ibid., 1676–7.

120 Ibid., 1260–70.

121 Ibid., 1276.

122 AO, RG 4-2, file 80.1, 'Criminal Sexual Psychopaths and Sex Offenders 1956.'

123 *Transcripts*, 627–32.

124 Paul W. Tappan, 'Some Myths about the Sex Offender,' *Federal Probation* 19, no. 2 (June 1955): 7–12.

125 *Transcripts*, 727–30.

126 See the 1970 Report of the Canadian Committee on *Youth, Drugs and the Drug Culture* (Ottawa, 1970). The government of Canada also launched a commission of inquiry into the problem of illegal drug use in the late 1960s. The commission issued its final report in 1973. See Canada, *Commission of Inquiry into the Non-Medical Use of Drugs: Final Report* (Ottawa: Information Canada, 1973).

127 Anthony Marcus, 'A Multi-Disciplinary Two Part Study of Those Individuals Designated Dangerous Sexual Offenders Held in Federal Custody in British Columbia, Part I,' *Canadian Journal of Corrections/Revue canadienne de criminologie* 8, no. 2 (April 1966): 90.

128 *Report*, 76–7.

129 *Transcripts*, 546.

130 *Report*, 55, 84, 117.

131 In April 1958, the same year the *Report* was submitted to Parliament, a British Columbia magistrate found Francis Stewart Saunders, who had pled guilty to one charge of gross indecency for engaging in sex with an adult male, to be a criminal sexual psychopath. He was sentenced to an indefinite term. It is not known when he was released, but in 1969 Saunders unsuccessfully appealed the preventive detention sentence. *R. v. Saunders* (1965), [1966] 2 C.C.C. (N.S.) 345 (B.C.S.C).

132 For an example of how the dangerous sexual offender law was later applied to a man who engaged in consensual homosexual relations with men under the age of twenty-one, see Kinsman, *Regulation of Desire*, 257–64.

133 Estelle Freedman, '"Uncontrolled Desires": The Response to the Sexual Psychopath, 1920–1960,' in *Passion and Power: Sexuality in History*, ed. Kathy Peiss and Christina Simmons (Philadelphia: Temple University Press, 1989), 199–225; Chauncey, 'The Postwar Sex Crime Panic'; Robertson, 'Separating the Men from the Boys.'

134 Philip Girard, 'Gays and Lesbians and the Legal Process since 1945' (unpublished paper, Canadian Lesbian and Gay Archives), 98.

135 If current statistical studies are to be believed, we would do well to begin by discarding the erroneous belief that most if not all men who sexually assault a child will repeat the crime. See Karl Hanson and Monique T. Bussiere, 'Predicting Relapse: A Meta-analysis of Sexual Offender Recidivism,' *Journal of Consulting and Clinical Psychology* 66, no. 2 (1998): 348–62.

136 House of Commons, *Debates*, 7 October 1994, 6741.

4 The Mad and the Bad

1 Benjamin Karpman, 'Sex Life in Prison,' *Journal of Criminal Law and Criminology* 38, no. 5 (1948): 476.

2 Bruno Cormier and Siebert P. Simons, 'The Problem of the Dangerous Sexual Offender,' in *Social Deviance in Canada*, ed. W.E. Mann (Toronto: Copp Clark, 1971): 343.

3 The annual reports provide a breakdown of diagnoses for new cases, and list new patients according to sex, but these are not cross-referenced. Individual case files are not accessible at this time. Interviews confirmed that while it is possible women sought or were ordered to get treatment for lesbianism, none of those interviewed could recall a single case, nor could they recall any female patients convicted of a sex crime of any other nature. P.J. Thomson, telephone interview by the author, 1998; R.E. Turner, interview by the author, Toronto, 1998; and J.H. Mohr, interview by the author, Wolfe Island, ON, 15 September 1998.

4   California, Department of Mental Hygiene, 'Part C: A Summary of the Study
    of Child Victims of Adult Sex Offenders,' in *Final Report on California Sexual
    Deviation Research* (Sacramento: Assembly of the State of California, 1954),
    59–62; 'Crime in California,' *Time Magazine*, 2 March 1953, 42. A 1975 study
    of incest cases at the Forensic Clinic claimed that removing the father from
    the family was 'inadequate,' since the behaviour was part of a 'family
    dynamic' of which a lack of sexual activity between husband and wife was a
    part. Atcheson et al., *Incest* (Toronto: The Institute, 1975), 13.
5   The historical literature is vast. On medical approaches to sex crime in gen-
    eral, see Frank Mort, *Dangerous Sexualities: Medico-Moral Politics in England
    since 1830* (New York: Routledge, 2000); Stephen Robertson, 'Separating the
    Men from the Boys: Masculinity, Psychosexual Development, and Sex Crime
    in the United States, 1930s–1960s,' *Journal of the History of Medicine and Allied
    Sciences* 56, no. 1 (January 2001): 3–35; and Estelle Freedman, '"Uncontrolled
    Desires": The Response to the Sexual Psychopath, 1920–1960,' in *Passion and
    Power: Sexuality in History*, ed. Kathy Peiss and Christina Simmons (Philadel-
    phia: Temple University Press, 1989), 199–225. Homosexual crimes attracted
    the most attention. Two particularly useful texts on their treatment in the
    pre–Second World War period include Harry Oosterhuis, *Stepchildren of
    Nature: Krafft-Ebing, Psychiatry and the Making of Sexual Identity* (Chicago: Uni-
    versity of Chicago Press, 2000); and Jennifer Terry, *An American Obsession: Sci-
    ence, Medicine and Homosexuality in Modern Society* (Chicago: University of
    Chicago Press, 1999). On the history of eugenics, see Ian Robert Dowbiggin,
    Keeping America Sane: Psychiatry and Eugenics in the U.S. and Canada (Ithaca,
    NY: Cornell University Press, 1997); Angus McLaren, *Our Own Master Race:
    Eugenics in Canada, 1885–1945* (Toronto: McClelland and Stewart, 1990);
    Nancy Ordover, *American Eugenics: Race, Queer Anatomy, and the Science of
    Nationalism* (Minneapolis: University of Minnesota Press, 2003); P.R. Reilly,
    The Surgical Solution: A History of Involuntary Sterilization in the United States
    (Baltimore: Johns Hopkins University Press, 1991).
6   Mark Linsky, 'The Most Critical Option: Sex Offences and Castration in San
    Diego, 1938–1975,' *Journal of San Diego History* 35, no. 4 (1989): 248–57;
    Angela Gugliotta, '"Dr. Sharp and His Little Knife": Therapeutic and Puni-
    tive Origins of Eugenic Vasectomy, Indiana, 1892–1921,' *Journal of the History
    of Medicine* 53 (October 1998): 371–406.
7   Marie E. Kopp, 'Surgical Treatment as a Sex Crime Prevention Measure,'
    Journal of Criminal Law and Criminology 28, no. 5 (January–February 1938):
    692–706.
8   Kopp, 'Surgical Treatment as a Sex Crime Prevention Measure,' 701–6.
9   Ontario, Royal Commission on Public Welfare, *Royal Commission on Public*

Welfare – Report to the Lieutenant-Governor in Council (Toronto: King's Printer, 1930), 9.

10 Archives of Ontario (hereafter AO), RG 20-15, acc. 23851, TB 6, 'Parents Action League of Ontario,' C.O. Dean, Gateway, Ontario to Minister J. Foote, 30 January 1956.

11 Ibid., Minister J. Foote to C.O. Dean, 15 February 1956.

12 AO, RG 4-2, file 80.1, 'Criminal Sexual Psychopaths and Sex Offenders 1956.' Some psychiatrists, however, were willing to castrate sex criminals as late as 1944. See R. v. Belt (1944), 84 C.C.C. 403 B.C.C.A), cited in Alex K. Gigeroff, *Sexual Deviations in the Criminal Law: Homosexual, Exhibitionistic, and Pedophilic Offences in Canada* (Toronto: University of Toronto Press, 1968), 104.

13 Doug Owram, *Born at the Right Time: A History of the Baby Boom Generation* (Toronto: University of Toronto Press, 1996): 40; Terry, *An American Obsession*, 297–8; McLaren, *Our Own Master Race*, 168; Allen M. Hornblum, 'They Were Cheap and Available: Prisoners as Research Subjects in Twentieth Century America,' *British Medical Journal* 315 (29 November 1997): 1437–41.

14 Library and Archives Canada (hereafter LAC), RG 33/131, acc. 83-84/253, 'Report of the Organization Meeting, Ottawa, March 29 & 30, 1954,' Private Hearings, Winnipeg, Regina and Edmonton, 2–9 September 1954, Interview with Dr G.F. Nelson, 107–8. See also Archives of Ontario (hereafter AO), RG 10-107-0-784, Committee on the Sex Offender, 'Interim Report,' unpublished photocopy (Toronto: Canadian Penal Association, June 1948).

15 California Department of Mental Hygiene, *Final Report on California Sexual Deviation Research* (Sacramento, CA: Assembly of the State of California, 1954), 32; F.L. Golla and R.S. Hodge, 'Hormone Treatment of Sexual Offenders,' *Lancet* 1 (1949): 256, 1006–7, cited in Charles W. Cabeen, 'Factors Related to Improvement of Sex Offenders in Therapy' (PhD diss., University of California, Los Angeles, 1955); G.N. Thompson, 'Electroshock and Other Therapeutic Consideration in Sexual Psychopathy,' *Journal of Nervous and Mental Disease* 109 (1949): 531–9. For lobotomy, see J.W. Friedlander and R.S. Banay, 'Psychosis Following Lobotomy in a Case of Sexual Psychopathy,' *Archives of Neurology and Psychiatry Chicago* 59 (1948): 302–21.

16 AO, RG 10-107 B.7, gen. 1-9-8, 19 August 1948, Memo Dr R.C. Montgomery to Ontario Hospital Superintendents; see also Committee on the Sex Offender, 'Interim Report,' 13.

17 Transcripts of the Hearings of the Royal Commission on the Criminal Law Relating to Criminal Sexual Psychopaths, Osgoode Hall Law Library (hereafter *Transcripts*), 610.

18 Psychiatry in Canada was still closely linked to neurology in this period, though the 1950s was the decade in which those ties were ultimately severed.

See, for example, AO, RG 10-107-0-997, President of the Ontario Neurological Association to Aldwyn B. Stokes, September 1956; and AO, RG 10-22-0-169, 'Psychiatry – University of Toronto,' Report to the Dean, Academic Year 1960-61.

19 Canada, *Report of the Royal Commission on the Criminal Law Relating to Criminal Sexual Psychopaths* (Ottawa: Queen's Printer, 1958), 103.

20 On the rise of psychology, see Steven C. Ward, *Modernizing the Mind: Psychological Knowledge and the Remaking of Society* (Westport, CT: Praeger, 2002); Stewart Justman, *The Psychological Mystique* (Evanston, IL: Northwestern University Press, 1998). On treatment for sex deviation, see Terry, *American Obsession*, chs. 9–12; Paul Robinson, *The Modernization of Sex: Havelock Ellis, Alfred Kinsey, William Masters and Virginia Johnson* (Ithaca: Cornell University Press, 1989); Donna Penn, 'The Meanings of Lesbianism in Post War America,' *Gender and History* 3, no. 2 (summer 1991): 190–203; and Gary Kinsman, '"Inverts," "Psychopaths" and "Normal" Men: Historical Sociological Perspectives on Gay and Heterosexual Masculinities,' in *Men and Masculinities: A Critical Anthology*, ed. Tony Haddad (Toronto: Canadian Scholars' Press, 1993), 3–35.

21 California, Department of Mental Hygiene, *Final Report on California Sexual Deviation Research* (Sacramento, CA: Assembly of the State of California, 1954), 71. Much has been written about how cold war anticommunist rhetoric dovetailed neatly with the rather hysterical language used to describe sex deviants. While there is a strong case to be made on this point, it bears repeating that psychiatrists consistently called for compassionate understanding toward sexual deviation, even to the point of arguing that this should be made easier by the knowledge that virtually everyone was susceptible to becoming a 'sadistic killer.'

22 On the role of the family and the psychiatrist, see J.D. Atcheson, 'Social Aspects of Sexual Behaviour,' *Criminal Law Quarterly* 3, no. 4 (February 1961): 455–61.

23 Freud did not see male homosexuality as particularly problematic, even though a strict interpretation of his theory might suggest otherwise. See especially his oft-reprinted 1935 'Letter to an American Mother,' http://www.psychpage.com/gay/library/freudsletter.html.

24 See, for example, *Careers and Cradles*, film, directed by Jack Olsen (Toronto: National Film Board of Canada, 1947); John Nash, 'It's Time Father Got Back in the Family,' *Maclean's Magazine*, 12 May 1956, 28–9, 82–3, 85.

25 AO, RG 20-16-2, file 52.5, General – Inmates 1951–52 Report Submitted to Col. G. Hedley Basher, Deputy Minister, Department of Reform Institutions, 28 March 1952.

26 J.W. Mohr, R.E. Turner, and J.R. Ball 'Exhibition and Pedophilia,' *Corrective Psychiatry and Journal of Social Therapy* 8, no. 4 (1962): 172–86.

27 A. Gigeroff, J. Mohr, and R. Turner, 'Sex Offenders on Probation: Heterosexual Pedophiles,' *Federal Probation* 32, no. 4 (December 1968): 17–21.

28 J.H. Mohr, R.E. Turner and M.B. Terry, *Pedophilia and Exhibitionism: A Handbook* (Toronto: University of Toronto Press, 1964).

29 Ibid., 5.

30 Mohr, interview by the author, 1998.

31 Much is made of the American Psychiatric Association's *Diagnostic and Statistical Manual of Mental Disorders* in defining sexual pathology, but it is worth pointing out that the clinic relied on the *International Statistical Classification of Diseases and Related Health Problems* authored by the World Health Organization. Furthermore, as was the case with many European sexologists, working with people who were criminally prosecuted for their sexual activities led forensic sexologists to critiques of the way the criminal justice system perpetuated a politics of fear.

32 J.W. Mohr and R.E. Turner, 'Sexual Deviations Part 1 – Introduction,' *Applied Therapeutics* 9, no. 1 (January 1967): 78–81.

33 Mohr, interview by the author, 1998.

34 J.W. Mohr and R.E. Turner, 'Sexual Deviations Part 3 – Exhibitionism,' *Applied Therapeutics* 9, no. 3 (March 1967): 263–5.

35 Marc Stein, *City of Sisterly and Brotherly Loves: Lesbian and Gay Philadelphia, 1945–1972* (Chicago: University of Chicago Press, 2000), 122–7.

36 See 'Panel Discussion,' *The Ladder* 3, no. 6 (March 1959): 7–12.

37 For a detailed examination of Hooker's work, see Henry Minton, *Departing from Deviance: A History of Homosexual Rights and Emancipatory Science in America* (Chicago: University of Chicago Press, 2002), chapter 8.

38 Gary Kinsman, *The Regulation of Desire: Homo and Hetero Sexualities,* 2nd ed. (Montreal: Black Rose Books, 1996), 240. Many leading homophile groups, including the Daughters of Bilitis and the Mattachine Society, regarded treatment experts as sympathetic to homosexuals, and as a useful community resource.

39 See especially Daniel Paitich, 'Attitude toward Parents in Male Homosexuals and Exhibitionists' (PhD diss., University of Toronto, 1964).

40 J.W. Mohr and R.E. Turner, 'Sexual Deviations Part 2 – Homosexuality,' *Applied Therapeutics* 9, no. 2 (March 1967): 167.

41 J.W. Mohr and R.E. Turner, 'Sexual Deviations Part 4 – Pedophilia,' *Applied Therapeutics* 9, no. 4 (April 1967): 363.

42 Turner and Mohr, *Exhibitionism and Pedophilia,* 120–1.

43 Ibid., 124–6.

44 *Toronto Star*, 4 August 1965, 24.

45 Ibid.

46 A 1975 research study on incest cases at the Forensic Clinic also implicated wives and daughters in their own victimization. See J.D. Atcheson et al., *Incest* (Toronto: The Institute, 1975).

47 AO, RG 10-22-0-153, 'A Study of Forensic Cases 1954,' Department of Psychiatry, University of Toronto, Gordon Watson, MA, STB, John Rich, MD, PhD, DPM, K.G. Gray, 10.

48 Terry Copp and Bill McAndrew, *Battle Exhaustion: Soldiers and Psychiatrists in the Canadian Army, 1939–1945* (Montreal and Kingston: McGill-Queen's University Press, 1990), 23.

49 Michael D. Tuchtie, 'A Symposium on the Sex Offender: Forensic Inpatient Service,' *Criminal Law Quarterly* 3, no. 4 (February 1961): 451. See also J.L. Paras, 'Sodium Amytal Narcosis in the Psychotherapy of a Sex Offender,' *Diseases of the Nervous System* 15, no. 6 (June 1954): 180–3.

50 *Transcripts*, 122.

51 It was also used in prison treatment programs at the Ontario Reformatory at Guelph and New Jersey's Menlo Park Diagnostic Center for sex offenders. See Albert Ellis, 'A Study of 300 Sex Offenders,' *International Journal of Sexology* 4, no. 3 (February 1951): 127–35.

52 J.R. Ball and Jean J. Armstrong, 'The Use of L.S.D. 25 (D-Lysergic Acid Diethylamide) in the Treatment of the Sexual Perversions,' *Canadian Psychiatric Association Journal* 6, no. 4 (August 1961): 231–5.

53 Jonathan Metzl, '"Mother's Little Helper": The Crisis of Psychoanalysis and the Miltown Resolution,' *Gender and History* 15, no. 2 (August 2003): 240–67.

54 Joseph Wolpe, *Psychotherapy by Reciprocal Inhibition* (Stanford, CA: Stanford University Press, 1958).

55 Toronto Psychiatric Hospital Outpatient Forensic Clinic, *Annual Report* (Toronto, 1959), 12.

56 Ibid., 21. Wolpe's approach was well received in the United States as well. Marc Stein notes that he was hired at Temple University in 1965 and awarded the American Psychological Association's Distinguished Scientific Award for the Applications of Psychology in 1979. Stein, *City of Sisterly and Brotherly Loves*, 122.

57 I.K. Bond and H.C. Hutchison, 'Application of Reciprocal Inhibition Therapy to Exhibitionism,' *Canadian Medical Association Journal* 83 (1960): 23–5; reprinted in H.J. Eysenck, ed. *Experiments in Behavior Therapy* (New York: Pergamon Press, 1964), 80–6. The failure of the treatment is described in Douglas A. Quirk, 'A Follow-Up on the Bond Hutchison Case of Systematic Desensitization with an Exhibitionist,' *Behavior Therapy* 5 (1974): 428–31.

58 Toronto Psychiatric Hospital Outpatient Forensic Clinic, *Annual Report* (Toronto, 1960), 12.

59 Hans Mohr, 'A la Recherche,' in *Breaking the Chains: Bruno M. Cormier and the McGill University Clinic in Forensic Psychiatry*, ed. Renée Fugère and Ingrid Thompson-Cooper (Westmount, QC: R. Davies Multimedia Publishing, 1998), 146.

60 For a recent discussion assessing the use of LSD and ECT in a prison setting in this period, see Norbert Gilmore and Margaret A. Somerville, *A Review of the Use of LSD and ECT at the Prison for Women in the Early 1960s* (Ottawa: Correctional Service of Canada, 1998).

61 There are many studies in this field. The most pertinent to Ontario and Canada is R. Karl Hanson, Richard A. Steffy, and Rene Gauthier, 'Long-Term Recidivism of Child Molesters,' *Journal of Consulting and Clinical Psychology* 61 (1993): 646–52. See also L.S. Grossman, B. Martis, and C.G. Fichtner, 'Are Sex Offenders Treatable? A Research Overview,' *Psychiatric Services* 50, no. 3 (March 1999): 349–61.

62 Of all the clinics and treatment facilities, it seems that in Canada only the TPH Forensic Out-Patient Clinic came anywhere close to achieving the dream of a combined research and treatment institute, likely because it was part of the provincial hospital system and not the Department of Reform Institutions. This meant that the treatment staff were neither compelled nor cajoled into working in the interests of the prison, and that adequate staffing numbers permitted them to pursue research and publishing.

63 The majority of the volunteer patients were men seeking treatment for homosexuality. See Forensic Clinic *Annual Reports*. On counselling Catholic priests, see Mohr, interview by the author, 1999.

5 Sex Deviant Treatment in Ontario Prisons

1 Archives of Ontario (hereafter AO), RG 20-16-2-0-96.3, General Psychologists, file 1954-55, 'Research and Treatment Department of Reform Institutions Policy and Organization.'

2 AO, RG 20-16-0-189.3, Conferences, 1959–60, Justin Ciale, 'Problems in Establishing a Therapeutic Relationship in a Prison Community,' 1.

3 Art Gordon and Frank J. Porporino, 'Managing the Treatment of Sex Offenders: A Canadian Perspective' (no. B-05, Research and Statistics Branch Correctional Service of Canada, May 1990), http://www.csc-scc .gc.ca/text/rsrch/briefs/b5/b05e_e.shtml, Individual therapy with the prison psychiatrist was available to about half of the federal inmates serving an indefinite sentence under criminal sexual psychopath and dangerous sex-

ual offender legislation. Library and Archives Canada (hereafter LAC), RG 73, vol. 81, file 1-1-68, Policy, Psychological Services, 1960–63, 'Memorandum to the Minister, 16 October 62, from the Commissioner.'

4 LAC, RG 73, vol. 138, file 1-21-12, pt 2, 'Memo,' 23 December 1963. The reference to the BC program can be found in LAC, RG 73, vol. 81, file 1-1-68, Policy, Psychological Services, 1960–63, A.M. Trono, 'Reply,' 10 October 1962.

5 LAC, RG 73, acc. 1980–81/039, vol. 322, file 13-32, vol. 1, Memorandum re the 5th and 6th meetings of the Committee on Sexual and Dangerous Sexual offenders, 11 April 1973, p. 2.

6 AO, RG 20-16-2, file 113.3, Memo from A.R. Virgin to G.H. Basher, 6 May 1947.

7 Maeve Winifred McMahon, 'Changing Penal Trends: Imprisonment and Alternatives in Ontario, 1951–1984' (PhD diss., University of Toronto, 1988), 104–5.

8 For a full account, see chapter 2.

9 AO, RG 20-16-2, file 113.2, 'General Mr. Potts and Dr. van Nostrand,' Memo, van Nostrand to the Minister of the DRI, 20 February 1956.

10 AO, RG 20-16, file 96.3, Memo, G. Hedley Basher to Superintendent, Industrial Farm, Burwash, 9 September 1954; AO, RG 20-16-2, file 113.3, Memo, F.H. Potts to G. Hedley Basher, 6 May 1947. On Basher's surly personality, see AO, RG 20-148, Minister Advisory Council on the Treatment of the Offender, Subgroup 1.2, Council Minutes 1960, 10.

11 'MP Backs the Idea Conjugal Jail Visits Raised In Ottawa,' *Toronto Telegram*, 19 June 1965, 65. For a transcript of the debate in the House of Commons, see Canada, Parliament, House of Commons, *Debates*, 18 June 1965, 2618–26.

12 On van Nostrand's military career, see Terry Copp and Bill McAndrew, *Battle Exhaustion: Soldiers and Psychiatrists in the Canadian Army, 1939–1945* (Montreal and Kingston: McGill-Queen's University Press, 1990).

13 Eric Cummins, *The Rise and Fall of California's Radical Prison Movement* (Stanford, CA: Stanford University Press, 1994), 16.

14 Group therapy first began as a psychoanalytic treatment method in the interwar period, and became more widespread in army mental health hospitals during the Second World War. See Cummins, *The Rise and Fall of California's Radical Prison Movement*, 14.

15 Maxwell Jones, *Therapeutic Community: A New Treatment Method in Psychiatry* (New York: Basic Books, 1953).

16 Ibid.

17 AO, RG 10-107-0- 224, 'Sex Criminals, 1947–1954.'

18 Ibid. Doctors and psychiatrists across Canada shared this view. See chapter 3.

19 AO, RG 20-16-2-52.5, 'General – Inmates, 1951–52,' F.H. Potts, 'Treatment for Sex Offenders' Report submitted to Col. G. Hedley Basher, Deputy Minister, Department of Reform Institutions, 28 March 1952. Incidentally, Potts suggested the clinic be established in an existing storage building at the Industrial Farm in Burtch. Similarly, Bruno Cormier's internationally acclaimed forensic psychiatric clinic at McGill University began in 1955 as an office in an unused stable on McGill property, indicating that while mental health experts assumed enormous cultural authority in the postwar era, they did so with very limited institutional resources.

20 George W. Henry, 'The Homosexual Delinquent,' *Mental Hygiene* 25, no. 3 (July 1941): 420–42. See also Joseph F. Fishman, *Sex in Prison: Revealing Sex Conditions in American Prisons* (New York: National Library Press, 1934); and Samuel Kahn, *Homosexuality and Mentality* (Boston: Meador Publishing, 1937).

21 The DRI was also responsible for juvenile delinquents, and young offenders were throughout the twentieth century the primary object of concern over homosexual corruption, thus the reference to boys. AO, RG 20-16-2 52.5, 'General Inmates 1951–1952,' F.H. Potts, Treatment for Sex Offenders, 28 March 1952.

22 Chapter 6 explores prison sex culture in detail. Many postwar psychologists and sociologists believed these 'relationships' were consensual, but a more accurate depiction is found in the film *Fortune and Men's Eyes*. The original play was written by John Herbert, a gay man from Ontario who served time in the Guelph Reformatory in the late 1940s. *Fortune and Men's Eyes*, film, directed by Harvey Hart (Metro-Goldwyn-Mayer, 1971).

23 AO, RG 20-16-2-0-60.3, Guelph – Inmates 1952–53, Psychologists Report, 24 July 1952.

24 AO, RG 49-131, 'Proceedings of the Select Committee Appointed by the Legislative Assembly of the Province of Ontario, to Study and Report upon Problems of Delinquent Individuals and Custodial Questions, and the Place of Reform Institutions Therein' (hereafter Select Committee Proceedings), 2704–5.

25 Select Committee Proceedings, 6539.

26 Ontario, Legislative Assembly, Select Committee to Study and Report upon Problems of Delinquent Individuals and Custodial Questions, and the Place of Reform Institutions Therein, *Report* (Toronto: Queen's Printer, 1954), 309–19.

27 AO, RG 20-16-2-215.5, 'General Potts Alton,' Memo to the Superintendent, O.R. Guelph RE: New directive on Sex Offenders, 8 June 1960.

28 AO, RG 20-16-2 132.3, 'Guelph Neuro Psychiatric Clinic, 1957–1958,' Dr

Buckner, Report on the Neuro Psychiatric Centre, Guelph, 1 June 1955–31 May 1957. For a historical examination of these films, see Helen Harrison, 'In the Picture of Health: Portraits of Health, Disease and Citizenship in Canada's Public Health Information, 1920–1960,' (PhD diss., Queen's University, 2001).

29 AO, RG 10-163-0-316, 'American Psychiatric Association,' Bernard A. Cruvant, Milton Meltzer, Francis J. Tartaglino, 'An Institutional Program for Committed Sex Deviants' (paper delivered at the 106th Annual Meeting of the American Psychiatric Association, Detroit Michigan, 1–5 May 1950); LAC, RG 33/131, acc. 83-84/253, 'Report of the Organization Meeting, Ottawa, March 29 & 30, 1954,' Testimony of Dr Gendreau, 30 March 1954.

30 L.J. Meduna, ed., *Carbon Dioxide Therapy: A Neurophysiological Treatment of Nervous Disorders*, 2nd ed. (Toronto: Ryerson Press, 1958).

31 Roger Caron, *Go-Boy!* (Toronto: McGraw-Hill Ryerson, 1978), 61.

32 Ibid., 64–6.

33 See Robert P. Odenwald, 'Carbon Dioxide Treatment of Sex Deviations,' in *Carbon Dioxide Therapy: A Neurophysiological Treatment of Nervous Disorders*, 2nd ed., edited by L.J. Meduna (Toronto: Ryerson Press, 1958), 256–65.

34 AO, RG 20-16-2-132.3, Guelph Neuropsychiatric Clinic, 1957–1958, Memo, F.H. Potts to Deputy Minister, 16 May 1957.

35 Ibid.

36 AO, RG 20-42-3, Millbrook Inmate Files, #MA 487. This continues to remain a problem. See Charles Schwaebe, 'Learning to Pass: Sex Offenders' Strategies for Establishing a Viable Identity in the Prison General Population,' *International Journal of Offender Therapy and Comparative Criminology* 49, no. 6 (2005): 614–25.

37 Jones, *Therapeutic Community*, 126–8.

38 AO, RG 20-16-2-144.5, 'General "Potts" – "Van" "Wilson" 1957–58,' Confidential Memo, F.H. van Nostrand to J. Foote, 18 November 1957.

39 AO, RG 20-16-0-132.3, Memo, F.H. van Nostrand to G.H. Basher, 7 June 1957.

40 On the 'piling up of sex cases,' see AO, RG 20-16-2-0-198.2, 'Guelph NPC Clinic 1960–61,' 30 June Staff Conference Minutes. Once an inmate was in prison, it was very difficult to secure a transfer to a mental ward in a general hospital; mentally disturbed patients languished in both provincial and federal prisons, and few received anything approaching medical care. The NPC stood out as an exceptional facility for this reason. According to most psychiatrists servicing federal institutions, they had time only for the most disturbed inmates. See Bruno Cormier quoted in Robert Fulford, 'What We Can Learn from the Tragic History of a Sex Criminal,' *Maclean's*, 21 September 1963, 24, 46–7.

41 AO, RG 20-16-2-215.5, 'General – "Potts" – "Alton"' Memo from Potts to
    Guelph Superintendent and NPC Staff, New Directive on Sex Offenders, 8
    June 1960. What is particularly noteworthy about this revised directive is that
    it identified inmates not according to the crime for which they were found
    guilty, but by the 'deviant' sexual object choice (i.e., a person of the same
    sex).

42 Dr R.E. Turner, 'Sex Offender Course in Criminology and Corrections,' 22
    March 1961, author's personal files.

43 AO, RG 20-16-2-198.2, 'Guelph NPC 1960–1961,' Staff Conference Minutes, 6
    May 1960.

44 In a memo to NPC staff, Potts complained that one inmate who was serving
    time for having sexual relations with his sister should have at least received
    some instruction in sex education. AO, RG 20-16-2-198.2, 'Guelph NPC
    Clinic 1960–1961,' Memo, Potts to Deputy Minister, 7 September 1960.

45 Norwalk was renamed the Metropolitan State Hospital in 1953. Kinsey Insti-
    tute Archives (hereafter KIA), Robert E. Wyers, 'Sex Offenders Help Orga-
    nize Their Own Treatment' (unpublished paper, 1953), 4.

46 Lorraine M. Williams recounts her experience replying to a 'men only' posi-
    tion at the TPH Outpatient Forensic Clinic in 'Setting Up Social Work at the
    Forensic Clinic,' *TPH: History and Memories of the Toronto Psychiatric Hospital,
    1925–1966*, ed. Edward Shorter (Toronto: Wall and Emerson, 1996), 253–8.

47 Bruno M. Cormier, *The Watcher and the Watched* (Montreal: Tundra Books,
    1975), 139–71.

48 Significant contributions were made by women in the pre–Second World
    War era. See Jennifer Terry's *An American Obsession: Science, Medicine and
    Homosexuality in Modern Society* (Chicago: University of Chicago Press, 1999)
    for a discussion of anthropologists Margaret Mead and Ruth Benedict (163–
    8), psychologists Catherine Cox Miles (163–77) and Lura Beam (143–54), as
    well as the contribution made by medical practitioner Katherine Bement
    Davis (126–35). Evelyn Hooker, who did not enter the field until the late
    1950s, had an enormous impact on studies of homosexuality. Hers were the
    only substantive published contributions made by a woman in the two and a
    half decades following the Second World War. Based on examinations of
    homosexuals *not* culled from the patient lists of treatment experts, Hooker
    concluded that social struggle rather than psychotherapy was the 'appropri-
    ate healing tool.' See Ronald Bayer, *Homosexuality and American Psychiatry:
    The Politics of Diagnosis* (New York: Basic Books, 1981), 49–53.

49 KIA, SO1, folder 2, 'Prison Staff Interviews.'

50 Ibid.

51 The idea that prisons should be provided with female sexual contacts was in

fact very popular in the 1950s, and had Canadian advocates as well. See chapter 6.

52 'Dancing, Beauty Aid Held Mental Help,' *Toronto Daily Star*, 17 June 1939.

53 KIA, Bessant, 'Therapy Program, part II,' (unpublished paper, 1955).

54 KIA, SO1, folder 2, 'Prison Staff Interviews.'

55 Ibid.

56 Cormier, *The Watcher and the Watched*, 125–38.

57 Ibid., 170.

58 AO, RG 20-16-2-114.6, 'Annual Reports for 1955–56,' Millbrook Annual Report, 14 May 1958.

59 AO, RG 20-16, file 60.3, Special Investigation File, Riot of 5 July 1952, 1952–1953.

60 AO, RG 20-16-2-146.2, 'Requests for Information,' Sentencing, Transferring, Sorting and Subsequent Procedures, 5.

61 AO, RG 20-16-2-154.16, 'Millbrook – Miscellaneous, 1957–1958,' Maximum Security, Millbrook, Ontario, Canada; AO, RG 20-16-2-200.6, 'Millbrook – Miscellaneous, 1960–61,' Inmate Rules and Regulations, 2.

62 AO, RG 20-43-3, Millbrook Inmate Case Files #SC 299 n.d. [1959?]. Mail was subject to censorship. This letter likely remained in the writer's file because the contents cast the institution in a negative light, and thus was never sent to its intended recipient.

63 AO, RG 20-16-2 155.3, Letter, 'Millbrook Inmates Removal Warrants,' F.E. Webb to W.A. Cardwell, 17 November 1958.

64 A 'special diet' consisted of a single meatloaf cut into three pieces and served with bread for breakfast, lunch, and dinner. AO, RG 20-16-2-168.3, 'General – Rules and Regulations 1958 to 1959,' Ontario Official Rules and Regulations for the Guidance of Employees of Provincial Correctional Institutions for Male Persons.

65 AO, RG 20-16-2-155.3, 'Millbrook Inmates 1960–61,' Progressive Stage System.

66 AO, RG 20-148, Correctional Services, file 11.5, 'Sexual Psychopaths, Observations by Judge Helen Kinnear,' Observations by Her Honour Judge Helen Kinnear Concerning the Work of the Royal Commission on the Criminal Law Relating to Criminal Sexual Psychopaths, 8.

67 AO, RG 20-16, file 215.5, General Potts-Alton, W.T. McGrath, 'Planning Canada's Correctional System' (address to the Annual Meeting of the John Howard Society of Peterborough, 12 April 1960), 3.

68 AO, RG 20-16-2-0-134.3, 'Millbrook – Inmates, 1957–58,' Minutes of Meeting held 18 February 1957.

69 AO, RG 20-16-0-132.3, Memo, van Nostrand to the Deputy Minister, 7 June

1957. In 1961 the department went even further, and limited Group II transfers to *only* homosexual men.

70 AO, RG 20-16-2 155.3, 'Millbrook Inmates Removal Warrants.'

71 AO, RG 20-16-2-155.3, 'Millbrook Inmates Removal Warrants,' Letter, Paterson to Basher, 22 January 1959.

72 AO, RG 20-16-2-0-154.16, 'Millbrook – Miscellaneous, Visitors, Chaplains, Religious Items, 1957–58,' Maximum Security Reformatory, Millbrook, Ontario, Canada.

73 AO, RG 20-16-2-167.5, 'General 29 1958-1959 Conferences,' F.H. Potts to W.T. McGrath, 13 May 1958.

74 AO, RG 20-43-3, Millbrook Inmate Case Files, KD, #269.

75 AO, RG 20-43-3, Millbrook Inmate Case Files, NTH, #223.

76 AO, RG 20-42-3, Millbrook Inmate Case Files, KBL, #2480. In a separate case, a Toronto-born inmate of Italian descent was reported by the presiding physician to be 'resentful to the guards because they want to have his haircut. He takes great pride in letting his hair grow long and looking after the waves in his hair. There is no tendency toward homosexuality here.' AO, RG 20-16-2-0-60.4, Guelph – Inmates 1952–53.

77 AO, RG 20-16-2-154.16, 'Millbrook – Miscellaneous, Visitors, Chaplains, Religious Items, 1957–58,' Maximum Security Reformatory, Millbrook, Ontario, Canada.

78 AO, RG 20-16-2-258.1, Memo, F.H. Potts to G. Hedley Basher, 8 May 1962.

79 AO, RG 20-16-2-287.3, Memo, B.A. Kelly to J. Marsland, 30 January 1964.

80 AO, RG 20-16-2-155.3, 'Millbrook Inmates Removal Warrants,' Memo, Atcheson to Basher, 29 April 1958.

81 Popular journalist Pierre Burton wrote an article exposing the use of the strap in Ontario reformatories, prompting many citizens of that province to write letters to the minister of reform institutions protesting its use. For the article, see *Toronto Star*, 4 December 1958, 21. For the letters of protest, see AO, RG 20-16-2-0-152.17, 'Guelph – Miscellaneous – Visitors – Chaplains – Religious Items 58–59.'

82 AO, RG 20-16-2-186.4, 'Superintendent's Conference, 1959–1960,' Transcript, 2 July 1959. See Pott's response, AO, RG 20-16-2-176.11, Memo, Potts to Basher, 21 September 1959.

83 AO, RG 49, press clippings, MS 755, reel 145, 'Health, Sex Deviates,' *Peterborough Examiner*, 13 July 1965. Colonel Paterson's enthusiastic support for transforming the prison into a therapeutic community is documented in his 1958 Annual Report, AO, RG 20-16-2 168.4, Annual Reports, 1958–59, 1.

84 AO, RG 20-16-2-258.1, 'Millbrook Inmates, 1962–63,' Minutes of the Monthly Treatment Meeting, 1 May 1962.

85 AO, RG 20-16-2-298.4, 'Staff: General Correspondence, 1963–64,' R.R. Ross to F.H. Potts, 28 August 1963.

86 Dr Richard Steffy, telephone interview by the author, 2 March 2001. See also comments by MPP George Ben, reported in the *Peterborough Examiner*. AO, RG 49, Press Clippings, MS 755, Reel 145, 'Health, Sex Deviates,' *Peterborough Examiner*, 8 October 1967.

87 Millbrook still stands today. The inmates who set the fire were sentenced to an additional two years incarceration, but they got two of their wishes: to expose the brutality at Millbrook, and to be transferred to Kingston Penitentiary – Canada's oldest penitentiary – where they believed they would have a better quality of life. See AO, RG 49, press clippings, MS 755, reel 145, 'Health, Sex Deviates,' 'No Treatment Given - Men are Just Broken,' *Peterborough Examiner*, 12 July 1965; and 'Hearts of Prison Staff Being Broken,' 13 July 1965. For 'Alcatraz of Ontario,' see 'Millbrook Reformatory … or Deformatory? A Dormant Volcano,' *Toronto Telegram*, 13 August 1965.

88 'All but Two Resign from Clinic,' *Globe and Mail*, 2 February 1961, 5.

89 'Punishment vs. Treatment in Prison,' *Globe and Mail*, 4 January 1963, 7.

90 Reverend S.G. West, an expert in corrections chaplaincy, argued that the Ontario public was a victim of a 'giant "snow job"' when it came to provincial prison reform. See the 'Foreword,' in W.E. Mann, *Society Behind Bars: A Sociological Scrutiny of Guelph Reformatory* (Toronto: Social Science Publishers, 1967), ix.

91 AO, RG 20-16-2-0-240.7, 'Misc Speeches and Press Releases, 1961–62,' Speech by the Minister to the Canadian Club, Sioux Ste Marie, 5 October 1961. On Potts's 1947 hiring, see AO, RG 20-16-2-0-276.2, 'Requests for Information, 1962–63,' Graham to Dr Lewison, 3 April 1963.

92 Guy Richmond, *Prison Doctor: One Man's Story That Must Be Told in Canada Today* (Surrey, BC: Nunaga Publishing, 1975).

93 Anthony Marcus, *Nothing Is My Number: An Exploratory Study with a Group of Dangerous Sexual Offenders in Canada* (Toronto: General Publishing, 1971), 58–9.

94 Canada, Canadian Committee on Corrections, *Toward Unity: Criminal Justice and Corrections* (Ottawa: Queen's Printer, 1969).

95 In 1964 the Sexual Offender Group (a misnomer, given that seven of the eighty-three in this group were not convicted of sexual offences) was organized into four groups. Of the total group population, 20 per cent were assigned to the pedophile group; 15 per cent to the character disorder group; 25 per cent to the homosexual group (it is not known how many of these were effeminate homosexuals who were traditionally segregated from the main population, and how many were 'wolves,' or sexual predators); and

40 per cent to the neurotic psychopathic group. It is not clear if all homosexuals were in the homosexual group, or if some were categorized as neurotic psychopathic or character disorders. AO, RG 20-148, 11.3, Sexual Offender Group, Millbrook, 31 January 1964.

96 Hans Jurgen Eysenck is considered the 'founding father' of the behaviour therapy movement. See his *Behaviour Therapy and the Neuroses: Readings in Modern Methods of Treatment Derived from Learning Theory* (New York: Pergamon Press, 1960). On Steffy's pedophile program, see Richard A. Steffy and Rene Gauthier, 'Report of the Alex G. Brown (AGB) Memorial Clinic Pedophile Treatment Program, 1965-1973' (unpublished manuscript, University of Waterloo, Waterloo, Ont., June 1976).

97 Steffy, telephone interview by the author, 2001.

98 Ibid.

99 Allen M. Hornblum, 'They Were Cheap and Available: Prisoners as Research Subjects in Twentieth Century America,' *British Medical Journal* 315 (29 November 1997): 1437–41.

100 *A Clockwork Orange*, film, produced and directed by Stanley Kubrick (1971).

101 A study of the records of provincial hospitals has yet to be done, but Toronto artist Jack Pollock described his experiences undergoing aversion therapy to treat his homosexuality while a patient in the provincial mental health care system. Jack Pollock, presentation at the Research-in-Progress Conference, Queen Street Mental Health Centre, Toronto, 1993.

102 On aversion therapy in Philadelphia, see Marc Stein, *City of Sisterly and Brotherly Loves: Lesbian and Gay Philadelphia, 1945–1972* (Chicago: University of Chicago Press, 2000), 122.

103 Don Jackson, 'Dachau in America,' in *Gay Roots: Twenty Years of Gay Sunshine,* ed., Winston Leyland (San Francisco: Gay Sunshine Press, 1991), 264–6.

104 Steffy, telephone interview by the author, 2001.

105 Critiques specifically aimed at prison psychiatry include a June 1974 feature issue of *Psychiatric Opinion* 11, no. 3 (June 1974); and Jessica Mitford, *Kind and Usual Punishment: The Prison Business* (New York: Alfred A. Knopf, 1973).

106 Phyllis J. Lundy and Peter R. Breggin, 'Psychiatric Oppression of Prisoners,' *Psychiatric Opinion* 11, no. 3 (June 1974): 35. Patuxent was one of the clinical programs Ontario doctors maintained ties with. See Toronto Psychiatric Hospital Outpatient Forensic Clinic, *Annual Report* (Toronto: University of Toronto, Department of Psychiatry, 1962), 21.

107 Steffy, telephone interview by the author, 2001. Interestingly, after leaving Mimico, Steffy used aversion therapy to help people quit smoking. The program was not successful.

108 Records of the actual number of people convicted under these laws are not
     easy to find. The number 109 comes from the National Parole Board files
     and covers the period from 1948 when criminal sexual psychopath legisla-
     tion was first introduced to 1977 when the dangerous sex offender designa-
     tion was abandoned in favour of 'dangerous offender' (the law remains
     unchanged since then). See Cyril Greenland, 'Dangerous Sexual Offender
     Legislation in Canada, 1948–1977: An Experiment that Failed,' *Canadian
     Journal of Criminology* 26, no. 1 (January 1984): 2–3. A 1977 report by the
     Inmate Programs Branch of the Solicitor General's Office indicated that in
     August 1977 there were 68 dangerous sexual offenders in the penitentiary
     system. If these two numbers are correct, then by 1977, 39 of the 109 (less
     than 40 per cent) had been paroled. LAC, RG 73, Records of the Solicitor
     General, acc. 1980-81/039, vol. 322, file 13-32, 'Inmate Programs Branch
     Paper on the Treatment of Sexual Offenders 3 October 1977,' 26.
109 *Regina v. Tilley* (1952), [1953] 104 C.C.C. 315 (Ont. Div. Ct.). 'Sex Attack
     Nets Indefinite Term,' *Globe and Mail,* 13 November 1952, 12.
110 Greenland, 'Dangerous Sexual Offender Legislation in Canada,' 1–12.
111 The law continues to be used primarily for sex offenders. Bonta et al. found
     that between 1977 and 1985, 78 per cent of dangerous offenders were con-
     victed of a sexual offence. In 1992, 90 per cent of dangerous offenders had
     committed a sexual offence. See James Bonta, Andrew Harris, Ivan Zinger,
     and Debbie Carriere, 'The Crown Files Research Project: A Study of Dan-
     gerous Offenders' (report no. 1996-01, cat. no. JS4-1/1996-1, Solicitor
     General of Canada), http://ww2.ps-sp.gc.ca/publications/corrections/
     199601_e.asp. On the practice of singling out sex offenders in prison, see
     chapter 6.
112 Jacqueline Faubert, 'The Emergence and Consequences of Risk Thinking
     in British Columbia Dangerous Offender Hearings, 1978–2000' (PhD diss.,
     Simon Fraser University, 2003), 217.
113 Ibid., 98.
114 Statistics Canada, 'Adult Correctional Services, 2004/2005,' *The Daily,*
     11 October 2006, http://www.statcan.ca/Daily/English/061011/
     d061011a.htm.

6 Compulsory Heterosexuality and the Limits of Forensic Sexology

1 Adrienne Rich, 'Compulsory Heterosexuality and Lesbian Existence,' *Signs:
   Journal of Women in Culture and Society* 5 (summer 1980): 631–60. Reprinted
   in *Journal of Women's History* 15, no. 3 (autumn 2003): 11–48, references are
   to this edition.

2 Rich, 'Compulsory Heterosexuality,' 20.

3 Ibid., 22.

4 Ibid., 37.

5 Race and ethnicity are also significant variables, particularly in the United States. However, a review of the Ontario provincial reformatory admission log books for this period shows that the inmate population was remarkably homogenous. Most inmates were Canadian-born Anglo-Protestants. A much more recent survey of Canada's federal prison population showed that 84.3 per cent were 'Caucasian,' 3.6 per cent 'North American Indian,' 1.0 per cent 'Asiatic,' 7.3 per cent 'Black,' and 3.1 per cent 'other.' Correctional Services of Canada, Offender Population Profile Report (Ottawa: Correctional Service of Canada, 31 March 1991). See also Dennis Cooley, 'Social Control and Social Order in Male Federal Prisons' (PhD diss., University of Manitoba, 1995), 118, 145–8. It is reasonable to assume that finer lines were drawn between French, English, and immigrant inmates, but more research is needed before developing an understanding of this aspect of inmate culture. American sociologists have taken a much more active interest in the racialization of prison sex culture since at least the 1970s, and historians are now beginning to pay serious scholarly attention to these questions. See Estelle Freedman, 'The Prison Lesbian: Race, Class, and the Construction of the Aggressive Female Homosexual, 1915–1965,' *Feminist Studies* 22, no. 2 (summer 1996): 397–423; Sarah Potter, '"Undesirable Relations": Same-Sex Relationships and the Meaning of Sexual Desire at a Women's Reformatory During the Progressive Era,' *Feminist Studies* 30, no. 2 (2004): 394–415; Angela Y. Davis, 'Race, Gender, and Prison History: From the Convict Lease System to the Supermax Prison,' in *Prison Masculinities*, ed. Don Sabo, Terry A. Kupers, and Willie London, 35–45 (Philadelphia: Temple University Press, 2001); William F. Pinar, *The Gender of Racial Politics and Violence in America: Lynching, Prison Rape and the Crisis of Masculinity* (New York: Peter Lang, 2001).

6 United States, District Attorney (Philadelphia Eastern District), *Report on Sexual Assaults in the Philadelphia Prison System and in Sheriff Vans* (Philadelphia: Philadelphia's District Attorney's Office, 1968). The letters are housed at the Kinsey Institute for the Study of Sex, Gender and Reproduction Archives. In the interests of privacy, I am unable to identify the prisons where these letters were collected.

7 Joseph F. Fishman, *Sex in Prison: Revealing Sex Conditions in American Prisons* (National Library Press, 1934). See also Harry Elmer Barnes and Negley K. Teeters, *New Horizons in Criminology* (New York: Prentice-Hall, 1943), 623.

8 Fishman, *Sex in Prison*, 148.

9 George Chauncey, *Gay New York: Gender, Urban Culture and the Making of the Gay Male World, 1890–1940* (New York: Basic Books, 1994), 93.

10 Fishman wrote his book to correct what he felt was inaccurate coverage. According to Fishman, the segregated homosexual population did not have the kind of freedom the news media suggested. Fishman, *Sex in Prison*; see also Chauncey, *Gay New York*, 92.

11 Fishman, *Sex in Prison*, 148–9.

12 Samuel Kahn, *Homosexuality and Mentality* (Boston: Meador Publishing, 1937).

13 See, for example, J.G. Wilson and M.J. Pescor, *Problems in Prison Psychiatry* (Caldwell, ID: Caxton Press, 1939); George W. Henry, 'The Homosexual Delinquent,' *Mental Hygiene* 25, no. 3 (July 1941): 420–42. On women's institutions, see Freedman, 'The Prison Lesbian,' 397–423.

14 At least one session at the 1945, 2nd Annual Superintendents' Conference, held in the United States, was devoted to the topic of sex in prison. In his report to the deputy minister, Guelph Superintendent Dr Heaslip wrote 'nearly all troubles discussed are common to us as Superintendents, whether one comes from South Carolina, Illinois or Canada.' AO, RG 20-16-2, Correspondence and Administration Files on Training Schools and Other Institutions – Microfilm Reel MS 3167, 'Minutes of the 2nd Annual Superintendents' Conference, 14–16 February 1945.'

15 Oswald C.J. Withrow, *Shackling the Transgressor: An Indictment of the Canadian Penal System* (Toronto: Thomas Nelson and Sons, 1933), 178.

16 Harvey Blackstock, *Bitter Humour: About Dope, Safe Cracking and Prisons* (Toronto: Burns and MacEachern, 1967), 109, 113.

17 According to the psychologists' report, homosexual charges constituted 18 per cent of the total charges laid. Archives of Ontario (hereafter AO), RG 20-16-2-0-90.2, 'Guelph – Inmates, 1954–55.'

18 AO, RG 20-155-0-3, Province of Ontario, Official Rules and Regulations for the Guidance of Officers and Employees of Reformatories and Industrial Farms for Male Prisoners, 1944.

19 AO, RG 20-16-2-0-89.13, 'Guelph Miscellaneous 1954–55,' 25 May 1954.

20 Roger Caron, *Go-Boy!* (Toronto: McGraw-Hill Ryerson, 1978), 23–24. See also the report of a Guelph inmate who committed suicide while in solitary confinement, AO, RG 20-16-2-0-90.2, 'Guelph – Inmates 1954–55,' 7 January 1955.

21 AO, RG 20-16-2-0-152.2, 'Guelph – Inspections (1) 1958-59,' E.H., Sworn Statement.

22 AO, RG 20-16-2, Correspondence and Administration Files on Training Schools and Other Institutions – Microfilm Reel MS 3167: 'Minutes of the 2nd Annual Superintendents' Conference, 14–16 February 1945.'

23 On the creation of the Kingston Prison for Women, see Kelly Hannah-Moffat, *Punishment in Disguise: Penal Governance and Federal Imprisonment of Women in Canada* (Toronto: University of Toronto Press, 2001), 80–91. On the movement as a whole, see Lucia Zedner, 'Wayward Sisters: The Prison for Women,' in *The Oxford History of the Prison: The Practice of Punishment in Western Society*, ed. Norval Morris and David J. Rothman (New York: Oxford University Press, 1995).

24 AO, RG 20-26-1-0-45.13, 'Guelph – Inmates 1951-52,' Neelands to Basher, 17 May 1951. For an early example of complaints about immorality in prison dorms, see Donald G. Wetherell, 'To Discipline and Train: Adult Rehabilitation Programs in Ontario Prisons, 1874–1900,' *Histoire sociale/Social History* 23, no. 12: 145–65.

25 See, for example, Blackstock, *Bitter Humour*, 102–3.

26 AO, RG 20-16-2-0-105.6, 'Guelph – Inmates 1955–56,' G.E. Jacobs to Chief Inspector, 26 May 1955.

27 Caron, *Go-Boy!*, 120. Problems in management and reform in prisons were approached in two ways: provide people-based programs or provide new structures. In the history of the prison, most problems were met with architectural, not program-based, solutions. See Eric Cummins, *The Rise and Fall of California's Radical Prison Movement* (Stanford, CA: Stanford University Press, 1994), 6.

28 Chauncey, *Gay New York*, 54.

29 AO, RG 20-42-3, Millbrook Case Files, KHD # 300.

30 These practices occurred in prisons across Canada and the United States. See Millbrook inmate files and William H. Haines and John J. McLaughlin, 'Treatment of the Homosexual in Prison,' *Diseases of the Nervous System* 3, no. 3 (March 1952): 85–87; Fishman, *Sex in Prison*, 60.

31 AO, RG 20-42-3, Millbrook Inmate Case Files, KBL, #2480.

32 Chauncey, *Gay New York*, 57

33 Kahn, *Homosexuality and Mentality*, 14.

34 What special rights Kahn had in mind, he does not say. Kahn, *Homosexuality and Mentality*, 160.

35 Edwin Johnson, 'The Homosexual in Prison,' *Social Theory and Practice* 1, no. 4 (fall 1971): 87.

36 Fishman, *Sex in Prison*, 22.

37 At the Ontario Reformatory in Guelph, 24 of the institution's 373 individual cells were set aside for homosexuals. AO, RG 20-16-105.4, 'Guelph – Inspections, 1955–56,' Accommodation. 'Gunzil' is more properly spelled as 'gunsel.' At the beginning of the twentieth century, prisoners and hoboes called young, inexperienced boys, especially homosexuals, gunsels. Today, how-

ever, it means merely second-rate criminal. See Robert Hendrickson, *Facts on File Encyclopedia of Word and Phrase Origins* (New York: Facts on File, 1987); 'Lover's Lane' is cited from Caron, *Go-Boy!*, 21, 22; 'Queen's Row' is cited from Johnson, 'The Homosexual in Prison,' 83.

38 For historical accounts of how the field of sexology was built on descriptions of the existing homosexual culture(s) including interviews and correspondence with homosexual men and women see Harry Oosterhuis, 'Richard von Krafft-Ebing's "Step-Children Of Nature": Psychiatry and the Making of Homosexual Identity,' in *Science and Homosexualities*, ed. Vernon A. Rosario (New York: Routledege, 1997), 89–107 and Terry, *An American Obsession*, especially chapter 7.

39 On declaring one's homosexuality as a survival strategy, see Allen Young, 'Sissy in Prison: An Interview with Ron Vernon,' *Out of the Closets: Voices of Gay Liberation*, ed. Karla Jay and Allen Young (1972; repr., New York: New York University Press, 1992).

40 AO, RG 20-16-2-0-90.2, 'Guelph – Inmates, 1954–55,' G.E. Jacobs to Chief Inspector, 26 May 1955.

41 AO, RG 20-16-2-0-155.3, 'Millbrook,' F.E. Webb to W.A. Cardwell, 17 November 1958.

42 *Toronto Telegram*, 28 September 1965.

43 AO, RG 49, press clippings, MS 755, reel 145, 'Health, Sex Deviates,' *Peterborough Examiner*, 12 July 1965.

44 Benjamin Karpman, 'Sex Life in Prison,' *Journal of Criminal Law and Criminology* 38, no. 5 (January–February 1948): 482. See also the report of G.E. Jacobs, inspector, concerning homosexual activity at Guelph: 'the measures found necessary by the Superintendent in routine treatment and punishment of sex deviates, were often in conflict with those procedures favoured by the Psychologists.' AO, RG 20-16-2-0-105.6, 'Guelph – Inmates 1955–56,' 26 May 1955.

45 Fishman, *Sex in Prison*, 133–9.

46 Karpman, 'Sex Life in Prison,' 477–8. Fishman pointed out that it was the usual practice in the Navy to discourage abnormal sex by 'keep[ing] the men occupied mentally and physically almost to the point of exhaustion.' Fishman, *Sex in Prison*, 20. See also Charles Ford, who gave similar advice to wardens of women. Charles Ford, 'Homosexual Practices of Institutionalized Females,' *Journal of Abnormal Psychology* 23 (1929): 448.

47 AO, RG 49-131, 'Proceedings of the Select Committee Appointed by the Legislative Assembly of the Province of Ontario, to Study and Report upon Problems of Delinquent Individuals and Custodial Questions, and the Place of Reform Institutions Therein' (hereafter Select Committee Proceedings), 28: 6546–7.

48 Deidre Foucauld, 'Prison Labour: Punishment or Reform: The Canadian Penitentiary System 1867–1960' (MA thesis, University of Ottawa, 1982). See also John Kidman, *The Canadian Prison: The Story of a Tragedy* (Toronto: Ryerson Press, 1947), 66–70.

49 On the role of mental health experts screening inductees in the United States, see Allan Berube's *Coming Out Under Fire: The History of Gay Men and Women in World War Two* (New York: Free Press, 1990). On the Canadian military experience, see Gary Kinsman, *The Regulation of Desire: Homo and Hetero Sexualities,* 2nd ed. (Montreal: Black Rose Books, 1996).

50 Select Committee Proceedings, 6510, 6512. When the example of the Women's Army Corps was raised, the chairman instructed the recording secretary to temporarily refrain from transcribing the rest of the discussion, presumably to avoid besmirching the reputation of that arm of the military.

51 William H. Haines and John J. McLaughlin, 'Treatment of the Homosexual in Prison,' *Diseases of the Nervous System* 13, no. 3 (March 1952): 2.

52 Robert Linder, 'Sex in Prison,' *Complex* 6 (1951): 5–20.

53 See also Bernard Glueck Jr, 'An Evaluation of the Homosexual Offender,' *Minnesota Law Review* 41, no. 2 (1957): 194.

54 This 'condition,' though never delimited from the broader diagnosis of an acute panic episode, has recently re-emerged as Homosexual Advance Defense (HAD). Lawyers have argued with varying success that their clients' violent attacks on gay men were caused by their repressed homosexual feelings. See also Eve Sedgewick on homosexual panic, *Epistemology of the Closet* (Berkeley and Los Angeles: University of California Press, 1990), 187–92.

55 Terry Copp and Bill McAndrew, *Battle Exhaustion: Soldiers and Psychiatrists in the Canadian Army, 1939–1945* (Montreal and Kingston: McGill-Queen's University Press, 1990), 6.

56 Bernard C. Glueck Jr and Russell H. Dinerstein, 'Sub-coma Insulin Therapy in the Treatment of Homosexual Panic States,' *Journal of Social Therapy* 1 (1955): 182–6. Linder, 'Sex in Prison,' 5–20.

57 AO, RG 20-16-2-0-134.3, 'Millbrook – Inmates, 1957–58,' Draft Copy of the Millbrook Policy, 2.

58 Wilson and Pescor, *Problems in Prison Psychiatry,* 208–9; cited in Henry, 'The Homosexual Delinquent,' 432.

59 An excellent source for up-to-date information on legal challenges and inquiries into sexual assault in American prisons is the human rights organization Stop Prisoner Rape (http://www.spr.org), founded in 1980 by Russell Dan Smith, himself a prison rape survivor. No similar organization exists in Canada.

60 AO, RG 20-16-2-0-134.3, 'Millbrook – Inmates, 1957–58,' Minutes of Meeting held 18 February 1957.

61 Other repressive measures psychologists and psychiatrists 'approved' as having no long-term harmful effects were the use of the strap in corporal punishment and the use of solitary confinement and windowless cells. AO, RG 20-16-2-0-90.2, 'Guelph – Inmates, 1954–55.' See also George D. Scott, *Inmate: The Casebook Revelations of a Canadian Penitentiary Psychiatrist* (Montreal: Optimum Publishing International, 1982).

62 AO, RG 20-8, Incidences of Homosexuality, 1973–1974, Memo from H. Garraway to H.S. Cooper, 12 November 1973.

63 AO, RG 20-42-3, Millbrook Inmate Case Files, KHD, #300, Probation Officer's Report, 12 November 1958.

64 AO, RG 20-148, Correctional Services File 11.3, Sexual Offender Group, Millbrook, 31 January 1964, Kelly to J. Marsland, 30 January 1964.

65 Kinsey Institute Archives (hereafter KIA), Anonymous, 'Prison Diaries,' 1951, unaccessioned.

66 KIA, Anon., 'Homosexuality in Prison' (1964), 6. This is an essay an inmate wrote as a contribution toward a collection of writing by inmates. The warden refused to allow him to submit it, another indication of prison administrators' attempts to keep a lid on the sex problem.

67 Select Committee Proceedings, 6497–9.

68 AO, RG 20-16-2-0-60.3, 'Guelph – Inmates 1952–53,' Psychologists Report, 24 July 1952.

69 Ibid., Minutes of Meeting held 18 February 1957.

70 AO, RG 20-16-2-0-200.10, 'Millbrook – Inmates – Removal Warrants, 1960–61,' 9 February 1961.

71 AO, RG 20-16-2-0-200.10, 'Millbrook – Inmates – Removal Warrants, 1960–61.'

72 Wardell Pomeroy, 'Sex in Prison' (KIA, audiotape of a presentation at a meeting of the Federal Warden's Institute, University of Colorado, 26 June 1962).

73 Samuel Kahn's 1920s study of homosexuals revealed that many of them feared being 'bugged,' by which they meant having their mind or brain somehow altered or disturbed, when they were being examined for their homosexuality. Kahn, *Homosexuality and Mentality*, 24. Other reports of inmates being threatened with electroconvulsive therapy and other psychiatric treatments can be found in Roger Caron's *Go-Boy!* and in KIA, 'Charles,' interview by Bruce Jackson, tape recording, 1962. For some patients, however, a transfer to a psychiatric ward was a welcome respite.

74 AO, RG 20-16-2-0-90.2, 'Guelph – Inmates 1954–55'; 105.6, 'Guelph – Inmates 1955–56.'

75 LAC, RG 73, acc. 1980-81/039, vol. 89, file 8-206, 'Joint House Senate Committee on Penitentiaries.'

76 Edwin Johnson, 'The Homosexual in Prison,' 87.

77 KIA, SO-1, folder 2, 'Prison Staff Interviews.'

78 AO, RG 20-42-3, Millbrook Case Files MQN, #692.

79 Comment from unidentified audience member. Pomeroy, 'Sex in Prison.'

80 Mary Louise Adams, *The Trouble with Normal: Postwar Youth and the Making of Heterosexuality* (Toronto: University of Toronto Press, 1997).

81 Wake's interest in questions about gender and sexuality was established at least by the mid-1950s when he undertook research for the Royal Commission on the Criminal Law Relating to Criminal Sexual Psychopaths. He went on to create Canada's infamous 'fruit machine.' See Gary Kinsman and Patrizia Gentile, '*In the Interests of the State*': *The Anti-gay, Anti-lesbian National Security Campaign in Canada: A Preliminary Research Report* (Sudbury, ON: Laurentian University, 1998); Daniel J. Robinson and David Kimmel, 'The Queer Career of Homosexual Security Vetting in Cold-War Canada,' *Canadian Historical Review* 75, no. 3 (September 1994): 319–45.

82 F.R. Wake, 'Normal Aggression and Delinquency,' *Bulletin of the Maritime Psychological Association* 8 (1959): 52.

83 Ibid., 55.

84 Ibid., 57.

85 'Societal guilt, rather than looking for someone to blame, or some impersonal economic system to make responsible, can be turned to a stronger, more determined effort to reduce the number of errors involved in the teaching of aggression.' Ibid., 58.

86 Pomeroy, 'Sex in Prison.'

87 It is hard to know exactly how Kinsey would have felt about Pomeroy's advice to Terre Haute officials. In 1954 Kinsey strongly but privately opposed the army's new policy to control homosexuality, which, he argued, 'appear[s] to be inspired by moral and traditional considerations, rather than by a desire to maintain and improve the efficiency of the Armed Forces.' Yet he was also concerned about inmates' sex lives. In a letter to one prison administrator, he explained that sexual readjustment upon release from prison is an issue 'that we have not reached an understanding of in our own minds,' suggesting that his approach to understanding human sexuality did not blind him to the complexity of prison sex culture. KIA, Correspondence files, letter to Manfred Guttmacher, 1 December 1954; letter to Mr Teets, 26 September 1949.

88 Fishman, *Sex in Prison*, 174–5.

89 'MP Backs the Idea Conjugal Visits Raised in Ottawa,' *Toronto Telegram*, 19 June 1965, 65.

90 'Cleric Denies He Backs Prostitution,' *Toronto Telegram*, 19 June 1965, 21.

91 'Prisoners Get 72-hour Passes to Visit Wives,' *Toronto Telegram*, 2 September 1965, 14.

92 Canada, Canadian Committee on Corrections, *Toward Unity: Criminal Justice and Corrections* (Ottawa: Queen's Printer, 1969), 315.

93 Ironically, prisoners in Canadian penitentiaries currently enjoy the right to same-sex conjugal visits as a result of the human rights protections enshrined in the Canadian Constitution. However, they are not extended this privilege if their spouse is another inmate. *Globe and Mail*, 4 September 2000, A-6.

94 The Macdonald Institute for Domestic Science opened in 1903 on the campus of the Ontario Agricultural College in Guelph, Ontario. Established by Adelaide Hoodless, it provided training for domestic science and home economics teachers. 'Macdonald Institute for Domestic Science,' http://www.mala.bc.ca/homeroom/Content/PostSec/macinst.htm (accessed 25 June 2001).

95 Allan Grossman, 'Brief to the Select Committee on Youth,' *Toronto Telegram*, 21 October 1965, 9. Ontario was not alone in this venture. In the United States a number of federal prisons experimented with 'cocorrections' in the 1970s. See John Ortiz Smykla, *Cocorrections: A Case Study of a Coed Federal Prison* (Washington: University Press of America, 1978).

96 Joan W. Scott, 'Gender as a Category of Analysis,' in *Gender and the Politics of History*, rev. ed. (New York: Columbia University Press, 1999).

97 Caron, *Go-Boy!*, 21.

98 Ibid., 70.

99 AO, RG 20-8, 'Incidences of Homosexuality, 1973–74,' Report of 11 July 1973.

100 Scott, *Inmate*.

101 AO, RG 20-16-2-0- 227.3, Memo to Potts from Sanderson, 28 June 1961. See also Caron, *Go-Boy!*, 160; and Scott, *Inmate*, 111.

102 George Devereux and Malcolm M. Moos, 'The Social Structure of Prisons, and the Organic Tensions.' *Journal of Criminal Pathology* 5, no. 4 (October 1942): 317.

103 Caron, *Go-Boy!*, 107.

104 Alfred Kinsey received donations of a wide range of illicit (and contraband) material found in the possession of inmates. Love letters were among them. The Kinsey Institute Archives restricts me from revealing which U.S. institutions this material was confiscated from.

105 KIA, Diaries collection, 48-B Prison – SQ – Inmate letters, 11 October 1950.

106 KIA, Diaries collection, 80-TI n.d. [1960?].

107 See T. Dunbar Mooie, 'Migrancy and Male Sexuality on the South African Gold Mines,' *Journal of South African Studies* 14, no. 2 (1998): 228–56.

108 AO, RG 20-16-2-0-227.3, 'Guelph – Inmates,' Minutes of the Staff Conference held on 2 February 1962.'

109 Caron, *Go-Boy!*, 107.

110 Guy Richmond, *Prison Doctor: One Man's Story That Must Be Told in Canada Today* (Surrey, BC: Nunaga Publishing, 1975), 101–2. According to Edwin Johnson, 'as on the outside, the marriage demonstrated stability within the inmate society.' Johnson, 'The Homosexual in Prison', 86.

111 Devereux and Moos, 'The Social Structure of Prisons', 306–24.

112 Philip Jenkins, *Moral Panic: Changing Concepts of the Child Molester in Modern America* (New Haven, CT: Yale University Press, 1998), 15.

113 AO, RG 20-16-2-0-60.4, 'Guelph – Inmates 1952–53,' Psychologists report on the July riot, 24 July 1952; ibid., G.E. Jacobs to Chief Inspector, 26 May 1955.

114 Interestingly, unlike the outside world, where different types of 'deviant' behaviour were often blurred under the broader category of 'sexual deviancy,' distinctions inside prison were made between different groups. Though considered 'sex deviants' on the outside, effeminate homosexuals (fairies and queens) were desirable as sexual partners, not reviled as sexual deviants. Queens and fairies were also the source of entertainment. During a 1971 riot at Kingston Penitentiary, the queens entertained the rioters by celebrating a mock mass in Catholic vestments. See Fred Desroches, 'Patterns in Prison Riots,' *Canadian Journal of Criminology and Corrections* 16, no. 4 (1974): 336–7.

115 Following the recommendations of the Royal Commission on the Criminal Law Relating to Criminal Sexual Psychopaths, 'criminal sexual psychopath' was changed to 'dangerous sexual offender,' and was later changed again to 'dangerous offender,' a category which included, but was not exclusively aimed at, sexual offenders. See Cyril Greenland, 'Dangerous Sexual Offender Legislation in Canada, 1948–1977: An Experiment that Failed,' *Canadian Journal of Criminology* 26, no. 1 (January 1984): 1–12.

116 Anthony Marcus, *Nothing Is My Number: An Exploratory Study with a Group of Dangerous Sexual Offenders in Canada* (Toronto: General Publishing, 1971), 72.

117 Ibid., 20.

118 Ibid., 29.

119 See also 'The Homosexual and the Prison System,' *TWO* (July/August) n.d. [1966?]: 5–6. In describing his experience in prison, the anonymous author claimed the 'prison head-shrinker' and visiting 'specialists' are 'more than eager to interview [homosexuals] on tape ... and then use their "material"

for learned discussions in the classroom, or medical lounges. But interest in
you, or your woes ... *certainly not.*'

120   Marcus, *Nothing Is My Number,* 24.

121   Ibid., 68–69.

122   Ibid., 17.

123   Accounts of the riot are taken from Roger Caron, *Bingo!* (Toronto: Methuen, 1985); Fred Desroches, 'The April 1971 Kingston Penitentiary Riot,'
Canadian Journal of Criminology and Corrections 16, no. 4 (1974): 317–31; *Globe
and Mail* daily coverage; and journalist and Citizen Committee member
Ron Haggart's account, 'Ninety Hours of Rebellion,' *Weekend Magazine,* 22
no. 16 (17 April 1972).

124   Caron, *Bingo!,* 128.

125   *Globe and Mail,* 19 April 1971, 1, 3; Caron, *Bingo!,* 178–86; Desroches, 'The
April 1971 Kingston Penitentiary Riot,' 317–31. The subsequent inquiry into
the riot avoided discussing these events, since criminal charges were still
pending against those involved. See Canada, *Report of the Commission of
Inquiry into Certain Disturbances at Kingston Penitentiary during April 1971*
(Ottawa: Information Canada, 1973).

126   Desroches, 'The April 1971 Kingston Penitentiary Riot,' 328.

127   Caron, *Go-Boy!,* 231–2; see also Haggart, 'Ninety Hours of Rebellion.'

128   Caron, *Bingo!,* 128.

129   Desroches, 'The April 1971 Kingston Penitentiary Riot,' 336.

130   The classic film *Fortune and Men's Eyes* offers brilliant insight into exactly this
issue. It is based on a play by John Herbert, who was a fairy, and who served
time in Ontario's Guelph Reformatory in the late 1940s. *Fortune and Men's
Eyes,* directed by Harvey Hart (Metro-Goldwyn-Mayer, 1971).

131   Alan J. Davis, 'Sexual Assaults in the Philadelphia Prison System and Sheriff's Vans,' *Trans-action* (December 1968): 8–16. Davis was the main investigator. For the full report, see United States, District Attorney (Philadelphia
Eastern District), *Report on Sexual Assaults in the Philadelphia Prison System and
in Sheriff's Vans* (Philadelphia: Philadelphia's District Attorney's Office,
1968).

132   Davis, 'Sexual Assaults,' 13.

133   Ibid., 15–16.

134   Ibid., 17. The report also identified race as a significant factor in the organization of sexual violence. Davis reported that in the Philadelphia prison system, 56 per cent of sexual assaults involved African American aggressors and
white victims. For Davis, however, this was little surprise, given that 80 per
cent of the prison population was black. 'It is safer for a member of any race
to single out for attack a member of a vastly outnumbered minority race,' he

argued. 'It also seems to reflect the current racial tensions and hostilities in the community.' Later studies would come to the same conclusion.

135 See especially Anthony M. Scacco, *Rape in Prison* (Springfield, IL: C.C. Thomas, 1975); Wayne S. Wooden and Jay Parker, *Men behind Bars: Sexual Exploitation in Prison* (New York: Plenum Press, 1982); Carl Weiss and David James, *Terror in the Prisons: Homosexual Rape and Why Society Condones It* (Indianapolis: Bobbs-Merrill, 1974).

136 Susan Riley, 'Stockwell Day Isn't a Candidate, but Then No One Is,' *Ottawa Citizen*, 28 January 2000, A16.

137 Janice Irvine, *Disorders of Desire: Sexuality and Gender in Modern American Sexology*, rev. ed. (Philadelphia: Temple University Press, 2005), 331.

Conclusion

1 Peter Briken, Andreas Hill, and Wolfgang Berner, 'Abnormal Attraction,' *Scientific American Mind* (February/March 2007): 58–63.

2 Results are measured by rates of recidivism. For an article that discusses the shortcomings of this method of assessment, and which describes almost no gains in treatment but which remains committed to its continued development, see L.S. Grossman, B. Martin, and C.G. Fichtner, 'Are Sex Offenders Treatable? A Research Overview,' *Psychiatric Services* 50, no. 3 (March 1999): 349–61.

3 W. Marshall and H. Barbaree, "The Long-Term Evaluation of a Behavioural Treatment Program for Child Molestors," *Behaviour Therapy Research* 26 (1988): 499–511; W. Marshall and S. Barrett, *Criminal Neglect: Why Sex Offenders Go Free* (Toronto: Doubleday, 1990).

4 Vernon L. Quinsey, Arunima Khanna and P. Bruce Malcolm, 'A Retrospective Evaluation of the Regional Treatment Centre Sex Offender Treatment Program,' *Journal of Interpersonal Violence* 13, no. 5 (October 1998): 640.

5 Toby Melville, unpublished AFP Photo, Paulsgrove, England, 11 August 2000.

6 Chas Critcher, 'Media, Government and Moral Panic: The Politics of Pedophilia in Britain 2000–1,' *Journalism Studies* 3, no. 4 (2002): 521–35.

7 The Circle of Support and Accountability is a faith-based program that operates in the 'Gospel tradition of radical hospitality.' It is currently supported by Corrections Canada. It expresses values similar to those of the Parents' Action League in that they see communities as organic and believe society bears a responsibility toward both offenders and victims of sex crimes. Begun by a Mennonite pastor in 1993, it has spread quickly to the United Kingdom and the United States, where they also have earned the

support of government agencies and are officially recognized as an integral part of the rehabilitation process. The reference to radical hospitality can be found in Correctional Services Canada, 'Circles of Support and Accountability: Guide to Project Development,' (2003), http://www.csc-scc.gc.ca/text/ prgrm/chap/circle/proj-guid/3_e.shtml. For general overviews of the Circles, see Robin J. Wilson, Janice E. Picheca, Michelle Prinzo, 'Circles of Support and Accountability: An Evaluation of the Pilot Project in South-Central Ontario' (Ottawa: Correctional Service of Canada, Research Branch, 2005), http://www.csc-scc.gc.ca/text/rsrch/reports/r168/r168_e.pdf; Quaker Peace and Social Witness, 'Circles of Support and Accountability in the Thames Valley: The First Three Years, April 2002 to March 2005' (London: Quaker Communications for Quaker Peace & Social Witness, 2005), http:// www.quake r.org.uk/shared_asp_files/uploadedfiles/82F718A7-9344-4A5C-A4A7-4B053FF22239_CirclesofSupport-first3yrs.pdf.

  8 In 2006 Whitmore kidnapped and sexually assaulted two boys aged fourteen and ten. He was captured and returned to prison.

  9 In 2007 the Associated Press reported that five convicted sex offenders were living under a highway bridge as a result of local ordinances. *Globe and Mail*, 9 April 2007, A11; 'Developments Bar Sex Offenders,' *USA Today*, 16 June 2006, 3A. See also Human Rights Watch, *No Easy Answers: Sex Offender Laws in the US* 19, no. 4(G) (September 2007): 95–110.

10 Morgan Day, 'What Does Your License Plate Say about You?' *kentnewsnet.com* (15 March 2007), http://media.www.kentnewsnet.com/media/storage/ paper867/news/2007/03/15/News/What-Does.Your.License.Plate .Say.About.You-2776494.shtml.

11 Human Rights Watch, *No Easy Answers*, 24.

12 Ibid., 7.

13 *Globe and Mail*, 8 August 2005, 8.

14 'Sex Offenders Living Under Miami Bridge,' *New York Times*, 17 April 2007, http://www.nytimes.com/2007/04/08/us/08bridge.html.

15 Michael Petrunik, 'Models of Dangerousness: A Cross Jurisdictional Review of Dangerousness Legislation and Practice' (Ottawa: Policy Branch, Ministry of the Solicitor General of Canada, 1994), 49.

16 'Ontario to Set Up Canada's First Sex Offender Registry,' CBC News, 10 November 2000, http://www.cbc.ca/canada/story/1999/04/16/ offenders99041.html. As was the case in the 1950s, calls for new legislation tend to be made following a local violent assault, usually involving a minor. The current trend is to name such laws after the victim. Simon A. Cole, 'From the Sexual Psychopath Statues to "Megan's Law": Psychiatric Knowledge in the Diagnosis, Treatment and Adjudication of Sex Criminals in New Jersey, 1949–1999,' *Journal of the History of Medicine* 55 (July 2000): 306.

17 Canada, Parliament, House of Commons, *Debates*, 25 March 1996, Val
    Meredith (Surrey-White Rock-South Langley).
18 Public Safety Canada, *Corrections and Conditional Release Statistical Overview
    Annual Report* (Ottawa: Public Works and Government Services Canada,
    2007), 103.
19 Criminal Code of Canada, Section 753.1.
20 Public Safety Canada, *Corrections and Conditional Release Statistical Overview*, 105.
21 For a general overview of current treatment techniques, see Linda S. Gross-
    man, Brian Martis, and Christopher G. Fichtner, 'Are Sex Offenders Treat-
    able? A Research Overview,' *Psychiatric Services* 50, no. 3 (March 1999): 349–
    61, http://psychservices.psychiatryonline.org/cgi/content/full/50/3/349.
22 Joanna Meyerowitz, *How Sex Changed: A History of Transsexuality in the United
    States* (Cambridge, MA: Harvard University Press, 2002).
23 Kate Bornstein, *Gender Outlaw: On Men, Women, and the Rest of Us* (New York:
    Routledge, 1994).
24 Noteworthy critiques of contemporary approaches to sex offender treatment
    and the use of pedophilia as a diagnostic term are Lea H. Studer and A.
    Scott Aylwin, 'Pedophilia: The Problem with Diagnosis and Limitations of
    CBT in Treatment,' *Medical Hypotheses* 67 (2006): 774–81; Jon Kear-Colwell
    and Douglas P. Boer, 'The Treatment of Pedophiles: Clinical Experience
    and the Implications of Recent Research,' *International Journal of Offender
    Therapy and Comparative Criminology* 44, no. 5 (2000): 593–605.
25 Dany Lacombe, 'Managing Fantasies: An Analysis of Prison Treatment Pro-
    grams for Sex Offenders' (unpublished paper presented at the Law's
    Empire conference, Harrison Hot Springs, BC, June 2005).
26 The issue caused tremendous controversy in gay and lesbian communities.
    See David Thorstad, 'Man/Boy Love and the American Gay Movement,'
    Journal of Homosexuality 20 (1990): 251–74.
27 Frits Bernard, 'The Dutch Pedophile Emancipation Movement,' *Paidika: The
    Journal of Pedophilia* 1, no. 2 (autumn 1987): 35–45.
28 'Court Refuses to Ban Dutch Pedophile Party,' *International Herald Tribune*,
    18 July 2006, http://www.iht.com/articles/2006/07/17/news/dutch.php.
29 Although the Outpatient Forensic Clinic staff never took on a proactive role
    in pushing for changes to the Criminal Code, staff collaborated with Alex K.
    Gigeroff, who argued for the decriminalization of homosexuality in his book
    *Sexual Deviations in the Criminal Law: Homosexual, Exhibitionistic and Pedophilic
    Offences in Canada* (Toronto: University of Toronto Press, 1968).
30 It is worth pointing out that many homosexuals, including American sexolo-
    gist George Henry's assistant Albert Gross, considered discretion to be an
    appropriate adaptation to homosexual life. On Gross and Henry's collabora-
    tion, see Henry L. Minton, 'Henry and Gross and the Study of Sex Offend-

ers, 1937–72,' chap. 5 in *Departing from Deviance: A History of Homosexual Rights and Emancipatory Science in America* (Chicago: University of Chicago Press, 2002), 94–121.

31 Psychopathy continues to be used, and psychologists and psychiatrists continue to debate its validity. See Grant T. Harris, Tracey A. Skilling, and Marnie E. Rice, 'The Construct of Psychopathy,' *Crime and Justice* 28 (2001): 197–264.

32 Kinsey Institute Archives, General Correspondence, Letter to Paul Gebhard, October 1977.

33 For details concerning the police standoff, see the court transcript at http://mikeoncrime.com/article/3229/whitmore-pleads-guilty-entire-transcript-of-crowns-submission-at-pedophile-sentencing. On his later suicide attempt, see 'Pedophile Seeks Chemical Castration for Sexual Urges,' *Winnipeg Free Press*, 27 July 2007, A4; 'Suicide Attempt,' *The Star Phoenix*, 22 May 2007, http://www.canada.com/saskatoonstarphoenix/story.html?id=6b15d49e-d905-4879-b8f3-ac5602496ac8&k=62874.

34 Petrunik, 'Models of Dangerousness,' 4.

35 Ibid., 43–4.

36 One of the earliest and most influential feminist analyses of rape was Susan Brownmiller's *Against Our Will: Men, Women and Rape* (New York: Bantam, 1975), where she argued that rape was a crime of violence, not a sex crime. Legal theorist Catharine A. Mackinnon challenged that view in her highly influential *Toward a Feminist Theory of the State* (Cambridge, MA: Harvard University Press, 1989).

Bibliography

Primary Sources

Atcheson, J.D. 'Social Aspects of Sexual Behaviour.' *Criminal Law Quarterly* 3, no. 4 (February 1961): 455–61.

Atcheson, J.D., et al. *Incest.* Toronto: The Institute, 1975.

Ball, J.R., and Jean J. Armstrong. 'The Use of L.S.D. 25 (D-Lysergic Acid Diethylamide) in the Treatment of the Sexual Perversions.' *Canadian Psychiatric Association Journal* 6, no. 4 (August 1961): 231–5.

Barnes, Harry Elmer, and Negley K. Teeters. *New Horizons in Criminology.* New York: Prentice-Hall, 1943.

Berman, Leo H., and Lawrence Zelic Freedman. 'Clinical Perception of Sexual Deviates.' *Journal of Psychology* 52 (July 1961): 157–60.

Blackstock, Harvey. *Bitter Humour: About Dope, Safe Cracking and Prisons.* Toronto: Burns and MacEachern, 1967.

Bond, I.K., and H.C. Hutchison. 'Application of Reciprocal Inhibition Therapy to Exhibitionism.' In *Experiments in Behavior Therapy*, edited by H.J. Eysenck, 80–6 (New York: Pergamon Press, 1964).

Boyd, Robert N. 'Sex Behind Bars.' In *Gay Roots: Twenty Years of Gay Sunshine*, edited by Winston Leyland, 272–8. San Francisco: Gay Sunshine Press, 1991.

Brillinger, H. Roy. 'The Judge and the Psychiatrist – Toward Mutual Understanding.' *Canadian Journal of Corrections* 1, no. 2 (January 1959): 1–9.

Burns, K. Phyllis. 'What's Happening to Canada's Children?' In *Social Problems: A Canadian Profile*, edited by Richard Laskin, 316–23. New York: McGraw-Hill Company of Canada, 1964.

Cabeen, Charles W. 'Factors Related to Improvement of Sex Offenders in Therapy.' PhD diss., University of California, Los Angeles, 1955.

California, Department of Mental Hygiene. *Final Report on California Sexual Deviation Research.* Sacramento, CA: Assembly of the State of California, 1954.

Callihoo, Robert, and Robert Chalifoux. 'A Native Viewpoint.' Unpublished
   paper, Drumheller Institution, 1972.
Canada. *Commission of Inquiry into the Non-Medical Use of Drugs: Final Report.*
   Ottawa: Information Canada, 1973.
Canada. *Report of the Commission of Inquiry into Certain Disturbances at Kingston Pen-
   itentiary during April 1971.* Ottawa: Information Canada, 1973.
Canada. *Report of the Royal Commission on the Criminal Law Relating to Criminal Sex-
   ual Psychopaths.* Ottawa: Queen's Printer, 1958.
Canada. *Report of the Royal Commission to Investigate the Penal System of Canada.*
   Ottawa: Queen's Press, 1938.
Canada, Canadian Committee on Corrections. *Toward Unity: Criminal Justice and
   Corrections.* Ottawa: Queen's Printer, 1969.
Canadian Criminal Cases. (C.C.C.) Toronto: Canada Law Book, 1948–77.
Canadian Federation of Home and School and Parent-Teacher Associations.
   Canadian Family Study, 1957–1960. Toronto: The Federation, 1960.
Cappon, Daniel. *Toward an Understanding of Homosexuality.* Englewood Cliffs, NJ:
   Prentice-Hall, 1965.
Caroll, Leo. 'Race and Sexual Assault in a Maximum Security Prison.' Photocopy,
   1974. Kinsey Institute Archives.
Caron, Roger. *Bingo!* Toronto: Methuen, 1985.
– *Go-Boy!* Toronto: McGraw-Hill Ryerson, 1978.
Ciale, Justin. *Tales of St Vincent de Paul Penitentiary.* Toronto: Legas, 1997.
Clemmer, Donald. *The Prison Community.* New York: Holt, Rinehart and Winston,
   1958.
Committee on the Sex Offender. 'Interim Report.' Toronto: Canadian Penal
   Association, 1948. Unpublished photocopy, Archives of Ontario, RG 10-107-0-
   784.
Cormier, Bruno M. *The Watcher and the Watched.* Montreal: Tundra Books, 1975.
Cormier, Bruno, and Siebert P. Simons. 'The Problem of the Dangerous Sexual
   Offender.' In *Social Deviance in Canada*, edited by W.E. Mann, 342–9. Toronto:
   Copp Clark, 1971.
Cradles and Careers. Directed by Jack Olsen. National Film Board of Canada, 1947.
Cruvant, Bernard A., Milton Meltzer, Francis J. Tartaglino. 'An Institutional Pro-
   gram for Committed Sex Deviants.' Paper presented at the 106th Annual
   Meeting of the A.P.A., Detroit, 1–5 May 1950. Kinsey Institute Archives.
Danziger, Peter L. 'Sexual Assaults and Forced Homosexual Relationships in
   Prison: Cruel and Unusual Punishment.' *Albany Law Review* 36, no. 2 (1971):
   428–38.
Davis, Katharine Bement. *Factors in the Sex Lives of Twenty-Two Hundred Women.*
   New York: Harper and Brothers, 1929.

Desroches, Fred. 'The April 1971 Kingston Penitentiary Riot.' *Canadian Journal of Criminology and Corrections* 16, no. 4 (1974): 317–31.
– 'Patterns in Prison Riots.' *Canadian Journal of Criminology and Corrections* 16, no. 4 (1974): 332–51.
Devereux, George, and Malcolm M. Moos. 'The Social Structure of Prisons, and the Organic Tensions.' *Journal of Criminal Pathology* 5, no. 4 (October 1942): 306–24.
Ellis, Albert. 'A Study of 300 Sex Offenders.' *International Journal of Sexology* 4, no. 3 (February 1951): 127–35.
Ellis, Albert, and Ralph Brancale. *The Psychology of the Sex Offender.* Springfield, IL: Charles C. Thomas Publishing, 1956.
Eysenck, Hans Jurgen. *Behaviour Therapy and the Neuroses: Readings in Modern Methods of Treatment Derived from Learning Theory.* New York: Pergamon Press, 1960.
– *The Causes and Cures of Neurosis: An Introduction to Modern Behaviour Therapy Based on Learning Theory and the Principles of Conditioning.* London: Routledge and Paul, 1965.
– *Experiments in Behaviour Therapy: Readings in Modern Methods of Treatment of Mental Disorders Derived from Learning Theory.* New York: Pergamon, 1964.
Fishman, Joseph F. *Sex in Prison: Revealing Sex Conditions in American Prisons.* New York: National Library Press, 1934.
Ford, Charles. 'Homosexual Practices of Institutionalized Females.' *Journal of Abnormal and Social Psychology* 23 (1929): 442–8.
Fortune and Men's Eyes. Directed by Harvey Hart. Metro-Goldwyn-Mayer, 1971.
Freud, Sigmund. 'Letter to an American Mother.' http://www.psychpage.com/gay/library/freudsletter.html.
Friedlander, J.W., and R.S. Banay. 'Psychosis Following Lobotomy in a Case of Sexual Psychopathy.' *Archives of Neurology and Psychiatry Chicago* 59 (1948): 302–21.
Fugère, Renée, and Ingrid Thompson-Cooper, eds. *Breaking the Chains: Bruno M. Cormier and the McGill University Clinic in Forensic Psychiatry.* Westmount, QC: R. Davies Multimedia Publishing, 1998.
Gebhard, Paul, John H. Gagnon, Wardell B. Pomeroy, and Cornelia V. Christianson. *Sex Offenders.* New York: Harper and Row and Paul B. Hoeber Medical Books, 1965.
Gigeroff, Alex K. *Sexual Deviations in the Criminal Law: Homosexual, Exhibitionistic, and Pedophilic Offences in Canada.* Toronto: University of Toronto Press, 1968.
Gigeroff, A., J. Mohr, and R. Turner. 'Sex Offenders on Probation: Heterosexual Pedophiles.' *Federal Probation* 32, no. 4 (December 1968): 17–21.
Glueck, Bernard Jr. 'An Evaluation of the Homosexual Offender.' *Minnesota Law Review* 41, no. 2 (1957): 187–210.

Glueck, Bernard C. Jr, and Russell H. Dinerstein. 'Sub-coma Insulin Therapy in the Treatment of Homosexual Panic States.' *Journal of Social Therapy* 1 (1955): 182–6.

Gray, Kenneth G. 'Psychiatric Examination of Sex Offenders.' In *Proceedings of the 83rd Annual Congress of Correction of the American Association*, 174–7. New York: Central Office, 1953.

– 'Psychiatry and the Criminal Code.' *Ontario Journal of Neuro-Psychiatry* 5 (December 1935): 44–53.

– 'Sexual Deviation: Problem and Treatment.' *Saturday Night Magazine*, 26 November 1955, 9–10.

Gray, Kenneth G., and Harry Hutchinson. 'The Psychopathic Personality: A Survey of Canadian Psychiatrist's Opinions.' *Canadian Psychiatric Association Journal* 9, no. 6 (1966): 452–61.

Group for the Advancement of Psychiatry. 'The Public Relations Problem of Psychiatry.' *Report* 5 (April 1948): 6–7.

Haggart, Ron. 'Ninety Hours of Rebellion.' *Weekend Magazine* 22, no. 16 (17 April 1972): 1–10.

Haines, William H., and John J. McLaughlin. 'Treatment of the Homosexual in Prison.' *Diseases of the Nervous System* 13, no. 3 (March 1952): 2–4.

Hartman, Valdemar. 'Group Psychotherapy with Sexually Deviant Offenders (Pedophiles).' *Proceedings of the 4th Research Conference on Delinquency and Criminology*, 259–72. Montreal, 1964.

Hendrickson, Robert. *Facts on File Encyclopedia of Word and Phrase Origins*. New York: Facts on File, 1987.

Henry, George W. 'The Homosexual Delinquent.' *Mental Hygiene* 25, no. 3 (July 1941): 420–42.

Huffman, Arthur V. 'A Report of a Study of Sex Offenders in Illinois.' In *Proceedings of the 83rd Annual Congress of Correction of the American Association*, 178–85. New York: Central Office, 1953.

Hutchison, H.C. 'A Case of Pedophilia in Which the Initiation of Assertive Behaviour Resulted in Significant Improvement.' *Mental Health Services* 1, no. 1 (March–April 1963): 14–15.

– 'Group Techniques with Wives of Sexual Deviates.' *Canada's Mental Health* 7, no. 5 (October 1959): 6.

Jackson, Don. 'Dachau in America.' In *Gay Roots: Twenty Years of Gay Sunshine*, edited by Winston Leyland, 264–6. San Francisco: Gay Sunshine Press, 1991.

Johnson, Edwin. 'The Homosexual in Prison.' *Social Theory and Practice* 1, no. 4 (fall 1971): 83–95.

Jones, Maxwell. *Therapeutic Community: A New Treatment Method in Psychiatry*. New York: Basic Books, 1953.

Kahn, Samuel. *Homosexuality and Mentality*. Boston: Meador Publishing, 1937.

Karpman, Benjamin. 'Sex Life in Prison.' *Journal of Criminal Law and Criminology* 38, no. 5 (January–February 1948): 475–86.

Kelleher, E. 'The Role of Psychiatry in Programs for the Control and Treatment of Sex Offenders.' Paper presented at the Institute on the Illinois Penal and Correctional System, 18 May 1952. Kinsey Institute Archives.

Kidman, John. *The Canadian Prison: The Story of a Tragedy*. Toronto: Ryerson Press, 1947.

Kilgour, A.J. 'Sex Delinquency: A Review of 100 Court Cases Referred to the Toronto Psychiatric Hospital.' *Ontario Journal of Neuro-Psychiatry* (September 1933): 34–50.

Kinsey, Alfred, Wardell B. Pomeroy, Clyde E. Martin, and Paul H. Gebhard. *Sexual Behavior in the Human Male*. Philadelphia: W.B. Saunders, 1948.

Kinsey, Alfred, et al. 'Concepts of Normality and Abnormality in Sexual Behaviour.' In American Psychological Association, *Psychosexual Development in Health and Disease: The Proceedings of the Thirty-Eighth Annual Meeting of the American Psychopathological Association, Held in New York City, June 1948* (New York: Grune and Stratton, 1949), 11–32.

Knowles, John A. 'The Role of the Prison Psychologist.' *Proceedings of the Oklahoma Academy of Science* 30 (1949): 172–5.

Kofsky, Sidney, and Albert Ellis. 'Illegal Communication among Institutionalized Female Delinquents.' *The Journal of Social Psychiatry* 48 (1958): 155–60.

Kopp, Marie E. 'Surgical Treatment as a Sex Crime Prevention Measure.' *Journal of Criminal Law and Criminology* 28, no. 5 (January–February 1938): 692–706.

Kubrick, Stanley. *A Clockwork Orange*. Produced and directed by Stanley Kubrick. 1971.

Laskin, Richard, ed. *Social Problems: A Canadian Profile*. New York: McGraw-Hill of Canada, 1964.

Laycock, S.R. 'Parents Share in Training for Citizenship.' *Canadian Home and School* 12, no. 4 (March–April 1953): 4–6.

Leznoff, Maurice. 'The Homosexual in Urban Society.' MA thesis, Sociology Department, McGill University, 1954.

Lindner, Robert M. *Rebel without a Cause: The Hypnoanalysis of a Criminal Psychopath*. New York: Grune and Stratton, 1944.

Lundy, Phyllis J., and Peter R. Breggin. 'Psychiatric Oppression of Prisoners.' *Psychiatric Opinion* 11, no. 3 (June 1974): 30–7.

Maletzky, Barry M. 'The Treatment of Homosexuality by "Assisted" Covert Sensitization.' *Behaviour Research and Therapy* 11, no. 4: 655–7.

Mann, W.E. *Society behind Bars: A Sociological Scrutiny of Guelph Reformatory*. Toronto: Social Science Publishers, 1967.

Mann, W.E., ed. *Social Deviance in Canada.* Toronto: Copp Clark, 1971.

March, R.E. 'The Classification Program in Canadian Federal Penitentiaries.' In *Proceedings of the 83rd Annual Congress of Correction of the American Association*, 47–54. New York: Central Office, 1953.

Marcus, Anthony. 'A Multi-Disciplinary Study of Those Individuals Designated Dangerous Sexual Offenders and held in Federal Custody in British Columbia, Part I.' *Canadian Journal of Corrections/Revue canadienne de criminologie* 8, no. 2 (April 1966): 90–103.

– 'Dangerous Sex Offender Project, Part II.' *Canadian Journal of Corrections/Revue canadienne de criminologie* 11, no. 3 (July 1969): 198–205.

– *Nothing Is My Number: An Exploratory Study with a Group of Dangerous Sexual Offenders in Canada.* Toronto: General Publishing, 1971.

McGee, Richard A. 'Prisons at the Crossroads.' In *Proceedings of the 83rd Annual Congress of Correction of the American Association*, 12–23. New York: Central Office, 1953.

McGrath, W.T. 'Planning Canada's Correctional System.' Address to the Annual Meeting of the John Howard Society of Peterborough, 12 April 1960. Archives of Ontario, RG 20-16, file 215.5, General Potts-Alton.

Meduna, L.J., ed. *Carbon Dioxide Therapy: A Neurophysiological Treatment of Nervous Disorders*, 2nd ed. Toronto: Ryerson Press, 1958.

Meredith, W.C.J. 'Law and the Sex Criminal.' *Saturday Night Magazine*, 18 October 1952.

Mohr, Hans. 'A la Recherche.' In *Breaking the Chains: Bruno M. Cormier and the McGill Clinic in Forensic Psychiatry*, 137–61. Westmount, QC: Robert Davies Multimedia Publishing, 1998.

Mohr, Johann. 'The Contribution of Research to the Selection of Appropriate Alternatives for Sexual Offenders.' *Criminal Law Quarterly* 4 (January 1962): 317–28.

Mohr, J.W., and R.E. Turner. 'Sexual Deviations Part I – Introduction.' *Applied Therapeutics* 9, no. 1 (February 1967): 78–81.

– 'Sexual Deviations Part II – Homosexuality.' *Applied Therapeutics* 9, no. 2 (February 1967): 165–8.

– 'Sexual Deviations Part III – Exhibitionism.' *Applied Therapeutics* 9, no. 3 (February 1967): 263–5.

– 'Sexual Deviations Part IV – Pedophilia.' *Applied Therapeutics* 9, no. 4 (April 1967): 363.

Mohr, J.W., R.E. Turner, and J.R. Ball. 'Exhibitionism and Pedophilia.' *Corrective Psychiatry and Journal of Social Therapy* 8, no. 4 (1962): 172–86.

Mohr, J.W., R.E. Turner, and M.B. Terry. *Pedophilia and Exhibitionism: A Handbook.* Toronto: University of Toronto Press, 1964.

Nagler, Ernest J. 'Male Homosexuality in Toronto – A Sociological and Social Problems Overview and Perspective.' 30 June 1971. Canadian Lesbian and Gay Archives, Community Homophile Association of Toronto.

Nash, John. 'It's Time Father Got Back in the Family.' *Maclean's Magazine*, 12 May 1956, 28–29, 82–83, 85.

Oliver, Bernard Jr. *Sexual Deviation in American Society*. New Haven, CT: College and University Press, 1967.

Ontario. *Royal Commission on Public Welfare – Report to the Lieutenant-Governor in Council*. Toronto: Royal Commission on Public Welfare, 1930.

Paitich, Daniel. 'Attitude toward Parents in Male Homosexuals and Exhibitionists.' PhD diss., University of Toronto, 1964.

'Panel Discussion.' *The Ladder* 3, no. 6 (March 1959): 7–12.

Paras, J.L. 'Sodium Amytal Narcosis in the Psychotherapy of a Sex Offender.' *Diseases of the Nervous System* 15, no. 6 (June 1954): 180–3.

Pomeroy, Wardell. 'Sex in Prison.' Audiotape of a presentation at a meeting of the Federal Warden's Institute, University of Colorado, 26 June 1962. Kinsey Institute Archives.

Potts, F.H. 'Treatment for Failure'. In *Proceedings of the 83rd Annual Congress of Correction of the American Association*, 127–30. New York: Central Office, 1953.

Psychiatric Opinion 11, no. 3 (June 1974). Special Issue on Treatment in Prison.

Quirk, Douglas A. 'A Follow-Up on the Bond Hutchison Case of Systematic Desensitization with an Exhibitionist.' *Behavior Therapy* 5 (1974): 428–31.

Reifen, D. 'Protection of Children Involved in Sexual Offences: A New Method of Investigation in Israel.' *Journal of Law, Criminology, and Police Science* 49 (1958): 223–9.

Rhodes, Robert J. 'Homosexual Aversion Therapy, Electric Shock Technique.' *Journal of the Kansas Medical Society* 74 (March 1973): 103–5.

Richmond, Guy. *Prison Doctor: One Man's Story That Must Be Told in Canada Today*. Surrey, BC: Nunaga Publishing, 1975.

Riordan, Michael. 'Blessed Are the Deviates: A Post-Therapy Check-Up on My Ex-Psychiatrist.' In *Flaunting It! A Decade of Gay Journalism from The Body Politic*, edited by Ed Jackson and Stan Persky, 14–20. Toronto: Pink Triangle Press, 1982.

Rodgers, R.S. *Sex and Law in Canada*. Ottawa: Policy Press, 1962.

Saunders, D.E. 'Sentences of Homosexual Offenders.' *Criminal Law Quarterly* 10, no. 1 (1967): 25–9.

Scacco, Anthony M. *Rape in Prison*. Springfield, IL: C.C. Thomas, 1975.

Scott, George D. *Inmate: The Casebook Revelations of a Canadian Penitentiary Psychiatrist*. Montreal: Optimum Publishing International, 1982.

Seeley, John R., Alexander Sim, and Elizabeth W. Loosley. *Crestwood Heights: A Study of the Culture of Suburban Life.* New York: Basic Books, 1956.

Smith, Charles E. 'The Homosexual Federal Offender: A Study of 100 Cases.' *Northwestern University Journal of Criminal Law, Criminology and Police Science* 44, no. 5 (January–February 1954): 582–91.

Stafford-Clark, David, Bernard L. Mallett, and James H.P. Willis. 'A Follow-up Study of Criminal Psychopaths.' *British Journal of Delinquency* 6 (1955): 126–36.

Stern, William. *Jugendliche Zeugen in Sittlichkeitsprozessen: ihre Behandlung und psychologische Begutachtung; ein Kapitel der forensischen Psychologie* [Juvenile Witnesses in Sex Crime Proceedings: Their Treatment and Psychological Assessment]. Leipzig: Quelle and Meyer, 1926.

Stevenson, George Herbert. 'Psychiatry and Sexual Offenders.' Paper presented at the Ontario Neuro-Psychiatric Association, 16 January 1948. Archives of Ontario.

Stevenson, George H., and Leola E. Neal. *Personality and Its Deviations: An Introduction to Abnormal and Medical Psychology.* Toronto: The Ryerson Press, 1950.

Sutherland, Edwin H. 'The Diffusion of Sex Psychopath Laws.' *American Journal of Sociology* 56 (1950): 142–8.

Sykes, Gresham M. *The Society of Captives: A Study of a Maximum Security Prison.* Princeton, NJ: Princeton University Press, 1958.

Szasz, Thomas S. *The Age of Madness: The History of Involuntary Mental Hospitalization, Presented in Selected Texts.* Garden City, NY: Anchor Books, 1973.

– *The Manufacture of Madness: A Comparative Study of the Inquisition and the Mental Health Movement.* New York: Harper and Row, 1970.

– *The Myth of Mental Illness: Foundation of a Theory of Personal Conduct.* New York: Harper and Row, 1961.

Tappan, Paul. *The Habitual Sex Offender: Report and Recommendations of the Commission on the Habitual Sex Offender.* Trenton, NJ: New Jersey Commission on the Habitual Sex Offender, 1950.

– 'Sentences for Sex Criminals.' *Journal of Criminal Law and Criminology* 42 (1951): 332–7.

– 'Some Myths about the Sex Offender.' *Federal Probation* 19, no. 2 (June 1955): 7–12.

– 'Treatment of the Sex Offender in Denmark.' *American Journal of Psychiatry* 108 (1951): 241–9.

Thompson, G.N. 'Electroshock and Other Therapeutic Consideration in Sexual Psychopathy.' *Journal of Nervous and Mental Disease* 109 (1949): 531–9.

Thompson, P.J. 'Discussion.' *Canadian Psychiatric Association Journal* 9, no. 6 (December 1964): 539–40.

Topping, Wesley. 'The Rise of the New Penology in British Columbia, Canada.' *British Journal of Delinquency* 5 (1955): 180–9.

Tuchtie, Michael D. 'A Symposium on the Sex Offender: Forensic Inpatient Service.' *Criminal Law Quarterly* 3, no. 4 (February 1961): 448–54.

Turner, R.E. 'The Group Treatment of Sexual Deviations.' *Canadian Journal of Corrections* 3, no. 4 (October 1961): 485–91.

– 'Psychiatric Treatment as an Alternative to Imprisonment.' *Criminal Law Quarterly* 4, no. 3 (January 1962).

– 'Treatment of the Sex Offender.' *Criminal Law Quarterly* 3, no. 4 (February 1961): 416–72.

Tyhurst, James Stewart. *More for the Mind: A Study of Psychiatric Services in Canada.* Toronto: Canadian Mental Health Association, 1963.

Wake, F.R. 'Normal Aggression and Delinquency.' *Bulletin of the Maritime Psychological Association* 8 (1959): 50–9.

Walker, Edward L. 'The Terman-Miles "M-F" Test and the Prison Classification Program.' *Journal of Genetic Psychology* 59 (1941): 27–40.

Watson, Gordon, John Rich, and K.G. Gray. 'A Study of Forensic Cases.' Unpublished report to the Department of National Health and Welfare, re: Mental Health Training Grant. Archives of Ontario, Ministry of Health.

Weiss, Carl, and David James. *Terror in the Prisons: Homosexual Rape and Why Society Condones It.* Indianapolis: Bobbs-Merrill, 1974.

White, James C. *The Autonomic Nervous System: Anatomy, Physiology, and Surgical Treatment.* New York, 1935.

Williams, Dalton Loyd. 'Prison Sex at Age 16.' In *Gay Roots: Twenty Years of Gay Sunshine*, edited by Winston Leyland, 279–86. San Francisco: Gay Sunshine Press, 1991.

Williams, Lorraine M. 'Setting Up Social Work at the Forensic Clinic.' In *TPH: History and Memories of the Toronto Psychiatric Hospital, 1925–1966*, edited by Edward Shorter. Toronto: Wall and Emerson, 1996.

Wilson, J.G., and M.J. Pescor. *Problems in Prison Psychiatry.* Caldwell, ID: Caxton Press, 1939.

Withrow, Oswald C.J. *Shackling the Transgressor: An Indictment of the Canadian Penal System.* Toronto: Thomas Nelson and Sons, 1933.

Wolpe, Joseph. *Psychotherapy by Reciprocal Inhibition.* Stanford, CA: Stanford University Press, 1958.

Wooden, Wayne S., and Jay Parker. *Men behind Bars: Sexual Exploitation in Prison.* New York: Plenum Press, 1982.

Wyers, Robert E. 'Sex Offenders Help Organize Their Own Treatment.' Unpublished paper, photocopy, 1953, Kinsey Institute Archive.

Wylie, Philip. *Generation of Vipers.* New York: Rinehart, 1942.

Young, Allen. 'Sissy in Prison: An Interview with Ron Vernon.' In *Out of the Closets: Voices of Gay Liberation*, edited by Karla Jay and Allen Young. 1972. Reprint, New York: New York University Press, 1992.

Secondary Sources

Adams, Mary Louise. *The Trouble with Normal: Postwar Youth and the Making of Heterosexuality.* Toronto: University of Toronto Press, 1997.

Annau, Catherine. 'Eager Eugenicists: A Reappraisal of the Birth Control Society of Hamilton.' *Social History* 27, no. 53 (1994): 111–33.

Arnup, Katherine. *Education for Motherhood: Advice for Mothers in Twentieth-Century Canada.* Toronto: University of Toronto Press, 1994.

Bayer, Ronald. *Homosexuality and American Psychiatry: The Politics of Diagnosis.* New York: Basic Books, 1981.

Bernard, Frits. 'The Dutch Pedophile Emancipation Movement.' *Paidika: The Journal of Pedophilia* 1, no. 2 (autumn 1987): 35–45.

Berube, Allan. *Coming Out Under Fire: The History of Gay Men and Women in World War Two.* New York: Free Press, 1990.

Black, Edwin. *War against the Weak: Eugenics and America's Campaign to Create a Master Race.* New York: Four Walls Eight Windows, 2003.

Blanchette, Kelley. 'Sex Offender Assessment, Treatment and Recidivism: A Literature Review.' Correctional Services Canada, August 1996. http://www.csc-scc.gc.ca/text/rsrch/reports/r48/r48e_e.shtml (accessed 26 November 2007).

Bliss, Michael. '"Pure Books on Avoided Subjects": Pre-Freudian Sexual Ideas in Canada.' *Historical Papers* (1970): 89–108.

Boag, Peter. *Same-Sex Affairs: Constructing and Controlling Homosexuality in the Pacific Northwest.* Berkeley: University of California Press, 2003.

Bonta, James, Andrew Harris, Ivan Zinger, and Debbie Carriere. 'The Crown Files Research Project: A Study of Dangerous Offenders.' Public Safety Canada, report no. 1996-01, cat. no. JS4-1/1996-1. http://ww2.ps-sp.gc.ca/publications/corrections/199601_e.asp.

Bornstein, Kate. *Gender Outlaw: On Men, Women, and the Rest of Us.* New York: Routledge, 1994.

Bothwell, Robert. *The Big Chill: Canada and the Cold War.* Toronto: Irwin Publishing, 1998.

Boyer, Patrick. *A Passion for Justice: The Legacy of James Chalmers McRuer.* Toronto: University of Toronto Press, 1994.

Briken, Peter, Andreas Hill, and Wolfgang Berner. 'Abnormal Attraction.' *Scientific American Mind* (February/March 2007): 58–63.

Brownmiller, Susan. *Against Our Will: Men, Women and Rape.* New York: Bantam, 1975.

Bumstead, J.M. 'Canadian and American Culture in the 1950s.' In *Interpreting Canada's Past,* vol. 2, edited by J.M. Bumstead, 398–411. Toronto: Oxford University Press, 1986.

Callihoo, Robert, and Robert Chalifoux. 'A Native Viewpoint.' Unpublished paper, Drumheller Institution, 1972. Archives of Ontario, Ministry of Corrections.

Calzavera, Liviana M., and Ted Myers. *Understanding HIV-Related Risk Behaviour in Prisons: The Inmates' Perspective.* Ottawa: National AIDS Clearinghouse, 1997.

Capshew, James H. *Psychologists on the March: Science, Practice and Professional Identity in America, 1929–1969.* New York: Cambridge University Press, 1999.

Champagne, Robert. 'Psychopaths and Perverts: The Canadian Royal Commission on the Criminal Law Relating to Criminal Sexual Psychopaths, 1954–1958.' *Canadian Lesbian and Gay History Network Newsletter* 2 (September 1986): 7–9.

Chapman, Terry L. 'Early Eugenics Movement in Western Canada.' *Alberta History* 25, no. 4 (1977): 9–17.

Chauncey, George Jr. *Gay New York: Gender, Urban Culture and the Making of the Gay Male World, 1890–1940.* New York: Basic Books, 1994.

– 'The Postwar Sex Crime Panic.' In *True Stories from the American Past,* edited by William Graebner, 160–78. New York: McGraw-Hill, 1993.

Chenier, Elise. 'Seeing Red: Immigrant Women and Sexual Danger in Toronto's Postwar Daily Newspapers.' *Atlantis: A Women's Studies Journal* 24, no. 2 (spring 2000): 51–60.

Christie, Nancy, and Michael Gauvreau. 'Introduction.' In *Cultures of Citizenship in Postwar Canada, 1940–1955,* edited by Nancy Christie and Michael Gauvreau. Montreal: McGill-Queen's University Press, 2003.

Chunn, Dorothy E. 'Secrets and Lies: The Criminalization of Incest and the (Re)formation of the "Private" in British Columbia, 1890–1940.' In *Regulating Lives: Historical Essays on the State, Society, the Individual and the Law,* edited by John McLaren, Robert Menzies, and Dorothy E. Chunn, 120–44. Vancouver: UBC Press, 2002.

Cohen Stanley. *Folk Devils and Moral Panics: The Creation of the Mods and Rockers,* 3rd ed. New York: Routledge, 2002.

Cole, Simon A. 'From the Sexual Psychopath Statute to "Megan's Law": Psychiatric Knowledge in the Diagnosis, Treatment, and Adjudication of Sex Criminals in New Jersey, 1949–1999.' *Journal of the History of Medicine and Allied Sciences* 55 (July 2000): 292–314.

Collins, Anne. *In the Sleep Room: The Story of the CIA Brainwashing Experiments in Canada.* Toronto: Lester and Dennys, 1988.

Committee on Sexual Offences against Children and Youths. *Sexual Offences against Children: Report of the Committee on Sexual Offences against Children and Youths.* Ottawa: Minister of Supply and Services Canada, 1984.

Cooley, Dennis. 'Social Control and Social Order in Male Federal Prisons.' PhD diss., University of Manitoba, 1995.

Copp, Terry, and Bill McAndrew. *Battle Exhaustion: Soldiers and Psychiatrists in the*

Canadian Army, 1939–1945. Montreal and Kingston: McGill-Queen's University Press, 1990.

Critcher, Chas. 'Media, Government and Moral Panic: The Politics of Pedophilia in Britain 2000-1.' *Journalism Studies* 3, no. 4 (2002): 521–35.

Cummins, Eric. *The Rise and Fall of California's Radical Prison Movement.* Stanford, CA: Stanford University Press, 1994.

Davis, Angela Y. 'Race, Gender, and Prison History: From the Convict Lease System to the Supermax Prison.' *Prison Masculinities,* edited by Don Sabo, Terry A. Kupers, and Willie London. Philadelphia: Temple University Press, 2001.

Delhi, Kari. 'Women and Class: The Social Organization of Mother Relations to Schools in Toronto, 1915–1940.' PhD dissertation, Ontario Institute for Studies in Education, 1988.

D'Emilio, John. 'The Homosexual Menace: The Politics of Sexuality in Cold War America.' In *Passion and Power: Sexuality in History,* edited by Kathy Peiss and Christina Simmons, 226–40. Philadelphia: Temple University Press, 1989.

– *Sexual Politics, Sexual Communities: The Making of a Homosexual Minority in the United States 1940–1970.* Chicago: University of Chicago Press, 1983.

D'Emilio, John, and Estelle B. Freedman. *Intimate Matters: A History of Sexuality in America,* 2nd edition. Chicago: University of Chicago Press, 1998.

Dowbiggin, Ian Robert. *Keeping America Sane: Psychiatry and Eugenics in the U.S. and Canada.* Ithaca, NY: Cornell University Press, 1997.

Duberman, Martin. *Cures: A Gay Man's Odyssey.* New York: Dutton, 1991.

Dubinsky, Karen. *Improper Advances: Rape and Heterosexual Conflict in Ontario, 1880–1929.* Chicago: University of Chicago Press, 1993.

Eskridge, William M. Jr. 'Privacy Jurisprudence and the Apartheid of the Closet, 1946–1961.' *Florida State University Law Review.* 1997. http://www.law.fsu.edu/journals/lawreview/frames/244/eskrfram.html (accessed 8 June 2001).

Fabiano, Elizabeth A., Frank J. Porporino, and David Robinson. 'Rehabilitation Through Clearer Thinking: A Cognitive Model of Correctional Intervention.' Research and Statistics Branch, Correctional Service of Canada, 1990. http://www.csc-scc.gc.ca/text/rsrch/briefs/b4/b04e_e.shtml (accessed 26 November 2007).

Fadel, Alec. 'Homosexual Offences in Ottawa, 1950–1967: The Medicalization of the Legal Process.' MA thesis, Concordia University History Department, 1994.

Fahrni, Magda. 'Counting the Costs of Living: Gender, Citizenship, and a Politics of Prices in 1940s Montreal.' *Canadian Historical Review* 83, no. 4 (December 2002): 483–504.

Faubert, Jacqueline. 'The Emergence and Consequences of Risk Thinking in British Columbia Dangerous Offender Hearings, 1978–2000.' PhD diss., Simon Fraser University, 2003.

Fejes, Fred. 'Murder, Perversion, and Moral Panic: The 1954 Media Campaign against Miami's Homosexuals and the Discourse of Civic Betterment.' *Journal of the History of Sexuality* 9, no. 3 (July 2000): 305–47.

Foucauld, Deidre. 'Prison Labour: Punishment or Reform: The Canadian Penitentiary System 1867–1960.' MA thesis, University of Ottawa, 1982.

Foucault, Michel. 'About the Concept of the "Dangerous Individual" in 19th-Century Legal Psychiatry.' *International Journal of Law and Psychiatry* 1 (January 1978): 1–19.

– *Discipline and Punish: The Birth of the Prison*, trans. Alan Sheridan. New York: Vintage Books, 1979.

– *History of Sexuality, Volume One.* New York: Vintage Books, 1990.

Freedman, Estelle. 'The Prison Lesbian: Race, Class, and the Construction of the Aggressive Female Homosexual, 1915–1965.' *Feminist Studies* 22, no. 2 (summer 1996): 397–423.

– '"Uncontrolled Desires": The Response to the Sexual Psychopath, 1920–1960.' In *Passion and Power: Sexuality in History*, edited by Kathy Peiss and Christina Simmons, 199–225. Philadelphia: Temple University Press, 1989.

Garland, David. *Punishment and Welfare: A History of Penal Strategies.* London: Gower Publishing, 1985.

Gerassi, John G. *The Boys of Boise: Furor, Vice and Folly in an American City.* 1966. Reprint, Seattle: University of Washington Press, 2001.

Gigeroff, Alex. 'The Evolution of Canadian Law with Respect to Exhibitionism, Homosexuality and Pedophilia.' In *Research Conference on Delinquency and Criminology, Proceedings / 4e Colloque de Recherche sur la Delinquance et la Criminalite, Montreal 1964*, 299–308. Ottawa: Societe de Criminologie du Quebec, avec la collaboration de l'Institute Philippe Pinel, 1965.

Gilmore, Norbert, and Margaret A. Somerville. *A Review of the Use of LSD and ECT at the Prison for Women in the Early 1960s.* Ottawa: Correctional Service of Canada, 1998.

Girard, Philip. 'Gays and Lesbians and the Legal Process since 1945.' Unpublished paper (photocopy). Canadian Lesbian and Gay Archives.

Gleason, Mona. *Normalizing the Ideal: Psychology, Schooling, and the Family in Postwar Canada.* Toronto: University of Toronto Press, 1999.

Golz, Annalee. 'Family Matters: The Canadian Family and the State in the Postwar Period.' *Left History* 1, no. 2 (fall 1993): 9–49.

Gomez, Alan Eladio. 'Resisting Living Death at Marion Federal Penitentiary, 1972.' *Radical History Review* 96 (fall 2006): 58–86.

Gordon, Art, and Frank J. Porporino. 'Managing the Treatment of Sex Offenders: A Canadian Perspective.' No. B-05, May 1990, Research and Statistics Branch, Correctional Service of Canada. http://www.csc-scc.gc.ca/text/rsrch/briefs/b5/b05e_e.shtml.

Gordon, Linda. *Heroes of Their Own Lives: The Politics and History of Family Violence, Boston, 1880–1960*. London: Vigaro, 1989.

Gosselin, Luc. *Prisons in Canada*. Montreal: Black Rose Books, 1982.

Greenland, Cyril. 'Dangerous Sexual Offender Legislation in Canada, 1948–1977: An Experiment that Failed.' *Canadian Journal of Criminology* 26, no. 1 (January 1984): 1–12.

– 'Dangerous Sexual Offenders in Canada.' In *Studies on Imprisonment*, edited by Law Reform Commission of Canada, 247–81. Ottawa: Supply and Services Canada, 1976.

– 'Is There a Future of Human Sexuality?' In *Sexual Behaviour in Canada: Patterns and Problems*, edited by Benjamin Schlesinger, 279–90. Toronto: University of Toronto Press, 1977.

Grekul, Jana, Harvey Krahn, and Dave Odynak. 'Sterilizing the "Feeble-Minded": Eugenics in Alberta, Canada, 1929–1972.' *Journal of Historical Sociology* 17, no. 4 (2004): 358–84.

Grossman, L.S., B. Martis, and C.G. Fichtner. 'Are Sex Offenders Treatable? A Research Overview.' *Psychiatric Services* 50, no. 3 (March 1999): 349–61.

Group for the Advancement of Psychiatry. *Psychiatry and Sex Psychopath Legislation: The 30s to the 80s*, vol. 9. New York: Group for the Advancement of Psychiatry, 1977.

Guard, Julie. 'Canadian Citizens or Dangerous Foreign Women? Canada's Radical Consumer Movement, 1947–50.' In *Sisters or Strangers? Immigrant, Ethnic, and Racialized Women in Canadian History*, edited by Marlene Epp, F. Iacovetta, and F. Swyripa, 161–89. Toronto: University of Toronto Press, 2004.

Gugliotta, Angela. '"Dr. Sharp and His Little Knife": Therapeutic and Punitive Origins of Eugenic Vasectomy, Indiana, 1892–1921.' *Journal of the History of Medicine* 53 (October 1998): 371–406.

Hannah-Moffat, Kelly. *Punishment in Disguise: Penal Governance and Federal Imprisonment of Women in Canada*. Toronto: University of Toronto Press, 2001.

Hanson, Karl, and Monique T. Bussiere. 'Predicting Relapse: A Meta-analysis of Sexual Offender Recidivism.' *Journal of Consulting and Clinical Psychology* 66, no. 2 (1998): 348–62.

Hanson, R. Karl, Richard A. Steffy, and Rene Gauthier. 'Long-Term Recidivism of Child Molesters.' *Journal of Consulting and Clinical Psychology* 61 (1993): 646–52.

Harris, Grant T., Tracey A. Skilling, and Marnie E. Rice. 'The Construct of Psychopathy.' *Crime and Justice* 28 (2001): 197–264.

Harrison, Helen. 'In the Picture of Health: Portraits of Health, Disease and Citizenship in Canada's Public Health Information, 1920–1960.' PhD diss., Queen's University, 2001.

Hogeveen, Bryan. '"The Evils with Which We Are Called to Grapple": Elite

Reformers, Eugenicists, Environmental Psychologists, and the Construction of Toronto's Working-Class Boy Problem, 1860–1930.' *Labour/Le Travail* 55 (2005): 37–68.

Hornblum, Allen M. *Acres of Skin: Human Experiments at Holmesburg Prison: A True Story of Abuse and Exploitation in the Name of Medical Science.* New York: Routledge, 1998.

– 'They Were Cheap and Available: Prisoners as Research Subjects in Twentieth Century America.' *British Medical Journal* 315 (1997): 1437–41.

Human Rights Watch. *No Easy Answers: Sex Offender Laws in the US* 19, no. 4(G) (September 2007).

Hunt, Arnold. '"Moral Panic" and Moral Language in the Media.' *British Journal of Sociology* 48, no. 4 (December 1997): 634–5.

Iacovetta, Franca. 'Making "New Canadians": Social Workers, Women, and the Reshaping of Immigrant Families.' In *A Nation of Immigrants: Women, Workers, and Communities in Canadian History, 1840s–1960s,* edited by Franca Iacovetta et al., 482–513. Toronto: University of Toronto Press, 1998.

Irvine, Janice M. *Disorders of Desire: Sex and Gender in Modern American Sexology.* Philadelphia: Temple University Press, 1990.

Jackson, Michael. 'The Paul Callow Files: A Documentary Review.' 5 June 2007. http://www.justicebehindthewalls.net/resources/news/callow.pdf.

Jenkins, Philip. *Moral Panic: Changing Concepts of the Child Molester in Modern America.* New Haven, CT: Yale University Press, 1998.

John Howard Society of Alberta. 'Sex Offender Treatment Programs: An Evaluation.' 1994. Access to Justice Network Publications. http://129.128.19.162/docs/sexofjhs.html (accessed 8 June 2001).

Justman, Stewart. *The Psychological Mystique.* Evanston, IL: Northwestern University Press, 1998.

Kaledin, Eugenia. *Mothers and More: American Women in the 1950s.* Boston: Twayne Publishers, 1984.

Kear-Colwell, Jon, and Douglas P. Boer. 'The Treatment of Pedophiles: Clinical Experience and the Implications of Recent Research.' *International Journal of Offender Therapy and Comparative Criminology* 44, no. 5 (2000): 593–605.

Kennedy, Elizabeth Lapovsky, and Madeline Davis. *Boots of Leather, Slippers of Gold: The History of a Lesbian Community.* New York: Routledge, 1993.

Kinsman, Gary. '"Inverts," "Psychopaths" and "Normal" Men: Historical Sociological Perspectives on Gay and Heterosexual Masculinities.' In *Men and Masculinities: A Critical Anthology,* edited by Tony Haddad, 3–35. Toronto: Canadian Scholars' Press, 1993.

– *The Regulation of Desire: Homo and Hetero Sexualities,* 2nd ed. Montreal: Black Rose Books, 1996.

– 'The Sexual Regulation of Family Relations: The "Public" Construction of Sexual Danger in Canada, 1950–1965.' Paper presented at the History of the Family Conference, Ottawa, 1994.

Kinsman, Gary, Dieter K. Buse, and Mercedes Steedman. *Whose National Security? Canadian State Surveillance and the Creation of Enemies*. Toronto: Between the Lines Press, 2000.

Kinsman, Gary, and Patrizia Gentile. '"In the Interests of the State": The Anti-gay, Anti-lesbian National Security Campaign in Canada: A Preliminary Research Report.' Sudbury, ON: Laurentian University, 1998.

Kittrie, Nicholas N. *The Right to Be Different: Deviance and Enforced Therapy*. Baltimore: Johns Hopkins University Press, 1971.

Knupfer, Anne Meis. '"To Become Good, Self-Supporting Women": The State Industrial School for Delinquent Girls at Geneva, Illinois, 1900–1935.' *Journal of the History of Sexuality* 9, no. 4 (October 2000): 420–46.

Korinek, Valerie J. *Roughing It in the Suburbs: Reading Chatelaine Magazine in the Fifties and Sixties*. Toronto: University of Toronto Press, 2000.

Kunzel, Regina. 'Situating Sex: Prison Sexual Culture in the Mid-Twentieth-Century United States.' *GLQ: A Journal of Lesbian and Gay Studies* 8, no. 3 (2002): 253–70.

Lacombe, Dany. 'Managing Fantasies: An Analysis of Prison Treatment Programs for Sex Offenders.' Unpublished paper presented at the Law's Empire conference, Harrison Hot Springs, BC, June 2005.

Ladd-Taylor, Molly. 'Saving Babies and Sterilizing Mothers: Eugenics and Welfare Politics in the Interwar United States.' *Social Politics* 4, no. 1 (1997): 136–53.

Levine, Helen. *The Power Politics of Motherhood: A Feminist Critique of Theory and Practice*. Ottawa: Carleton University, Centre for Social Welfare Studies, 1981.

Li, Peter S. *The Making of Postwar Canada*. Toronto: Oxford University Press, 1996.

Linsky, Mark. 'The Most Critical Option: Sex Offences and Castration in San Diego 1938–1975.' *Journal of San Diego History* 35, no. 4 (1989): 248–57.

Loo, Tina, and Carolyn Strange. *Making Good: Law and Moral Regulation in Canada, 1867–1939*. Toronto: University of Toronto Press, 1997.

Low, Brian J. *NFB Kids: Portrayals of Children by the National Film Board of Canada, 1939–1989*. Waterloo: Wilfred Laurier University Press, 2002.

Lunbeck, Elizabeth. *The Psychiatric Persuasion: Knowledge, Gender, and Power in Modern America*. New Jersey: Princeton University Press, 1994.

MacKinnon, Catharine A. *Toward a Feminist Theory of the State*. Cambridge, MA: Harvard University Press, 1989.

Marshall, Dominique. 'Reconstruction Politics: The Canadian Welfare State and the Formation of Children's Rights, 1940–1950.' In *Family Matters: Papers in*

Post-Confederation Canadian Family History, edited by Lori Chambers and Edgar-Andre Montigny, 135–56. Toronto: Canadian Scholars' Press, 1998.

Marshall, John. 'Pansies, Perverts and Macho Men: Changing Conceptions of Male Homosexuality.' In *The Making of the Modern Homosexual*, edited by Kenneth Plummer, 133–54. London: Hutchinson, 1981.

Marshall, W., and H. Barbaree. 'The Long-Term Evaluation of a Behavioural Treatment Program for Child Molestors.' *Behaviour Therapy Research* 26 (1988): 499–511.

Marshall, W., and S. Barrett. *Criminal Neglect: Why Sex Offenders Go Free*. Toronto: Doubleday, 1990.

May, Elaine Tyler. *Homeward Bound: American Families in the Cold War Era*. New York: Basic Books, 1988.

Maynard, Steven. '"Horrible Temptations": Sex, Men, and Working-Class Male Youth in Urban Ontario, 1890–1935.' *The Canadian Historical Review* 78, no. 2 (June 1997): 191–235.

– 'On the Case of the Case: The Emergence of the Homosexual as a Case History in Early Twentieth-Century Canada.' In *On the Case: Explorations in Social History*, edited by Franca Iacovetta and Wendy Mitchinson, 65–87. Toronto: University of Toronto Press, 1998.

– 'Through a Hole in the Lavatory Wall: Homosexual Subcultures, Police Surveillance, and the Dialectics of Discovery, Toronto, 1890–1930.' *Journal of the History of Sexuality* 5, no. 2 (1994): 207–43.

McLaren, Angus. 'The Creation of a Haven for "Human Thoroughbreds": The Sterilization of the Feeble-Minded and the Mentally Ill in British Columbia.' *Canadian Historical Review* 67, no. 2 (1986): 127–50.

– *Our Own Master Race: Eugenics in Canada, 1885–1945*. Toronto: McClelland and Stewart, 1990.

– *The Trials of Masculinity: Policing Sexual Boundaries, 1870–1930*. Chicago: University of Chicago Press, 1997.

– *Twentieth Century Sexuality: A History*. Malden, MA: Blackwell Publishers, 1999.

McMahon, Maeve Winifred. 'Changing Penal Trends: Imprisonment and Alternatives in Ontario, 1951–1984.' PhD diss., University of Toronto, 1988.

Metzl, Jonathan. '"Mother's Little Helper": The Crisis of Psychoanalysis and the Miltown Resolution.' *Gender and History* 15, no. 2 (August 2003): 240–67.

Meyerowitz, Joanne. 'Beyond the Feminine Mystique: A Reassessment of Postwar Mass Culture, 1946–1958.' *Journal of American History* 79, no. 4 (March 1993): 1455–82.

– *How Sex Changed: A History of Transsexuality in the United States*. Cambridge, MA: Harvard University Press, 2002.

– *Not June Cleaver: Women and Gender in Postwar America.* Philadelphia: Temple University Press, 1994.

Miller, Neil. *Sex Crime Panic: A Journey to the Paranoid Heart of the 1950s.* New York: Alyson Books, 2002.

Mills, Allen George. *Fool for Christ: The Political Thought of J.S. Woodsworth.* Toronto: University of Toronto Press, 1991.

Minton, Henry. *Departing from Deviance: A History of Homosexual Rights and Emancipatory Science in America.* Chicago: University of Chicago Press, 2002.

Mitford, Jessica. *Kind and Usual Punishment: The Prison Business.* New York: Alfred A. Knopf, 1973.

Mooie, T. Dunbar. 'Migrancy and Male Sexuality on the South African Gold Mines.' *Journal of South African Studies* 14, no. 2 (1998): 228–56.

Moran, James E. *Committed to the State Asylum: Insanity and Society in Nineteenth Century Quebec and Ontario.* Montreal: McGill-Queen's University Press, 2001.

Mort, Frank. *Dangerous Sexualities: Medico-Moral Politics in England since 1830.* New York: Routledge, 2000.

National Commission for the Protection of Human Subjects of Biomedical and Behavioural Research. 'Prisoners as Research Subjects.' In *Crime and Justice*, vol. 3, 2nd ed., edited by Sir Leon Radzinowicz and Marvin E. Wolfgang, 312–31. New York: Basic Books, 1977.

Oliver, Peter. *Unlikely Tory: The Life and Politics of Allan Grossman.* Toronto: Lester and Orpen Dennys, 1985.

Oosterhuis, Harry. 'Richard von Krafft-Ebing's "Step-Children of Nature": Psychiatry and the Making of Homosexual Identity.' In *Science and Homosexualities*, ed. Vernon A. Rosario. New York: Routledge, 1997.

– *Stepchildren of Nature: Krafft-Ebing, Psychiatry and the Making of Sexual Identity.* Chicago: University of Chicago Press, 2000.

Ordover, Nancy. *American Eugenics: Race, Queer Anatomy, and the Science of Nationalism.* Minneapolis: University of Minnesota Press, 2003.

Owram, Doug. *Born at the Right Time: A History of the Baby Boom Generation.* Toronto: University of Toronto Press, 1996.

Parenti, Christian. *Lockdown America: Police and Prisons in the Age of Crisis.* New York: Verso, 1999.

Parr, Joy, ed. *A Diversity of Women: Ontario, 1945–1980.* Toronto: University of Toronto Press, 1995.

Penn, Donna. 'The Meanings of Lesbianism in Post War America.' *Gender and History* 3, no. 2 (summer 1991): 190–203.

Petrunik, Michael. *Models of Dangerousness: A Cross Jurisdictional Review of Dangerousness Legislation and Practice.* Policy Branch, Ministry of the Solicitor General of Canada, 1994.

Pinar, William F. *The Gender of Racial Politics and Violence in America: Lynching, Prison Rape and the Crisis of Masculinity.* New York: Peter Lang, 2001.

Pon, Madge. 'Like a Chinese Puzzle: The Construction of Chinese Masculinity in *Jack Canuck.*' In *Gender and History in Canada,* edited by Joy Parr and Mark Rosenfeld, 88–100. Toronto: Copp Clark, 1996.

Porter, Roy. *The Greatest Benefit to Mankind: A Medical History of Humanity.* New York: W.W. Norton, 1997.

Potter, Sarah. '"Undesirable Relations": Same-Sex Relationships and the Meaning of Sexual Desire at a Women's Reformatory During the Progressive Era.' *Feminist Studies* 30, no. 2 (2004): 394–415.

Prentice, Alison, et al. *Canadian Women: A History.* Toronto: Harcourt Brace Jovanovich, 1988.

Prentice, Susan. 'Workers, Mothers, Reds: Toronto's Postwar Daycare Fight.' *Studies in Political Economy* 30 (1989): 115–41.

Public Safety Canada. *Corrections and Conditional Release Statistical Overview Annual Report.* Ottawa: Public Works and Government Services Canada, 2007.

Quaker Peace and Social Witness. 'Circles of Support and Accountability in the Thames Valley: The First Three Years, April 2002 to March 2005.' London: Quaker Communications for Quaker Peace and Social Witness, 2005. http://www.quaker.org.uk/shared_asp_files/uploadedfiles/82F718A7-9344-4A5C-A4A7-4B053FF22239_CirclesofSupport-first3yrs.pdf.

Quinsey, Vernon L., Arunima Khanna, and P. Bruce Malcolm. 'A Retrospective Evaluation of the Regional Treatment Centre Sex Offender Treatment Program.' *Journal of Interpersonal Violence* 13, no. 5 (October 1998): 621–44.

Rich, Adrienne. 'Compulsory Heterosexuality and Lesbian Existence.' *Signs: Journal of Women in Culture and Society* 5 (summer 1980): 631–60.

Reilly, P.R. *The Surgical Solution: A History of Involuntary Sterilization in the United States.* Baltimore: Johns Hopkins University Press, 1991.

Roberts, Barbara. 'Women's Peace Activism in Canada.' In *Beyond the Vote: Canadian Women in Politics,* edited by Linda Kealey and Joan Sangster, 276–308. Toronto: University of Toronto Press, 1989.

Robertson, Stephen. 'Separating the Men from the Boys: Masculinity, Psychosexual Development, and Sex Crime in the United States, 1930s–1960s.' *Journal of the History of Medicine and Allied Sciences* 56, no. 1 (January 2001): 3–35.

Robinson, Daniel J., and David Kimmel. 'The Queer Career of Homosexual Security Vetting in Cold-War Canada.' *Canadian Historical Review* 75, no. 3 (September 1994): 319–45.

Robinson, Paul. *The Modernization of Sex: Havelock Ellis, Alfred Kinsey, William Masters and Virginia Johnson.* Ithaca: Cornell University Press, 1989.

Rutherdale, Robert. 'Fatherhood and the Social Construction of Memory: Breadwinning and Male Parenting on a Job Frontier 1945–1966.' In *Gender and History in Canada*, edited by Joy Parr and Mark Rosenfeld, 357–75. Toronto: Copp Clark, 1996.

Sabo, Don, Terry A. Kupers, and Willie London. *Prison Masculinities*. Philadelphia: Temple University Press, 2001.

Schmidt, Sarah. '"Private" Acts in "Public" Spaces: Parks in Turn-of-the-Century Montreal.' In *Power, Place, and Identity: Historical Studies of Social and Legal Regulation in Quebec*, edited by Tamara Myers, Kate Boyer, Mary Anne Poutanen, and Steven Watt, 129–49. Montreal: Montreal History Group, 1998.

Schwaebe, Charles. 'Learning to Pass: Sex Offenders' Strategies for Establishing a Viable Identity in the Prison General Population.' *International Journal of Offender Therapy and Comparative Criminology* 49, no. 6 (2005): 614–25.

Scott, Joan. 'Gender as a Category of Analysis.' In *Gender and the Politics of History*, rev. ed. New York: Columbia University Press, 1999.

Sedgewick, Eve. *Epistemology of the Closet*. Berkeley and Los Angeles: University of California Press, 1990.

Setliff, Eric. 'Sex Fiends or Swish Kids? Gay Men in Hush Free Press, 1946–1956.' In *Gendered Pasts: Historical Essays in Femininity and Masculinity in Canada*, edited by Kathryn McPherson, Cecilia Morgan, and Nancy M. Forestall, 158–78. Toronto: Oxford University Press, 1999.

Shorter, Edward. *A History of Psychiatry: From the Era of the Asylum to the Age of Prozac*. New York: John Wiley and Sons, 1997.

– ed. *TPH: History and Memories of the Toronto Psychiatric Hospital, 1925–1966*. Toronto: Wall and Emerson, 1996.

Smith, Geoffrey S. 'National Security and Personal Isolation: Sex, Gender, and Disease in the Cold War United States.' *International History Review* 14, no. 2 (May 1992): 307–37.

Smykla, John Ortiz. *Cocorrections: A Case Study of a Coed Federal Prison*. Washington: University Press of America, 1978.

Snell, James G. 'The White Life for Two: The Defence of Marriage and Sexual Morality in Canada, 1890–1914.' *Histoire Sociale/Social History* 16, no. 31 (May 1983): 111–28.

Statistics Canada. 'Adult Correctional Services, 2004/2005.' *The Daily*, 11 October 2006, http://www.statcan.ca/Daily/English/061011/d061011a.htm.

Stein, Marc. *City of Sisterly and Brotherly Loves: Lesbian and Gay Philadelphia, 1945–1972*. Chicago: University of Chicago Press, 2000.

Stewart, Lorne. 'The History of the Juvenile and Family Court of Toronto.' Unpublished paper, Centre of Criminology, University of Toronto, 1971.

Strange, Carolyn. *Toronto's Girl Problem: The Perils and Pleasures of the City, 1880–1930*. Toronto: University of Toronto Press, 1995.

Strong-Boag, Veronica. 'Home Dreams: Women and the Suburban Experiment in Canada, 1945–60.' *Canadian Historical Review* 4 (1991): 471–504.

Struthers, James. '"Lord Give Us Men": Women and Social Work in English Canada, 1918–1953.' In *The Benevolent State: The Growth of Welfare in Canada*, edited by Allan Moscovitch and Jim Albert, 126–43. Toronto: Garmond Press, 1987.

Studer, Lea H., and A. Scott Aylwin. 'Pedophilia: The Problem with Diagnosis and Limitations of CBT in Treatment.' *Medical Hypotheses* 67 (2006): 774–81.

Terry, Jennifer. *An American Obsession: Science, Medicine and Homosexuality in Modern Society.* Chicago: University of Chicago Press, 1999.

Thorstad, David. 'Man/Boy Love and the American Gay Movement.' *Journal of Homosexuality* 20 (1990): 251–74.

Trent, James W. 'To Cut and Control: Institutional Preservation and the Sterilization of Mentally Retarded People in the United States, 1892–1947.' *Journal of Historical Sociology* (Great Britain) 6, no. 1 (1993): 56–73.

Valverde, Mariana. 'Building Anti-Delinquent Communities: Morality, Gender, and Generation in the City.' In *A Diversity of Women, Ontario, 1945-1980*, edited by Joy Parr, 19–45. Toronto: University of Toronto Press, 1995.

– *Diseases of the Will: Alcohol and the Dilemmas of Freedom.* New York: Cambridge University Press, 1998.

Verdun-Jones, Simon N., and Russell Smandych. 'Catch-22 in the Nineteenth Century: The Evolution of Therapeutic Confinement for the Criminally Insane in Canada, 1840–1900.' *Criminal Justice History: An International Annual,* 2 (1981): 85–108.

Vickers, Jill McCalla. 'Feminist Approaches to Women in Politics.' In *Beyond the Vote: Canadian Women and Politics*, edited by Linda Kealey and Joan Sangster, 16–36. Toronto: University of Toronto Press, 1989.

Walkowitz, Judith R. *City of Dreadful Delight: Narratives of Sexual Danger in Late-Victorian London.* Chicago: University of Chicago Press, 1992.

Ward, Steven C. *Modernizing the Mind: Psychological Knowledge and the Remaking of Society.* Westport, CT: Praeger, 2002.

Weeks, Jeffrey. *Sex, Politics and Society.* London: Longmans, 1981.

Wetherell, Donald G. 'To Discipline and Train: Adult Rehabilitation Programs in Ontario Prisons, 1874–1900.' *Histoire sociale/Social History* 23, no. 12: 145–65.

Whitaker, Reg, and Gary Marcuse. *Cold War Canada: The Making of a National Insecurity State, 1945–1957.* Toronto: University of Toronto Press, 1994.

Wilson, Robin J., Janice E. Picheca, Michelle Prinzo. 'Circles of Support and Accountability: An Evaluation of the Pilot Project in South-Central Ontario.' Ottawa: Correctional Service of Canada, Research Branch, 2005. http://www.csc-scc.gc.ca/text/rsrch/reports/r168/r168_e.pdf.

Wright, Mary J., and C. Roger Myers, eds. *The History of Academic Psychology*. Toronto: C.J. Hogrefe, 1982.

Zedner, Lucia. 'Wayward Sisters: The Prison for Women.' In *The Oxford History of the Prison: The Practice of Punishment in Western Society*, edited by Norval Morris and David J. Rothman, 329–61. New York: Oxford University Press, 1995.

Index

STUDIES IN GENDER AND HISTORY

General editors: Franca Iacovetta and Karen Dubinsky

Cure mental
health
Why? 32

Homosexuality)